A Generous Donation
Given In Memory Of

Ernest J. Allen

Long-Time Resident of Valley Center
and
Local Dairyman
Has Provided This Library Material
For Your Use and Enjoyment

Arizona

Arizona: A History

is published with a generous gift from

the Salt River Project,

whose contribution is matched by a Challenge Grant

from the National Endowment for the Humanities

to support publishing in the humanities by

the University of Arizona Press.

Thomas E. Sheridan

ARIZONA

* * * *A History*

The University of Arizona Press ✳ Tucson

Second paperbound printing 1996

The University of Arizona Press
Copyright © 1995
The Arizona Board of Regents
All rights reserved
♾ This book is printed on acid-free, archival-quality
paper.
Manufactured in the United States of America
99   98   97   96   5   4   3   2
Library of Congress Cataloging-in-Publication Data
Sheridan, Thomas E.
   Arizona : a history / Thomas E. Sheridan.
     p.   cm.
   Includes bibliographical references and index.
   ISBN 0-8165-1056-3 (alk. paper). —
   ISBN 0-8165-1515-8 (pbk. : alk. paper)
   1. Arizona—History.   I. Title.
F811.S465   1995   94-18712
976.1—dc20   CIP

British Cataloguing-in-Publication Data
A catalogue record for this book is available from the
British Library.

To my daughter, Rachel

I hope the wild places will still be there

when you're old enough to need them.

Contents

Preface

Like most Arizonans, my life is a web of contradictions, and those contradictions influence how I perceive the state. I work in Tucson but live thirty-five miles to the southwest so my family and I can listen to coyotes instead of police helicopters at night. My neighbors are fourth-generation Arizona ranchers and retirees from Illinois. I want to hear Mexican wolves howl once again in the Altar Valley, but I also want those ranchers to keep on running their cattle on public lands. Biological diversity may be the new mantra, but cultural heritage needs to be preserved as well. We should be seeking balance, not exclusion.

But balance in Arizona is hard to find. The boom brought me to the state when I was three years old, and I've been living off it and seeking refuge from it ever since. My father was in the savings-and-loan business when it was still a conservative little industry dominated by the Federal Home Loan Bank Board. He died the year before deregulation and never lived to see his competitors, or the companies he ran, go belly up. My parents were honest and ethical, but they also went to cocktail parties with people who later became Watergate co-conspirators or targets of the RTC. My mother tells great stories about Phoenix in the 1950s, when a friend with unexplained entrées into unusual places would call up the day after Christmas and say, "Let's fly to Vegas for New Years' Eve." They'd get front-row seats. Anyone who didn't live in Phoenix during the boom has a hard time understanding how honest businessmen and businesswomen could rub shoulders with people like Bugsy Siegel and Ned Warren. But they did. It was a wide-open town.

Beyond that town, however, was a world still rooted in the nineteenth century. I first explored the Arizona backcountry with my grandfather, Maurice Maney, who tried to teach me trout fishing and dragged me into a lot of dark Western bars. We started out fishing Tonto Creek at the Baptist Bridge, where our neighbor Harry Robertson had a ramshackle log cabin on Forest Service lease land. Harry and my grandfather both fly-fished, and they both drank. No matter what stream we fished—Tonto or Christopher Creek or the East Verde— we always ended up in the old Kohl's Ranch bar. The smell of beer and the firm, damp smell of gutted trout intermingle in those memories.

Since then I've backpacked or hunted other wild stretches of the state alone or with a few good companions, especially Tom Barnes, Fritz Jandrey, Neal Ackerley, John Higgins, Kim Clifton, Dave Philips, Tom McGuire, and my wife, Chris Szuter. Fr. John Howard took me across the Grand Canyon when I was twelve. My passion for Arizona comes from those trips.

Many others have helped me learn more about the state's human and natural history, including Bunny Fontana, Jim Officer, Kieran McCarty, Jim Griffith, Carmen Villa Prezelski, Hank Dobyns, Bob Euler, George Gumerman, Amadeo Rea, Bruce Dinges, Diana Hadley, Peter Warshall, Tom McGuire, Eric Henderson, Nancy Parezo, Gary Nabhan, Dick Felger, Bob Webb, Julio Betancourt, Tony Burgess, Muffin Ames Burgess, Don Bufkin, Pat Preciado Martin, Ken Chilton, Jim Chilton, Dave Yetman, Ken Nichols, Art Carrillo Strong, Conrad Bahre, Chuck Bowden, Bill Doelle, Joe Wilder, Paul Martin, Tom Saarinen, Dick Reeves, and the late Ned Spicer and Leland Sonnichsen. A few good institutions have taught me as well—Brophy College Prep, Prescott College in its first incarnation, the Southwestern Mission Research Center, the Arizona Historical Society, where I directed the Mexican Heritage Project from 1982 to 1984, and the Arizona State Museum at the University of Arizona, where I work now. Barbara Bush and Susan Peters, at the Arizona Historical Society, and Chris Marin and Edward Oetting, at Archives and Manuscripts in the University Libraries at Arizona State University, assisted me in selecting the historical photographs. I thank David Weber, Suzanne Fish, Paul Fish, Greg McNamee, Tom McGuire, Hartman Lomawaima, and Peter Iverson for reading sections of the manuscript. Bruce Dinges and Steve Cox read the entire book, chapter by chapter. Their comments and criticisms were invaluable. I would also like to acknowledge the assistance of Joe Wilder and the Southwest Center of the University of Arizona in supporting the preparation of the index for the book. Finally, I would like to thank Alan Schroder, manuscript editor and historian, for reading the final manuscript with such thoroughness and care.

I also want to acknowledge a few of the places that have shaped me as much as any person: the Mazatzals, Galiuros, Sierra Anchas, Cerro Colorados, the Blue River country, Houston Mesa, Club Cabin, Davenport Wash, Deadman Creek, Hopi Spring, Powers Garden, Deer Creek, Holdout Spring, KP Creek, Mud Spring, Moonshine Park, Paradise Park, White Oak Spring, Maple Peak, Pueblo Canyon, and Edward Spring. These hidden places and many others are the Arizona I love. I hope they stay hidden for a long time to come.

Diamond Bell, Arizona
February 10, 1994

Introduction

I grew up in Phoenix, a child of the boom in a subdivision carved out of citrus groves just south of the Arizona Canal. Soon after my family moved there in 1955, we began making pilgrimages up the Beeline Highway to a neighbor's log cabin under the Mogollon Rim. I remember sitting beside my mother on a chaise longue in the back of a pickup as we drove up Oxbow Hill to Payson. The Tonto Basin seemed to stretch around us forever in a series of yellow hills that led to mysterious places like Punkin Center or the Sierra Anchas, but the country that captured my imagination most of all was the Mazatzal mountain range, whose blue outline dominated the western horizon. The Mazatzals were dark and deep, and to my young eyes, they embodied all the mystery and grandeur of the West. No one took me into them then. That came later. For thirteen years they fermented into that most powerful of drugs—wilderness—only in my mind.

Then, when I was sixteen, I made my first forays into their rattlesnake-infested heart. I started by switchbacking up the Barnhardt Trail west of Rye, past south-facing slopes bristling with agave and north-facing crevices where once, in January, I found a waterfall completely captured by ice. That trail led me around Mazatzal Peak and brought me to a little clearing where Chilson Cabin used to stand—a plank shed guarding a trickle of water dripping from a pipe. I remember camping there one moonlit night and watching a doe step out of the junipers to feed. Fifty miles to the southwest, Phoenix glittered, but I wanted the doe's world then. The doe and Chilson Cabin belonged to an Arizona I hungered to become a part of before it disappeared.

Ever since then the Mazatzals have been my touchstone in a state I call home. I return to them year after year—from Lion Mountain, Horseshoe Dam, and Sheep's Bridge, from Polles Mesa down the Gorge and the East Verde River to its confluence with the Verde. I have carved part of my own personal history into the soft wood of the door to Club Cabin, a line shack below Table Mountain where ranchers, hunters, and backpackers have weathered snowstorms and sunstroke for nearly a century. The Mazatzals are therefore a good place for me to begin a history of Arizona because they are real, while Arizona, after all, is only a set of arbitrary lines on a map. Arizona as a geographical concept did not exist until the nineteenth century. It was not a political reality until 1863. Even then, almost all the important forces that have shaped Arizona have washed across much larger areas as well. There is no way to confine precolumbian Indian societies or Spanish imperial expansion or Anglo American manifest destiny to Arizona's boundaries. When you write about the history of Arizona, you have to write about other places too.

There is also the inescapable arrogance of the term itself. If you hike into the Mazatzals, you pass jagged outcrops of rock that are nearly two billion years old. Those rocks were Arizona long before Arizona had a name, and they will be Arizona long after the name has disappeared. All of us—Paleolithic mammoth hunters, Hohokam farmers, Mexican ranchers, Anglo American dam builders and city dwellers—are light dust on those rocks. The land should make us humble, but it rarely does.

Yet we still need to tell our stories. This one begins with the killing of an animal that stood twelve feet tall at the shoulder and ends with the construction of a canal 335 miles long. Both were acts of either hubris or vision, depending on your point of view. In between, there was more hubris, more vision, more folly, bravery, greed, and sacrifice. The history of Arizona is not a linear progression from wilderness to civilization. Instead it is a series of advances and retreats, accommodations and blunders, booms and busts. Many peoples have lived here over the past twelve thousand years or more, but the overwhelming impression their history conveys is the transitory nature of human occupation in this arid, rugged land. That is why history is so important. The lessons of the past may not prevent mistakes in the future, but at least they can help us inhabit a particular landscape and learn a little about its mysteries, beauties, and cruelties. Otherwise, we are nothing more than carpetbaggers or tourists.

This book interprets the past by organizing it into three major phases—incorporation, extraction, and transformation—that mark Arizona's integration into what Immanuel Wallerstein calls the modern world-system. Beginning in the fifteenth century, Europe completed the transition from feudalism to capitalism and began expanding across the globe in search of new commodities and new markets. During the next five hundred years, ties of commerce, conquest, and biological interchange linked Europe, Asia, Africa, and the Americas, including Arizona. As the world-system changed because of political realignments and technological change, its links with Arizona changed as well. Arizona has never developed in isolation, not even during precolumbian times. Other cultures, other centers of power, and other economic and political demands have always shaped the people living here, and those demands have accelerated with each phase. As they have, relations of race, class, gender, and ethnic identity in Arizona have changed as well.

During the first phase—incorporation—the integration was shifting, tenuous, and incomplete. Until the late nineteenth century, Arizona was a frontier in the most basic sense of the term. It was not a border between civilization and wilderness, or civilization and savagery, because those terms were nothing more than the value judgments of the conquerors. Instead, it was contested ground, a place where no one group—tribe, nation-state, or empire—held uncontested sway. During those four centuries, three major cultures—Athapaskans, Hispanics, and Anglo Americans—converged on the region. They and the people who were already living here—Hopis, River Yumans, Upland Pais, and O'odham —fought, slept, and traded with one another, exchanging ideas, rituals, seeds, and genes. But none of the groups established dominion over the entire area until the U.S. military won the Indian wars of the 1860s through the 1880s. When Geronimo surrendered to General Nelson Miles in 1886, the frontier came to an end.

That same decade, the extractive phase began as the Southern Pacific and the Atlantic & Pacific (later called the Santa Fe) transcontinental railroads breached Arizona's isolation and bound it to the rest of the nation with iron rails. The railroads allowed capitalists in California, Chicago, the eastern United States, and western Europe to convert Arizona's natural resources into commodities that could be shipped someplace else for finishing and processing. During the extractive period, the railroads, copper companies, cotton farmers, and ranchers dominated Arizona politics and pitted Mexican and Anglo workers against one another to break the unions and keep wages down. The result was the creation of a class system organized largely along ethnic lines.

By the early twentieth century, however, some people were beginning to view Arizona as more than a bundle of resources to be plundered. People with tuberculosis and other respiratory diseases set up tent cities on the outskirts of Phoenix and Tucson to cure themselves in the desert air. And as the federal government set aside Arizona's most spectacular scenery and archaeological sites as national forests, parks, and monuments, tourists arrived as well. New constituencies were being formed, many of them outside the state. Eventually those constituencies would challenge the miners, ranchers, loggers, and farmers for the right to determine how Arizona's natural resources were utilized, especially on public lands. The third phase—the great transformation from extractive colony to urban Sunbelt society—had begun.

It was a long, complex process of negotiation to define Arizona's identity, and it was mediated every step of the way by the federal government. Many Arizonans still believe in the mystique of the Old West, with its rugged individualists and its wide-open spaces. The wide-open spaces are still there, at least for a time, but behind every rugged individual is a government agency. The federal government conquered the Indians, regulated grazing and logging on federal lands, built Arizona's enormous water control systems like the Salt River Project and the Central Arizona Project, and even triggered the transition from the rural to the urban by establishing air bases and defense plants around Phoenix and Tucson during World War II. More than most places, modern Arizona would not exist without federal support.

To examine those processes of incorporation, extraction, and transformation, I employ a theoretical approach I call political ecology, by which I mean the ongoing interplay between global political and economic forces and local cultural, demographic, and ecological factors. Every social system draws matter and energy from the natural world, relying on its climate, soils, plants, animals, mineral deposits, and sources of water. That natural world sets limits on what people can and cannot do. True dry farming, for example (farming that depends on direct rainfall alone), is impossible over most of Arizona. If you want to raise crops, you have to furnish them with more water than direct rainfall alone. Irrigation and water control therefore become ecological imperatives.

But the magnitude of water control, the types of crops grown, and the uses to which they are put depend on factors that often transcend local ecosystems and local societies. Arizona farmers cultivated very little cotton until World War I, when the British embargoed Egyptian long-staple cotton at a time when the U.S. military desperately needed long-staple fiber for tires and airplane fabric. As a result, the government and the tire companies turned to the deserts of Arizona, which offered the long, hot, dry growing season long-staple cotton required. By then the Salt River Project was already in place and there was a ready supply of cheap, seasonal labor just across the border in Mexico. Global disruption created national demand, and national demand intersected with regional climatic factors, river systems, irrigation networks, and labor patterns to produce Arizona's cotton boom.

The cotton boom, in turn, generated its own momentum as well as its own tensions and contradictions, just as the copper and cattle booms had done forty years earlier. But each commodity imposes different demands and requires different intersections of the global and the local, all of which influence relations of race, class, and gender in different ways. Another definition of political ecology, then, is the historical dialectic that determines how and why certain natural resources are converted into commodities at particular places and times, and how commodity production transforms local ecosystems and local societies.

This book pays particular attention to the commodification of Arizona's "four C's"—copper, cattle, cotton, and climate—as Arizona moved through the three phases of incorporation, extraction, and transformation outlined above. It also explores how the exploitation of those resources affected the political struggles and daily lives of people across the state, including Native Americans, Mexicans, African Americans, and women. I have not treated these groups in separate chapters because I believe that would have marginalized them. Instead, I have tried to embed social relations and social identities within the larger political, economic, and cultural contexts that affected them at different stages in Arizona's history.

One final comment is necessary. This book begins and ends with the natural world, which is easy to overlook, especially today, when dams have domesticated Arizona's rivers and refrigeration has tamed the desert's heat. Historians, anthropologists, and other social scientists pay a great deal of attention to how people accommodate, resist, or manipulate one another, yet nature, the ultimate Other, often remains trapped in a conceptual limbo—passive rather than active, reactor rather than actor, background rather than foreground, feminine rather than the gendered and ungendered collection of beings and forces that it is. Yet nature in Arizona has made its own demands.

Perhaps one of nature's most important demands is also one of the subtlest— the growing belief among many people that Arizona has a value that transcends commodification or cost-benefit analysis. Native Americans invest plants, animals, and places with spiritual power—places like *waw kiwulk,* or Constricted Hill (Baboquivari Peak), where the Tohono O'odham believe I'itoi, the creator of human beings, lives. Anglo Americans, on the other hand, establish national parks and pass endangered species acts. The culture of business and government speaks the language of the ledger, but that language does not express many of our deepest needs. Perhaps Annie Peaches, a Western Apache, said it best when she told anthropologist Keith Basso, "The land is always stalking people. The land makes people live right. The land looks after us." History lets Arizona stalk us through its past.

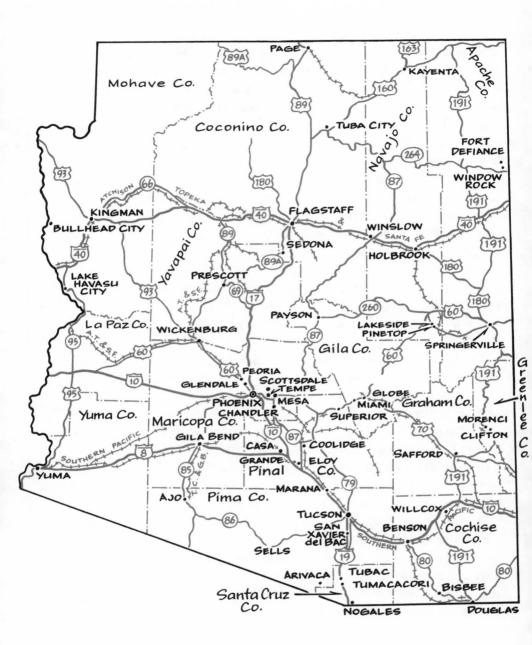

A Political Map of Arizona

Arizona

A group of Chiricahua Apaches at Fort Bowie in 1886 after their surrender. (Courtesy of the Arizona Historical Society)

I INCORPORATION

1

The Native Americans

The mammoth was huge, perhaps twelve feet tall at the shoulder. Its forelegs were the forelegs of a behemoth. Its long, curved tusks swept the space in front of it like the antennae of an insect frozen in ivory. And even though it fed on grasses, not flesh, one blow from its feet or one swing of its tusks would have crushed any predator foolish enough to threaten it. Yet somehow, 11,000 years ago, a small band of hunters crept close enough to this massive creature to hurl at least eight stone-tipped spears into the upper right side of its body. The spears may not have killed the mammoth, at least not immediately. The bones that eroded out of an arroyo a mile north-west of Naco, Arizona, on the modern Mexican border show no signs of butchering. But even if the mammoth eluded its pursuers to die alone, the audacity of those ice-age hunters still transfixes our imaginations. Armed with nothing more powerful than wood and stone, they stalked an animal that was larger than any land mammal alive today.

The fluted spear points these paleolithic people left behind are the first incontrovertible evidence we have of human society in the Southwest. Arizona history did not begin when emigrants from Europe first put pen to paper, but its early chapters are written in stone and clay, not ink. Some call this prehistory to distinguish it from the written record that followed hundreds of generations later, but the distinction is an artificial one. The Naco mammoth is a text to be interpreted, just as a seventeenth-century letter from a Jesuit missionary or a federal census manuscript from the late nineteenth century must be interpreted, not just read, for its full meaning to become clear. All tell the story of people through space and time. All are history—Arizona history—a part of our past.

*   *   *   Paleo-Indians and Archaic Peoples

Some scientists argue that small bands of men, women, and children wandered across the deserts of southwestern Arizona and northwestern Mexico 10,000 to 20,000 years earlier than the mammoth hunters. According to the best available archaeological and geological evidence, however, paleolithic hunters and their families moved into northwestern North America sometime between 16,000 and 10,000 B.C. In central Alaska, they found their passage south blocked by a huge ice sheet until a temporary recession in the last ice age opened up an ice-free corridor through northwestern Canada, allowing bands to fan out across the rest of the continent. In the opinion of geoscientist Paul Martin, these bands, armed with Clovis spear points (named for the site near Clovis, New Mexico, where the first point was found) encountered mammoths, camels, ground sloths, and horses who had never faced sophisticated big-game hunters before. The result was "Pleistocene overkill"—the rapid and systematic decimation of nearly all the species of large ice-age mammals in North America by 8,000 B.C. In a sense, the hunters who pursued the Naco mammoth may have represented the first of Arizona's many cycles of boom and bust, creating a society that relentlessly exploited a single resource until that resource was depleted or destroyed.

Archaeologists call the 7,000 years between the disappearance of the big-game hunters and the emergence of pottery-making societies around 100–200 A.D. the Archaic period. Most Archaic groups survived by becoming generalists rather than specialists, foraging in seasonal movements across the deserts, mountains, and plateaus. They did not abandon hunting, but they depended to a much greater degree upon wild plant foods and small game. Their tools became more varied, with grinding and chopping implements becoming more

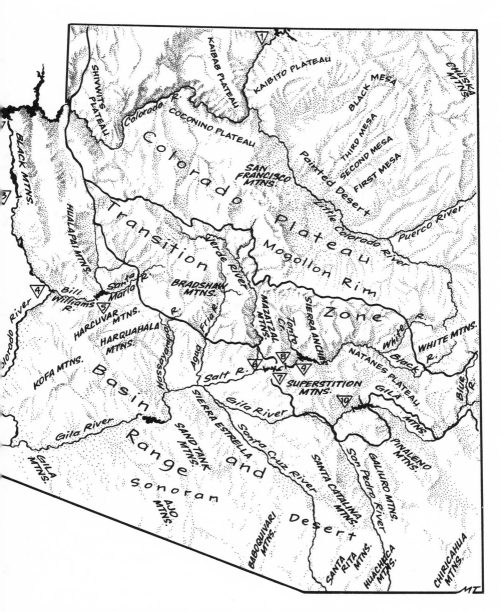

Glen Canyon Dam / Lake Powell	6. Stewart Mtn. Dam / Saguaro Lake
Hoover Dam / Lake Mead	7. Morman Flat Dam / Canyon Lake
Davis Dam / Lake Mohave	8. Horse Mesa Dam / Apache Lake
Parker Dam / Lake Havasu	9. Theodore Roosevelt Dam / Theodore Roosevelt Lake
Alamo Dam / Alamo Lake	10. Coolidge Dam / San Carlos Lake

A Physiographic Map of Arizona

common—a sure sign that seeds, fruits, and greens constituted a greater proportion of their diet. Such a way of life may not seem as exciting to us as big-game hunting, but it lasted for a much longer time.

Climatic changes drove this transition. When the first big-game hunters entered Arizona, forests and woodlands could be found as much as 3,000 feet lower than today. In the Sonoran Desert, piñon, juniper, and oak woodlands extended as far down the slopes as 1,800 ft (the elevation of the lower slopes of Camelback Mountain in Phoenix), while desert grasslands studded with Joshua trees, beargrass, and yucca carpeted the valleys below. The great ponderosa pine forests of the Colorado Plateau did not exist. Instead, the Mogollon Rim supported vast stands of mixed conifers such as Douglas fir, blue spruce, and Rocky Mountain juniper—trees characteristic of higher altitudes today. Even the giant saguaro—the plant that most symbolizes Arizona in people's minds—had largely taken refuge south of the modern border with Mexico.

Nonetheless, temperatures were rising and the seasonal distribution of precipitation had begun to change, causing major changes in vegetation as well. The Clovis people were stalking mammoths and other ice-age species in southeastern Arizona at a time when many streams were drying up, forcing the animals to concentrate around springs and seeps. The growing aridity of the region therefore coincided with the arrival of hunters who specialized in the pursuit of large mammals. It is possible that climate and humans acted together to bring about the extinction of those species.

Arizona grew even more arid after the last ice age came to an end. Summers grew wetter but warmer, so rainfall evaporated more quickly. Winters became considerably drier, making less moisture available to plants. In southern Arizona valleys, woodlands gave way to desert grasslands, and desert grasslands gave way to desert scrub. Important Sonoran Desert species like saguaro and brittlebush recolonized the region from the south, while ponderosa forests and piñon-juniper-oak woodlands climbed back onto the Colorado Plateau. By 2000 B.C., the modern plant communities of Arizona had been established, and an essentially modern climate prevailed.

The early Archaic peoples of Arizona survived these changes by adapting to the cycles of plants and animals rather than by trying to make the plants and animals adapt to them. In the woodlands they gathered acorns in July and August, and piñon nuts and juniper berries in November. In the deserts they picked the leaves of annual plants like chenopodium (goosefoot) and amaranth (pigweed). They also roasted agave in rock-lined pits in the spring and collected cactus fruit and harvested the pods of mesquite in the summer. Because of their dependence on scattered and seasonal resources, Archaic groups did not occupy permanent settlements. Instead, they wandered from camp to camp in search of water and wild foods.

Their tools reflected their economy: ground stones (manos and metates) for grinding seeds into flour, scrapers for working hide and wood, and projectile points—smaller and cruder than the earlier Clovis and Folsom points—for hunting large and small game. The varying proportions of such tools at different sites suggest that people moved back and forth between different environmental zones in order to exploit particular resources.

But while their tools may have been crude and their settlements temporary, Archaic societies still fashioned artifacts that demonstrated their capacity for wonder and their quest for supernatural power. Most spectacular are the giant intaglios found on both sides of the Colorado River in southeastern California and southwestern Arizona. From 10 to 100 feet in length, these figures emerge out of the desert pavement like images from dreams—lines, circles, and spirals; stylized rattlesnakes, thunderbirds, phalluses, and human forms. We do not know what the intaglios symbolized for the people who made them, but we do know they demanded great investments of time and labor from their creators—investments that had no clearcut relation to material gain. As such, they serve as poorly understood windows on a world of symbol and power where rivers had not been tamed by dams and energy could not be harnessed in webs of electric lines.

* * * The Introduction of Agriculture

The power of the intaglios was elusive, however. For most of the Archaic period, people were not able to transform the environment in any fundamental way. Many archaeologists, in fact, assumed that the Archaic cultures of Arizona were evolutionary dead ends. They believed that groups from outside the region, particularly from Mesoamerica (central and southern Mexico and part of Central America), introduced major innovations like agriculture into the Southwest. According to this model, corn first put down Southwestern roots in the highlands of western New Mexico and eastern Arizona—the pre-Hispanic culture area known as the Mogollon—where Archaic populations began growing a small and primitive variety of maize at places like Bat Cave as early as 3500 B.C. From there, corn spread slowly to more arid lowland areas such as the Sonoran Desert.

During the 1980s these early maize dates were challenged by a refinement in radiocarbon dating using the accelerator mass spectrometer (AMS) technique. Accelerator dates reveal that the first corn from Bat Cave and other highland sites appeared about 1,000 B.C., 2,500 years later than previously thought. Moreover, a number of sites excavated in southern Arizona demonstrate that Archaic farmers were cultivating corn in the Tucson Basin about the same time as well. At the Milagro site along Tanque Verde Creek, for example, a Late Archaic population built pit houses, dug bell-shaped storage pits, and planted corn around 850 B.C. Beginning about three thousand years ago, then, Archaic groups were already making the transition from food gatherers to food producers. They also possessed many of the cultural features that accompany semisedentary agricultural life—storage facilities, more permanent dwellings, larger settlements, and even cemeteries.

Despite the early advent of farming, however, Late Archaic groups still exercised relatively little control over their environment. Furthermore, wild food resources remained important components of the diet even after the invention of pottery and the development of irrigation. The introduction of agriculture never meant the complete abandonment of hunting and foraging regardless of the size of pre-Hispanic societies.

Nonetheless, major changes were taking place in Arizona—changes that reflected larger populations, increasing technological sophistication, and greater contact with people outside the region, especially the complex societies of Mesoamerica. During the first millennium A.D., at least three major cultural traditions flourished in the Southwest: the Anasazi, the Hohokam, and the Mogollon. These are the cultures that left behind such spectacular manifestations of their societies as the cliff dwellings of Betatakin and Canyon de Chelly, the canal systems of the Salt River Valley, and the exquisite black-on-white pottery of the Mimbres region. In the minds of many people, the Anasazi, Hohokam, and Mogollon epitomize the very Southwest itself.

❋   ❋   ❋   The Anasazi

Of the three cultural traditions, none has captured the imagination of both scholars and the general public more completely than the Anasazi of the Colorado Plateau. Anasazi groups ranged from the Rio Grande Valley to the Grand Canyon. Their architecture was breathtaking, their religion a mosaic of bewildering complexity. Like the Hohokam and Mogollon, they originally lived in semisubterranean pit houses, but as they moved their dwellings to the surface, their religious rituals remained rooted in circular or rectangular chambers known as kivas, which were often built below ground. It was a religion that dominated daily life and linked families and clans to communities, and human beings to the natural world. It was also a religion with a fascinating array of supernatural figures we can speculatively reconstruct from rock art and kiva murals or watch spring to life in ceremonies from the Hopi Mesas to Taos. Unlike the two other major traditions, the Anasazi are the only pre-Hispanic group who indisputably left behind modern descendants. Archaeologists may debate whether the Akimel and Tohono O'odham developed out of the Hohokam, but no one denies the cultural and biological connections between the Anasazi and the Hopi, Zuni, Acoma, and Pueblo peoples of the Rio Grande.

Like all complex civilizations, the Anasazi's origins were humble. Between 600 B.C. and A.D. 550 (the dates vary from region to region), the earliest Anasazi lived in relatively small, mobile groups. During the summer they migrated to the lowlands, camping in dry rock shelters above watercourses, beside which they planted their crops. During the fall and winter they moved back into the uplands to harvest piñon nuts and other wild foods and, as noted above, dwelled in semisubterranean circular pit houses that insulated them against the cold. Both their settlement patterns and their artifacts indicate that they followed a seasonal round of activities that depended on both agriculture and foraging. They made no pottery. Instead, they stored their food and transported their goods in light, durable nets and baskets that gave them their archaeological name, the Basketmakers.

Beginning around A.D. 550, one of the Southwest's periodic cycles of arroyo cutting came to an end as water tables rose and the arroyos began to fill with sediment. As a result, Anasazi agriculture intensified and people settled for the first time in permanent communities on mesas above rivers and streams. Slab-lined pit houses became more elaborate, and the size of many communities grew, with some encompassing as many as a hundred structures. Bows and arrows supplanted atlatls (spear-throwers) as the most common hunting weapons. People domesticated turkeys and added beans to their agricultural crops. More significantly, fragile and less portable ceramic vessels replaced baskets as the most ubiquitous containers, a sure sign that life was becoming more settled. People who did less wandering from camp to camp could afford to carry large numbers of pots.

These developments continued during the ninth and tenth centuries A.D. Pottery became more sophisticated, with black-on-white and red-on-black designs decorating the ware. Settlements expanded not only in size but in number as Anasazi groups pushed west to the Colorado and Virgin rivers and south to the Hopi Buttes. While pit houses remained the predominant form of dwelling among Anasazi on the Colorado Plateau in northern Arizona, people at Chaco Canyon in northwestern New Mexico and Mesa Verde in southwestern Colorado constructed single-story masonry pueblos composed of contiguous rooms.

In many respects, the period from A.D. 1000 to 1150 represented the peak of Anasazi society. Anasazi populations known as the Kayenta fanned across the entire Colorado Plateau, occupying both rims of the Grand Canyon as well as upland areas such as northern Black Mesa. The transition from pit houses to pueblos also became widespread. In contrast to later Anasazi settlements in Arizona, however, most pueblos on the Colorado Plateau consisted of masonry structures that rarely exceeded a dozen rooms. To the east, in Chaco Canyon, huge multistoried villages such as Pueblo Bonito rose on the high New Mexican desert, connected to other communities by an elaborate system of roads and signaling stations. But the "Chaco Phenomenon" largely bypassed the Anasazi of northern Arizona. As populations increased and agriculture intensified, the Kayenta broke into relatively small groups and expanded their territory, not the size of their communities. Yet the different Anasazi branches shared numerous cultural traditions, including widespread religious ceremonies and beliefs. Families and clans constructed subterranean ceremonial chambers known as kivas. A few villages even built so-called great kivas, which may have integrated entire communities or even networks of communities. This architectural and religious tradition culminated during the eleventh and twelfth centuries, when enormous great kivas, such as those in Chaco Canyon (which are 15 to 20 meters in diameter), served to bring together large numbers of people, including those from different clans and perhaps different ethnic and linguistic groups. Anasazi communities oriented themselves around these sacred spaces with as much symmetry as any Spanish community laid out around a central plaza and church. Plazas, in fact, began to appear in Chaco communities in the eleventh century and spread to other Anasazi regions in the centuries to come.

Both Chaco fusion and Kayenta fission were successful developments, at least for a time, but both had their hidden costs as well. Populations expanded in areas that had a marginal environment for intensive agriculture. The demand for local resources rose, and when demand exceeded local supply, the exchange of not only luxury goods but basic items increased. The Anasazi brought more fields into production and built more diversion dams to channel runoff onto thirsty crops. In Chaco Canyon alone, they used 200,000 to 215,000 wooden beams to construct the massive multistoried pueblos. And while they hewed many of those beams from forests as far as fifty miles away, the insatiable demand for fuel wood decimated the ponderosa pine and piñon-juniper stands in and around the canyon itself. The removal of so much timber may have contributed to increased runoff and thus soil erosion and arroyo cutting, which, combined with a prolonged drought between 1130 and 1180 A.D., lowered water tables and made farming more precarious. People moved out of the Chaco core, deserting many settlements.

The Kayenta Anasazi also suffered from drought and arroyo cutting during the twelfth and thirteenth centuries. Abandoning many peripheral areas, they withdrew to areas with permanent springs or perrenial streams, where they built larger settlements and extensive systems of water distribution and erosion control: terraces, checkdams, irrigation ditches, and masonry-lined reservoirs. Fission gave way to fusion, a trend that developed into something of a juggernaut even after environmental conditions temporarily improved in the early 1200s. Although they could have dispersed into smaller communities at that time, the Anasazi, like many complex societies, had reached a point where internal dynamics overwhelmed external influences. They were gambling on a strategy of population concentration and agricultural intensification, betting that more complex forms of technology and social organization could keep the environment at bay. For a brief period, the gamble paid impressive returns; ultimately, it risked abandonment and collapse.

A case in point are the spectacular ruins of Tsegi Canyon just south of the Utah-Arizona border in Navajo National Monument. The cliff dwellings of Kiet Siel and Betatakin appear to be timeless extensions of the great sandstone escarpments to which they cling. Nevertheless, dates from tree rings cored from their timbers reveal that their entire period of habitation lasted less than fifty years. Anasazi first occupied the cave sheltering Betatakin in 1250, but construction of the masonry structure itself did not begin until 1267, when families erected three groups of rooms. A fourth followed in 1268, and at least ten rooms and a kiva were added in 1275. Both dwellings and population peaked the next decade. By the end of the century, Betatakin was deserted.

✳   ✳   The Hohokam

One of the paradoxes of Anasazi civilization is the illusion of permanence some of their most ephemeral communities convey. We walk through Betatakin or stare down at Antelope House in Canyon de Chelly and feel that we are coming face to face with an eternal past. In reality, however, most Anasazi groups moved frequently in their search for water and arable land. The average length of settlement for the dated sites on the Colorado Plateau was eighty years, an average biased by the inclusion of large sites inhabited for longer periods of time. When only small sites of ten rooms or less are examined, the average drops to thirty-four years.

The second major pre-Hispanic culture in Arizona was characterized by a greater degree of stability even though its architecture was evanescent. At sites such as Snaketown along the Gila River, people known as the Hohokam lived in the same settlements for centuries, scattering their dwellings around a central plaza and building their pit houses on top of one another generation after generation. The Hohokam therefore represent a remarkably successful adaptation to desert life.

That adaptation was based on a mastery of canal irrigation. With nothing more than wooden digging sticks, the Hohokam excavated ditches as large as ten feet wide and fifteen feet deep. Archaeologists have traced nearly a hundred miles of such canals around Florence and anywhere from 125 to 315 miles in the Phoenix area. Estimates of total land under irrigation range from 65,000 to 250,000 acres in the Salt River Valley alone. Several of the canals, in fact, served as prototypes for the ambitious waterworks of the Salt River Project. In the core Hohokam area along the Salt and Gila rivers, multisettlement "irrigation communities" developed along major canal systems. One such irrigation community linked the settlements of Pueblo Grande, La Ciudad, and Las Colinas north of the Salt River in the Phoenix Basin. Another stretched along a canal running south of the Gila River past Florence and Casa Grande. The Hohokam devised the most extensive system of water control on the North American continent, including Mesoamerica. Only the major hydraulic societies of Peru dug more earth and moved more water.

Because of the sophistication of that system, many archaeologists believed that the Hohokam were Mesoamerican immigrants who brought their knowledge of irrigation with them when they settled in the Southwest. Hohokam material culture did, in fact, possess a distinctly Mesoamerican flavor: three-dimensional clay figurines, palettes, censors, pyrite-backed mirrors, and, above all, ballcourts, platform mounds, and large canals. Those artifacts and forms of public architecture reveal more cultural affinity with societies to the south than they do with the Anasazi or the Mogollon. But most archaeologists have now discarded the immigration hypothesis, arguing that the Archaic peoples of south central Arizona developed into the Hohokam about A.D. 200 rather than 300 B.C., as was earlier thought. Goods and ideas moved from Mesoamerica to the Southwest and back again, but not populations.

The Hohokam did not live by irrigation alone. Where abundant surface water was available, they dug canals. Where such water was absent, they channeled the flow of arroyos onto alluvial deltas or constructed hillside terraces known as *trincheras* to retard runoff and retain moisture. They also manipulated a wide variety of wild or semidomesticated plants—including little barley, chenopods, amaranth, panic grass, devil's claw, and agave—to extract more food and fiber from them. Along the western margins of the Tortolita Mountains near Marana, for example, archaeologists Paul and Suzanne Fish have discovered an estimated 42,000 Hohokam rock piles extending across more than two square miles. Nearby are huge roasting pits that consistently yield agave remains. According to the Fishes and their colleagues, the Hohokam of the northern Tucson Basin were cultivating agave on a massive scale—a form of agriculture that could be carried out on the rocky bajada of a mountain range miles away from the Santa Cruz River because the agaves did not need to be irrigated. The rock piles served as a cover to reduce evaporation and protect the bases of the stems and the roots of the agaves from rodents. Perhaps no other site better demonstrates the agricultural diversification of the Hohokam.

Their ingenuity extended to wild resources as well. No matter how large their settlements grew, the Hohokam continued to harvest the bounty of the desert, especially mesquite pods, saguaro fruit, cholla buds, and the greens of wild plants. They also hunted large and small game, developing different strategies for the pursuit of each. Archaeologist Frank Bayham has shown that Ventana Cave in the arid Papaguería served as a base camp from which the Hohokam could hunt deer and bighorn sheep. Christine Szuter, on the other hand, argues that the very act of clearing the desert for cultivation may actually have increased the densities of jackrabbits and rodents. That allowed the Hohokam, including women and children, to practice "garden hunting" that could be carried out in conjunction with agricultural tasks.

The Hohokam needed these wild resources to buffer them against environmental fluctuations even their impressive systems of water control could not overcome. A detailed examination of the irrigation network at La Ciudad along the Salt River revealed that sections had to be rebuilt or abandoned after floods. Through the analysis of tree rings from the Salt and Verde drainages, dendrochronologist Donald Graybill and his colleagues were able to pinpoint some of the floods by reconstructing the annual flow of the Salt River from A.D. 740 to 1370. They found that numerous large floods surged down the Salt between 798 and 805, apparently forcing many Hohokam populations to leave the Salt River Valley and settle along the Agua Fria, Verde, and New rivers, and in the Tonto Basin. Then, in 899, the largest floods in the entire 630-year span roared out of the mountains, devastating canal systems and making irrigation agriculture impossible for several years. Like the farmers of Phoenix and Tempe in the late nineteenth century, the Hohokam learned that the Salt could ravage as well as sustain them.

Nonetheless, they persevered and expanded. Between A.D. 700 and 1150,

Hohokam red-on-buff pottery dominated the ceramics of communities from what is now Flagstaff to the Santa Cruz Valley. Ballcourts also proliferated. By the eleventh century there were more than 200 of these oval, bowl-shaped structures in the Hohokam region. Most scholars believe that some variant of the Mesoamerican rubber ballgame was played on these earthen courts. Furthermore, they speculate that the rituals associated with the games were one of the primary mechanisms by which the Hohokam created a regional social system that stretched across the Sonoran Desert and beyond. The regularity of their spacing—with about 5.5 kilometers between ballcourts in the Salt River Valley—may reflect some similarity in the size of basic Hohokam political and economic units. But ballcourts may also have brought different groups together to watch the games and to exchange goods at trade fairs that grew up around them. At a time when floods periodically forced the Hohokam to decentralize their "irrigation communities," the ritualized games maintained their social and cultural cohesion.

After A.D. 1100, however, social and ecological forces transformed Hohokam society. North of the Salt and Gila river valleys, red-on-buff ceramics almost disappeared. In the Salt-Gila heartland, Hohokam congregated into larger settlements straddling longer and more interconnected canals. Platform mounds surrounded by walled compounds replaced ballcourts as the most prominent form of public architecture. The distribution of luxury and ceremonial items became far less uniform, suggesting that Hohokam society was growing more centralized and more hierarchical, with groups fighting over strategic resources. The traditional concept of the Hohokam as egalitarian desert farmers now seems too simplistic, and it appears that coercion as well as cooperation characterized Hohokam life, at least during the Classic Period of A.D. 1150 to 1450.

*   *   *   The Mogollon

Even more radical changes rocked the third major pre-Hispanic culture of the Southwest: the Mogollon. The Mogollon ranged across the mountains and desert of southeastern Arizona, southwestern New Mexico, and northern Mexico, the region that later became known as the Apachería when Athapaskan-speaking groups moved into the area in the seventeenth century. Like the Anasazi and the Hohokam, the Mogollon probably represented an extension of late Archaic ways of life, gradually making the transition from hunting and gathering to agriculture during the first millennium B.C. By A.D.

200 they were at least semisedentary, living in pit-house settlements on high mesas or knolls towering above valley floors.

These early villages averaged only about seventeen pit houses, but as the Mogollon mastered the techniques of mountain agriculture, the size of their communities gradually increased. One of these techniques may have been small-scale irrigation, but more important were forms of dry or runoff farming, especially the construction of contour terraces on gentle mountain slopes and checkdams along upland drainages. The Mogollon intensified their agriculture by exploiting a wide variety of environmental niches, including mesas and hill slopes at higher elevations, where rainfall was greater. Nonetheless, like the Anasazi, they also had to move frequently in response to changing environmental conditions.

Mogollon communities, many of them oriented around great kivas, grew steadily after A.D. 750. Then, about A.D. 1000, a residential transition from pit houses to aboveground masonry pueblos began. In the north, the rapid penetration of Mogollon territory by Anasazi groups accompanied this trend, and many archaeologists believe that the Anasazi eventually assimilated the northern Mogollon. Whatever the processes—colonization, displacement, or amalgamation—cultural boundaries between the Anasazi and the northern Mogollon blurred during the late pre-Hispanic period.

Mogollon groups to the south, on the other hand, continued to maintain a distinct identity during the Classic Mimbres period (A.D. 1000–1150). In southwestern New Mexico, southeastern Arizona, and northern Chihuahua, their communities flourished, with large pueblos, such as Galaz, consisting of six to eight separate clusters of rooms containing more than thirty rooms apiece. There was also a pronounced shift in ceremonial architecture as great kivas gave way to plazas, a change that may have taken place in order to accommodate more people at community-wide ceremonies. At the same time, however, small subterranean kivas once again appeared, suggesting that some sort of ritual organization existed below the village level. If so, Mogollon religion may have been growing more elaborate, perhaps in response to the increasing complexity of Mogollon society in general.

No better indication of the society's sophistication can be found than the pottery the Mogollon produced. Beginning in the eleventh century, potters in the Mimbres Valley achieved an unrivaled mastery of proportion and pictorial representation. Alternating between bold geometric designs and naturalistic renditions of Southwestern animals, Classic Mimbres black-on-white bowls crawl and swirl with scorpions, turtles, waterfowl, and jackrabbits. There are batlike monsters, coupling antelopes, and human fetuses struggling to escape from the eggs of four-legged creatures. The images range from the mundane to the fantastic, but all share a cleanness of line that makes Mimbres pottery one of the great achievements of Southwestern art.

Like most such florescences, however, the Mimbres tradition proved as transient as the society that created it. The Classic Southern Mogollon lasted little more than a century, flowering in the 1000s and withering by 1150. And although many Mimbres sites were reoccupied during the late 1100s, the inhabitants did not exercise the same triumphant command over clay. On the contrary, new and inferior ceramic traditions moved into the area, accompanied by changes in architecture, burial customs, and settlement patterns. Whatever motivated the Mimbres potters to transform utilitarian vessels into art was gone, almost as if their imaginations had drained away through the "kill holes" punched in the center of bowls entombed in Mimbres graves.

* * *   Shifting Populations and Power in the Late Prehistoric Period

The decline of the Southern Mogollon raises some fascinating questions about parallel developments in the Southwestern archaeological record. If the dating is correct, the Mimbres culture disappeared about the same time that Anasazi and Hohokam groups were contracting their territories. Those developments also coincided with the collapse of the remarkable civilization at Chaco Canyon. Were such events strictly fortuitous? Most archaeologists don't think so. Instead, they believe that broad regional factors must have affected societies throughout the Southwest, displacing many people and transforming the societies of others.

One possible factor was climate change. We have already seen that a long drought imposed intolerable stresses on many Kayenta Anasazi communities in the 1100s. Growing aridity also destroyed the delicate balance of adaptation at Chaco, a balance made ever more precarious by wood cutting and soil erosion. Similar processes—shifting precipitation patterns, the denuding of nearby trees and shrubs, crop failures, periodic famines—apparently affected the Mimbres region as well. But while comparable trends have been postulated for peripheral areas occupied by the Hohokam, no direct evidence of environmental stress has yet been found below the Colorado Plateau. On the contrary, prehistoric populations were actually increasing in the Verde Valley, along the San Pedro, and in the northern Tucson Basin. Environmental conditions may have been more localized than was previously thought. Consequently, any model based on one region cannot be uncritically applied across the Southwest as a whole.

Recently, however, a number of archaeologists have proposed another explanation for the displacements of the early 1100s, one that involves social rather than natural perturbations. According to this theory, trade with Mesoamerica played a critical role in Southwestern societies, and Chaco dominated that trade during the tenth and eleventh centuries. Because of the number of Mexican trade items (copper bells and macaws, for example) and Mesoamerican architectural traits (core veneer masonry, colonnades, and T-shaped doorways), scholars such as Charles DiPeso and Robert Lister even believed that Mesoamerican merchants known as *pochteca* actually took up residence at Chaco to direct the flow of goods and information. The position of the Mimbres Mogollon in this regional system is unclear, but we know that the Hohokam functioned as important middlemen between the Chaco elite and the Mesoamerican societies of western Mexico. They did so by controlling the production and distribution of shell artifacts from the Gulf of California, which they traded to Chaco for items the Mesoamericans wanted, particularly turquoise. When Chaco crumbled, the Hohokam suffered as well, losing both their most stable market and their integral position in the network of regional exchange.

The last few centuries before the arrival of the Spaniards present a complex and confusing puzzle to archaeologists. It was a time characterized by dramatic realignments of both population and power across the Southwest, a time when pre-Hispanic groups abandoned certain areas and converged on others. The Tonto Basin became the location of a number of major settlements during the 1300s, as did upland areas to the east. Grasshopper Pueblo near modern Cibecue, Arizona, had 500 rooms. The largest of the Homol'ovi settlements northeast of Winslow along the Little Colorado River possessed more than 700 structures. Many small sites were abandoned. Most large sites were located near major springs and streams.

Among the Hohokam, a new form of public architecture came into being: the multistoried "big house" best exemplified by the ruins at Casa Grande. Moreover, elite groups began living, not just conducting ceremonies, on platform mounds surrounded by walls or palisades. Social stratification increased as political power became concentrated in fewer and fewer hands. Among the Western Anasazi, in contrast, pueblos grew up around large plazas where the entire population could gather to participate in public rituals. About the same time, rectangular kivas appeared, suggesting that Anasazi religion, like the katsina ceremonies today, had private as well as public functions.

Such reorganization involved changes in the way people thought as well as in the way they lived. During the 1300s a number of Mexican motifs suddenly emerge in the rock art, kiva murals, and pottery designs of people living from the Mogollon Rim to the Rio Grande Valley. There are plumed serpents, parrots, macaws, and, above all, masked figures—precursors of the katsinam who are an integral part of the religious rituals of the western Pueblos today. Among groups like the Hopi, katsinam are supernatural beings who possess a wide range of powers—the power to cure, the power to insure fertility, and, most important, the power to bring rain. The katsinam also represent a form of ancestor recognition—a profound link with people who have gone before. That link connects modern clans, communities, and institutions with the prehistoric leaders who transformed Anasazi and Mogollon society in the thirteenth and fourteenth centuries. Nowhere is the bond between the past and the present more vibrant.

Archaeologist E. Charles Adams has traced the diffusion of belief in the katsinam across the prehistoric Southwest. He believes it developed along the upper Little Colorado River in east central Arizona between A.D. 1275 and 1325. That is where three major features associated with it—enclosed plazas, rectangular kivas, and representations of katsinam and katsina masks on Four-mile Polychrome pottery—first converged. From there, the belief system spread north to the Homol'ovi area and the Hopi Mesas and east to Zuni villages. Adams also argues that the katsinam may have been transformed from an earlier emphasis on warfare and death into a magnificent obsession with rain. When Hopis die, part of their essence becomes clouds. When katsinam are present, the clouds gather. Both the ancestors and the katsinam are bearers of prosperity, including rain, one of the greatest gifts supernaturals can bestow on an arid land.

It was no accident that the emphasis on rain developed during the fourteenth and fifteenth centuries. Drought struck the Hopi Mesas in the 1370s, the 1430s, the 1440s, and from 1455 to 1465. Similar episodes of aridity desiccated the Zuni and Rio Grande regions during much the same period. As their crops shriveled and their storehouses emptied, people strengthened their faith that the presence of the katsinam brought rain.

The more people believed, the greater the power of the religious leaders grew. The Anasazi developed strategies to monitor harvests, redistribute food, increase trade, and organize communal work projects such as cleaning springs and repairing reservoirs and dams. The religion itself developed into one of the central integrating principles of Pueblo society, reinforcing and crosscutting the ties of kinship and clan. It also brought people together to carry out the complex ceremonies the katsinam demanded. Participation in the belief system was a powerful way of incorporating newcomers into a community and reducing conflict over scarce and necessary resources, particularly agricultural land. Settlements grew larger in the process, a trend that accelerated as sources of water dried up and people congregated around the springs that still seeped and the streams that continued to flow. Thus the Anasazi and Mogollon appropriated symbols and supernaturals from Mesoamerica and transmuted them into something uniquely Puebloan, a cycle of rituals that wove living and dead into an enduring plea for rain.

Those early katsinam may never have presented themselves to the Hohokam. Nevertheless, they too must have prayed for rain. Sometime in the fifteenth or early sixteenth century, Hohokam platform-mound communities disintegrated and their canal systems fell into disuse. The irrigation societies that had endured for a millennium dried up and disappeared. Some scholars argue that prolonged irrigation rendered fields too saline for cultivation. Others contend that unregulated competition for irrigation water caused the progressive abandonment of downstream canals and the settlements they supported. Entrenched inside their "big houses," conflicting elites may have destroyed the very civilization they sought to control.

Whatever the exact nature of the Hohokam demise, Native Americans in central and southern Arizona were following very different ways of life when the Jesuit missionary Eusebio Francisco Kino and his companions rode into the area two hundred years later. By then the people of the Sonoran Desert were Piman speakers who may or may not have been descendants of the Hohokam. Like the Hohokam, they raised corn, beans, squash, and cotton along the rivers of the region. Unlike the Hohokam, they constructed no ballcourts, platform mounds, or large canals. Most archaeologists believe that the differences between the two were the result of developments that predated the arrival of the Europeans. But as the following chapter suggests, Spaniards may have had a tremendous impact on Native Americans in Arizona long before they actually colonized the region. Culture change does not necessarily require the direct encounter of two groups. On the contrary, one culture may transform—even devastate—another generations before the two meet.

2

The Arrival of the Europeans

Before they learned to read and write in government schools, Akimel O'odham (River People, or Pima Indians) living along the Gila River recorded their history by carving notched symbols into the soft wood of willow or the ribs of the giant saguaro. Caressing these mnemonic marks, Piman keepers of the sticks would then "tell" the events of the past. The narratives do not march to the same rhythm as Western histories. There are no "great men," no prime movers, no sweeping sense of historical progress. Instead, isolated occurrences are simply described—a battle, a harvest, a strange plague.

Nevertheless, certain trends emerge from those terse recitations —trends that resonate with the fatalistic power of global forces glimpsed only at the local level. The earliest of the surviving calendar sticks begins in 1833, the year of a great meteor shower. Nearly seventy years later, when a tubercular anthropologist named Frank Russell wrote down the stick's telling, the only entry for 1901 and 1902 was the opening of a day school in a nearby Maricopa Indian village. In between, there are stories about Apache attacks and epidemics, battles with the Mohave and Quechan Indians of the Colorado River, and the arrival of telegraph lines and railroads. Seven decades of Arizona history are refracted through the lenses of people who began the century as proud and independent farmers, and who ended it as impoverished wards of the state. The notches on the calendar sticks are therefore both epigrams and elegies. The world they describe was already in the process of being transformed when the records begin. By the time the sticks were entombed in a museum collection, the world was gone.

❋ ❋ ❋ The Columbian Exchange in Arizona

It was a world perched on the periphery of a periphery, a frontier between the colonial expansion of Europe and the last defiant stand of native North America. Even though they had never been conquered or missionized, the Akimel O'odham had been drawn into the European orbit. In 1837–38, for example, the oldest Pima calendar stick recorded the following incident:

> One cold night in the spring a Pima at Rso'tuk was irrigating his wheat field by moonlight. Without thought of enemies he built a fire to warm himself. This the Apaches saw and came about him in the thicket. Hearing the twigs cracking under their feet, he ran to the village and gave the alarm. The Pimas gathered in sufficient numbers to surround the Apaches, who attempted to reach the hills on their horses. Two horses stumbled into a gully, and their riders were killed before they could extricate themselves. The others were followed and all killed.

There is no mention of white men in this short narrative. But the reasons the Pimas and Apaches were fighting, and the very way they fought, demonstrate how thoroughly the worlds of both had been transformed by what historian Alfred Crosby calls the Columbian Exchange. Take, for example, Apache methods of transportation. In 1541 the expedition of Francisco Vázquez de Coronado ventured onto the western fringes of the Great Plains after wintering among the Pueblo Indians of northern New Mexico. There Coronado and his men encountered Native Americans they called Querechos. The Querechos may have been Athapaskan-speaking ancestors of the Apaches, but they traveled on foot, their belongings pulled by dog train, as they pursued the great herds of bison across the plains. The daring Indian horsemen who struck terror into European settlers from Canada to northern Mexico were creations of the conquest. Like the Apaches who raided the Pimas, they did not exist until Indians learned how to steal or break wild Spanish horses.

And what of the lone Pima irrigating his wheat field that cold spring night? Neither he nor his Apache assailants had ever lived in a mission or paid homage to a Spanish king. Yet the very crop he cultivated came from seed introduced by missionaries like Padre Eusebio Francisco Kino in the seventeenth and eighteenth centuries. Prior to the arrival of the Europeans, the major Pima food crops had been corn, beans, and squash. Those cultigens could only be grown during spring and summer months when frosts were not a danger. Wheat, on the other hand, could be sown in December and harvested in June, enabling the Pimas to farm year-round. That allowed them to live in larger, more permanent settlements—a crucial defensive measure against their Indian enemies. Both the Pimas and the Apaches saw their lives transformed by Old World animals and Old World plants.

Those material changes were more important than the exploits of individual European military or religious leaders. The explorations of *conquistadores* like Coronado may capture our imaginations, but in terms of their historical impact, they were little more than ripples on the surface of a deep, dark lake. The events that truly revolutionized human society in Arizona took place quietly, without notice: the exchange of seeds, the theft of a horse herd, the introduction of an iron plow. Those were the acts that changed people's lives, even people who never lived under the flags of Mexico or Spain.

One of the most devastating consequences of European contact occurred unintentionally, at the microbial level. When Columbus crossed the Atlantic in 1492, the peoples of North and South America had been biologically isolated for at least 10,000 years. Melting ice sheets and rising oceans had severed them from their Eurasian kinsmen, so they never participated in the genetic changes taking place in the Old World.

Perhaps the most important of these changes was the development of partial immunity against so-called childhood diseases, such as smallpox, measles, and influenza. Many of the plagues that swept across Europe, Asia, and Africa originated among animals, especially those that lived in herds. Old World peoples had grown up with horses, sheep, goats, and cattle for hundreds of generations. They had been infected by, and had developed relatively successful adaptations to, many of the microbes that spread from animals to humans and back again in an exchange that produced smallpox and cowpox; measles, distemper, and rinderpest; and the constantly mutating strains of influenza.

The people of the New World were not so resistant. The few animals they had domesticated—dogs and turkeys in North America, guinea pigs and llamas on the southern continent—did not host the sort of viruses that could ravage human populations. Consequently, epidemic disease was relatively unknown in the Americas before the Europeans arrived.

Once Eurasian epidemics arrived, however, they breached the genetic insularity of the New World with terrifying rapidity. Smallpox first broke out in the Caribbean in 1518. Two years later it spread to Mexico, where it pustulated into a great pandemic, sapping the strength of the Aztec and Tarascan empires and weakening the Incas nearly a decade before Pizarro and his men ever reached Andean South America. The results were catastrophic: drastic population decline and the disintegration of many Indian societies. Indian populations declined by 66 to 95 percent during the sixteenth, seventeenth, and eighteenth centuries.

We may never know when the first wave of disease spread across Arizona. Because no Europeans lived among the Indians of Arizona for most of the sixteenth and seventeenth centuries, the documentary record remains largely mute. Nevertheless, Old World diseases like smallpox, measles, and influenza must have taken their toll. A few anthropologists even speculate that the collapse of supposedly pre-Hispanic civilizations like the Hohokam may have been caused, at least in part, by such epidemics. Most archaeologists contend that the Hohokam were gone by A.D. 1450, but Hohokam chronologies are notoriously imprecise. It is conceivable that some communities survived into the sixteenth century only to wither under pestilential winds.

✸   ✸   ✸   The Early Spanish Entradas

Unfortunately, the records left by Spanish explorers shed little light on the controversy. The narratives are vague, contradictory, and full of gaps. Fading memories, a faulty knowledge of geography, and a desire to tell superiors what they wanted to hear often worked against their historical reliability. And yet these early narratives have their own strengths and fascination. During the sixteenth century, tiny bands of conquistadores from the Iberian Peninsula toppled empires and spanned the globe. It was an explosion of conquest and exploration unparalleled in the history of the world, and it flashed across Arizona, creating legends that enticed other Europeans and Euro-Americans for generations to come.

The first visitors from the Old World may have been Alvar Núñez Cabeza de Vaca and his three companions, including a North African named Estevan. Shipwrecked off the Gulf coast of what is now Texas in 1528, the *náufragos*

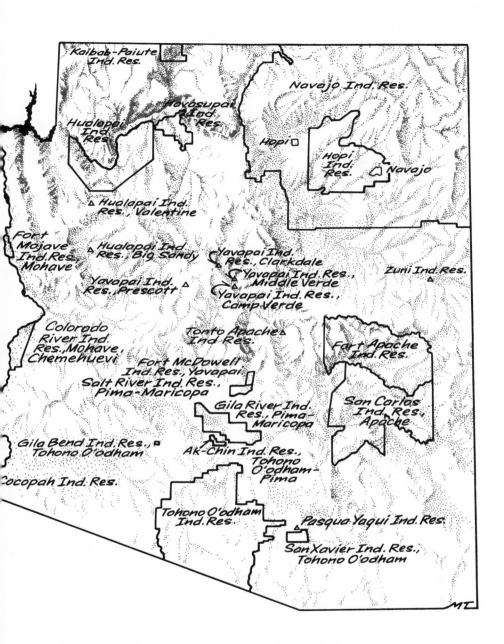

Indian Reservations in Arizona

(shipwrecked ones) survived as slaves and shamans before trekking across half a continent. Some scholars believe they crossed Texas into New Mexico, perhaps nicking the southeastern corner of Arizona before turning south into Sonora. Others argue that they followed a more southerly route across Coahuila and Chihuahua. Regardless of where they went, however, Cabeza de Vaca and his comrades heard stories of Indian kingdoms to the north "where there were towns of great population and great houses." When they finally ran into a Spanish slaving party north of Culiacán, Sinaloa, eight years later, they and their tales reached Mexico City. Those stories launched the first documented penetrations of Arizona.

Fray Marcos de Niza led the initial expedition. Because Viceroy Antonio de Mendoza wanted to find his own Tenochtitlán while keeping rival Hernán Cortés at bay, the Franciscan and his guide, Estevan, slipped quietly out of Mexico City and up the west coast of New Spain. As adventurous as the friar was cautious, Estevan plunged on ahead, traveling as far north as the Zuni pueblos. But the luck that had won him fame as a curer in Texas ran out among the Zunis, who pierced him with arrows. No one knows what Estevan saw or learned before he died.

Fray Marcos was more fortunate, but he may not have had as much to tell. The Franciscan claimed to have followed in Estevan's footsteps until he came to a hill across from the Zuni pueblo of Cíbola, which he described as "larger than the city of Mexico." A number of researchers, however, question whether he left Sonora at all. They agree with Coronado, who called Fray Marcos a liar.

Regardless of his veracity, the Franciscan's glowing description of Cíbola—just one of seven cities that he called "the greatest and best" of all Spanish discoveries in the New World—triggered the *entrada* of Francisco Vázquez de Coronado in 1540. Governor of Nueva Galicia in western Mexico, Coronado led more than 300 Spaniards, including at least three women, and more than a thousand Indians on a bold, well-organized venture that took them from southern Nayarit to central Kansas. And the excursions of his lieutenants extended Coronado's own travels. Melchor Díaz crossed the Colorado River into California. Pedro de Tovar fought a pitched battle with the Hopi Indians. García López de Cárdenas became the first European to see the Grand Canyon. Hernando de Alarcón sailed up the Gulf of California and navigated the shoals of the lower Colorado. Together or in small groups, Coronado's party made the first systematic European exploration of the Southwest.

Apparently Arizona did not fire their imaginations. With the exception of Alarcón, who quizzed the Yuman-speaking Indians along the Colorado about their methods of curing, their sexual practices, and their chronic warfare with one another, most members of the Coronado expedition showed little interest in the Native Americans there. It is also difficult to reconstruct their route through the state. Historian Herbert Eugene Bolton and geographer Carl Sauer believed that they ascended the San Pedro River, but Charles DiPeso argued that they crossed into Arizona near the modern town of Douglas. With no archaeological evidence to corroborate Coronado's passage through Arizona, the documentary evidence is like pieces of a puzzle without a frame.

What we do know is this: Coronado's failure to find great cities of gold and silver put an end to Spanish designs on the region for the next forty years. No other Europeans entered Arizona until the 1580s, and then they came from New Mexico, not Sonora. The fantasy of Cíbola could not compare with the fortunes being made in Zacatecas, Guanajuato, and San Luis Potosí. Because of those great silver strikes, Mexico's bonanza lay forever to the south.

Yet Spanish interest in Arizona still flickered. In 1583, Antonio de Espejo led nine soldiers and more than a hundred Zunis on a search for precious metals through the north central part of the state. Espejo traded with the Hopis and claimed their territory for Philip II of Spain. He also discovered silver and copper deposits in the vicinity of Jerome, east of Prescott. Both actions rekindled Spanish curiosity about Arizona, but neither resulted in a permanent Spanish presence here.

An expedition of more far-reaching consequences was Juan de Oñate's colonization of northern New Mexico in 1598. Oñate and his large party of men, women, and livestock left the mining communities of southern Chihuahua in late January of that year. By November the Spaniards were in Hopi country, chasing after Espejo's ore. But a bitter northern Arizona winter drove them back to the Zuni pueblos and eventually to the Rio Grande. Oñate therefore commissioned one of his captains—Marcos Farfán de los Godos—to search for the minerals instead.

Farfán and eight companions, along with some Hopi guides, rode southwest across the Little Colorado into the timbered country of the Mogollon Rim. There he and his party encountered Jumana Indians, who may have been Yuman-speaking Yavapais. The Jumanas daubed themselves with minerals of various colors, wore skins of deer and beaver, and lived on a diet of venison, wild plant foods, and maize. A stark contrast to the sedentary Hopis, with their multistoried pueblos and their abundant fields, the Jumanas led Farfán to the valley of the Verde River.

The Verde enchanted Farfán, who waxed eloquent about its "splendid pastures, fine plains, and excellent land for farming." The river also passed within a few miles of the mineral deposits discovered by Espejo, which were being mined by the Indians themselves. Farfán wrote, "These veins are so long and wide that one-half of the people in New Spain could stake out claims in this land." His description made the Verde Valley sound like an Eden where Spaniards could find two of the things—water and silver—that they loved most. The legend of Arizona's fabulous mineral wealth was being born.

* * * The Athapaskans

Despite Farfán's paean, the Verde Valley never became a part of the Spanish empire. Like the rest of Arizona north of the Gila River, it remained in the hands of Native Americans for the next three hundred years. By 1600, however, the Spaniards had encountered most of the Indians—Pais, River Yumans, and Hopis—who emerge more clearly in later historical records. But none of the early explorers recorded any contacts with two of Arizona's largest and most famous Native American peoples—the Athapaskan-speaking Navajos and Apaches—at least not on Arizona soil. To Coronado, in fact, much of what later became the Apachería (Apache territory) was rugged *despoblado*—an unpopulated terrain of pine forests and rushing rivers the Spaniards were only too happy to leave.

It is possible that the ancestors of the Apaches and Navajos simply stayed out of the Spaniards' way. Coronado crossed paths with the Apachean Querechos in northeastern New Mexico, and Espejo fought people who were probably Athapaskans in northwestern New Mexico. But Apaches apparently did not move south of the Little Colorado until the 1600s. Like the Spaniards, the Athapaskans were relative latecomers to the Southwest.

They were also consummate opportunists. Linguists have shown that all Navajo and Apache groups spoke dialects of a single language, one related to those spoken by Athapaskan hunters and gatherers in northern Canada. In other words, the people who later became the Navajos and Chiricahua, Jicarilla, Lipan, Mescalero, Kiowa, and Western Apaches migrated south along the western edge of the Great Plains at about the same time. Trains of coyote- and wolf-sized dogs carried their belongings. Bison provided them with meat and hides. Because of their dependence on the huge "cows" of the prairie, Oñate dubbed them the "Vaquero Apache."

Once they reached the Southwest, however, the Athapaskans diverged as they absorbed many of the traits of their neighbors. Some groups established strong trading relationships with the Pueblo peoples, exchanging salt, bison hides, and deer skins for cotton blankets and agricultural produce. They also began farming in well-watered locations throughout the Four Corners area, including Arizona. By the 1630s, Spaniards in New Mexico were referring to them as Apaches de Nabajú.

Pueblo influences only deepened after the 1680 Pueblo Revolt, which temporarily drove the Spaniards out of northern New Mexico. When the Spaniards reconquered the area in 1694, many rebels took refuge among the Apaches de Nabajú, teaching them how to make pottery, weave close-coiled baskets, and perform complex ceremonies, and inspiring them to organize themselves into matrilineal clans. Puebloan and Athapaskan elements fused to create a new system of action and belief that became Navajo culture.

The Navajos also took much of value from the Spaniards, particularly a thorough knowledge of domestic animals. Horses enabled them to raid their neighbors. Sheep and goats allowed them to fan out across the mesa and canyon country of the Colorado Plateau. By the end of the eighteenth century, they were even carrying on a brisk trade in woolen blankets with Spanish communities in New Mexico. Hunters and gatherers by origin, the Navajos quickly transformed themselves into the greatest Indian pastoralists in North America.

Contact with the Pueblo peoples and the Spaniards revolutionized Apache society as well. During the seventeenth century, small Apache groups continued their southward migrations. As bands splintered and drifted away from one another, cultural and linguistic differences developed. The Western Apaches, who settled in the White Mountains, adopted matrilineal clans and ceremonial masked dancers from their Pueblo neighbors. The Chiricahua Apaches, on the other hand, never organized themselves into clans, indicating that their relations with the Pueblo Indians were more tenuous.

But the Chiricahuas did ally themselves with small groups of Uto-Aztecan hunters and gatherers in southeastern Arizona and northern Mexico known as the Sumas, Mansos, Janos, and Jocomes. When the Spaniards appeared, these groups and the Apache newcomers joined together to raid Spanish herds. The Sumas and Mansos died out or were absorbed into Apache society, but the Chiricahuas prospered. They became the specters that rode through Hispanic nightmares for the next two hundred years.

❋ ❋ The Missionization of the Pimería Alta

By the late 1600s, the Apaches and their allies had begun preying upon the Piman communities of southern Arizona. In March 1699, the Jesuit missionary Eusebio Francisco Kino and Juan Mateo Manje, the second-highest civil official in Sonora, visited O'odham settlements in the Tucson Basin. Manje reported that O'odham along the San Pedro River had "just finished devastating

a ranchería of Apaches, capturing some children and other booty. This was in response to an Apache attack on the pueblo of Santa María three weeks earlier, when the enemies ran off the few horses the community had. The people of Humari [a Pima chief] had gone forth to avenge that raid, just as these Pimans would do now."

Earlier, the Spaniards had tried to bring the Hopis into their sphere of influence. In 1629 the Franciscans founded a mission at Awatovi, followed by additional missions at Shongopovi and Oraibi. But the Hopis soon began to resist the gray-robed friars in a variety of ways, poisoning one of the first missionaries and protesting the abuses of others. When the Pueblo Revolt broke out, the Hopis swiftly dispatched the four Franciscans living among them. Then, in 1700, to make sure the missionaries never regained a foothold in their territory, they destroyed the Christian village of Awatovi and killed its men. Both the Franciscans and the Jesuits made sporadic attempts to return to the Hopi mesas, but their attempts failed.

As a result, the Sonoran Desert rather than the Colorado Plateau became the focus of missionary activity in Arizona for the rest of the colonial period. Missionaries and Spanish officials alike dreamed of extending the empire to the Gila River, to Hopi country, and beyond, but Apache resistance halted the Spanish advance in what came to be called the Pimería Alta.

Even there the European presence was precarious. Beginning in 1687, Kino and his colleagues established missions among O'odham living in the river valleys of northern Sonora. Some of the new converts rebelled in 1695, but the missions weathered that storm and Kino pushed onward. He explored Tohono O'odham (Papago) country as far west as the Colorado River, visited the Sobaipuri Pimas along the Santa Cruz and San Pedro, and traveled as far north as the Salt River Valley, where he preached to the Gileños, as the Akimel O'odham living along the Salt and Gila rivers were called. Nearly everywhere he and his companions went, the O'odham welcomed them with food, arches made of branches, and simple wooden crosses. The tall Jesuit was as charismatic as he was energetic, and the Pimas responded to his warmth and his drive.

They also appreciated the material gifts he gave them: grain seeds, vegetables, fruit trees, and small herds of livestock. Kino and his fellow missionaries knew that in order to convert the Indians, they had to change the way they lived as well. The foundation of their efforts therefore became the policy of *reducción*, which involved "reducing" the Indians to village life, in which they could be catechized and controlled. The O'odham moved to gathering camps each year to harvest mesquite pods, cholla buds, saguaro fruit, and other wild foods. It was part of their seasonal round, but the Jesuits feared such movement because they believed that the Indians reverted to their "pagan" habits away from mission discipline.

In northern Sonora, most Pimas accepted, or were forced to accept, Spanish ideas about the way civilized people should live. In Arizona, on the other hand, missionization proceeded more slowly. Kino founded missions San Xavier and San Miguel at the Piman communities of Bac and Guevavi along the Santa Cruz, but the Jesuits soon abandoned those northern outposts. They were not re-staffed until 1732, twenty-one years after Kino died.

The rest of Pimería Alta never came under Spanish control. Nonetheless, both the Sobaipuris along the San Pedro River and the Gileños along the Gila became staunch allies of the Spaniards, fighting the Apaches and trading with the communities of Tucson and Tubac. In the words of historian Kieran McCarty, the Pimas served as "the perennial listening post during both the Spanish and Mexican periods for situations developing beyond the frontier." Without the O'odham allies, Hispanic Arizona would not have survived.

*   *   *   The Beginnings of Hispanic Arizona

Spaniards did not establish towns for themselves in southern Arizona until the second half of the eighteenth century. By the late 1600s, however, a few settlers were grazing their stock on the lush grasslands drained by the headwaters of the Santa Cruz. Ten years before Kino and Manje explored the Pimería Alta, José Romo de Vivar was running cattle at the southern end of the Huachuca Mountains. A prominent Sonoran rancher and miner, he may have been southern Arizona's first Hispanic pioneer.

More colonists trickled into the region after the Jesuits reestablished the missions of Bac and Guevavi in 1732. But the most important impetus to Spanish settlement was the discovery of large chunks (*bolas*) and slabs (*planchas*) of silver lying on the ground near a mining camp called Arizonac, which was located in Sonora a few miles southwest of modern Nogales. The name may have come from two Piman words, *ali* and *shonak*, which mean "small springs." Or prominent Basques in the area, including Juan Bautista de Anza the Elder, father of the founder of Alta California, may have called the camp "valuable rocky places" (*arritza onac*) or "good oaks" (*aritz onac*). Whatever its linguistic origin, the designation bequeathed both its name and its legend to the territory that took shape to the north more than a century later.

The discovery of the silver itself was made by a Yaqui Indian in 1736. Prospectors streamed into the region, creating Arizona's first mining boom. But Anza decided that the silver was buried treasure, not a natural deposit. He did so to defend the interests of his king, who was entitled to half of any treasure but only a fifth of the proceeds from any mine. Because Anza commanded the *presidio* (garrison) of Fronteras and also served as *justicia mayor,* or chief justice, of Sonora, his authority carried great weight. Disappointed miners soon left for other bonanzas, and Arizonac sank back into obscurity. But the name and the images it conjured wormed their way into the lore of the time, tantalizing prospectors with the promise of veins so rich you could pick up the silver with your bare hands. Like Espejo's ore, that lure became part of Arizona's myth. The dream of lost Spanish mines even danced in the heads of the railroad speculators who pressured President James Buchanan to buy southern Arizona from Mexico in the early 1850s.

By its very nature, however, prospecting was a nomadic and evanescent occupation. Most of the pioneers who remained in Arizona made their living as subsistence farmers and small ranchers, not miners. These were the families that cleared the fields, built up the herds, and constructed homes for themselves along the Santa Cruz and its tributaries. The mission registers of Guevavi recorded their names—Ortega, Bohórquez, Gallego, Covarrubias. They also chronicled the ceremonies that marked the end of one generation and the beginning of another.

The generations faced extinction on several occasions. The first was in 1751, when O'odham led by Luis Oacpicagigua rebelled against the harsh discipline of several Jesuit missionaries. Luis and his followers killed two priests and more than a hundred Spanish settlers before the revolt dissipated and Luis surrendered to the Spaniards at the Pima community of Tubac along the Santa Cruz River. To prevent future uprisings among the O'odham, the Spanish Crown established a new *presidio* (garrison of professional soldiers) at Tubac in 1752. It was the first permanent Spanish settlement in Arizona and the northernmost military outpost of Spanish Sonora.

Like most frontier communities, Tubac was an ethnic melting pot, its population composed not just of Spaniards but also of *coyotes* (Spanish-Indian offspring), mulattos (Spanish-black offspring), *moriscos* (Spanish-mulatto offspring), and Indians from various tribal groups. The captains of the presidios may have been peninsular Spaniards or *criollos* (Spaniards born in the New World). Most *gente de razón* ("people of reason"; non-Indians), in contrast, were products of that fusion of the European, Indian, and African that made colonial Mexico such a vital and fluid society during the Spanish colonial period.

For the next century, these Hispanic pioneers fought a grueling battle for survival along the Santa Cruz River. The dream of northward expansion still flickered. In 1775, Juan Bautista de Anza led a group of Spanish colonists from

Tubac to San Francisco Bay. The Spaniards tried to secure that route five years later by settling along the lower Colorado, but the Yuman-speaking Quechan Indians soon grew tired of Spanish livestock trampling their fields and Franciscan missionaries telling them how to live. Veterans of countless battles against their Cocopa, Maricopa, and O'odham enemies, the Quechans bided their time until the morning of July 17, 1781. Then, in the heat of a desert summer, they surprised the Spaniards during mass and slaughtered them, including the Franciscan missionary Francisco Garcés. According to historian David Weber, the Yuma revolt turned California into an "island" and Arizona into a "cul de sac," severing the Arizona-California connection before it could be firmly established. José de Zúñiga, captain of the Tucson presidio, blazed a trail between Tucson and the Zuni pueblos in 1795, but Apache hostilities prevented that route from becoming well traveled. In the Southwest, Hispanic pioneers moved north–south, not east–west, sealing the isolation of the northwestern provinces.

✳ ✳ ✳ The Apachería

The failure to open those routes left Arizona exposed and beleaguered on the edge of a twisted upthrust of mountain ranges and river gorges known as the Apachería. The region was both a homeland and refuge for the Apaches, to whom livestock raiding became as important as gathering agave or harvesting corn. The Apaches even referred to the people of northern Mexico as their "shepherds"—their arrogance the arrogance of all mounted warriors, whether Scythian, Mongol, or Comanche, who had been preying on farmers and pastoralists since plants and animals were first domesticated in the neolithic Near East.

Because of their bloodthirsty reputation, however, no other Native American group has been as misrepresented or misunderstood. Raiding—"to search out enemy property" in the language of the Western Apaches—was an economic activity, one usually carried out by five to fifteen men. Raids were designed to run off livestock, not to shed the blood of the stock raisers themselves. War, on the other hand, meant "to take death from an enemy," and Apaches waged it to seek revenge for the murder of a kinsman. Blood vengeance was a common theme in Native American cultures across North America. It set the Hurons against the Iroquois Confederacy in the Northeast and the Quechans and Mohaves against the Maricopas and Gila Pimas in the Southwest. It was also one of the few cultural mechanisms that united large numbers of Apaches in a common cause.

The differences between raiding and warfare shed considerable light on the structure of Apache society itself. Like most other Indian groups, kinship was the fundamental principle of Apache culture. There were no hereditary kings or priests, no formal councils of government. In contrast to the Spaniards, the Apaches did not think of themselves as a nation or an empire. On the contrary, the Apaches, like their O'odham enemies, resided in small local groups that were essentially independent of one another. Composed of people related by either blood or marriage, local groups controlled their own farming sites and hunting territories. They also chose their own chiefs, a political reality few Europeans understood. The Apaches recognized larger groupings among themselves, but those entities were more linguistic and geographic than political. Local groups carried out nearly all the important activities of Apache life, including raids.

Warfare, in contrast, transcended the local group. Apaches were matrilineal, meaning they traced their family lines through women. The Western Apaches also organized their matrilineages into clans, an extension of kinship that cut across the boundaries of local groups and bands. According to legend, each clan descended from women who had cleared land for cultivation in a certain area. Clan members could not marry each other, because they were relatives. For the same reason, they were obliged to avenge a clan member's murder. Consequently, many large-scale Apache attacks were organized for the purpose of blood revenge.

The fluidity of Apache society confounded the Spaniards, who had spent seven centuries forging a national identity during the Reconquista (the reconquering of the Iberian Peninsula from Islamic invaders). Like most people, the Iberians interpreted the actions of others through the lens of their own customs and beliefs. Hierarchical and bureaucratic, they attempted to impose hierarchy on the Native Americans they encountered. But the Apaches slipped through Spanish preconceptions as easily as they penetrated the Spanish line of presidios along the frontier. Treaties made with the chief of one local group were not binding on any other group, not to mention the Apaches as a whole. The Apaches broke apart and came together again in patterns of alliance that defied the comprehension of their Spanish adversaries. The Iberians may have considered themselves Basques, Andalusians, or Castilians, but they also swore allegiance to both Majesties—the Spanish Crown and the Roman Catholic Church —whose authorities were absolute in temporal and spiritual affairs.

Apache autonomy ultimately proved to be a fatal weakness. Clan affiliations only partially counterbalanced intense loyalty to the local group. The stable pattern was raiding, not warfare. The various Apache bands never forged a common identity strong enough to drive the Spaniards, Mexicans, or Anglo

Americans out of the Southwest. On the contrary, the Spaniards, and later the Anglo Americans, defeated the Apaches by exploiting divisions among the Indians themselves.

That strategy did not evolve until late in the colonial period, however. Throughout most of the eighteenth century, the Spaniards had to overcome other threats to their northwestern frontier: the Yaqui revolt of 1740, the Pima rebellion of 1751, and the bitter guerrilla warfare of the Seris and Lower Pimas during the 1750s and 1760s. Not until the Seris had been worn down by the largest military campaign in Sonoran colonial history, in fact, were the Spaniards able to turn their full attention to the Apaches. Even then, it took more than twenty years of intense military pressure before the Spaniards and the Apaches achieved a fragile peace.

✻   ✻   ✻   **The Bourbon Reforms**

The first thing the Spaniards did was to realign their presidios. In 1765, Charles III of Spain commissioned the marqués de Rubí to make a sweeping inspection of the northern presidios. Rubí's recommendations resulted in the Reglamento of 1772, a major reorganization of the presidial system carried out by Hugo O'Conor, one of the "Wild Geese" who fled English-occupied Ireland to fight for the Catholic kings of Spain. O'Conor transferred the presidio of Terrenate north to the west bank of the San Pedro in 1776. It survived for less than five years before the garrison limped back to Sonora, decimated by Apache attacks. O'Conor was more successful in 1775 when he relocated the presidio of Tubac forty miles to the north. There, at the new site of San Agustín de Tucson, the soldiers were closer to the Western Apaches, enabling them to mount offensive campaigns into Apache territory more easily. They also had good wood and water and the comforting presence of several nearby O'odham communities. Tucsonenses (Hispanic residents of Tucson) and Pimas fought Apaches together for the next hundred years.

But presidial realignments were only part of much broader shifts in Spanish policy that were known as the Bourbon Reforms (because they took place under the Bourbon kings of Spain). In 1776, Carlos III placed the *provincias internas* (the "interior" or northern provinces, including Sonora) under the direct jurisdiction of the Spanish Crown rather than the viceroy in Mexico City. The king then created the office of *comandante general* to streamline the administration of the provincias internas by giving one official broad civil and military powers. The comandante general was supposed to take decisive action against both Indian and European antagonists, including the Russians on the Pacific coast and the British in the Mississippi Valley. Spanish officials feared that the expansion of the Russians and the British might threaten not only the northern provinces but also the rich silver-mining areas of Zacatecas and San Luis Potosí. Militarization replaced missionization as the dominant philosophy of conquest along the frontier.

The expulsion of the Jesuits in 1767 foreshadowed that change. Missionaries from the Society of Jesus first entered northwestern New Spain in the 1590s. Believing that most soldiers and settlers were bad influences on Native Americans, they tried to establish autonomous mission communities where they could isolate and protect their Indian converts. In areas where they were successful, such as the valley of the Río Yaqui and the Pimería Alta, they also dominated Indian land and labor. But as Spanish ranchers and miners settled along the mission frontier, bitter competition for Indian resources broke out between the missionaries and the colonists. The Jesuits won many of the skirmishes with colonial officials, but in 1767 they lost the war.

The Spanish Crown allowed gray-robed Franciscans to replace the Jesuits, but the friars never had a chance to exercise the power their black-robed predecessors had enjoyed. Immediately after the expulsion of the Jesuits, in fact, Spanish officials toyed with the idea of abolishing the missions once and for all. They abandoned that scheme as soon as they realized that the missions were the cheapest and most effective way to control Christianized Indians. Nonetheless, a new order had arisen in northern New Spain, one that reflected a fundamental transformation of European society and the colonies Europe controlled. The world economy was growing more and more capitalistic as medieval privileges crumbled. Consequently, resources such as land and labor became commodities in the marketplace rather than rights and duties locked up in a feudal order. The Jesuit dream of independent missions contradicted the entrepreneurial dream of abundant land and a mobile labor force. With the Jesuits gone and the Franciscans weakened, it became much easier for Spanish settlers to exploit that land and labor for private gain.

＊　　＊　　＊　Pacification and Expansion

For a time, the new order worked extremely well. Beginning in the 1770s, soldiers from presidios and "flying companies" (*compañías volantes*) scoured the Apachería. At Tucson, Captain Pedro Allande y Saabedra mounted nearly a dozen major forays against the Apaches between 1783 and 1785 alone. Haughty, domineering, and wracked by wounds, Allande was a nobleman who had fought everyone from the Portuguese to the Seri Indians during his long career. He capped that career in Tucson by impaling the heads of his Apache enemies on the palisades of the presidio walls.

Juan Bautista de Anza was an even more successful adversary. As governor of New Mexico during the 1780s, Anza severed an alliance between the Navajos and the Western Apaches. He then employed Navajos as auxiliaries in his campaigns against Apache groups living along the headwaters of the Gila River. Other Spanish commanders formally incorporated Native Americans into the military as well, with Opatas manning the flying company at Bavispe and Pimas serving at the reinstated garrison of Tubac. Indeed, the use of one Indian group to fight another was a very old strategy in northern New Spain, one that dated from the Chichimec wars of the 1500s. But commanders like Anza raised it to an art form, persuading Navajos, Utes, and Comanches to stop fighting the Spaniards and carry the battle to their Apache foes.

Spanish officials did not rely on the sword alone, however. In 1786, Viceroy Bernardo de Gálvez instituted a cynical but effective policy of bribery, instructing his military commanders to offer Apaches who agreed to stop fighting "defective firearms, strong liquor, and such other commodities as would render them militarily and economically dependent on the Spaniards." This Machiavellian approach evolved into a full-fledged rationing system in 1792, when a native of the Canary Islands named Pedro de Nava became comandante general of the provincias internas. Apaches were already living in *establecimientos de paz,* or peace camps, near the garrisons of Janos, Fronteras, Bacoachi, Santa Cruz, and Tucson, but Nava made the peace camps one of the cornerstones of Spanish Apache policy. At the camps the Indians received beeves, flour, brown sugar, and tobacco. With the threat of fire and blood hanging over them, the Spaniards hoped that rations would take the place of raids.

Many Apaches never accepted the Spanish program, but a number of the peace camps were remarkably successful. In 1793, for example, more than a hundred Western Apaches from the Aravaipa band left their territory in the Galiuro Mountains and sued for peace at the Tucson presidio. José Ignacio Moraga, the officer in command, gave chief Nautil Nilché a suit of clothes in honor of the occasion. The Apache leader reciprocated by handing Moraga six pairs of enemy Apache ears. Common currency on the frontier, the grisly trophies symbolized Nautil Nilché's new loyalties. He and his kinsmen and kinswomen settled north of the presidio along the floodplain of the Santa Cruz River, where they formed the nucleus of an Apache Manso (Tame Apache) community that remained a part of Tucson's frontier population for the next half century.

Because of the success of the Apache peace program, Hispanic Arizona flourished modestly during the last years of Spanish rule. A few adventurous pioneers grew crops, raised stock, or operated small gold and silver mines in outlying areas such as Arivaca and the San Pedro Valley, but most Spaniards continued to live along the Santa Cruz. The total non-Indian population hovered around 1,000, with 300 to 500 people at Tucson, 300 to 400 at Tubac, and less than 100 at Tumacacori. The rest of Arizona remained in Native American hands.

Despite their small size, communities like Tucson and Tubac were as tenacious as the mesquite trees that provided most of their shade. Their appearance was not impressive: flat-roofed adobe buildings clustered beside a ragged patchwork of fields. As Tucson's Captain José de Zúñiga noted in an official report to the Real Consulado (Royal Board of Trade) in 1804, "We have no gold, silver, iron, lead, tin, quicksilver, copper mines, or marble quarries." He went on to say, "The only public work here that is truly worthy of this report is the church at San Xavier del Bac." Built by O'odham under the direction of Franciscans between 1779 and 1797, Bac was a baroque glory. Zúñiga dismissed the other missions along the Santa Cruz as mere chapels.

Beneath the dust and manure and sun-baked bricks, however, the roots of Hispanic Arizona spread wide and deep. Spanish frontiersmen were as tough as any pioneers on the North American continent. They knew the desert and they knew the Indians—fighting, sleeping, and dying with Tohono O'odham from the western deserts, Pimas from the San Pedro Valley, Apaches from the eastern mountain ranges, and even Yaquis from southern Sonora and Yumans from the Colorado River. Tucson, Tubac, Guevavi, and other settlements along the Santa Cruz were multi-ethnic communities in every sense of the term.

Nevertheless, divisions of class did exist. Soldiers may have belonged to every racial category under the Spanish sun, but most presidial officers were full-blooded Spaniards or their descendants. As anthropologist James Officer notes, the Elías González, Urrea, Comadurán, Zúñiga, and Pesqueira families belonged to a far-flung elite that linked Hispanic Arizona with Arispe, Altar, Alamos, and other important Sonoran centers of power. Members of this small but proud aristocracy intermarried, formed business partnerships, and helped one another fight for control over Sonora's military and economic affairs. One native Tucsonense, José de Urrea, nearly became president of Mexico itself during the civil wars following independence from Spain.

Most Hispanic residents of Arizona, on the other hand, found their lives circumscribed by river, desert, and the Apaches. Theirs was largely a subsistence economy, one wedded to the floodplain of a shallow intermittent stream. The most important crop was wheat, followed by corn, beans, and squash. The most important animals were cattle and horses, although a herd of 5,000 sheep at Tubac produced enough wool for 600 blankets in 1804. During times of relative peace, farming and ranching expanded along the Santa Cruz and spilled over into other watersheds. But whenever Apache raiding intensified, herds dwindled, fields were abandoned, and families took refuge behind presidio walls.

It was a harsh, hardscrabble way of life, one that swung like a pendulum between flood and drought, peace and war. Nonetheless, it endured. The people of Hispanic Arizona may not have been able to extend the empire, but they held on to their little piece of it in the face of great odds. Like rawhide, the sinews of their culture bound them together and bound them to the land.

Those sinews were to be strained to the limit in the years to come.

3

Mexican Arizona and the Anglo Frontier

The year 1826 was a bad one for Mexican Arizona. Five years earlier, Mexico had won its independence from Spain after a decade of bloody struggle. The revolution had destroyed the colonial silver mining industry and had bankrupted the national treasury. Along the northern frontier, funds that had supported missions, presidios, and Apache peace camps dried up and nearly disappeared. As a result, the Apaches began raiding once again, running off horse herds and killing anyone unlucky enough to be caught outside the protection of presidial walls.

Then, in early November, Ignacio Pacheco, the *alcalde de policía* (mayor) of Tucson, reported that "the Gila Pimas, represented by a village governor and two of his men, arrived at this presidio with news of sixteen foreigners bearing arms along the banks of their river. The Gila governor demanded papers of identification. . . . Their leader replied that they came only to visit Indians along the

Gila in order to obtain mules and horses from them and to find out where there might be other rivers abounding in beaver."

Those cryptic words signaled the beginning of a new era in Arizona history. The foreigners Pacheco referred to were a group of Anglo American trappers led by Ceran St. Vrain and William Sherley Williams, better known to his fellow mountain men as Old Bill. They were not the first Anglos to slip into Arizona from their outposts in northern New Mexico, nor would they be the last. At a time when Mexico was sinking into political and economic chaos, another American colossus was stirring east of the Mississippi River, spitting forth pioneers in search of virgin rivers and cheap land. The movement began as a trickle—a few trappers and traders blazing the Santa Fe Trail—but the trickle soon became a torrent. Ten years after Pacheco warned about foreigners in Arizona, an army of largely Anglo rebels wrested Texas from Mexican hands. In 1848, Mexico ceded more than half its territory to the United States, including Arizona north of the Gila River. By 1856 the Stars and Stripes was flying over Tucson itself. Pacheco and his countrymen did not know it then, but the days of Mexican Arizona were numbered. Their nation was on the defensive. Arizona was already part of the Anglo frontier.

✳   ✳   ✳   **The Trappers**

The first Anglo frontiersmen were hardly an invading army. On the contrary, they were a ragtag collection of misfits, adventurers, and businessmen romanticized by later generations as mountain men. From their headquarters in Taos, New Mexico, the mountain men entered Arizona for one purpose and one purpose only: to rip the "hairy banknotes," as they called beavers, from every watercourse between the upper Gila and the Colorado delta. No single individual was their leader, but Old Bill Williams can serve as their prototype. A young New England writer named Albert Pike described him as "gaunt, and red-headed, with a hard, weather beaten face, marked deeply with the smallpox. He is all muscle and sinew, and the most indefatigable hunter and trapper in the world." At a time when William Henry Ashley, John Jacob Astor, and the Hudson's Bay Company dominated most of the great trapping grounds in Canada and the Pacific Northwest, independent trappers like Old Bill flourished in the Southwest, at least until gentlemen in Europe and the eastern United States donned hats made of silk instead of beaver felt. The mountain men were both capitalists and refugees from corporate capitalism. They prized their self-reliance, yet they were as dependent upon the market as any other commodity producers across the world.

The first to set foot on Arizona soil were Sylvester Pattie and his son James, who spent the winter of 1825–26 trapping along the San Francisco, Gila, and San Pedro rivers. James left an imaginative account of his travels, full of dramatic encounters with bears, "panthers," bloodthirsty Indians, and "wild hogs," or javelina, whose tusks "were of a size so enormous, that I am afraid to commit my credibility, by giving the dimensions." Pattie was the first Anglo to describe Arizona and the first of many to exaggerate the ferocity of its human and animal inhabitants. The myth of the savage land springs to life in his pages.

Despite its embellishments, however, Pattie's narrative constitutes the most extensive firsthand account of early trapping in the Southwest, which was much different from trapping in the north, where Indians participated in the trade and formed close relationships with many non-Indian trappers. During the winter of 1826–27, for example, Pattie returned to Arizona with a group of French trappers led by Miguel (Michel) Robidoux, one of six brothers who had grown up trapping and trading along the Missouri River. After visiting a village of Spanish-speaking Pimas who cultivated wheat, corn, and cotton along the south bank of the Gila, Robidoux and his companions made their way to a "Papawar" settlement about a mile up the Salt River. The Indians were probably Yuman-speaking Maricopas, allies of the Pimas who had engaged in extensive warfare with their Mohave and Quechan enemies for centuries. That evening, they turned their war clubs on the trappers, killing everyone except Pattie, Robidoux, and another Frenchman. Fleeing the carnage, the three men stumbled upon the camp of another group of trappers, led by Ewing Young. The trappers soon returned to exact their revenge. By the time the slaughter was over, Pattie claimed that 110 Indians lay dead.

No other encounter between mountain men and Native Americans matched the brutality of the Robidoux massacre or its retaliation. Nonetheless, similar hostilities broke out whenever trappers traveled through the Apachería or trapped beaver in Mohave territory along the Colorado. Because French and Anglo American mountain men did their own trapping, the Indians must have perceived them as invaders rather than traders—heavily armed strangers who entered their lands without permission to seize beavers from their rivers and streams. Not surprisingly, the Native Americans often responded by attempting to kill the trappers or drive them away.

But they kept on coming, exploring Arizona and pushing on to California, where they sold their furs to the ships trading with the Mexican settlements of the Pacific coast. By the time the Southwestern fur trade had declined in 1833, many of the most famous mountain men in Western history had passed through Arizona. Besides Old Bill Williams, Ceran St. Vrain, Michel Robidoux, and Antoine Leroux, there was Milton Sublette, Christopher "Kit" Carson, and Ewing Young, a Tennessee carpenter who crisscrossed Arizona more than anyone else. Reviled as a smuggler and a scoundrel by New Mexican officials, who called him "Joaquín Yon," Young epitomized the single-minded ruthlessness of the trappers. He fought with Apaches and Mohaves. He quarreled incessantly with Mexican authorities. He pioneered a grueling trail up the Verde River and west to California across the Mojave Desert. The lure of beaver-laden rivers was too strong to be dampened by the danger of Indian attack or the tenuous legality of Mexican claims. Men like Young saw an opportunity, and they took it any way they could.

In their wake they left a few depleted streams and not much more. The mountain men's impact upon Arizona was not profound. Because they exported their pelts through northern New Mexico or California, they had little reason to visit Tucson or Tubac. As a result, the trappers avoided confrontations with the Mexicans along the Santa Cruz. And even though they decimated beaver populations along many Arizona rivers, those populations had apparently recovered a decade later when the next swell of Anglo Americans surged across the area. Restless and ambitious, the mountain men simply did not stay in Arizona long enough to transform either its economy or its ecology.

Nonetheless, their presence presaged the shape of things to come. For all their vaunted independence, the mountain men were servants rather than masters—advance men for an economic system that viewed land, water, and wild animals as commodities to be exploited rather than resources to be distributed among neighbors and kin. By usually ignoring demands to present their passports at the presidio of Tucson, the trappers made a mockery of Mexican pretensions to control Arizona beyond the Santa Cruz Valley. Their example would be followed, in a more direct and violent fashion, by merchants and frontiersmen moving into California, New Mexico, and Texas. A New York editor expressed the sentiments of most Anglo pioneers when he wrote, "There is no such thing as title to the wild lands of the new world, except which actual possession gives. They belong to whoever will redeem them from the Indian and the desert, and subjugate them to the use of man." The mountain men may not have subjugated Arizona, but through their contempt for Mexican territorial claims and their relentless commercial exploitation of a single resource, they set the pattern for their countrymen in the years to come.

❋   ❋   ❋   Mexicans and Apaches

During the 1830s and early 1840s, however, Apaches, not Anglos, threatened the Mexican settlers of southern Arizona. As early as 1824, Apaches began running off horse herds from Tumacacori and other Santa Cruz communities. Then, to the south, a charismatic Yaqui leader named Juan Banderas envisioned a pan-Indian nation taking shape in northwestern Mexico and launched a series of revolts in Sonora. Antuna, chief of Tucson's Apache Mansos, warned that the Yaquis were planning to attack Tucson in alliance with Tohono O'odham, Yumas, and Western Apaches. That assault never materialized, but the tenuous peace of the late colonial period was crumbling. The bitter decades had begun.

During those decades just about every institution that had held the Spanish frontier together disintegrated as the new Republic of Mexico plunged into bankruptcy and civil war. The first to collapse was the *provincias internas* (the "interior," or northern, provinces), which had centralized political and military power in the north under the authority of the comandante general. In 1824, Mexico dismembered the system and partitioned itself into states, which frequently acted independently of one another even in military affairs. In April 1835, for example, Chihuahuan authorities negotiated a peace treaty with Chiricahua Apaches (so-called Mimbreños, Gileños, and Mogolloneros) led by "General" Juan José Compá and sixteen other chiefs at the mining community of Santa Rita del Cobre in southwestern New Mexico. That left the Chiricahuas free to raid Sonoran communities like Sahuaripa on the western slopes of the Sierra Madre. Sonoran officials protested the treaty and mounted a counterattack against the Chiricahuas, but Chihuahuan forces did not join their countrymen. Centralized leadership and coordinated military campaigns were vestiges of the colonial past. Mexican authority became almost as diffuse as authority among the Apaches.

Struggles for power within the Mexican states compounded disunion among the states themselves. In Sonora a series of *caudillos,* or military strongmen, dominated politics during the nineteenth century. These caudillos, including José de Urrea, Tucson's native son, and Manuel María Gándara, who owned a hacienda at the old mission of Calabasas, manipulated factions among the Yaquis, Opatas, and Apaches to advance their own ends. They also drew presidial forces into their interminable civil wars, leaving the northern frontier exposed and defenseless for months at a time. In 1832 many families had to abandon Tubac because its garrison had been reduced to the captain, his aide, and three retired soldiers. The Tubaqueños probably sought refuge with their Tucson neighbors, hoping that strength of numbers, if not strength of arms, would keep the Apaches at bay.

But the biggest single blow was the dismantling of the Apache rationing program in 1831. The ethnohistorian William Griffen estimated that 2,496 Apaches received weekly supplies of beef, corn, sugar, and other foodstuffs from presidial commanders in Chihuahua, Sonora, and New Mexico in 1825. Such rations had been an important part of the economy of many Apache groups since the 1790s. Their abrupt withdrawal forced the Apaches to leave the peace camps and return to their old pursuits.

In such a fragmented political and economic atmosphere, betrayals proliferated and peace talks occasionally turned into massacres. One particularly brutal incident occurred on April 22, 1837, when a group led by John Johnson, an Anglo living in Sonora, pursued an Apache raiding party that had stolen Sonoran cattle. Johnson's party followed the cattle tracks into the Animas Mountains in southwestern New Mexico, where it encountered the camp of Juan José Compá, the same Apache who had made peace with the Chihuahuans the year before. For two days Johnson and the Apaches talked, and then Juan José and other chiefs relaxed enough to gather around some *panocha* (brown sugar) and *pinole* (parched corn) Johnson offered. When they did, Johnson turned what may have been a swivel gun upon them and cut down at least twenty Apaches, including Juan José. The massacre burned itself into the memories of Chiricahuas like Mangas Coloradas. Apache and Mexican children learned to demonize one another. Once again, the bloody cycle of attack and counterattack was renewed.

That cycle accelerated during the 1830s and reached its zenith the following decade. The attacks were particularly devastating because of one new development—the presence of Anglo American gunrunners in New Mexico. With the opening of the Santa Fe Trail in 1821, Anglo American traders began exchanging firearms and ammunition for stolen horses and mules. Comanches received the weapons first, followed by Navajos, Apaches, and Utes. While Mexico reeled from one coup after another, Indian access to firearms transformed the balance of power in the Southwest. The Apaches lost the battle against the Comanches for control of the Southern Plains, but they held their ground in the mountains of Arizona and New Mexico until long after the Apachería became part of the United States.

Not all Mexican-Apache alliances broke down during the 1830s, however. When Apaches from most of the peace camps rose in revolt, many Apache Mansos in Tucson under the leadership of Chief Antuna resisted the call to arms. At a parley with the Pinal Apaches, a band who lived near modern Globe, violence erupted when the Tucson contingent refused to join their kinsmen. One Manso and one Pinal were killed. Thereafter, Antuna and his people served as scouts for the Tucsonenses, extending the effective range of the Tucson presidio far beyond the valley of the Santa Cruz.

Tucson in the 1830s was as much an Apache as a Mexican community. The

Sonoran census of 1831 listed only 465 Mexican inhabitants, whereas Tucson's Apache Manso community in 1835 was said to include 486 individuals. Many lived north of the presidio along the east bank of the Santa Cruz. Some cultivated their own fields or occasionally worked for Mexican farmers, and they also moved freely back and forth between Tucson and the surrounding mountains, hunting deer and bighorn sheep, gathering cactus fruit and roasting agave. During the first half of the nineteenth century, their way of life remained remarkably Apachean despite the fact that they were allies, not enemies, of the Mexicans along the Santa Cruz.

But if relations between the Mexicans and the Mansos continued to be favorable, those between the Mexicans and the Pimas steadily deteriorated. Hispanic settlers had been moving onto O'odham lands along the Santa Cruz River since the eighteenth century. Following Mexican independence, the pressure grew more intense, especially after the Franciscan missions began to wither and decay. By 1843, mesquite choked the fields of Tumacacori, while those at Calabasas, Guevavi, and Sonoita were completely deserted. At San Xavier only about one-eighth of the acreage previously cultivated for mission purposes lay under the plow. Throughout the colonial period, missions served as a precarious buffer between Indians and Hispanic settlers in the Pimería Alta. When the mission system crumbled, O'odham land tenure disintegrated as well.

The most blatant land grab occurred in 1844. Far to the south, in the port of Guaymas, the Mexican government declared that the mission lands of Tumacacori had been abandoned and auctioned them off for five hundred pesos to Francisco Alejandro Aguilar. The few Pimas who had not been driven away by Apache depredations neither knew about nor consented to the sale. Besides, Aguilar was the brother-in-law of Manuel María Gándara, one of the most powerful caudillos in Sonora. He turned Calabasas into his own private hacienda, and by the late 1840s Pima dispossession along the Santa Cruz was nearly complete. The Pimería Alta was shrinking, the victim of Apache hostilities and Mexican greed.

❋ ❋ The Land Grants

Mexican expansionism was not limited to the Santa Cruz Valley. During the 1820s and 1830s, Sonoran ranchers strove to colonize the grasslands of southeastern Arizona. Their legal tool was the land grant; their instrument of occupation, the tough and rangy *criollo,* or mixed-breed longhorn cow. Dismissed as little more than *cuernos, cuero, y cojones* (horns, hide, and balls), these longhorns, or their descendants, roamed the range as feral survivors long after their masters were gone.

Before Mexico won its independence from Spain in 1821, the Spanish government had made a few small grants of land in southern Arizona. In 1789, Toribio de Otero petitioned for a *solar* (lot) from the Tubac presidio in return for military service. The land remained in the Otero family until 1938. In 1807, the O'odham of the Tumacacori mission received title to a long strip along the Santa Cruz River south of Tubac encompassing the former mission lands of Tumacacori, Calabasas, and Guevavi. Part of this grant was the land auctioned off in Guaymas in 1846. Finally, in 1812, Agustín Ortiz purchased the site of Arivaca—an important mining and ranching center since the mid eighteenth century—at public auction. Charles Poston purchased that hacienda from Ignacio Ortiz in 1856 for $10,000.

Most of the grants in Arizona, however, were awarded after Mexican independence. In 1821, Tomás and Ignacio Ortiz received four *sitios* (a total of four square leagues, about 17,000 acres) known as San Ignacio de la Canoa and located between Tubac and modern Sahuarita. The following year, the great ranch of San Bernardino east of modern Douglas became the property of Lieutenant Ignacio Pérez. It totaled more than 73,000 acres in Arizona and northeastern Sonora. León Herreros acquired San José de Sonoita in 1825, while "Ramón Romero and other shareholders, their children, heirs, and successors" received title to San Rafael de la Zanja in the lush San Rafael Valley the same year. The Mexican government issued five more grants, including Buenavista, San Rafael del Valle, San Juan de las Boquillas y Nogales, Tres Alamos, and the enormous Babocómari ranch, between 1826 and 1831.

Not since the founding of the presidios at Tubac and Tucson had Hispanic Arizona embarked upon such an ambitious effort to roll back the borders of the Apachería. The land grants established Mexican title to much of the Santa Cruz and San Pedro valleys. They also extended Mexican domain over the high, yucca-studded plains south of the Chiricahua Mountains. The area included some of the best cattle country in the Southwest, most of which ended up in the hands of the powerful Elías-González family or their relatives. During the colonial period, the Spanish government supported the mission and presidial systems in order to insure royal control over the northern frontier. By the 1820s, however, private capital had become the cutting edge of colonization, and most of that capital belonged to a network of elite families who dominated northern Sonora at the time. They were the ones who provided the livestock and took the risks.

If the Elías-Gonzálezes and their neighbors had received the land grants twenty years earlier, when they would have been protected by the presidios and the Apache peace program, they might have succeeded. As it was, their ranches were little more than adobe islands in a desert sea—isolated, vulnerable, easily destroyed. Beginning in the late 1820s, the Apaches began to burn their buildings and kill their cowboys, run off their horses and slaughter their beef. By 1840 most of the grants had been abandoned. And even though the U.S. Court of Private Land Claims eventually confirmed eight of the Spanish and Mexican land grants in the early twentieth century, none of the descendants of the original grantees had managed to hold on to their titles. John Slaughter owned the San Bernardino Ranch north of the Mexican border, and Colin Cameron's San Rafael Cattle Company had acquired the San Rafael de la Zanja grant. Large-scale ranching did not return to the area until the 1880s, after most of the Apaches had been confined to reservations. When it did, Anglo land-and-cattle companies, not the Mexican elite, held sway.

The brief history of Mexican Arizona, then, can only be understood as a desperate seesaw for survival. The Apaches would attack. The Mexicans would counterattack. The Apaches would attack again, in larger numbers, with better guns. Some presidial soldiers were so poor they had to sell their weapons to feed their families. Relations with the Tohono O'odham of the western deserts were so bad the Mexican government had to campaign against their former allies in 1840–41. Meanwhile, the brief florescence of Hispanic Arizona withered under a harsh Athapaskan wind.

The little colony reached its nadir at midcentury. In 1843 the Apaches killed at least thirty shareholders of the San Rafael de la Zanja grant at La Boca de Noria near modern Lochiel. Ranching ceased in the San Rafael Valley. Five years later, at least fifteen Tucsonenses, including nine presidial soldiers, rode into ambush in the Whetstone Mountains. By the time the bodies could be recovered, they were so decomposed that the remains had to be carried back to the presidio of Santa Cruz in sacks. Tubac itself was abandoned once again after an Apache assault in January 1849. The communities of the Santa Cruz were reeling. The end of Mexican Arizona was near.

✳ ✳ The Mexican War and Arizona

In the mid-nineteenth century, a student of Argentine history coined the phrase, To govern is to populate. That principle proved as relentless in the North American deserts as it was on the South American pampas. The Spaniards had long been haunted by the fear that other European powers were planning to invade their sparsely populated northern frontier. They sparred with the French and English in the Mississippi Valley. They watched the Russians creep down the Pacific coast. In the end, however, Mexico won its independence from Spain, and another new American nation made those fears a reality. Uncle Sam, not John Bull, ripped Mexico in two.

The laceration began with Texas in 1836. Six years earlier, Mexico's secretary of state, Lucás Alamán, warned, "Where others send invading armies . . . [the North Americans] send their colonists." Alamán's admonition came too late. Desperate to fill in the empty spaces, Mexico invited Anglo American and other foreign colonists to settle in Texas in 1824. By 1830 there were already more than twice as many Anglos as Mexicans there (7,000 to 3,000). By 1836 the ratio had risen to ten to one. When Sam Houston led his rebels to victory at San Jacinto, their triumph simply formalized the demographic conquest of their country-men. Vastly outnumbered, the Mexicans of Texas soon became a despised mi-nority in their native land.

Texas remained an independent republic until 1845. Nonetheless, many cit-izens of the United States believed that they had a God-given mandate to extend their "area of freedom" across North America. On December 27, 1845, John L. O'Sullivan, editor of the *New York Morning News,* thundered that it was "our manifest destiny to overspread and to possess the whole of the continent which Providence has given us for the development of the great experiment of liberty and federated self-government entrusted to us." With such ideological fervor fueling economic self-interest, it is not surprising that rhetoric soon gave way to war. Mexico had already broken off relations with the United States in March 1845 after the annexation of Texas. Six months later, President James Polk sent John Slidell to Mexico City to buy California and New Mexico. When the Mexican government refused to negotiate, Polk ordered General Zachary Taylor to Texas to occupy disputed territory between the Nueces River and the Rio Grande and the United States declared war on Mexico in May 1846. But even though one of the motivations of the Mexican War was to seize control of that river, which many speculators compared to the Mississippi or the Hudson, the main prize was California. "They seem to look upon this beautiful land as their own Canaan," an observer of Anglo settlers in California wrote, "and the motley race around them as the Hittites, the Hivites, and the Jebusites, whom they are to drive out." The Mexican War therefore became a quasi-religious crusade as well as the most monumental land grab in North American history.

Arizona was never a prize in the conflict. On the contrary, most Anglo pioneers and politicians considered it a wasteland, a desert, an Indian-infested obstacle between Santa Fe and San Diego. Several U.S. military expeditions passed through the area on their way west, but they did so as quickly as possible, and none of them stayed.

General Stephen Watts Kearny, commander of the Army of the West, led the first group of soldiers. Following his conquest of New Mexico, Kearny and a detachment of "wilderness-worn dragoons" left Santa Fe on September 25, 1846. They were guided by a reluctant Kit Carson, who had been impressed into service along the way. Under Carson's able direction, Kearny and his men descended the Gila and spent the next two months following the river's long and tortuous passage to the Colorado. The expedition marched through the villages of the Gila Pimas, but it completely bypassed Tubac and Tucson. It therefore avoided any confrontation with Mexican troops. Yet it did give the soldiers their first taste of the Arizona desert. "Every bush is full of thorns . . . and every rock you turn over has a tarantula or a centipede under it," wrote Dr. John S. Griffin. "The fact is, take the country altogether, and I defy any man who has not seen it—or one as utterly worthless—even to imagine anything so barren."

The next expedition swung farther south, rolling through Tucson on its way to California. This was the famous Mormon Battalion, a company of Latter Day Saints from the Midwest who volunteered for duty in order to prove their patriotism and diffuse the religious hatred of their neighbors. The main purpose of their journey was to blaze a wagon trail across the southern Great Plains and the Southwest. When they reached Santa Fe, Lieutenant Colonel Philip St. George Cooke took command and led the battalion to San Diego. The Mormons left Santa Fe in October 1846. They had to double-team their wagons to get over the Sacramento Mountains in south central New Mexico and lower them by rope down Guadalupe Pass in the northern Sierra Madre. While their encounters with Indians were generally peaceful, the wild bulls of southeastern Arizona took an instant dislike to them, charging their caravan and goring their mules. According to chroniclers of the expedition, there were thousands of them, as fearless and dangerous as the grizzlies of the northern plains. Like many such travelers' accounts of the time, the numbers were undoubtedly exaggerated, but they gave birth to the myth of the great herds that supposedly roamed over southeastern Arizona during the Mexican period.

Because of Cooke's firmness, however, wild bulls were the only antagonists the battalion had to face. The Mormons were the first representatives of the U.S. government to meet the Mexican population of Arizona. The initial encounter, ironically enough, took place at a mescal distillery between the San Pedro and Santa Cruz valleys. There the teetotaling Mormons met a sergeant and several soldiers from the Tucson presidio. The sergeant politely requested that Cooke and his men make a detour around Tucson. Cooke politely declined. Several days of sparring followed as Tucson's veteran commander, Antonio Comadurán, attempted to persuade the battalion not to enter the community. When all threats and pleas for an armistice failed, Comadurán wisely withdrew his outnumbered garrison to San Xavier.

The result was a peaceful day of trading between the Mormons and the Mexican inhabitants of Tucson. The battalion lumbered into town on December 17. After some initial hesitation, the Tucsonenses offered the soldiers food and water, and the soldiers responded by bartering clothing for the beans and flour they needed. They also luxuriated in the comparative lushness of the little Sonoran Desert oasis. "It looked good to see young green wheat patches and fruit trees," Henry Bigler wrote, "and to see hogs and fowls running about, and it was music to our ears to hear the crowing of the cocks. Here are the finest quinces I ever saw."

By the time Cooke and his troops had left the next morning, the only shots that had been fired came from one of the battalion's pickets, who mistook returning civilians for Mexican soldiers during the night. No one was injured and no one died. Cooke even sent a note to Comadurán apologizing for the inconvenience. With it he enclosed a letter to the governor of Sonora. The letter assured the governor that Cooke had not come "as an enemy of the people whom you represent; they have received only kindness at my hands." The lieutenant colonel then concluded, "The unity of Sonora with the States of the north, now her neighbors, is necessary effectually to subdue these Parthian Apaches. Meanwhile I make a wagon road from the streams of the Atlantic to the Pacific Ocean, through the valuable plains, and mountains rich with minerals, of Sonora. This, I trust, will prove useful to the citizens of either republic, who, if not more closely, may unite in the pursuits of a highly beneficial commerce."

✳ ✳ ✳ The Forty-Niners

Cooke's words proved prophetic. After General Winfield Scott seized Mexico City in September 1847 after bloody hand-to-hand combat, Nicholas Trist sat down with Mexican authorities and hammered out the Treaty of Guadalupe-Hidalgo, which Congress ratified the following March. In return for $18,250,000 in cash payments and claims assumed by the U.S. government, the United States won confirmation of its title to Texas. It also annexed California and New Mexico, which included Arizona north of the Gila River. Many Anglo Americans wanted to press their advantage and seize all of Mexico, but for the moment they had to content themselves with a new frontier that stretched from the Gulf of Mexico to the Pacific coast. Canaan was at hand.

The following year, commerce did indeed unite people in both countries, at least for a time. The common lure was gold, enough gold to ignite the largest mining rush in American history. Spaniards had dreamed of Quivira and the Seven Cities of Cíbola since Coronado's expedition, but when the dream materialized at Sutter's Mill along the American River, Alta California belonged to the United States. "Now have the dreams of Cortez and Pizarro become realized," one newspaper wrote. The Gold Rush of 1849 sucked thousands of individuals, Anglos and Mexicans alike, into its vortex, pulling them across deserts, oceans, and plains. Gold-seekers left many towns in Sonora nearly depopulated. Argonauts plodding westward along the Gila Trail, in contrast, overwhelmed the little communities of southern Arizona. By the time the rush was over, 50,000 argonauts had tramped through the region on their way to the California goldfields.

It was a hellish journey at times. The Gila Trail crossed the Sierra Madre at Guadalupe Pass and swung down the Santa Cruz Valley, passing through Tumacacori, Tubac, and Tucson. From there it followed Cooke's wagon road north to the Pima villages and west to the junction of the Gila and the Colorado. The most brutal legs of the trail were two ninety-mile stretches without water, the first between Tucson and the Gila River, the second across the Mojave Desert west of the Colorado. Both men and mules lost their lives there. "What this God-forsaken country was made for," one forty-niner wailed, "I am at a loss to discover."

As parched and perilous as it was, however, the Gila Trail became the artery connecting Arizona to the United States. Flush with racism and victory, most Anglo Americans dismissed Mexicans and their settlements with contempt. John E. Durivage of the *New Orleans Daily Picayune* called Tucson "a miserable old place garrisoned by about one hundred men." But a few of the forty-niners noted the rich grasslands of southeastern Arizona or commented on the region's mineral wealth. "The whole country abounds in rich gold and silver mines," one chronicler wrote. "But as soon as a town or rancho is built, the Apaches tear it down and kill all the males and carry off all the females." The seeds of future settlement were planted, though it would be years before they took root.

The argonauts also provided valuable information about Arizona's Native Americans. The Gila Pimas, who sustained them with their wheat and corn, deeply impressed them. "Finding a heathen people so kind, good, sympathetic, simple, honest, and hospitable," Benjamin Butler Harris observed, "was indeed a surprise well worth the toil and privation of the trip, and calculated to make Christianity blush for its meager attainments and to revive hope for human Utopia." But they viewed the Quechans of the Colorado River with great suspicion. "The rascally Yumas would come boldly into camp, professing friendship, but woe betide a man's scalp were he caught out alone and unarmed," Harris commented. Harris also noted that the Quechans, who swam the forty-niners' mules across the river, "would invariably drown a fat one . . . so as to get the carcass for a feast."

The Apaches, on the other hand, left most of the argonauts alone, viewing the Anglo Americans as potential allies in their struggle against the Mexicans. After one inconsequential skirmish near Guadalupe Pass, the great Chiricahua war chief Mangas Coloradas told a group of Americans that he loved them. The Mexicans, in contrast, were *christianos malditos* (evil Christians) he planned to exterminate from the land.

❋ ❋ ❋ The Last Days of Mexican Arizona

Mangas Coloradas was undoubtedly indulging in a little hyperbole to impress his new American friends. Despite their hatred of the Mexicans, the Apaches depended upon Mexican livestock to flesh out their diet and see them through hard times. As one old man named Palmer Valor told anthropologist Grenville Goodwin in the early 1930s, "Our people used to go on raids down into Mexico to bring back horses, mules, burros, and cattle. This is the way we used to take the property of the Mexicans and make a living off them. There were no White people to take things from in those days." To the Apaches, Mexico was a vast and dangerous larder, as vital to their economy as the cornfields, agaves, and acorns of the Apachería itself.

The events of December 16, 1850, capture Athapaskan ambivalence toward their Mexican foes. About nine that morning, a large number of Apaches, perhaps as many as 361, swept out of the Catalina Mountains and caught Tucson by surprise. Surrounded and outgunned, the Tucsonenses fled to the presidio or to the large adobe *convento* (religious residence) on the west bank of the Santa Cruz River. There they watched helplessly while the Apaches rounded up their animals, killed four of their neighbors, and took two Mexican boys and four Apache Manso women captive.

Suddenly, however, the Apaches offered to make peace. Nine surprised soldiers ventured outside the presidial walls and embraced the enemies they had been fighting just minutes before. A treaty might even have been secured if O'odham had not ridden in from San Xavier and descended upon the Apaches, driving them away. In the chaos of mid-nineteenth-century Arizona, peace was often measured in hours, not years.

Even if the Apaches and the Mexicans had agreed to stop killing one another that winter day, their treaty would have been as ephemeral as a desert snowfall. Apaches made truces with one Mexican community in order to raid another. Livestock stolen in Sonora was bartered in Chihuahua or New Mexico. As Palmer Valor told Goodwin, "In the old days some Mexicans and also a few White people used to come from the north to get horses, mules, and burros from us that we had taken in Mexico. They used to trade us blankets, guns, and gunpowder for them." Conditions in the Southwest were too chaotic to allow a balance of power between Mexicans and Apaches to be achieved, especially when Anglo American scalp hunters like James Kirker and John Joel Glanton were playing one group against the other and stirring up the bloody pot.

No one captures the savagery of that period better than Cormac McCarthy in his novel *Blood Meridian*. McCarthy conjures up Glanton's murderous odyssey from Chihuahua City to his fatal confrontation with the Quechan Indians at Yuma Crossing. After leaving the Sonoran state capital of Ures with "a contract signed by the governor of the state of Sonora for the furnishing of Apache scalps," Glanton and his scabrous band massacre a village of black-haired Sonorans. Mexican troops pursue them. To escape, they follow the tracks of an Apache war party down the Santa Cruz Valley. After passing the bodies of their Delaware scouts "hanging head downward from the limbs of a blackened paloverde tree . . . gray and naked above the dead ashes of the coals where they'd been roasted until their heads had charred and the brains bubbled in the skulls and steam sang from their noseholes," Glanton's party rides past Mission San Xavier del Bac. The church was "solemn and stark in the starlight. Not a dog barked. The clusters of Papago huts seemed without tenant. The air was cold and clear and the country there and beyond lay in a darkness unclaimed by so much as an owl. A pale green meteor came up the valley floor behind them and passed overhead and vanished silently in the void."

Like an Old Testament prophet on mescaline, McCarthy writes with hallucinatory clarity. Anglos, Mexicans, and Indians alike are beyond redemption in his universe, which is pitiless and cruel. But McCarthy does not have to invent much. The barbarous acts he describes all happened at one time or another, even if they did not march to the chronology he invents. The terrible truth about *Blood Meridian* is its grounding in historical reality. The Southwest in the mid nineteenth century was a land where the old order had collapsed and a new order had not yet been created. The result was a political vacuum where the worst instincts often ruled.

As part of that vacuum, Mexican Arizona limped into the 1850s, maligned by gold seekers, lashed by Apache raids, ravaged by a cholera epidemic that broke out in 1851. The establishment of "military colonies" in Tucson and Tubac only aggravated an already desperate situation. To prevent the loss of any more territory, the Mexican government decided to grant each recruit a plot of land in return for a six-year tour of duty. In Tucson, however, military officials confiscated land already being cultivated by civilians or retired *presidiales,* turning farmers against the very soldiers who were supposed to protect them. The result was bitter conflict at a time when the survival of Mexican Arizona hung on a very thin thread.

It is not surprising, then, that many residents greeted the Treaty of Mesilla with relief. In 1853, President James Buchanan dispatched James Gadsden, a railroad speculator from North Carolina, to present Mexican president Santa Anna with five different plans to purchase more of northern Mexico. The most ambitious offered $50 million for Baja California and much of Sonora, Chihuahua, and Coahuila. The least extensive sought Arizona south of the Gila River and the Mesilla Valley of New Mexico. That was the one Santa Anna accepted. In return for $10,000,000, the United States received nearly 30,000 square miles of deserts and mountains. With it came Tucson, Tubac, and Tumacacori as well.

When the House of Representatives ratified the Gadsden Purchase on June 29, 1854, suddenly, with the stroke of a pen, Mexican Arizona became a part of the United States. After more than a century of precarious existence, what began as the outpost of an empire ended almost as an afterthought. The government of the United States had no great desire to acquire the settlements of the Santa Cruz. They just happened to be there—a handful of adobe communities lying along the route for an all-weather railroad.

Nonetheless, most inhabitants of the region welcomed the change. After years of isolation and neglect, Mexican Arizona fell under U.S. law and, presumably, U.S. protection. Perhaps there would be markets for beef and flour. Perhaps the Apaches would finally be kept at bay. Mexican troops remained in Tucson until March 1856, but when they headed south to Imuris, few civilians went with them. Sonora was the dangerous, poverty-stricken past. Arizona was the uncertain but hopeful future. Besides, the Santa Cruz Valley was their home. Their parents and children were buried there. They had defended it with their sweat and their blood.

As a result, when U.S. troops finally did ride into southern Arizona in late 1856 to take possession of the region, no mass exodus of Mexicans occurred. On the contrary, Mexican as well as Anglo immigrants began to trickle into the area, drawn by the promise of peace and prosperity. In the words of Carmen Lucero, who was a little girl at the time, "I have often heard my mother say that the coming of the Americans was a Godsend for Tucson, for the Indians had killed off many of the Mexicans and the poor were being ground down by the rich. The day the troops took possession there was lots of excitement. They raised the flag on the wall and the people welcomed them with a fiesta and they were all on good terms. We felt alive after the Americans took possession and times were more profitable."

4

Early Anglo Settlement and the Beginning of the Indian Wars

Mangas Coloradas (Red Sleeves) was at least six feet tall, with a powerful body and an enormous head. Anglo Americans regarded him as the greatest Apache leader of the mid nineteenth century. Indian agent Edward Wingfield called him "a noble specimen of the genus homo. He comes up nearer the poetic ideal of a chieftain . . . than any person I have ever seen." He was a war chief, diplomat, and consummate strategist—one who, according to legend, married one daughter to Cochise, another to a Navajo chief, and a third to a leader of the Western Apaches. In a kin-based society, Mangas Coloradas wove a web of obligations that extended from central Arizona to Chihuahua.

His life spanned three chaotic epochs in Southwestern history. He was born in the early 1790s at a time when Spanish soldiers were scouring the Apachería from Tucson to Texas. As a child he must have visited or perhaps even lived in the Apache peace camp near the presidio of Janos in northwestern Chihuahua, but he spent his adult years taking advantage of Mexican decline and decay. From his strong-holds in the mountains of western New Mexico, he raided as far south as Durango in north central Mexico.

During the Mexican War, Mangas Coloradas welcomed the Anglo American soldiers and urged General Stephen Watts Kearny to join with the Apaches and conquer northern Mexico once and for all. Over the next fifteen years, however, friendship degenerated into wariness and war. In 1861, Mangas Coloradas tried to persuade miners in southwestern New Mexico to leave Chiricahua territory. The miners allegedly tied him to a tree and whipped him, so he and his warriors drove them out with fire and blood. The next year, he and his son-in-law Cochise ambushed troops from General James H. Carleton's California Column in Apache Pass between the Dos Cabezas and Chiricahua Mountains. The sol-diers repulsed the ambush with howitzers, and Mangas Coloradas slipped away to nurse his wounds.

Finally, in January 1863 members of mountain man Joseph Walker's party of gold seekers lured the old chief into the deserted mining camp of Pinos Altos to talk peace. Instead, they seized him and delivered him to General Joseph R. West, who had orders from Carleton to "punish the Gila Apaches, under that notorious robber, Mangus Colorado." That evening, West placed Mangas Colo-radas under the guard of two soldiers. According to Daniel Ellis Conner, a member of the Walker party, "About 9 o'clock I noticed that the soldiers were doing something to Mangas, but quit when I returned to the fire and stopped to get warm. Watching them from my beat in the outer darkness, I discovered that they were heating their bayonets and burning Mangas's feet and legs. This they continued to do [until] Mangas rose upon his left elbow, angrily protesting that he was no child to be played with. Thereupon the two soldiers, without remov-ing their bayonets from their Minie muskets each quickly fired into the chief, following with two shots each from their navy six-shooters. Mangas fell back into the same position . . . and never moved."

✳   ✳   ✳   **The Struggle for the Colorado River**

Tales of Apache cruelty spread like smallpox on the frontier, but the Apaches never murdered a high-ranking U.S. officer during a peace negotiation. The savagery did not end with the Apache chief's death. First the soldiers scalped Mangas Coloradas with an "Arkansas toothpick," a Bowie knife. Then they cut off his head and boiled it in a pot so they could send his skull to a phrenologist, who determined that it was larger than Daniel Webster's. The man who had been hailed by Wingfield as "the Master Spirit amongst the Apaches" became a "robber" to be killed and a medical curiosity to be studied. The desecration of his corpse outraged the Chiricahuas as much as his betrayal and murder. Mangas Coloradas's revenge was a series of Chiricahua war chiefs—Cochise, Victorio, Juh—who carried on his fight for the next twenty-three years.

Throughout the 1850s, however, hostilities between Apaches and Anglo Americans were sporadic rather than sustained. The U.S. government established only two military posts in southern Arizona before the Civil War: Fort Buchanan at the headwaters of Sonoita Creek in 1856 and Fort Breckinridge along the San Pedro River in 1860. Civilians often had to defend themselves in Arizona during the Mexican period, and their self-reliance continued for the first decade of American rule.

Not that there were many civilians in Arizona to begin with. During the 1850s, the vast western half of the territory of New Mexico remained largely in Indian hands. A few merchants and artisans like Sam Hughes and Solomon Warner drifted into Tucson, engineers under the fitful direction of a former bookseller named John Russell Bartlett surveyed the U.S.-Mexican border, and military expeditions led by Captain Lorenzo Sitgreaves, Lieutenant Amiel Whipple, and Lieutenant Joseph Ives mapped out wagon roads and railroad routes across the Colorado Plateau. But the only areas where Americans attempted to create new settlements were a few mining communities in southern Arizona and a string of ports along the Colorado River. The rest of the region belonged to the Apaches, the Upland Yumans, the O'odham, and the Navajos.

The lower Colorado River Valley, in fact, became the first region settled by non-Indians since the Santa Cruz Valley in the eighteenth century and the first part of Arizona penetrated by the Industrial Revolution. At a time when the rugged terrain to the east could be traversed only by horseback or mule train, steamboats plied the shifting channels of the Colorado. During the early territorial period, water linked the deserts of Arizona to Sonora, California, and the rest of the world.

The Yuman-speaking Quechan and Mohave Indians did not surrender control of the valley without a fight. For centuries they had dominated the lower Colorado, massacring the Spaniards who settled among them in 1781 and carrying out raids and pitched battles with their Indian enemies, especially the Yuman-speaking Maricopas and their O'odham allies along the Gila River. War impregnated Yuman culture, engendering a class of professional warriors known as *kwanami*. Their culture hero, Kumastamxo, had created all peoples and had ordained who were friends and who were foes. He had also given the Quechans and Mohaves the power to dream war dreams—to determine the location of the enemy and to foresee the outcome of a campaign. War was not simply an economic or political activity. On the contrary, it was a mythological process, one that linked Quechans and Mohaves with the first moments of creation.

So when thousands of Americans began tramping across their territory in 1849, the River Yumans reacted with antagonism as well as enterprise. On the one hand, they prospered by swimming gold seekers and their livestock across the Colorado. On the other, they resented the newcomers, whose sheer numbers threatened their way of life. Early in 1850 a group of scalp hunters led by John Joel Glanton tried to monopolize the ferry business by assaulting a Quechan chief and threatening to kill an Indian for every Mexican carried across the river. The Quechans retaliated by splitting open the heads of the scalp hunters with clubs. Throughout the height of the Gold Rush, they maintained control over one of the most strategic river crossings in North America.

The American occupation of the lower Colorado Valley did not really begin until February 1852, when Major Samuel Heintzelman reestablished Fort Yuma on the California side of the river. Like many officers, Heintzelman spent as much time pursuing his business interests as his military duties, and he became a major investor in the Colorado Ferry Company, which wrested control of the crossing from the Quechans once and for all. As more and more Americans settled in the area, founding the community of Colorado City (modern Yuma), Quechan autonomy began to diminish and disappear.

One of the last spasms of that independence shook Yuman society five years later. On September 1, 1857, several hundred Quechan, Mohave, and Yavapai warriors crossed more than 160 miles of desert on foot to attack the Maricopas, who were living in two villages east of the Estrella Mountains near modern Phoenix. The Maricopas and Pimas counterattacked on horseback, killing more than a hundred of the Yuman invaders. It was the last major battle the River Yumans fought. The bones they left behind served as bloody epitaphs for a way of life outside the control of empires or nation-states.

The most important development in the conquest of the lower Colorado, however, was the arrival of steam-powered ships. In December 1852 a sixty-five-foot-long paddle wheeler named the *Uncle Sam* churned up the river as far as the Gila-Colorado confluence. It ran aground and sank the following spring, but the *General Jesup* took its place in 1854, pioneering steam transportation as far north as Mohave territory. By the 1870s, six steamers and five barges were calling upon ports as far north as Rioville near the mouth of the Virgin River. Shifting sandbars, scarce timber for fuel, and fluctuating water levels plagued their journeys, and relentless heat desiccated the passengers, who inched along the Colorado at fifteen miles a day. But until Chinese laborers completed the Southern Pacific Railroad in 1881, most of the goods entering Arizona were water-borne.

*   *   *   ## The Early Mining Frontier

One result of the steamboat trade was the establishment of ports and landings up and down the Colorado. Most were ramshackle affairs that served local mines, but a few developed into small towns: Yuma, La Paz, Ehrenberg, and Hardyville. No other stretch of Arizona was as hot, and the communities themselves offered few luxuries to the weary travelers who pulled up there. Army wife Martha Summerhayes even refused to get off the boat when she and her officer husband reached Ehrenberg in the late summer of 1874. "Of all the dreary, miserable-looking settlements that one could possibly imagine," Summerhayes wrote, "that was the worst. An unfriendly, dirty, and Heaven-forsaken place, inhabited by a poor class of Mexicans and half-breeds."

Nevertheless, the strategic importance of ports like Ehrenberg outweighed their inhospitable appearance. Steamboats deposited the bounty of the outside world along the riverbanks, where wagons freighted it to the forts, mines, and ranches of the interior. The Spanish empire was never able to conquer Arizona. With the aid of steamships and freight wagons, nineteenth-century industrial America completed the task in three and a half decades.

It did so for one reason: the lure of gold and silver. "We had one war with Mexico to take Arizona," General William Tecumseh Sherman allegedly snarled, "and we should have another to make her take it back." But Sherman's pessimism crumbled in the face of miners' greed. Jacob Snively made the first big strike in 1857 when he discovered gold along the Gila about twenty miles upstream from the junction with the Colorado. A year later more than a thousand people were panning for coarse grains in placers or preying upon those who did. Arizona's first boomtown had sprung to life, and its name was Gila City. According to journalist J. Ross Browne, "The earth was turned inside out. Rumors of extraordinary discoveries flew on the wings of the wind in every direction. Enterprising men hurried to the spot with barrels of whiskey and billiard tables; Jews came with ready-made clothing and fancy wares; traders crowded in with wagon-loads of pork and beans; and gamblers came with cards and monte-tables. There was everything in Gila City within a few months but a church and a jail, which were accounted barbarisms by the mass of the population."

Gila City also set the pattern for the boomtowns to come. A few prospectors made a killing. Most barely found enough gold to purchase food at the inflated prices that prevailed—bread for a dollar a loaf, beans at fifty cents a pound. By 1864, when Browne visited the site, the "promising Metropolis of Arizona consisted of three chimneys and a coyote."

But another type of mining community—the company town—also developed. These were corporate ventures, not ragtag assemblies of prospectors. And while most did not appear until railroads and a revolution in technology made large-scale copper mining feasible, a few, like the Sonora Mining and Exploring Company, represented corporate capitalism's first foray onto the Arizona frontier.

The endeavor began auspiciously. Two unlikely partners—Samuel Heintzelman (a hard-nosed Pennsylvania German) and Charles Debrille Poston (a scheming visionary from Kentucky)—started the company in Cincinnati in 1856. Poston and a German mining engineer named Herman Ehrenberg established the company's headquarters at the abandoned presidio of Tubac and purchased the 17,000-acre ranch of Arivaca from Tomás and Ignacio Ortiz. The following spring, another German engineer, Frederick Brunckow, discovered silver in the Cerro Colorado Mountains just north of Arivaca. Soon advertisements were trumpeting Poston and Heintzelman's venture as "the most important Mining Company on this Continent."

The Sonora Mining and Exploring Company was typical of Western entrepreneurship—a volatile mixture of ambition, promotion, and exaggeration that promised much more than it delivered. Heintzelman left Poston in charge of the mines while he attempted to raise money back east. That decision may have been a fatal mistake. More interested in self-promotion than production, Poston allowed his engineers to open too many mines without developing any of them and never completed the smelting works at Arivaca. Worst of all, he spent much more than he made. "Mr. Poston has done very well in many things," Heintzelman confided to his journal, "but is not the man to manage this business now after it has assumed this shape. He has that Southern or Kentucky slovenliness of doing business."

Meanwhile, the Panic of 1857 swept across the financial centers of the United States, and the business unraveled. While Heintzelman frantically tried to entice investors, banks failed, debts mounted, and work in the mines themselves proceeded at a snail's pace. In December, Heintzelman persuaded firearms inventor Samuel Colt to invest $10,000 in the company. By 1859, Colt had seized control of the company, but even his greater access to capital could not turn the Sonora Mining and Exploring Company into a success. Part of the problem was faulty machinery and primitive transportation. Colt imported new boilers, lathes, and steam-powered crushers and amalgamators, but ore still had to be shipped out by wagon across southern Arizona and loaded onto steamboats near Fort Yuma. The rail lines that transformed Arizona into a colony of industrial America had not yet been built. Heintzelman and Poston were pioneers a generation too early.

*   *   *   ## Mexican Labor and Ethnic Conflict in Southern Arizona

Heintzelman and Poston's most immediate problem, however, was men, not machines. Later, looking back on his days as manager of the mining company in Tubac, Poston rhapsodized, "We had no law but love, and no occupation but labor. No government, no taxes, no public debt, no politics. It was a community in a perfect state of nature." Reality was much harsher than Poston's memory. Like Sylvester Mowry's Patagonia mine, the Sonora Mining and Exploring Company relied heavily on Mexican labor—a precedent that would be followed by most of Arizona's extractive industries in the years to come. There were 231 males living at Tubac in 1860, only 23 of whom had been born outside Mexico or the territory of New Mexico. In the mining communities of Santa Rita, Arivaca, and Cerro Colorado, Mexicans constituted 70 percent of the labor force (67 of 96). Poston bragged of his paternalism, claiming that he married Mexican couples and baptized their children. Other managers despised their Mexican employees and never understood the fluid work patterns of the frontier. When Mexicans left the mines in late August for the fiesta of San Agustín in Tucson or made their annual pilgrimage to Magdalena, Sonora, to pay homage to San Francisco in early October, Heintzelman and his German engineers complained about Mexican laziness and unreliability. They never understood how fiestas knit families together and maintained bonds between people and powerful saints, making life bearable on such a dangerous frontier.

More serious was the exploitation of Mexican labor itself. According to mining engineer Raphael Pumpelly, Mexican workers received twelve to fifteen dollars per month, compared to thirty to seventy dollars per month for Anglo workers. Moreover, the mining companies often paid them "in cotton and other goods, on which the company made a profit of from one hundred to three hundred percent." Differential wage scales—combined with late pay, lead poisoning, malarial fevers, and abusive overseers—prompted Mexicans to strike for better conditions or simply to walk off the job. The "law of love" had a dark side. On several occasions, that dark side drove southern Arizona to the brink of ethnic war.

A case in point was the so-called Sonoita Massacre. On May 1, 1859, a ranch foreman named George Mercer whipped and shaved the heads of seven Mexican workers. Five days later, one of Mercer's friends was murdered at his ranch near Tumacacori. Enraged, Mercer and seven other armed men vowed to drive all Mexicans from the region. They rode up to a mescal distillery in the Sonoita Valley and opened fire, killing four Mexicans and one Yaqui Indian.

News of the attack spread rapidly, and many Mexicans fled to Sonora. Watching their workforce evaporate, mine owners condemned the massacre and workers trickled back to the mines. Nonetheless, acts of violence escalated. During the late 1850s and early 1860s, Mexicans murdered twenty-five people in Arizona, causing Anglo observers and later historians like Hubert Howe Bancroft to rail against that "vicious class" of Mexicans who were "always plotting to rob and kill." Yet Anglos—a small minority of Arizona's population—killed thirty-nine people during the same period, twenty-three of whom were Mexican. In many respects, then, southern Arizona resembled southern Texas. Both were regions where Anglos exploited Mexican laborers, and both were regions where Anglo as well as Mexican desperadoes slipped back and forth across the border to commit their crimes.

❋   ❋   ❋   **The Civil War and the Escalation of Apache Hostilities**

Without railroads or political stability, the early mining communities may never have turned a profit for their investors, but the point became moot with the intensification of Apache hostilities and the outbreak of the Civil War. Southern Arizona had belonged to the United States for less than a decade before the most traumatic conflict in the nation's history tore the Union in two. As the slaughter mounted at places like Bull Run and Antietam, the rest of the nation understandably ignored Arizona.

The biggest blow came in the spring and summer of 1861, when federal troops left Arizona and marched east to repel the Confederate invasion of New Mexico. At the time there were only five military posts in the entire region: Fort Buchanan and Fort Breckinridge in southern Arizona, Fort Mohave and Fort Yuma on the Colorado River, and Fort Defiance in Navajo country. As the soldiers rode away, the Indians watched them go and thought they had won their war against the whites.

Even before the federal troops left, however, Apaches were slashing at the settlers who dug their mines on Apache mountains and drove their cattle into Apache valleys. Both Anglos and Apaches belonged to aggressive, expansionistic societies, but those societies were based upon radically different political, economic, and cultural premises. Anglos believed in private property and market exchange. Land was something to be divided up and exploited for the production of commodities, whether it was hay and beef to sell to local military posts or precious metals for the international financial markets. Apaches were territorial as well, but in a different sense. Local groups shared the resources of certain areas, and kinship was the dominant organizing principle of Apache life. That meant that the accumulation of personal wealth, including stolen live-stock, was limited. Thus a kin-ordered society confronted a market-ordered society in a region ideally suited for guerrilla warfare.

Accustomed to preying off their enemies for the good of their kin, Apaches were not about to accept the restrictions on raiding imposed by the invaders. A military miscalculation known as the Bascom Affair touched off the conflagra-tion. On January 27, 1861, Apaches raided the ranch of John Ward eleven miles south of Fort Buchanan and stole a young Mexican boy named Félix Ward. First Lieutenant George Bascom marched to Apache Pass. There he met Cochise, the chief of the central band of the Chiricahuas, who called themselves the Choko-nens. Because Cochise had not led the raid, he agreed to enter Bascom's camp, bringing along members of his family. Cochise told Bascom that the White Mountain Apaches had taken the boy and that he would get him back within ten days. Bascom replied that Cochise and his family would be held hostage until the boy was returned.

That infuriated Cochise, who whipped out a knife and slashed a hole in the tent where he and Bascom were talking. He ran outside, pushed his way through the soldiers, and escaped even though they fired at least fifty shots at him and wounded him in the leg. Cochise demanded the release of his relatives. Bascom refused. The Apaches seized an employee of the Butterfield stage sta-tion. Cochise offered to exchange the prisoner for the Chiricahuas, and again Bascom turned him down.

The bloody spiral accelerated. Two days later, Cochise burned a wagon train, killing nine Mexicans and taking three Anglos prisoner. Then he attacked Bas-com's command. When Bascom repulsed the assault, Cochise executed the four Anglo prisoners and mutilated their bodies. The soldiers hung six Apache men in retaliation, including Cochise's brother and two nephews. Hostage taking and limited reprisals had become a war of blood vengeance. According to histo-rian Dan Thrapp, 150 whites were killed within sixty days.

✳ ✳ The Subjugation of the Navajos

The Bascom Affair and the murder of Mangas Coloradas two years later triggered a chain reaction of resistance that did not end until Geronimo surrendered to General Nelson Miles in 1886. Confederates under Captain Sherod Hunter, who occupied southern Arizona during the spring of 1862, bore orders to lure the Apaches into Tucson for peace talks and exterminate the adults. But Hunter's frontiersmen spent most of their time expelling Union supporters and skirmishing with Union troops, so the order was never enforced. A detachment of Colonel James Carleton's California Column, which drove the Confederates out of Tucson, fought the Battle of Apache Pass after being ambushed by Cochise and Mangas Coloradas. But even though the column withstood the Apaches and established Fort Bowie to secure the pass, Chokonens under Cochise, Chihennes (Eastern Chiricahuas) under Mangas Coloradas's successors, Nana and Victorio, and Nednhis (Southern Chiricahuas) under Juh continued the struggle.

The government had greater success in subduing another Athapaskan people, the Diné, or Navajos. Like the Apaches, the Diné ran off cattle, horses, and sheep from New Mexican settlements in the upper Rio Grande Valley. Lieutenant W. H. Emory of the Army of the West called them the "lords of New Mexico" because they attacked communities from Zuni to Santa Fe. Unlike the Apaches, however, the Navajos used stolen animals to replenish their own herds. According to Charles Bent, the first American governor of New Mexico, "It is estimated that the tribe possesses 30,000 head of horned cattle, 500,000 sheep and 10,000 head of horses, mules and asses, it not being a rare instance for one individual to possess 5,000 to 10,000 sheep and 400 to 500 head of other stock." Those herds enabled them to spread across a vast region that stretched from the Chama River to the Little Colorado.

The Diné also cultivated the soil more intensively than the Apaches, raising wheat, corn, beans, squash, melons, and peaches, especially in Canyon de Chelly. Anglo American observers emphasized Navajo raiding because raiding fit their preconceptions of Indian savagery, but the Navajo economy was far more complex, as were Navajo–New Mexican relationships. Both groups preyed upon the other, the Navajos raiding New Mexican herds, the New Mexicans rounding up Navajos as slaves. Yet they also traded with one another, with the Navajos producing woolen blankets of "rare beauty and excellence" for the New Mexican market in return for silver, metal goods, and other commodities. Along the Southwestern frontier, people could be enemies, allies, or trading partners depending on conditions at the time.

Once the United States invaded New Mexico during the Mexican War, however, U.S. military authorities attempted to end the raids. Their policy puzzled the Diné, who thought that Navajos and Anglo Americans were fighting a common foe. "This is our war," Navajo leader Zarcillos Largo told Colonel Alexander Doniphan in 1846. "We have more right to complain of you interfering in our war than you have to quarrel with us for continuing a war we had begun long before you got here."

For the next seventeen years, U.S.-Navajo relations oscillated between inconclusive peace negotiations and abortive military campaigns. Treaties were made at Jemez pueblo in 1852 and at Laguna Negra in 1855, but neither brought lasting peace. In 1858 a campaign led by Colonel Dixon Miles tried to track down Navajo war leader Manuelito. Two years later, Manuelito returned the favor by attacking and nearly overrunning Fort Defiance. Established in 1851, Fort Defiance lived up to its name—an isolated gesture of aggression against a people it could neither conquer nor control.

By the fall of 1860, the citizens of New Mexico were ready to take matters into their own hands. Five companies of volunteer militia commanded by Manuel Chaves scoured the Navajo country, killing any men they found and enslaving about a hundred women and children. The volunteers also destroyed Navajo cornfields and captured thousands of cattle, horses, and sheep. But a Yankee martinet and a legendary mountain man brought the Navajos to their knees. In October 1862, Brigadier General James Carleton took command of the military department of New Mexico after leading his California Column across the Mojave Desert and Arizona. A self-righteous, deeply religious New Englander, Carleton craved battle with the Confederates, whom he considered vile secessionists. By the time he arrived in Santa Fe, however, his predecessor, General Edward Canby, had already run the Confederates out of New Mexico. Carleton therefore turned his moral wrath on the Navajos and the Mescalero Apaches. Canby had advised him that the only way to deal with the Apaches and Navajos was to force them onto remote reservations, and Carleton knew just the spot—a wide stretch of floodplain along the Pecos River known as Bosque Redondo.

The man Carleton chose to carry out his plans was Christopher "Kit" Carson—beaver trapper, buffalo hunter, army scout, Taos pioneer. Carson was not a brutal man, but he carried brutal orders. Carleton commanded him to deliver an ultimatum to the Navajos. "Say to them: 'Go to the Bosque Redondo, or we will pursue and destroy you. We will not make peace with you on any other terms.'" Carson did what he was told. In July 1863 he reached Fort Defiance, which he renamed Fort Canby, with more than 700 soldiers and Ute Indian scouts. The Utes tracked down the Navajos, killed the men, and seized the women and children as slaves. The soldiers burned Navajo cornfields, slaughtered their sheep, and confiscated their cattle and horses. As summer became fall and fall became winter, small groups of starving Navajos straggled into Fort Canby to surrender. By the end of the year, the only refuge left was Canyon de Chelly.

Located in northeastern Arizona, Canyon de Chelly is shaped like the talon of a hawk. At its mouth it looks like just another desert wash, its cliffs about thirty feet tall. But with each twist and turn of Tsaile Creek or Chinle Wash, the sandstone cliffs rise higher. At Spider Rock they tower nearly a thousand feet above the canyon floor. After a bitter winter storm blanketed the canyon with snow, Carson's forces entered from the east and west. Carson fought no pitched battles with the Diné, but once again he systematically razed their fields and destroyed their herds. By February, hundreds of Navajos had embarked upon their Long Walk to the desolate Bosque Redondo—famished, freezing, driven into exile from their homeland. Carleton reported that Bosque Redondo held 8,354 of them by January 1865. With devastating suddenness, Navajo independence had disappeared. The Diné no longer were lords but smallpox-ridden wards of the state.

＊　　＊　　＊　　The Expansion of Mining in Central Arizona

Carleton's policy of exile or extermination pacified northeastern Arizona and southwestern New Mexico, at least for a time. The general had done his job with ruthless efficiency, but Carleton's determination to defeat the Athapaskans was fueled by more than a sense of military duty. Like so many of his fellow officers, he wanted riches as well as glory, so when the party of the gold seeker Joseph R. Walker called on him in New Mexico in 1862, Walker may have offered Carleton an unofficial partnership in return for military protection. Walker left for Arizona with Carleton's blessings, and in 1863 he and his men discovered gold along the north bank of the Hassayampa River five miles south of Prescott. Other prospectors made more strikes along Lynx, Weaver, and Big Bug creeks, which soon became known as the Walker Mining District. Carleton established Fort Whipple in Chino Valley later that year.

For the first time in Arizona's history, non-Indians came to the mountainous interior and stayed. After Ohio mining interests led by Samuel Heintzelman pushed the Arizona Organic Act through Congress in 1863, Fort Whipple even became the first capital of the new Arizona Territory. Then, the following year, both fort and capital were moved south to a new town named after William Hickling Prescott, author of *History of the Conquest of Mexico*. An aggressive community of miners, merchants, and territorial officials sprang up in the middle of Yavapai and Apache country, and one bonanza generated ripples of exploration that led to other bonanzas. Soon mines tunneled into some of the driest country in North America, and names like Hassayampa, Harquahala, and Castle Dome entered the legendary geography of the mining frontier. Like most other features of that geography, Arizona's early mines rarely developed into permanent communities. On the contrary, prospectors descended like locusts on one strike after another, stripping away the nuggets and surface veins, and leaving behind their sluice boxes and shacks. Arizona is lightly dusted with their traces—a mound of adobe, a scrap of rusted metal, a few weathered boards. They were as evanescent as spring rain.

What the prospectors did, however, was to pioneer hundreds of miles of mule trails and wagon roads across the western Arizona desert. The first route embarked from La Paz, the second from Fort Mohave, the third from Hardyville over a toll road that enabled great high-wheeled freight wagons to carry loads as heavy as 15,000 pounds. The journeys were bone-crunching and tissue-withering affairs, rough on oxen, mules, and men. For six months of the year, temperatures could rise above 100 degrees as the sun reflected off the desert pavement and the rocks of the low western mountains. Then the freighters had to double- or triple-team their wagons up inclines like Yarnell Hill to reach the ore-bearing high country of the interior. For centuries the promise of Espejo's silver had danced beyond the reach of Spaniards and Mexicans. But steamships on the Colorado and freight wagons straining across the basins and ranges of the Harcuvar, Aquarius, and Vulture mountains made Prescott the most important center of settlement north of the Santa Cruz Valley. They also led, inevitably and implacably, to the escalation of Arizona's Indian wars.

✳ ✳ ✳ Civilian Militias and the Arizona Volunteers

The first round of hostilities involved civilian militias, not army personnel. Carleton's California Volunteers established Camp Lowell in Tucson in 1862 after Captain Sherod Hunter evacuated his Confederates. They also founded Fort Bowie near Apache Pass and Fort Whipple near Prescott. But even though Carleton, like his Confederate counterpart, John Baylor, ordered the extermination of all hostile Apache men in Arizona, the California Volunteers were spread too thin to conquer the Yavapais and Apaches, or even to protect the settlers in outlying ranches and mines. Pioneers with time on their hands and a taste for blood therefore went Indian hunting—slaughtering men, women, and children wherever they found them. Native Americans responded with brutalities of their own. Scalping and the mutilation of corpses became commonplace as prospectors bored deeper and deeper into Hualapai, Yavapai, and Tonto Apache territory. Beaver trappers, forty-niners, and military surveyors had come and gone, but the miners would not fade away.

The most famous civilian Indian fighter of the 1860s was King S. Woolsey, a "large, hale, and hearty man" from Alabama who sold hay and other supplies to federal troops. He made money off the government, lost money in mining, and established two ranches, one of which was east of Prescott on the Agua Fria River. Woolsey hated the Yavapais and Apaches who ran off his stock, but he was a close friend of Juan Chivaria, a Maricopa war leader who fought alongside him and who, in the words of the *Phoenix Herald,* "wept like a child" at his funeral. The old pattern of alliances forged by the Spaniards of the Santa Cruz Valley prevailed. During the 1860s and early 1870s, Maricopas and Pimas often joined Anglos and Mexicans in short, savage campaigns against their Apache and Yavapai enemies.

In the short run, Woolsey's forays may have been successful. After a series of raids around Prescott in January 1864, Woolsey and sixty-nine other Anglos, Maricopas, and Gila Pimas pursued the attackers across the Agua Fria and Verde drainages to Fish Creek Canyon in the Salt River country. There they encountered about two hundred Apaches or Yavapais, and someone joked, "Now we have found the stock and more of it than we want." Both sides were darkly amused by the situation, but both agreed to talk. Then Woolsey touched his left hand to his hat, and his party opened fire. According to one eyewitness, "We made good Indians out of twenty-four of their number—or killed them which is the same thing—besides what got away packing lead."

In the long run, however, civilian reprisals merely stoked the flames of blood vengeance among the kinsmen of the dead. These were hit-and-run affairs, often degenerating into massacres of women and children as well as men. Many Indians died, but not enough to change the balance of power in the territory. "Savage civilized men are the most monstrous of all monsters," wrote Daniel Ellis Conner, who participated in Woolsey's "Massacre at Bloody Tanks." Atrocity bred atrocity as the body count on both sides climbed into the hundreds.

With the Civil War still grinding across the South and Carleton still fighting the Navajos, the regular army was not yet ready to elbow the civilians aside. The U.S. War Department therefore authorized Governor John Goodwin of Arizona to raise five companies of Arizona Volunteers in 1864. Recruitment was delayed for a year, but by the fall of 1865, more than 350 men had been mustered into service under the command of nine officers.

They were not the Anglo pioneers of Western myth. On the contrary, the overwhelming majority were Mexicans, many of them from Sonora, or O'odham and Maricopas from the Gila River villages. But even though some of them arrived in the recruitment camps with not a "shirt on their body nor any drawers at all," they had grown up fighting Yavapais and Apaches, as had their fathers and grandfathers. Many never received shoes or warm clothing. They lived in hovels and marched for days on beef jerky and *pinole* (parched cornmeal). But they carried .54-caliber rifles with plenty of ammunition, in addition to bows, arrows, and war clubs. For the next year, these tough native frontiersmen guarded wagon trains between Prescott and La Paz and campaigned relentlessly across central Arizona.

Their officers permitted them a few freedoms that made enlistment more tolerable. At the largely Mexican company of Camp Lincoln on the Verde River, for example, sixteen women joined the men. These women created a sense of community at the outpost, marching in procession behind an image of the Virgin of Guadalupe to meet the volunteers whenever they returned from the field. And when they took the field, the men's endurance and knowledge served them well. According to the Third Arizona Territorial Legislature, the volunteers inflicted "greater punishment on the Apaches than all other troops in the territory." Traveling "barefoot and upon half rations," they killed from 150 to 173 Apaches and Yavapais while losing only ten men in combat themselves. If their enlistments had been extended (as many territorial officials and army officers requested), that centuries-old alliance of Hispanic, O'odham, and Maricopa frontiersmen might have conquered the Apachería for the Anglo newcomers.

✻ ✻ The Hualapai War

After their year in service ended, however, the War Department disbanded the Arizona Volunteers. The official reason was bureaucratic: the army did not have the authority to retain native recruits. But racial and cultural prejudices undoubtedly played a role in the decision as well. Manifest Destiny had carried Anglo Americans across the continent and had won them more than half of Mexico. Now it was time to subjugate the wilderness and tame the Native Americans too. Indians and Mexicans might make good scouts, it was said, but they were too unreliable to make good soldiers. Frontier pragmatism was fine in its place, but institutional recognition of their fighting prowess would have threatened the racial hierarchy of American society. So the regular army lurched into action, doomed to learn and relearn lessons the Mexicans, Pimas, and Maricopas had known for two hundred years. During the mid-1860s, the army was too disorganized to take on the Apaches and Yavapais in a systematic fashion, so they turned their attention to the Pai Indians of northwestern Arizona. The so-called Hualapai War bloodied the regular soldiers and gave them a taste of the longer, bloodier campaigns to come.

Today the Yuman-speaking Pai are divided into two "tribes"—the Hualapai and Havasupai—but those divisions reflect U.S. policy rather than cultural or linguistic differences. When Anglos first moved into their territory, there were three major Pai subgroups: the Middle Mountain People (Witoov Mi'uka Pa'a), the Yavapai Fighters (too diverse to have a single name), and the Plateau People (Ko'audva Kopaya). The three subgroups were composed of thirteen bands, each of which numbered from 85 to 250 individuals and occupied distinct but overlapping ranges. Further, during much of the year each band broke into smaller camps of three or four related families. Nevertheless, all these scattered little groups of kin considered themselves a people—The People, Pai—distinct from their linguistic relatives, the Yavapai, who were known as Jiwha', or The Enemy. All believed that their territory had been given to them by Tudjupa, their creator, who said, "Here is the land where you will live. Go to the places where you find water. Mark off your land and live by the water. Name these places."

So they did, and each band christened itself after the places in turn—the Amat Whala Pa'a (Pine-Clad Mountain People), the Havasooa Pa'a (Blue-Green Water People), and the Teki'aulva Pa'a (Lower Big Sandy River People). During the summer months they irrigated their crops from creeks or springs. During the other seasons they moved from one wild plant harvest to another. Pai territory stretched from the Grand Canyon to the Bill Williams River—an immense territory considering the small number of Pais. The Hopis were their friends, the Yuman-speaking Mohaves and Yavapais their bitter enemies. Long before Anglos came to Arizona, the Pais defended their huge expanse of desert and mountain as God-given land, so when prospectors fanned out across their territory in 1863, many Pais—like Sherum, the chief of the Middle Mountain People—grew alarmed. Under his direction, Pais traded buckskins for Navajo blankets, which they traded to the Paiutes for Mormon guns.

Hostilities almost erupted in April 1865 when drunken Anglos murdered a Pai leader named Ana:sa. In retaliation the Pais severed transportation routes between Prescott and the Colorado River ports. Only the dollar diplomacy of freighter W. H. Hardy reopened the toll road between Prescott and Hardyville and prevented the conflict from spreading. But Hardy's peace lasted only about nine months. Chief Wauba Yuma of the Yavapai Fighters rode into Beale Springs to show a group of freighters a copy of the treaty with Hardy. A former member of the Walker party put a bullet through his lungs. This was the spark that ignited the tinder. Soon the Hualapai War burned like a series of brushfires across northwestern Arizona.

Like most such conflicts, the war rarely consisted of pitched battles. The Pais swooped down on freighters or stoned miners to death in their shafts. Cavalry detachments from Fort Mohave responded by attacking Pai rancherías, burning wikiups and cornfields, and capturing women and children. Mohaves occasionally joined these campaigns or mounted ones of their own, using the Hualapai War as a pretext to avenge themselves on their traditional adversaries. The army exploited these ancient antagonisms just as the Spaniards and Mexicans had done for nearly two hundred years. Arizona's Indians were never able to forge intertribal alliances. On the contrary, each group helped defeat the other in turn.

Nevertheless, the Pais held out for more than two years against their better-armed foes. Sherum in particular fought with tenacity and brilliance. On one occasion he mobilized several hundred Pais to attack soldiers at Beale's Springs. On several others he held off U.S. forces even though his warriors had only forty rifles and muskets among them. After one such engagement—a surprise attack on Sherum's own ranchería in the Cerbat Mountains—Captain Samuel Young confessed, "We had been fighting our best for one hour and twenty-five minutes when Indians made their appearance on both flanks and I withdrew slowly from that vestibule of death."

But the Pais were no match for the superior manpower of the "Grand Army of the Colorado," as Prescott's *Arizona Miner* acidly called the Fort Mohave troops. Between June 1867 and December 1868, cavalry columns destroyed at least sixty-eight Pai rancherías and killed about 175 Pais—nearly one fourth of the tribe. During the last summer of the war, an epidemic of whooping cough or dysentery further devastated the resistance fighters. Under Chief Leve Leve of the Yavapai Fighters, the Pais therefore began to surrender at Fort Mohave and were temporarily interned along the Colorado River. Even Sherum laid down his arms after twice escaping from soldiers who were trying to deport him to Angel Island in San Francisco Bay. A year later, fifty Pais were scouting for army forces campaigning against the Yavapais. Soon the military was ready to penetrate the Apachería itself.

5

The Military Conquest
of Indian Arizona

General George Crook came to Arizona in 1871, when Vincent Colyer and General O. O. Howard dominated U.S. Indian affairs. Both
helped shape President Ulysses S. Grant's Peace Policy, which sought
to replace armed force with peace negotiations, and corrupt Indian
agents with agencies run by Protestant denominations such as the
Quakers, the Episcopalians, and the Dutch Reformed Church.
Crook despised Colyer and sneered at Howard's pious Christianity,
dismissing the general as a pompous windbag who "told me that he
thought the Creator had placed him on earth to be the Moses to the
Negro. Having accomplished that mission, he felt satisfied his next
mission was with the Indian." Patient yet single-minded, the bushy-
bearded commander believed that the hostile Indians of Arizona
could only be pacified by relentless military campaigns.

Once the government turned him loose, that's exactly what he
did. First he defeated the Yavapais and Western Apaches between
1873 and 1875. Then, seven years later, he returned to Arizona to

track down the Chiricahua Apaches. Crook revolutionized military pack trains and developed a crack corps of Apache scouts. "There never was an officer so completely in accord with all the ideas, views, and opinions of the savages whom he had to fight or control," wrote his aide-de-camp Captain John Bourke. "In time of campaign this knowledge placed him, as it were, in the secret councils of the enemy." More than anyone else, Crook was the architect of the final military conquest of Indian Arizona.

Ironically, Crook fought his last battle in defense of Indian rights. Crook may have been stern and unsentimental, but he was a keen judge of human character. That judgment, and an unquenchable sense of fair play, led him to trust most Indians, even those who had been his foes. It galled him bitterly, then, when the U.S. government deported all the Chiricahuas to Florida, including his beloved scouts. Crook knew that Geronimo could never have been cornered in the Sierra Madre without the help of men like Chato, the Chiricahua war leader who became one of Crook's most trusted allies. Crook died knowing that Chato and the other scouts, as well as Chiricahuas who had been living peacefully on the San Carlos Reservation, were sweltering in a military prison near the Alabama gulf coast. They remained in exile until 1913, twenty-four years after the general's death. It was a sordid epilogue to a saga Crook helped to write. Like most Victorians, he never questioned the morality of conquering the Indians. The tragic irony of his life was that he wanted that conquest to be just.

❋ ❋ ❋ Federal Indian Policy and the Camp Grant Massacre

Before Crook took command, Indian affairs in Arizona lurched between peace and war. Each new general tried a different mixture of the carrot and the stick. Each new round of Indian hostilities brought increasing conflict between the settlers and the soldiers, leading General E.O.C. Ord to declare that war was the foundation of Arizona's economy and that civilians demanded more troops because they wanted profits, not peace. Westerners generally favored exterminating the Indians. Easterners vacillated between the ploughshare and the sword. The report of the Indian Peace Commission, in 1867, led to the creation of the Board of Indian Commissioners two years later. Investigating abuses within the Office of Indian Affairs, the commissioners, led by Colyer, spearheaded a growing movement for Indian rights that culminated in the "Quaker Policy" of President Grant's administration. That policy placed the appointment of Indian agents in the hands of Protestant religious organizations, not political patrons. Nothing infuriated frontiersmen more than to have Eastern clergymen telling them what to do.

The biggest problem Arizona's military faced, however, was one that had confounded the Spaniards and the Mexicans: too few soldiers confronting too vast a land. Most chronicles of the time identified the Apaches as the biggest menace, but Yuman-speaking Yavapais, who were usually identified as Apache Mohaves or Apache Yumas, resisted Anglo intruders just as tenaciously. Divided into four subtribes—the Tolkapaya (Western Yavapais), the Yavepe and the Wipukpaya (Northeastern Yavapais), and the Kewevkapaya (Southeastern Yavapais)—the Yavapais ranged from the Colorado River to the Tonto Basin. Like the Apaches, they were mobile and extremely independent, their only political authorities being war chiefs and advisory chiefs (older men who were often former war chiefs) selected by the local groups. That made it extremely difficult for the U.S. military to run down or negotiate with more than one Yavapai group at a time.

During the late 1860s and early 1870s, however, there were only a handful of garrisons in central Arizona. In Yavapai territory there was Fort Whipple (1863–1913), Camp Date Creek (1867–1873), Camp Verde (1865–1890), Camp Hualpai (1869–1873), and Fort McDowell (1865–1890). In Western Apache country there was Camp Reno (1867–1870), Fort Apache (1870–1922), Camp Goodwin (1866–1871), and Camp Grant (1865–1872). Troopers, many of them German and Irish immigrants, had to pursue their quarry across terrain where none of the folds of the earth were gentle, and the landscape was rarely green or kissed by rain. Not surprisingly, many of the soldiers deserted, fleeing places like Camp Grant, a bleak, sun-scorched collection of adobes that, in the words of Captain Bourke, was "recognized from the tide-waters of the Hudson to those of the Columbia as the most thoroughly Godsforsaken post of all those supposed to be included in the annual Congressional appropriations."

But the incident that best captured the confusion of the era was the Camp Grant Massacre. Early in 1871 a thirty-seven-year-old first lieutenant named Royal Emerson Whitman assumed command of Camp Grant on the San Pedro River about fifty miles northeast of Tucson. Whitman was a complex and driven man, a free thinker who joined the Maine volunteers to free the slaves during the Civil War and a hard drinker who scandalized his fellow soldiers by going on binges for two or three days at a time. On one occasion he pointed a derringer at his post surgeon in a drunken rage. On another, he denounced General Crook as "a damned son of a bitch." Such actions caused his superiors to court-martial him three times in nine months after the Camp Grant Massacre occurred.

Nevertheless, Whitman, in the words of Apache agent John Clum, "was the first man within my knowledge fully to comprehend and honestly to sympathize with the Apaches." In February 1871 five old Apache women straggled into Camp Grant to look for a son who had been taken prisoner. Whitman fed them and treated them kindly, so other Apaches from the Aravaipa and Pinal bands soon came to the post to receive rations of beef and flour. That spring, Whitman created a refuge along Aravaipa Creek about five miles east of Camp Grant for nearly 500 Aravaipa and Pinal Apaches, including Chief Eskiminzin. The Apaches began cutting hay for the post's horse herd and harvesting barley in nearby ranchers' fields.

Whitman must have suspected that peace could not last, because he urged Eskiminzin to move his people to the White Mountains near Camp (later Fort) Apache, which was established in 1870. Eskiminzin refused, saying, "That is not our country, neither are they our people. Our fathers and their fathers before them have lived in these mountains and have raised corn in this valley. We are taught to make mescal our principal article of food, and in summer and winter here we have a never-ending supply. At the White Mountains there is none, and without it we get sick."

The Aravaipas should have taken Whitman's advice. Camp Grant was too close to Tucson, where people had been fighting Apaches for a hundred years. During the winter and spring, William Oury and Jesús María Elías formed the Committee of Public Safety, which blamed every depredation in southern Arizona on the Camp Grant Apaches. After Apaches ran off livestock from San Xavier on April 10, Oury and Elías decided to take matters into their own hands. Elías contacted his old ally Francisco Galerita, leader of the Tohono O'odham at San Xavier. Oury collected arms and ammunition from his fellow Anglos. On the afternoon of April 28, six Anglos, forty-eight Mexicans, and ninety-four O'odham gathered along Rillito Creek and set off on a march to Aravaipa Canyon. At dawn on Sunday, April 30, they surrounded the Apache camp, ready to strike.

The cottonwood-shaded banks of the Aravaipa soon turned into a killing ground. As Apache women and children stirred in the semidarkness, O'odham bounded forward "like deer," clubbing, stabbing, raping, splitting heads open with rocks. Meanwhile, the Anglos and Mexicans picked off any Apaches who tried to escape. It was slaughter pure and simple because most of the Apache men were off hunting in the mountains or carrying out surreptitious raids. By the time the carnage ended, twenty-seven children had been captured and more than a hundred Aravaipas and Pinals had been mutilated and slain.

Whitman arrived at the scene a few hours later, appalled at what he found. All the wikiups were burning, and all but eight of the corpses were women and children. The shaken lieutenant searched for wounded, found none, and buried the bodies. Then he dispatched interpreters into the mountains to find the Apache men and assure them that his soldiers had not participated in the "vile transaction." The following evening, the surviving Aravaipas began trickling back to Camp Grant, "so changed in forty-eight hours as to be hardly recognizable."

Most of the settlers in southern Arizona considered the attack justifiable homicide. They agreed with Oury, who said it was "the killing of about 144 of the most bloodthirsty devils that ever disgraced mother earth." The U.S. military and the Eastern press, on the other hand, called it a massacre, and President Grant bluntly informed Governor A.P.K. Safford that if the perpetrators were not brought to trial, he would place Arizona under martial law. They were. The trial lasted five days. After deliberating for nineteen minutes, the jury acquitted each and every one of the more than one hundred defendants. Frontier vengeance was vindicated, and Tucson celebrated with many drinks.

Many army officers considered the trial a travesty. They also believed that a nefarious "Tucson Ring" of freighters and government contractors had encouraged the Camp Grant Massacre in order to provoke the Aravaipas and keep supplies flowing to the troops. But such arguments oversimplified the passions of the time. They also fell into a common trap of Western history by making Anglos the leading protagonists in the drama even though most of the participants were O'odham or Mexicans. Ever since the late 1600s, Apaches had run off livestock and O'odham and Hispanics had given pursuit. Both sides murdered adults and carried off children whenever they found them. Both sides sought vengeance for their dead. It was a brutal pattern of provocation and revenge but an understandable one, part of the age-old struggle between the sedentary and the nomadic, the periphery and the frontier. The number of bodies along Aravaipa Creek may have been greater than after most such assaults, but the motivations of the avengers were the same. Bloody as it was, the Camp Grant Massacre was no aberration. On the contrary, it was the culmination of two centuries of conflict on the Arizona frontier.

✳ ✳ Crook Takes Command

The massacre was also a stunning indictment of U.S. Indian policy. Southern Arizona had been a part of the United States for nearly two decades. Millions of dollars and hundreds of soldiers had poured into the territory, yet the army exercised little control over either Indians or civilians. Dissension continued to wrack the federal government as the "peace party" and the "war party" savaged each other in the White House, Congress, and the press.

Crook was the man who finally ironed out the wrinkles, taking command of the Department of Arizona in June 1871. He lost no time in siding with Oury and Elías against Whitman over the Camp Grant Massacre. But Crook was as deliberate as Whitman was rash. He was a careful, methodical commander who interviewed every officer in southern Arizona before deciding on a course of action. He realized that the Yavapais and Apaches had to be pursued into every corner of their territory before they would accept confinement on reservations. He also recognized that neither soldiers nor civilians knew the Apachería well enough to make that pursuit successful. After experimenting with Navajos and Mexicans, Crook turned to the Apaches themselves, enlisting members of the White Mountain bands as scouts. Other Spanish, Mexican, and Anglo military commanders had used Apaches to fight Apaches, but Crook systematized that strategy until it became an essential part of his campaign.

In the fall of 1872, the federal government finally unleashed Crook and his troops. Crook's plan was to sling a great noose of soldiers around the Yavapais and Western Apaches and then tighten it. Three columns left Camp Hualpai northwest of Prescott to sweep the area from Camp Verde to the San Francisco Peaks. Two detachments from Camp Date Creek and two from Camp Verde pursued Yavapais in the Hassayampa, Agua Fria, and Verde drainages. Other expeditions rode out from Camp Apache, Camp Grant, and Fort McDowell. By the end of the year, Crook had nine columns in the field. After scouring the margins of Yavapai and Apache country, the saddle-hardened veterans slowly began to converge upon the Tonto Basin, where the Tonto Apaches lived. Starvation and cold became pitiless allies of the soldiers as they forced the Indians out of the desert and onto higher ground.

The offensive turned out to be a bloody, grueling success. "The officers and men worked day and night," Crook wrote in his annual report of 1873, "and with our Indian allies would crawl upon their hands and knees for long distances over terrible canyons and precipices where the slightest mishap would have resulted in instant death, in order that when daylight came they might attack their enemy and secure the advantage of surprise." Occasionally there were major battles such as the massacre at Skeleton Cave in the Salt River Canyon, where soldiers shot or stoned to death seventy-six Yavapais from the Kewevka-paya subtribe. Most engagements were less decisive. A few Indian men would be killed and a few women and children captured if the soldiers spared them. Sometimes, in the heat of battle, they did not. After his command fired into the huts of an Indian camp between Camp Verde and Fort McDowell, Lieutenant Walter Schuyler reported: "Two bucks and one squaw got away," implying that many other "squaws" did not. On another occasion, Schuyler wrote his father that after assaulting a Yavapai village and killing forty Indians, the soldiers left the children to fend for themselves. Other officers were not so callous. Horrified at finding an Apache baby trying to suckle her dead mother, Captain S.B.M. Young took her home to his wife, who raised the little girl until she died several years later.

More important than body counts, however, was the destruction of weapons, clothing, and food supplies. During the winter, the Apaches and Yavapais subsisted almost entirely upon stores of cornmeal, dried meat, wild seeds, and roasted mescal that had been pounded into cakes and spread out to dry. Once those caches were confiscated or burned, hunger haunted the Indians as terribly as the bullets and sabers of Crook's troops. Winter campaigning was one of the legacies of the Civil War—part of the concept of "total war" advocated by General William T. Sherman and General Philip Sheridan. Sherman and Sheridan had honed that concept on their marches through the South, and now they turned it against the Western Indians.

By the spring of 1873, Yavapai and Western Apache resistance was all but broken. After months in the saddle—and agonizing days on foot after an epidemic devastated army horse herds—Crook's cavalry had driven the Indians from the Bradshaws, Mazatzals, Sierra Anchas, Superstitions, and Pinals, and the foothills of the Mogollon Rim. The last war chief to surrender was Delshay, a Tonto Apache from the Mazatzals. According to Crook, Delshay said that "he had had 125 warriors last fall, and if anybody had told him he couldn't whip the world, he would have laughed at them, but now he had only twenty left. He said they used to have no difficulty in eluding the troops, but now the very rocks had gotten soft, they couldn't put their foot anywhere without leaving an impression by which we could follow."

❋ ❋ The Early Reservation System

The reason the rocks had "gotten soft" was Crook's reliance on Apache scouts. They understood the movements of their people, even if they were from different bands. "The longer we knew the Apache scouts," Bourke noted, "the better we liked them. They were wilder and more suspicious than the Pimas and Maricopas, but far more reliable, and endowed with a greater amount of courage and daring." Hostilities did not cease completely after

Crook's offensive, but the surrender of most of the surviving Yavapais and Western Apaches, and the increasing availability of Apache scouts, made life outside the reservations ever more dangerous. And while no final tally of the Apache and Yavapai dead was ever compiled, Bourke estimated that troops from Camp Grant alone killed more than 500 Indians.

Life in captivity often became a slow death itself. Early reservations in Arizona were sullen, miserable places. Soldiers herded Indians from many different bands and tribes together like cattle. Corrupt Indian agents cheated them out of their rations. Honest but overzealous ones tried to turn hunters, gatherers, and raiders into yeoman farmers. Worst of all, people who had never lived sedentary lives before suddenly found themselves forced to occupy one place year-round. Disease thrived in the cramped, dirty quarters, and epidemics swept across the reservations, killing hundreds.

Indians living on the early reservations had one advantage, however. Despite destitution and defeat, Yavapais from the Tolkapaya subtribe at Date Creek or the White Mountain Apaches at Camp Apache remained in their home ranges, surrounded by landmarks. A butte, a spring, a mesa, a mountain—all had names and meanings. These places were part of their origin, their very identity as a people. They constituted a moral as well as a physical geography for the Native Americans who lived there.

All that changed in 1874, when the government decided to consolidate many of the smaller reserves into one giant reservation where the Indians could be isolated and controlled. That reservation was San Carlos, the southern portion of the White Mountain Apache Reservation. San Carlos straddled the Gila River downstream from Safford, where Mexican and Mormon farmers were already diverting the Gila onto their fields. From there it stretched northward over the Gila Mountains to Ash Flat and the Natanes Plateau, a sea of piñon pine and juniper undulating in every direction. Then it descended into the pine-clad canyons of the Black River, which joined with the White River to form the Salt about twenty miles southwest of Camp Apache. Before relocation, this was the territory of the San Carlos band of the Western Apaches, who were closely related to the Pinal Apaches to the west and the Aravaipa Apaches to the south.

Beyond was a vast forest of piñon-juniper and ponderosa pine watered by streams that drained the great escarpment of the Mogollon Rim. To the north and west, bands of Carrizo, Cibecue, and Canyon Creek Apaches farmed pockets of alluvial soil along creeks of the same name. To the north and east were the Western and Eastern White Mountain Apaches, who cultivated their summer plots along the White River and Big Bonito Creek. They also stalked deer and elk in the White Mountains and the Blue Range, and they were the ones the other Apaches called the On Top of Mountain People because of the spruce- and fir-crowned peaks that dominated their territory. Mountains were sacred to the Western Apaches—sources of supernatural power and homes of the *gaan,* beings who lived in the region before the Apaches arrived. To be cut off from the mountains was to be cut off from the deepest sources of Apache identity and culture, to be less than whole.

Yet the federal government established the headquarters of San Carlos in one of the lowest and hottest portions of the reservation—a bleak creosote flat where San Carlos Creek trickled into the Gila. The spot was chosen for two reasons: first, because it was relatively close to Tucson, where powerful freighters and merchants lived; and second, because the terrain was open and the army could keep an eye on the Indians confined there. With those two forces in play, the government conducted an experiment in relocation unmatched in Arizona history until the internment of the Japanese during World War II, throwing thousands of Yavapais, Chiricahuas, and Western Apaches together with little regard for cultural, political, or linguistic differences. For the Pinal, San Carlos, and Aravaipa Apaches, the experiment was wrenching, but at least they were able to draw some solace from familiar country. For the Yavapais and the Tonto, White Mountain, and Chiricahua Apaches, on the other hand, San Carlos was a bitter exile. The land stalked the people, but the people could not stalk the land.

The first groups removed against their will were Yavapais and Tonto Apaches living near Camps Verde and Date Creek. The forced march from Camp Verde to San Carlos began on February 27, 1875. For eight days, 1,400 Yavapais and Tonto Apaches trudged across 180 miles of the roughest country in the territory, including the Tonto Basin. At one point a group of Yavapais and Apaches came to blows and seven Indians died. By the end of the journey, more than a hundred others had perished from malnutrition and cold. "It was an outrageous proceeding," Bourke wrote, "one for which I should still blush had I not long since gotten over blushing for anything that the United States Government did in Indian matters."

Almost as misguided was the relocation of the Indians at Camp Apache about sixty miles northeast of San Carlos. From its establishment by the War Department in 1870, the Camp Apache reservation was the closest thing to a success in the sorry history of Anglo-Apache affairs. The White Mountain bands had never relied as heavily upon raiding as their Pinal, Aravaipa, or

Chiricahua brethren. Nor had their territory been overrun with settlers like the country of the Yavapais and Tonto Apaches to the west. The White Mountain people were the first Apache bands to surrender and the first to have soldiers stationed in their midst. There, in the valley of the White River, where the post known successively as Camp Ord, Camp Mogollon, Camp Thomas, Camp Apache, and finally in 1879 Fort Apache was located, White Mountain Apaches had raised corn, beans, and squash for generations. Crook recruited most of his early scouts from their ranks.

During the early 1870s the reservation escaped much of the upheaval wracking the rest of the Apachería. The Dutch Reformed Church, which was given jurisdiction over the Apaches by the Grant administration, appointed James E. Roberts as agent in December 1872. Roberts encouraged stock raising and agriculture among the White Mountain people, convinced that the Indians would "become civilized just as soon as they became lovers of money." By the spring of 1874, Roberts's charges had dug more than five miles of canals and were irrigating more than 300 acres of land around Camp Apache. The military responded by purchasing 100 bushels of beans, 6,000 bushels of corn, and 150 tons of hay from the Apache farmers. In Roberts's mind, the first steps toward Apache capitalism had begun.

But then the soldiers started interfering in the internal affairs of the reservation. They undercut Roberts's authority to issue passes. They took over the dispensation of rations, the foundation of any Indian agent's power and influence. Finally, in 1874, Roberts became caught up in a complex scheme to reduce the size of the reservation because copper ore had been discovered near modern Clifton. Territorial officials, including Governor A.P.K. Safford and Delegate to Congress Richard C. McCormick, were attempting to return the area to the public domain, and Roberts, perhaps unwittingly, played along. He also grew increasingly unstable, which gave the military a convenient excuse to occupy agency buildings, remove Roberts from office, and seize control of the reservation itself. Once again conflict between civil and military authorities gutted any effort to hammer out a coherent Indian policy in Arizona.

❋ ❋ ❋ Cochise and the Chiricahua Reservation

To prevent a complete breakdown in civil-military relations, the Commissioner of Indian Affairs placed the White Mountain Apaches under the jurisdiction of the San Carlos agent, John Clum, a member of the Dutch Reformed Church. It turned out to be a wise decision. Unlike Roberts, Clum proved to be more than a match for the officers stationed along the Apache frontier. When he arrived at San Carlos in August 1874, Clum was not quite twenty-three years old—short, cocky, belligerent, convinced that the army did more harm than good on Indian reservations. He lost no time in establishing his influence among the Apaches, striking up a lifelong friendship with Eskiminzin and persuading many of the White Mountain people to move south to San Carlos. By visiting Apache camps without soldiers and by fiercely defending the Apaches against the military, Clum won the confidence of his charges. They responded by turning in their weapons, setting up a tribal court to try minor infractions, and organizing their own police force under Clum's command. The young agent soon had 4,200 Indians—Apaches and Yavapais—living on his huge, semi-arid reservation. Even the military grudgingly admitted that he was doing a good job.

But Clum could not solve the problem of the Chiricahuas. Unlike Eskiminzin, whose people had been shattered by the Camp Grant Massacre, the Chiricahua chiefs had not yet been broken by the new order taking shape in Arizona. For generations the Chiricahuas had immersed themselves in the treacheries of scalp hunter diplomacy on the frontier of the decaying Spanish empire. They had played off Chihuahuans and Sonorans against one another. They had raided when they could, made peace when they had to. They were political strategists as well as warriors, and they despised the arrogance of the young New Yorker. "Juh said that this boy thought that he knew more than Ussen Himself [Creator of Life] and that he could defy not only the Indians but the army," recalled Juh's son Asa Daklugie. Stout old Juh, perhaps the greatest guerrilla leader of all the Chiricahua chiefs except Victorio, knew better.

The Chiricahuas also hated San Carlos, where they first experienced the "shaking sickness" (malaria). According to Daklugie, "That was the worst place in all the great territory stolen from the Apaches. If anybody had ever lived there permanently, no Apache knew of it. . . . The heat was terrible. The insects were terrible. The water was terrible. . . . Insects and rattlesnakes seemed to thrive there; and no White Eye could possibly fear and dislike snakes more than do Apaches."

More than anything else, however, the Chiricahuas loved their mountain homelands and the access it gave them to both the United States and Mexico. For two hundred years they had raided Sonora and Chihuahua from their camps in the Mogollons, the Animas, the Chiricahuas, and the Sierra Madre. Then, after the Treaty of Guadalupe-Hidalgo and the Gadsden Purchase, Cochise, Juh, Victorio, and other chiefs had mastered the border game, retreating into Mexico whenever U.S. pressure got too intense. But in 1867, Benito Juárez and his followers drove the French out of Mexico and executed the French puppet, Maximilian. After years of fighting foreigners and one another, the Mexican people slowly put the pieces of their country back together again—a process that culminated in the Porfiriato (1876–1910), when Porfirio Díaz ruled Mexico with a velvet glove for foreign investment and an iron fist for internal dissent. Governor Ignacio Pesqueira reasserted his control over Sonora, and the Terrazas family imposed order and progress on Chihuahua. By the fall of 1868, Cochise had been forced to flee north instead of south, taking refuge in the Mogollon Mountains to escape a determined campaign by Jesús García Morales, the brutal commander of Pesqueira's forces who had just crushed a rebellion of Yaqui Indians in southern Sonora. Northern Mexico was no longer a sanctuary, and the border game grew ever more dangerous. By the early 1870s, many Chiricahua chiefs, including Cochise, were ready to talk peace.

According to legend, the key figure in these negotiations was Thomas Jonathan Jeffords, a redheaded steamboat captain on the Great Lakes who had drifted into Arizona during the Civil War. While working for the Southern Overland Mail, Jeffords supposedly rode into Cochise's camp alone in the early 1860s to persuade the chief to stop killing his riders. Cochise was so impressed with his bravery that the two men became close friends. The Bascom Affair made Cochise hate the Anglos; his friendship with Tom Jeffords made him trust them again. It was a moral fable simplified for Western novels and Hollywood movies. Thus, the movie myth of *Blood Brother* and *Broken Arrow* was born.

Like so many other legends in Arizona history, the Jeffords myth overemphasized the role of Anglo Americans on a complex political and ethnic frontier. It also ignored the political sophistication of Chiricahua leaders and the role of Mexicans in the Apache wars. Yet Cochise's biographer, historian Edwin Sweeney, concludes that Jeffords and Cochise probably did not meet until the early 1870s, when Cochise was already beginning to talk with U.S. authorities at the Cañada Alamosa Reservation in New Mexico. One of the few historians of the Apaches to comb Mexican records thoroughly, Sweeney emphasizes the toll Mexican campaigns had taken on Cochise's Chokonens and other Chiricahua bands. Cochise trusted Jeffords and arranged with him to negotiate with the U.S. military, but he did so because he and his people were being harassed from all sides by Chihuahuan scalp hunters, Sonoran soldiers, O'odham revenge parties, and even Manso Apaches from Tucson bankrolled by merchant Estevan Ochoa. Jeffords was the go-between, not the prime mover, of Cochise's final peace with the U.S. government.

That peace was not easily achieved. Cochise first met with army officers in late September 1871. The army wanted Cochise and the other Chiricahuas to settle at Tularosa, New Mexico. Cochise refused. A year later, General O. O. Howard met with Jeffords at Tularosa and told him he wanted to talk with Cochise. Jeffords said, "General Howard, Cochise won't come. The man that wants to talk to Cochise must go where he is." So Howard did, accompanied only by Jeffords, two Chiricahuas, and his aide, Lieutenant Joseph Sladen. The little party rode into the Dragoon Mountains east of the San Pedro River on September 30, 1872. The next day, Cochise came to the general's camp with his youngest wife, his youngest son, and his sister, a fifty-year-old widow who was one of his most trusted advisors. Sladen called her the "presiding genius" of Cochise's outpost in the Dragoons overlooking the road to Fort Bowie. She had "strongly marked, unprepossessing features giving evidence of a strong will," Sladen observed. He added that her "independence and force seemed to justify this faith in her ability."

Howard offered to meet Cochise's earlier demand and allow the Chiricahuas to move to Cañada Alamosa near the Black Range in New Mexico. Cochise countered with a proposal that surprised everyone, even Jeffords. "Why not give me Apache Pass?" he said. "Give me that and I will protect all the roads. I will see that nobody's property is taken by Indians." Howard was reluctant to do so at first, but Cochise persuaded him that many of the Chokonen Chiricahuas would never leave their homeland, not even for Cañada Alamosa. So Howard finally agreed to a reservation in Chokonen territory, one that ran from the Dragoon Mountains on the west to the Peloncillo Mountains on the east. It included the Chiricahua Mountains and ran all the way south to the Mexican border. Howard also promised rations of food and clothing to be distributed by Jeffords, who had already been appointed agent to the Chiricahuas. An eloquent orator, Cochise replied that "hereafter the white man and the Indian are to drink the same water, eat of the same bread, and be at peace."

Cochise kept his word, but the reservation was doomed from the very beginning because of its closeness to Mexico. Chokonen depredations in southern Arizona ceased, but the Chiricahuas continued to raid Sonora and Chihuahua just as they always had. "There are many young people whose parents and relatives have been killed by the Mexicans, and now these young people are liable to go down, from time to time, and do a little damage to the Mexicans,"

Cochise told a group of officers sent by Crook in January 1873. Cochise himself did not join the raiding parties, but neither he or Jeffords did much to discourage them.

By then, of course, Crook had launched his campaign against the Yavapais and Western Apaches and was searching for a legitimate excuse to take up arms against Cochise as well. He even formulated a plan to provoke Cochise by demanding that the Chiricahuas submit to a daily roll call. If they refused, he wrote Governor Pesqueira of Sonora, who was complaining bitterly about Chiricahua hostilities in his state, "I will commence hostilities against them without delay." But Cochise and Jeffords were able to fend off Crook and perform their remarkable balancing act for another year. By the end of 1873, Cochise had convinced many of his own people and some of the Nednhi Chiricahuas living on the reservation to stop their Mexican raids.

Nevertheless, when Cochise died of a stomach ailment complicated by heavy drinking on June 8, 1874, it was only a matter of time before the structure Cochise, Howard, and Jeffords had built came crashing to the ground. From the very beginning, the reservation in southeastern Arizona had been less a place than a web of trust—trust between Jeffords and Cochise, and between Cochise and the other Chiricahuas who roamed from the Mogollon Mountains to the Sierra Madre. Jeffords hung on for nearly two more years, but he never had the influence over the Apaches that Cochise had. Many Anglos did not trust him either, including Crook. When the government cut Jeffords's beef ration from 889,000 pounds to 650,000 in the spring of 1876, a few Chiricahuas resumed raiding in southeastern Arizona. Then Nicolas Rogers sold whiskey to a Chiricahua named Pionsenay and several companions at the Sulphur Springs stage station. Pionsenay killed him and his cook after Rogers refused to sell more.

Those hostilities gave the enemies of Jeffords the ammunition they needed. John Wasson, editor of the *Tucson Weekly Citizen,* thundered that Jeffords was an "incarnate demon" and accused him of a long list of crimes. He was a drunkard. He was in collusion with the whiskey peddlers and the ammunition dealers. He received gold and livestock stolen by the Chiricahuas in Mexico. The charges went on and on. Jeffords denied the accusations, and Captain C. B. McLellan of the Sixth Cavalry at Camp Bowie even wrote him a letter of support. But the damage was done. On May 3 the government ordered Clum to suspend Jeffords and, if "practicable," transfer the Chiricahuas to San Carlos. Jeffords's career as a mediator between the Chiricahuas and the U.S. government had come to an end.

✴   ✴   ✴   Victorio and the Failure of Relocation

After waiting for military reinforcements to arrive, Clum began the relocation in early June. Cochise's sons Taza and Naiche agreed to the move and killed several Chiricahuas, including Eskinya, Cochise's trusted ally, when he insisted they go to war. Nednhi Chiricahuas led by Juh also requested transfer. Unfamiliar with their fierce desire to remain free, Clum granted them three days to round up their kinsmen. They used that time to elude the cavalry and flee south. Of the more than 1,000 Chiricahuas enumerated in Jeffords's infrequent censuses, only 42 men and 280 women and children accompanied Clum north. Nonetheless, Clum later boasted: "The terrible shade of that tribe's dreaded name had passed away."

Nothing could have been further from the truth. The firing of Jeffords and the abolition of the reservation in southeastern Arizona drove the Chiricahuas deeper into Mexico or over to the Ojo Caliente reservation in New Mexico. In April 1877 the Interior Department ordered Clum to remove the bands at Ojo Caliente to San Carlos as well. Victorio and the Chihenne Chiricahuas acquiesced, at least at first. Geronimo, on the other hand, appeared "defiant" to the young agent, so Clum supposedly hid his Apache police in the commissary building at Ojo Caliente and surprised Geronimo, seizing his rifle and throwing him in shackles. "Thus was accomplished the first and only *bonafide capture* of GERONIMO THE RENEGADE," Clum crowed.

A total of 453 Chiricahuas—110 from Geronimo's band, the rest under Victorio—reached San Carlos in late May. From the very beginning they despised the reservation and quarreled with the other Apaches confined there. Meanwhile, Clum's feuds with the military escalated until he made good on one of his many threats to resign. On July 1, Clum left San Carlos, nearly three years after he had arrived. He was replaced by a series of agents who were renowned, perhaps unjustly, for their corruption. Two months later, Victorio, Loco, and 308 other Chiricahuas bolted for New Mexico, killing twelve ranchers before surrendering at Fort Wingate in early October.

Victorio and his people returned to Ojo Caliente, where they lived peacefully for less than a year before the government attempted to transfer them to San Carlos again in October 1878. Victorio escaped, and after a year of unsuccessful peace negotiations, he gathered Chiricahuas, Mescaleros, and even a few Comanches to his side and embarked upon one of the most remarkable guerrilla campaigns in American history. He and his men—125 to 150 strong—always traveled with women and children, some of whom, like Victorio's sister Lozen, were accomplished warriors themselves. Yet for more than a year Victorio's little band outran thousands of soldiers and killed hundreds of settlers across New Mexico and west Texas, becoming the very embodiment of Apache resistance in the Southwest. They were elusive. They were invulnerable. They were shadows moving across a sunlit land.

Or so it seemed. As long as Victorio remained in country he knew, he was able to slip through the net again and again. In July and August 1880, however, Black cavalrymen in West Texas relentlessly harried Victorio and his people, keeping them from the few sources of water in that hot, parched land. To escape them, Victorio crossed the Rio Grande near Fort Quitman and drifted south into the desolate deserts of northeastern Chihuahua. There he met his end at the hands of Mexican militia, not U.S. soldiers. On October 15, Joaquín Terrazas and 260 hard-riding Chihuahuans and Tarahumara Indians hunted the Apaches down on three rocky outcrops called Tres Castillos. Victorio and his band fought until their ammunition ran out, and then they died, seventy-eight of them, sixty-two of whom were men. Terrazas also took sixty-eight prisoners. Victorio was not one of the survivors.

✳   ✳   ✳   **The Last Stand of the Chiricahuas**

Despite Victorio's death, other Apaches continued to fight on. Nana, Victorio's rheumatic old lieutenant, carried out devastating raids in Chihuahua and New Mexico during the summer of 1881, covering more than a thousand miles and killing thirty to fifty Anglos. Even more incredible was the odyssey of five Apache women captured at Tres Castillos. Taken to Mexico City and sold as slaves, the women—including Siki, a daughter of Loco—endured captivity for three years until they had a chance to escape. Then they headed for the deserts of northern Mexico with only a blanket and a knife between them until they found Geronimo's band in the Sierra Madre. No other feat better symbolized the determination of the Apache rebels.

The Apaches at San Carlos, on the other hand, were thoroughly demoralized. Hungry, poorly clothed, wracked by disease and intertribal conflicts, they were also convinced that their agent, John Tiffany, was selling their rations to Anglos off the reservation. Most of the Apaches realized that armed resistance was futile, so they turned to a prophet, the Western Apache medicine man Noch-del-klinne. Slightly built but possessing the supernatural power (*diyih*) so important to Apaches, Noch-del-klinne told his followers that if they held dances similar to the Ghost Dance, two dead chiefs would be resurrected and the whites would be driven away. It was an attempt by desperate people to accomplish through religion what they could not achieve through force of arms, but as Noch-del-klinne's dances in the remote Cibecue Valley attracted more and more Apaches, General Eugene Carr at Fort Apache grew alarmed. In late August 1881, he organized an expedition of 117 troops to arrest the Apache leader. When he did, many of his Apache scouts rebelled. Shots were fired, people scattered, and both soldiers and Apaches were killed, including Noch-del-klinne. It was the only time during the history of the Apache Wars that Apache scouts turned against U.S. troops.

The consequences were as tragic as they were predictable. The scouts and many other Apaches fled, committing a few depredations around Fort Apache, and soldiers soon swarmed across the enormous reservation, trying to run them down. Crook believed that the scouts had been provoked and argued that "any attempt to punish any of the Indian soldiers for participation in it would bring on war." But the army court-martialed five of the scouts who surrendered anyway, sending two to the military prison at Alcatraz. The other three—Sergeant Dandy Jim, Sergeant Dead Shot, and Private Skippy—were hung at Fort Grant on March 3, 1882.

Many at San Carlos thought that the army intended to punish them as well, so Juh, Chato, Naiche, Geronimo and sixty-six other members of the Nednhi band slipped away in September 1881. For the next four years the Chiricahuas and their pursuers fought a brutal war of attrition, most of it on Mexican soil. In the winter of 1882, Juh ambushed and killed a party of Mexicans led by the veteran Indian fighter Juan Mata Ortiz, Terrazas's second-in-command at Tres Castillos. The following year, Chihuahuan militia surprised Juh's camp and killed his wife and young daughter. Sometime after that, Juh's horse slipped on a steep mountain trail above the Río Aros in northwestern Chihuahua, tumbling the heavyset old chief into the water. The other Chiricahuas tried to revive him, but he never recovered consciousness. From then on, Geronimo led most of the Chiricahuas who refused reservation life.

No other Apache was as notorious or as misunderstood. Geronimo was never a chief, not even of his own small Bedonkoke band. After Juh's death, the Chokonen and Nednhi Chiricahuas remaining in the Sierra Madre recognized Cochise's son Naiche as chief. Geronimo, in contrast, was a respected shaman with great power, including the power to foretell the future. And in a world fraught with danger, such power was an essential part of Apache leadership. "No White Eyes seem to understand the importance of that in controlling Apaches," Asa Daklugie confided to Eve Ball. "Naiche was not a Medicine Man; so he needed Geronimo as Geronimo needed him."

Geronimo's principal opponent was Crook, who returned to take over the Department of Arizona in September 1882. By then the border game was about to be closed down. On July 29, Mexico signed a treaty allowing U.S. troops to chase hostile Apaches across the international boundary. In May 1883, Crook gathered about fifty soldiers and two hundred Quechan, Mohave, and Apache scouts and rode up the rugged valley of the Bavispe River in northwestern Sonora until he turned east into the Sierra Madre itself. Captain Emmet Crawford and his scouts were the first to encounter the Chiricahuas, attacking the ranchería of Chato and Bonito. That turned out to be the only hostile engagement of the entire campaign. The penetration of their territory by U.S. troops was threat enough, and soon the Apaches, including Geronimo, made their way to Crook's camp in the Sierra Madre.

For the next several days, Crook and Geronimo sparred with one another over the details of the surrender. Crook realized that he was in no position to insist on complete submission. If he did, the Apaches would scatter into the mountains and the war would drag on for years. He therefore accepted Geronimo's promise to return to San Carlos on his own—a move that prompted his critics to charge that Geronimo had captured Crook rather than vice versa. Crook then led Nana, Loco, Bonito, and 225 other Chiricahuas back to Arizona, arriving at San Carlos on June 23.

At first it seemed that Crook's gamble had paid off. Confounding the skeptics, Geronimo kept his part of the bargain in late February 1884. He and the other Chiricahuas settled along Turkey Creek fifteen miles below Fort Apache, where they cultivated 4,000 acres and harvested 3,850,000 pounds of corn, 600,000 pounds of wheat and other cereals, 540,000 pounds of beans, 20,000 pounds of potatoes, and 200,000 pumpkins. Geronimo himself became one of the most proficient farmers. The transition from raider to husbandman seemed to be proceeding with remarkable speed.

But the bucolic tranquility was illusory. The officers at Fort Apache clashed incessantly with the agents at San Carlos. Accusations of corruption kept surfacing, and Alchisé, a friendly White Mountain chief, noted sardonically that the "Great Father" had given his people many cattle "older than this world," with "not a tooth in their heads." In May the humiliations of reservation life finally overwhelmed many of the Chiricahuas. Crook prohibited alcohol on the reservation, outlawing the brewing of *tizwin,* a fermented corn liquor much favored by the Apaches. Under the guise of preventing wife beating, the military also began to interfere in the personal affairs of Apache families themselves. On May 15 the Chiricahuas demonstrated their contempt for such meddling by getting drunk on tizwin and flaunting their disobedience. Two days later, Geronimo, Naiche, Nana, and 131 other Chiricahuas deserted the reservation.

Crook organized another expedition into northern Sonora, and once again Apache scouts, including former Chiricahua rebels like Chato, led the way. But when the general and Geronimo sat down in a cottonwood-shaded ravine called Cañon de los Embudos on March 25, 1886, the negotiations were doomed from the start. Crook's superiors wanted unconditional surrender; the Chiricahuas, an immediate return to San Carlos. Crook and Geronimo finally agreed to a compromise that would have allowed the Chiricahuas to return to the reservation after a two-year imprisonment back east, but as soon as General Philip Sheridan and President Grover Cleveland learned of the agreement, they rejected it. By then, however, Geronimo, Naiche, and forty other Chiricahuas, including fourteen women and six children, had slipped away.

That left Crook himself in an untenable position. When Sheridan heard that the peace talks had collapsed, he concluded that the Apache scouts had allowed Geronimo to escape and told Crook to use regular troops from then on. He also ordered Crook to load the rest of the Chiricahuas onto railroad cars and ship them to Fort Marion (now Castillo de San Marcos National Monument) in St. Augustine, Florida. This time there was to be no promise of return. In the face of Sheridan's criticism—and a direct order that required him to go back on his word to the Apaches—Crook asked to be relieved.

His successor was General Nelson Miles, a square-jawed Indian fighter from the Northern Plains with a walrus moustache and a penchant for self-glorification. Miles was given more than 5,000 soldiers—one-fourth of the entire U.S. army—to capture or kill Geronimo's little band. A more astute politician than Crook, Miles deployed his regulars with great fanfare and erected twenty-seven heliograph stations to keep track of the hostiles. In the end, however, two Chiricahua scouts under Captain Charles Gatewood—Kayitah and Martine—tracked Geronimo to the Torres Mountains southeast of Fronteras. Gatewood met with the Chiricahua leader in late August and persuaded him to surrender for the fourth and final time. Geronimo did so at Skeleton Canyon in the Peloncillo Mountains of southeastern Arizona on September 4, 1886.

＊ ＊ Exile in the East

The result was a train ride to Florida and an exile that lasted twenty-seven years. As hard-nosed as he was, Crook thought that the Chiricahuas could be trusted. Miles and the U.S. government did not. They believed that Arizona would not be secure until the Chiricahuas were deported, and their opinion prevailed.

The first to go were the seventy-seven Chiricahuas rounded up during Crook's second campaign. The government dispatched them to Fort Marion in April 1886. Miles then persuaded Sheridan that all the Chiricahuas in Arizona had to be removed. To his credit, Miles argued for Indian Territory in Oklahoma as their destination rather than mosquito-ridden Florida, where the Apaches "would in a short time most likely die." He even arranged to send Chato and twelve other Chiricahua leaders, including three women, on a tour of Indian Territory to persuade them to resettle there. Instead, President Cleveland brought Chato and the rest of the Chiricahua delegation to Washington, D.C., where Chato was presented with a silver medal. Cleveland asked him to persuade his people to move to Florida. Chato refused and demanded a "paper" allowing them to stay in Arizona. Cleveland responded by giving the illiterate scout a document that proclaimed he had visited the nation's capital. Then, after the fanfare was over and the Chiricahuas were on their way back to Arizona, Chato and the others were arrested as prisoners of war at Fort Leavenworth, Kansas.

Infuriated by the mistreatment of his scouts, Crook roared: "The surrender of Geronimo could not have been effected except for the assistance of Chato and his scouts. For their allegiance, they have been rewarded by captivity in a strange land." Cleveland and the War Department ignored him. Meanwhile, the military called in the rest of the peaceful Chiricahuas—and Indians married to Chiricahuas—for a "routine count" at Fort Apache and remanded them to Fort Marion as well. Geronimo and his tattered rebels were the last to go. By the end of the year, the government had confined nearly 500 Chiricahuas on the other side of the continent—the men at Fort Pickens near Pensacola, the women and children at Fort Marion on Florida's Atlantic coast. Arizona's Apache wars had finally come to an end.

Crook spent the last years of his life bitterly protesting the treatment of the Chiricahuas. On January 2, 1890, he even visited them at Mount Vernon, Alabama, where they had been transferred after 119 of the 498 exiles had died in the dank, malarial, overcrowded prisons of Florida. "Chatto came out, and went out to the General, and gave him a greeting that was really tender," one young officer wrote. "He took him by the hand, and with his other made a motion as if to clasp him about the neck. It was as if he would express his joy, but feared to take such liberty. It was a touching sight."

Crook returned to Washington to lobby for a bill to settle the Chiricahuas at Fort Sill in Oklahoma. But after he died on March 21 of that year, the bill expired as well. For the next four years the Apaches remained in Alabama, sweltering and dying in the Southern heat. Then, in 1894, the government finally heeded Crook's advice and sent them to Fort Sill, where they scattered across the reservation in "villages" that resembled their traditional local groups. But even though Indian agents helped them become farmers and ranchers, most remained refugees on the Southern Plains. In 1913 they were offered a choice: private land in Oklahoma or a part of the Mescalero reservation in central New Mexico. After living outside the Southwest for nearly three decades, 187 of the 271 surviving Chiricahuas, including Chato, chose to return home. No other Southwestern Indians had been moved so far or been gone for so long.

❋ ❋ ❋   The Rise and Fall of the Gila Pimas

As harsh as the deportation of the Chiricahuas was, however, other Native Americans suffered nearly as much. Navajos languished at Bosque Redondo until 1868, where insects ate their crops and Comanche raids and smallpox epidemics ravaged their numbers. When the army finally allowed them to return to their homeland, many families survived on rations dispensed from Fort Wingate and Fort Defiance because their fields had reverted to weeds and their herds had been destroyed.

The Yavapais interned at San Carlos also began to trickle back to their traditional ranges, but the government did not create reservations for them until 1904 at Fort McDowell, 1910 near Camp Verde, and 1935 at Prescott. Hualapais were a little luckier. Taken to La Paz on the Colorado River reservation in 1874, they escaped a year later, only to find their country overrun by ranchers. The stockmen monopolized their springs and ran cattle over their grasslands, destroying several of the wild plant species upon which the Hualapais relied. In order to contain them, the government established a small reservation along the south rim of the Grand Canyon in 1883.

But the cruelest fate awaited the Akimel O'odham. The Pimas had been allies of the Europeans ever since Kino rode through their country in the late seventeenth century. As noted earlier, during the California Gold Rush they fed thousands of Anglo and Mexican argonauts with the produce from their floodplain fields. Beginning in the late 1840s, in fact, the Pimas developed into the first agricultural entrepreneurs in Arizona. The market for their crops that had been created along the Gila Trail during the Gold Rush swelled with the establishment of a stagecoach route through Pima territory in 1857 and the outbreak of the Civil War in 1861. By 1870 the Pimas were selling or trading more than three million pounds of wheat a year. If their water rights had been respected, O'odham, not Anglos, might have been the ones to make Phoenix rise from the ashes of the Hohokam.

But that was not to be. During the late 1860s, Anglo and Mexican farmers settled upriver from the Pima villages around Florence and dug irrigation ditches that siphoned off the waters of the Gila. In 1873, Chief Antonio Azul led a delegation of Pimas to Washington, D.C. to protest the situation. The government responded by suggesting that the Pimas emigrate to Indian Territory in Oklahoma. The O'odham refused, but 1,200 did move north to the Salt River, where irrigation water was more plentiful. The rest strung out along the Gila and farmed the best they could wherever stretches of the river still flowed.

Then, in 1887, the construction of a large canal near Florence diverted the Gila once and for all. By 1895, conditions were so desperate that the government began issuing rations to the O'odham. Once the Pimas had fed the territory. Now they did not have enough water to feed themselves. In the span of a single generation, proud and independent farmers had gone from entrepreneurship to the dole. The desolate poignancy of that transformation was captured by Piman George Webb, who wrote:

> In the old days, on hot summer nights, a low mist would spread over the river and the sloughs. Then the sun would come up and the mist would disappear. On those hot nights the cattle often gathered along the river up to their knees in the cool mud.
>
> Soon some Pima boy would come along and dive into the big ditch and swim for awhile. Then he would get out and open the headgate and the water would come splashing into the laterals and flow out along the ditches. By this time all the Pimas were out in the fields with their shovels. They would fan out and lead the water to the alfalfa, along the corn rows, and over to the melons. The red-winged blackbirds would sing in the trees and fly down to look for bugs along the ditches. Their song always means that there is water close by as they will not sing if there is not water splashing somewhere.
>
> The green of those Pima fields spread along the river for many miles in the old days when there was plenty of water.
>
> Now the river is an empty bed full of sand.

Now you can stand in that same place and see the wind tearing pieces of bark off the cottonwood trees along the dry ditches.

The dead trees stand there like white bones. The red-wing blackbirds have gone somewhere else. Mesquite and brush and tumbleweeds have begun to turn those fields back into desert.

Mexican and Italian miners at the Clifton-Morenci strike in 1903. (Courtesy of the Arizona Historical Society, from the La Moine Collection)

EXTRACTION

6

The Freighters and
the Railroads

In 1875, at a time when, across the Southwest, Anglo Americans despised Mexicans as a "race of mongrels," the citizens of Tucson elected Don Estevan Ochoa mayor of the town by the overwhelming margin of 187 to 40. A native of Chihuahua who immigrated to the United States in the 1850s, Ochoa was a soft-spoken little man with dark, liquid eyes and a neatly trimmed beard. He was also Tucson's leading citizen during the 1860s and 1870s. He served in the territorial legislature for three terms; he helped found the Arizona public school system; and he and his partner Pinckney Randolph Tully built one of the largest, most diversified economic empires in the Arizona Territory, combining long-distance freighting with merchandizing, mining, and stock raising. At its peak, Tully, Ochoa & Company employed hundreds of men and owned more than $100,000 worth of freighting equipment. By 1880 the firm had become the largest taxpayer in Pima County.

Then the Southern Pacific Railroad arrived. Before the railroads, all goods reached the interior of Arizona by oxen or mule. Anyone with a wagon and a string of animals could become a freighter, and scores of independent operations lumbered across Arizona's rugged terrain. But the railroads sliced through the heart of the frontier, binding Arizona to the rest of the United States with bands of iron and steel. The Southern Pacific could transport goods for 1½ cents a pound and haul them from Yuma to Tucson in a day. Firms like Tully, Ochoa & Company charged 5½ to 14 cents per pound and took up to twenty days. Animal power simply could not compete with steam.

In November 1880 a Southern Pacific locomotive ploughed into two of Tully, Ochoa & Company's freight wagons, smashing the vehicles and killing their mules. That accident symbolized the end of an era and the passing of the frontier. For two decades Ochoa and his fellow freighters had dominated the isolated young territory, running its politics and getting rich off government contracts. But when the railroads unleashed their "irresistible torrent of civilization and prosperity," Ochoa and other merchants drowned. By 1888, the year he died in genteel poverty, Don Estevan and most of his contemporaries were relics of another age. They had become as obsolescent as Chato or Geronimo. The railroads destroyed them as surely as the frontier society they fought to build.

✳ ✳ ✳ Freighting on the Frontier

While it flourished, however, that society was more egalitarian than the extractive colony that took root in its corpse. During the 1860s and 1870s, Arizona was too isolated and dangerous to allow any major industries to develop, so the scale of the territory's economy remained small enough to prevent the entrenchment of a rigidly stratified social structure. Livestock were the natural prey of the Apaches. Agriculture was confined to streams like the Santa Cruz. Technological innovations had not yet transformed copper mining by allowing the extraction of low-grade ore.

Unless an individual struck it rich in the goldfields, the only way to make a fortune on the Arizona frontier was long-distance freighting. Nearly everything, including most basic foodstuffs, had to be imported from outside the territory. Wheat and corn came from Sonora and Chihuahua. Manufactured goods arrived from the eastern United States. Army posts were Arizona's biggest markets, and they received their clothing and equipment from San Francisco. But even though those supplies could be carried by ship around the Baja peninsula to the Colorado River and upriver by steamboat, they still had to be hauled by wagon or muleback across hundreds of miles of desert and mountain. The tide of the industrial age may have lapped at Arizona's western borders, but the great dry heart of the territory could only be penetrated by sweat and muscle, not steam.

For two-and-a-half decades, then, Arizona's most important vehicle of transportation was a wooden leviathan known as the Murphy wagon. Named after its inventor, Joseph Murphy of St. Louis, the Murphy wagon was designed to ride the waves of the Great Plains. Its bed was sixteen feet long and four feet wide. Its wooden sides rose six feet high. The rear wheels alone measured seven feet in diameter—taller than the tallest bullwhacker or muleskinner, even if he wore a ten-gallon hat and boots. A stout wagon could haul up to 12,500 pounds, and teamsters often hitched two or three of the rigs together and cracked their whips across the backs of as many as thirty-six mules. Curling across the countryside like enormous, slow-moving snakes, the wagon trains were the threads that wove the tenuous little web of forts and mines together on the Arizona frontier.

Along the trail the freighters encountered every hazard known to God or man. In December 1857, Solomon Warner was hauling three wagon loads of goods between Yuma and Tucson. Floods forced him to leave his two largest wagons behind near Maricopa Wells. Then the Apaches attacked, breaking into four barrels of whiskey and strewing 500 pounds of beads and 1,500 pounds of sugar across the sodden desert floor. Warner's men ran off the Indians before they could burn the wagons, but the barrel-chested merchant still suffered a $1,087 loss. Known for his droll sense of humor, Warner must have felt that the weather had conspired with the Apaches to strand his train in a region where heat and thirst were the usual foes.

But that was often the lot of the freighters. One year, the grasses withered and animals might die because there was no forage. The next year, winter storms or summer monsoons might sweep away teams and turn trails into muddy quagmires. Freighting was a hard way to make a living, and many freighters lost money along the way. Nevertheless, it was the one enterprise that every other business depended on in early territorial Arizona. Michael Goldwater of Ehrenberg, Charles Trumbull Hayden of Tempe, Tully, Ochoa & Company, Lord & Williams, and E. N. Fish & Company of Tucson all made long-distance freighting the foundation of their endeavors.

❋ ❋ The Army and Arizona's Economy

As important as it was, however, few of Arizona's pioneer entrepreneurs restricted themselves to freighting alone. Arizona's economy was too rudimentary to permit specialization. Businessmen therefore engaged in a diz-zying array of undertakings to turn a profit.

The range of Estevan Ochoa's investments exemplifies the restless entrepreneurial spirit of the time. Ochoa and his partner owned one of the largest stores in Tucson, selling everything from wagons and harnesses to, as his advertising noted, "Dry Goods, Clothing, Hardware, Glassware, Liquor, Boots, Shoes, and provisions." With additional establishments at Camp Grant and Fort Bowie, Tully, Ochoa & Company helped pioneer the business principle of vertical integration in Arizona. Tully and Ochoa also mined copper in the Santa Rita Mountains, operated two smelting furnaces in Tucson, and ran as many as 15,000 sheep on southern Arizona grasslands.

Other immigrants from Mexico were just as successful, at least in southern Arizona. The Aguirre brothers from Chihuahua—Epifanio, Pedro, Conrado, and Yjinio—cut their teeth freighting goods for their father from Missouri to Santa Fe along the Santa Fe Trail. Then they moved to Arizona and plunged into the livestock business, running thousands of head of cattle from Casa Grande to Sasabe. Their brother-in-law, Mariano Samaniego, a native of Sonora, was also a freighter and rancher. He operated stage lines from Tucson to nearby mining communities and went on to become the most successful Mexican politician in the territory. Finally there was Leopoldo Carrillo, Tucson's premier urban entrepreneur. Born in Moctezuma, Sonora, Carrillo settled in Tucson in 1859. By 1870 he had become the town's wealthiest individual, owning everything from a bowling alley and an ice cream parlor to nearly a hundred homes. A decade later the *Tucson City Directory* could not decide on a single label to describe Carrillo's many business enterprises, so it simply called him a capitalist. It was a designation he did his best to live up to until his death in 1890.

Perhaps the most remarkable entrepreneurs, however, were a group of Jewish merchants from German-speaking Europe. In 1848 a virulent wave of anti-Semitism broke out across Poland, Germany, and Russia. Many Jews were attacked and killed. Others fled their homelands to join the immigrant stream to the United States. Three such refugees were Philip Drachman and Joseph and Michael Goldwater, who booked steerage together on a ship to New York in 1852. Ten years later, all three men were freighting goods and running stores in La Paz, Ehrenberg, and Prescott, drawn by the goldfields and the hundreds of prospectors who toiled there. The Goldwaters soon settled in Prescott and founded one of the most successful mercantile chains in the territory. Drachman, on the other hand, eventually ended up in Tucson, where he and his younger brother Samuel raised their families, bid on government contracts, and won election to the territorial legislature.

Regardless of whether they were Jewish or Mexican immigrants or Anglos, however, these early entrepreneurs personified the economy of territorial Arizona before the coming of the railroads. Gold and silver may have lured thousands of prospectors to the frontier, but mining was a notoriously fickle mistress. For every miner who struck it rich, there were a hundred men who barely wrestled a living from the hard ground. Supplying them was a far more reliable way to make money. Many of the merchants settled and prospered. Most of the prospectors drifted away.

An even more lucrative source of income came from government contracts. In 1869, General William T. Sherman noted that it cost two to three times as much to support a soldier in Arizona as it did in Kansas or Nebraska because nearly everything the troops ate, wore, or fought with had to be freighted in from somewhere else. To cut costs, the army therefore encouraged local production, purchasing most of the crops and livestock raised in the territory. Woodcutters, charcoal makers, and lumber contractors also found a ready market for their goods.

A few figures demonstrate just how important the military was to Arizona's struggling young economy. In 1869 the army advertised its need for nearly seven million pounds of corn or barley. A year later the 1870 federal census reported a total crop of only 2.6 million pounds of barley and 1.5 million pounds of corn in the entire territory. In other words, Arizona farmers could not cultivate as much grain as army horse herds consumed. With demand exceeding production by more than one-third, farmers and stockmen naturally came to see the military as the fountain of their prosperity.

Again, however, the entrepreneurs dominated most economic transactions. Army quartermasters rarely bought directly from farmers and ranchers. On the contrary, they awarded contracts to the lowest bidders, who were usually the largest merchants. Once these merchants controlled the military market, they were able to dictate terms to the small producers hanging on by their ploughshares around Prescott, Tucson, and the Salt River Valley. In 1873, Tucson contractors paid only one cent per pound for barley in cash and two and a quarter cents in trade even though it cost at least that much to raise the grain. According to the Prescott *Weekly Arizona Miner,* such merchants were "too greedy and selfish to think of benefiting the country." "While engaged in the mad struggle to obtain contracts," the angry editors snarled, the merchants were "ever ready to sacrifice the bone and sinew of the country to their own shortsightedness and avarice."

Most army officers agreed with that assessment. General E.O.C. Ord bluntly proclaimed that war was the economic basis of the territory. Following that line of reasoning to its logical extreme, General John Schofield argued that the Camp Grant Massacre took place because contractors wanted Apache hostilities to continue, not cease. Tension between big business and the federal government—so characteristic of Arizona history in the twentieth century—crackled just as strongly during the early territorial period.

That tension gave rise to one of Arizona's most enduring myths: that the notorious "Tucson Ring" of merchants and federal officials were in collusion with one another in the awarding of government contracts. Military men like Crook, who opposed the concentration of Apaches at San Carlos and who wanted the War Department, not the Interior Department's Indian Bureau, to oversee Arizona's Indians, first perpetrated the myth. But unlike many of the other accusations that flew about in that vituperative era, the reality of this shadowy cabal quickly became unquestioned dogma, part of the very canon of Arizona history. As historian C. L. Sonnichsen wryly pointed out, "the myth of the Tucson Ring is so commonly accepted that many a popular novelist would have trouble plotting his stories if he were deprived of the wicked ring as a whipping boy."

Yet the existence of the ring has never been proved. After carrying out an exhaustive study of the military supply system in the Southwest, historian Darlis Miller concluded: "Fraud was not rampant—a dishonest contractor was the exception rather than the rule." Miller believes that the image of the "corrupt contractor" should be replaced by "that of the frontier capitalist, investing money in a risky business, alternately assisted by and obstructed in his operations by an economy-minded War Department." She points out that the army had more problems with merchants who defaulted on their contracts because of droughts, Indian attacks, and other business reverses than with merchants who attempted to defraud the military by "salting" their contracts or bribing soldiers to record deliveries that were never made.

Cutthroat competition, in fact, seemed to characterize the freighting business far more than collusion. Barron Jacobs developed his own secret code to send business messages to his father in San Francisco. Lord & Williams bid against E. N. Fish and Tully, Ochoa & Company. Even relatives, like the Zeckendorf brothers and their nephew, Albert Steinfeld, dissolved partnerships and went into business for themselves because of disagreements and family feuds. Arizona during the 1860s and 1870s was too chaotic to sustain the sort of oligarchic conspiracy attributed to the merchants and their friends in the federal government. The myth of a Tucson Ring imposes too much order on the messy and dangerous realities of the time.

❋   ❋   Territorial Society on the Eve of the Railroads

Regardless of their honesty, however, most of the early entrepreneurs invested their lives as well as their fortunes in Arizona Territory. They were the ones who ran municipal governments and founded public schools, and who built churches, stores, and banks. They may have had partners in San Francisco or New York, and they may have depended on contracts from the federal government, but they were tied to Arizona in a way that the next wave of businessmen never were.

One striking aspect of territorial society on the eve of the railroads was how intensely personal it was. Men knew one another on many different levels—as neighbor, business partner, and drinking companion; as cousin, brother-in-law, or *compadre* (the relationship between the father and godfather of a child). Mariano Samaniego and Yjinio Aguirre went into the freighting business together in Mesilla, New Mexico, in 1865. Three years later Samaniego wed Dolores, Yjinio's sister, and the young couple moved to Tucson, where Yjinio's brothers Pedro and Epifanio were already making their mark as freighters and ranchers. Similar ties linked Jewish businessmen in the territory. Hyman Goldberg, an immigrant from Russian Poland, wed Augusta Drachman in 1852. Hyman and Augusta had four children. One son married the daughter of Isador Solomon, the founder of Solomonville near Safford, and a daughter wed Hugo Zeckendorf, thus uniting three of the most prominent Jewish families in Arizona.

Marriage also strengthened ties between ethnic groups, especially Anglos and Mexicans. Anglo women were practically unknown in early territorial Arizona. The 1860 federal census of Tucson reveals a total Anglo population of 168 individuals, 160 of whom were males. Consequently, the list of Anglo men who married Mexican women reads like a who's who of the Arizona territory. Sam Hughes and Hiram Stevens wed Atanacia and Petra Santa Cruz of Tucson. Peter Brady married Inez García of Durango. Governor A.P.K. Safford asked the seventh legislative assembly to grant him a divorce from his first wife, Jennie. The governor then wed Margarita Grijalva of Magdalena, who died in childbirth, and Soledad Bonillas, the sister of Ignacio Bonillas, a Tucson schoolteacher who became Mexico's ambassador to the United States during the Mexican Revolution. Pinckney Randolph Tully, Augustus Brichta, Fritz Contzen, James Douglass, Charles Etchells, William Oury, and John Sweeney also married into Mexican families. During the 1870s, 62 percent of all marriages involving Anglos in Pima County were marriages in which Anglo men wed Mexican women.

These unions gave cities like Tucson, Florence, and Yuma a bicultural vitality unique in the southwestern United States outside of New Mexico or the Mexican stronghold of San Antonio in Texas. In a sense, Mexicans assimilated Anglos rather than the other way around. Spanish was the lingua franca. Adobe remained the most common building material. 'Dobe dollars' (Mexican pesos) served as a common medium of exchange, and Sonora became one of the biggest markets, representing $50,000 worth of trade a month in Tucson alone.

Underlying everything, however, was the pervasiveness of Mexican culture, which permeated the domestic realm and spilled out into the streets, the stores, the churches, and the bars. Gamblers played monte, a card game of Spanish origin. Drinkers swigged moonshine mescal. The most popular social events were Mexican fiestas such as *el día de San Juan* (the feast day of St. John the Baptist, June 24) or *la fiesta de San Agustín* (the fiesta of St. Augustine, Tucson's patron saint, August 28), which almost always culminated in a series of match races between local horses. Rooted in the horse culture of northern Mexico, these races were passionate affirmations of masculine status on a frontier where horses represented beauty, freedom, wealth, and even survival. Men wagered thousands of pesos as bands played and liquor flowed.

The strongest representatives of Mexican culture in this fragile bicultural society were the Mexican women who married Anglo men. We know very little about them—what they thought, how they felt, how much they influenced their husbands' business affairs. Male preoccupations and pursuits dominated the official records of the frontier. Moreover, most Mexican women grew up in a culture that kept the domains of men and women rigidly separate. On September 2, 1877, for example, in an essay entitled "The Mission of a Woman," Tucson's first Spanish-language newspaper, *Las Dos Repúblicas*, proclaimed that the man must be the master of the household, supporting the family and disciplining the children. Because of her "weakness" and "natural timidity," in contrast, the woman should restrict herself to "the interior arrangement of the house, the purchase of provisions, the care of animals, the maintenance and cleaning of the furniture, the supervision of domestic help and the early education of the children." Even if they accepted these restrictions, however, Mexican women opened many doors for their Anglo spouses throughout southern Arizona and northern Mexico. *Confianza,* or mutual trust, was a vital aspect of financial as well as personal transactions, and nothing bolstered business relationships better than family ties.

Even more important was the influence of these women on their children. Both sons and daughters of Anglo-Mexican unions grew up speaking Spanish, receiving Catholic sacraments, eating Mexican food like flour tortillas and *ca-*

zuelas (meat soups), and learning Mexican songs, legends, and proverbs (*dichos*). These offspring were U.S. citizens and were fluent in English, yet many chose to identify with the culture of their mothers rather than their fathers. And they continued to do so even after the bicultural society withered and discrimination against Mexicans intensified. Carlos Tully, the adopted son of P. R. Tully, sank his fortune and his career into a series of Spanish-language newspapers, starting with *Las Dos Repúblicas* in 1877. Bernabé Brichta was active in Mexican politics in Tucson. Both men helped found the Alianza Hispano-Americana, a mutual-aid society that fought discrimination across Arizona and the West. The language they loved, the rituals they cherished, the concepts that guided their lives were largely words and ceremonies and ideas they had learned from their mothers and the other Mexican women who had raised them. For them, *mexicanidad* was a heritage to be nurtured, not an impediment to be discarded.

Regardless of ethnicity, however, women faced special challenges on the frontier. If they were married, their husbands were often gone for weeks or months at a time. That left them to tend family businesses as well as care for the children and do all the household chores. If they lived on farms or ranches, they had to milk the cows, till the garden, jerk the meat, and scrub the clothes. For most Mexican women, making tortillas was a daily ritual that began before dawn, a ritual they often accompanied with gestures of faith such as adding salt to the dough in the form of a cross *para bendecir la masa* (to bless the dough). These acts of devotion sanctified the toil of daily life and made the dangers of the frontier less terrifying.

For many women, moreover, temporary separations often became permanent. In 1880, 16.7 percent of all Mexican households in Tucson were headed by widows who had lost their husbands to Apache attacks, mining accidents, or the hazards of chasing cattle across rough, broken terrain. When such domestic disasters occurred, women had to take in boarders or work outside the home as laundresses, seamstresses, or cooks. Speaking to oral historian Patricia Preciado Martin, Livia León Montiel recalled the life of her great grandmother, Anastasia Coronado, who raised her mother after Livia's grandmother died in childbirth. "When Francisco (Anastasia's husband) died—he was already elderly—my mother was about eleven or twelve. They had very little. My great-grandmother was able to make a living because she was a *partera* (midwife). She took care of women in childbirth, and they paid her with *frijol* [beans] and *maiz* [corn]." That was in Sonora, but the old woman continued to support her granddaughter and herself as a midwife after they moved to Tucson in 1900.

The lives of Indian women were even harsher, especially those who had to raise their families on the run. Most Native American societies valued women and the contributions they made. Hopis, Navajos, and Apaches traced descent through females. The most widespread and elaborate Apache ceremony was the *na ih es* ("getting her ready"), or puberty ceremony, which conferred long and healthy lives upon the girls who received the Gift of Changing Woman. But the pressures of the Apache wars made food gathering and child care ever more arduous and ever more dangerous. When Naiche and Geronimo were getting drunk and preparing to bolt after bargaining with Crook in Cañon de los Embudos, Naiche's wife Ha-o-zinne apparently could not face another flight to the Sierra Madre. She tried to escape, so Naiche shot her in the leg to keep her from warning Crook's Apache scouts. Ha-o-zinne and others like her had fought bravely and endured untold hardships, but they also knew that the frontier was closing in around them and chasing them down.

✳   ✳   ✳   Early Railroad Surveys

Except for the Native Americans, nearly everyone else in Arizona— Jew or Gentile, Anglo or Mexican—dreamed of the day when the frontier would come to an end. The Civil War had interrupted Manifest Destiny for five of the bloodiest years in the history of warfare, but America was finally getting back to business. There was gold to be dug, crops to be planted, beef to be raised. Arizonans did not want to be left behind as the nation chased prosperity with an abandon unparalleled in its restless, money-hungry history.

And what business demanded, more than anything else, was a way of linking California and Oregon with the states east of the Mississippi River. Ever since the 1840s, visionaries like Asa Whitney had called for the construction of a transcontinental railroad. Whitney, a China trader, favored a northern route from Lake Superior to the Northwest. Southerners, led by Secretary of War Jefferson Davis, fought for a line along the thirty-second parallel. Senator Thomas Hart Benton of Missouri championed the thirty-eighth parallel with an eastern terminus in St. Louis. During the 1850s, however, all the proposed routes became pawns in the struggle between the North and the South.

Congress gave the army $150,000 in 1853 to "ascertain the most practicable and economical route for a railroad from the Mississippi River to the Pacific Ocean." As a result, four small bands of army engineers and civilian scientists set off across the continent to survey passages along the forty-seventh, thirty-eighth, thirty-fifth, and thirty-second parallels. At first, Arizona was little more than a footnote in the grand design—an obstacle to be overcome rather than a destination to be reached. Yet two of the surveying parties spent much of their time tramping across Arizona terrain. The first, commanded by Lieutenant

Amiel Whipple, crossed Oklahoma, the Texas Panhandle, and New Mexico, picking up mountain man Antoine Leroux as a guide in Zuni. Leroux had led the party of Captain Lorenzo Sitgreaves down the Little Colorado River in 1851, but this time he and Whipple followed a more southerly trail. Riding across the vast juniper-studded mesas and ponderosa forests of northern Arizona, Whipple's expedition passed the site of modern Flagstaff and followed the Bill Williams River to the Colorado.

Whipple was extremely enthusiastic about northern Arizona as a railroad route. "The southern slopes of the mountains abound in permanent springs and streams, which renders the resort to wells unnecessary," he wrote. "No finer timber grows in the interior of our continent." Whipple's judgment proved accurate. The Mogollon Rim supported the largest stand of ponderosa pine in North America, and by the 1880s a booming lumber industry had developed around towns like Flagstaff and Williams.

But Whipple was interested in much more than trees for lumber and cross-ties. One member of his party was the Swiss geologist Jules Marcou. Another was artist-naturalist Heinrich Baldwin Mollhausen, who won fame as the "German Fenimore Cooper" after his novels about the American West captivated Europe. Whipple therefore headed one of the first scientific expeditions in Arizona history, setting a precedent that later made Arizona one of the greatest geological, biological, and anthropological laboratories in the world. Moreover, Whipple's final report was the most comprehensive description of the region to date, providing valuable information about northern Arizona's plants, animals, and climate. Nonetheless, the lieutenant made one damaging error: he estimated that the railroad would cost a whopping $169,210,265 rather than the $93,853,605 that he later realized was the more accurate figure. Consequently, the thirty-fifth parallel route, in many ways the most practical of the four, did not receive the attention it deserved.

The southernmost passage, on the other hand, was a favorite of Secretary of War Davis from the very beginning. Appointed by the newly elected Democratic administration, Davis represented Southern merchants, slave owners, and railroad speculators who saw a rail line along the thirty-second parallel as crucial to the Southern cause. These were the same individuals who wanted more of northern Mexico, so even before the Gadsden Purchase had been ratified, Davis commissioned three military expeditions to survey stretches of that route. By the time the nation was ready to begin its first great transcontinental road, however, the Civil War had destroyed any chance of immediate action on any route. The population of staunchly pro-Union California had swelled to more than 300,000 people, and fabulous mineral strikes like the Comstock Lode in

Nevada were making businessmen from Chicago to San Francisco eager to find a way to siphon that wealth into their own pockets. As a result, political support for a central route linking the Midwest with northern California quickly overwhelmed all other possibilities. Arizona's dreams of a railroad withered and nearly died with the Confederate cause.

❋   ❋   ❋   The Genesis of the Southern Pacific

Four Sacramento shopkeepers eventually revived those dreams. The unlikely railroad barons were Charles Crocker, a dry-goods merchant; Leland Stanford, a grocer; and Mark Hopkins and Collis P. Huntington, partners in a hardware store. They were neither railroad men nor wealthy San Francisco capitalists. But after their Central Pacific Railroad climbed the Sierra Nevada and joined the Union Pacific at a shantytown called Promontory, Utah, in 1869, the rest of the country referred to them as the Big Four.

Their interest in Arizona began in 1870, the year after Leland Stanford had taken the first swing at the golden spike in Utah and missed. The Big Four had done the impossible, carving a railroad across one of the steepest mountain ranges in North America. But now they were $24,000,000 in debt and controlled hundreds of miles of track that ran through nothing but open spaces. The only way to make their gamble pay off was to monopolize rail transport in California, so that's what they set out to do. First, they consolidated their control over San Francisco by acquiring the California Pacific and the San Francisco and San Jose railroads, their only major competitors. Then they decided to make sure no one else built a transcontinental railroad into the southern part of the state.

The instrument they used to accomplish that goal was a speculative little venture called the Southern Pacific Railroad Company. The Southern Pacific had been created to build a line from San Francisco to San Diego, where it was supposed to swing east. Congress even granted it a right-of-way and alternate sections of public land in California as long as it connected with another paper tiger known as the Atlantic & Pacific. The Atlantic & Pacific was stalled at a little town called Vinita in northeastern Indian Territory (Oklahoma). Nevertheless, the Big Four knew that unless they opened up southern California themselves, another rail line might grab a share of the promised land.

Their second major strategy, then, was to turn the Southern Pacific's legal fictions into realities of iron and steel. The obstacles were formidable: a national depression, the decline of mining activity in Nevada, and, strangely enough, the completion of the Suez Canal. By advertising itself as America's gateway to the Orient, San Francisco had seduced an entire nation into making it the western terminus of the transcontinental railroad. But when the Suez Canal opened, world trade shifted from the Pacific to the Mediterranean once again, diminishing San Francisco's commerce with Asia. All such setbacks shrank the supply of money available to an enterprise as desperate for credit as the Central Pacific. These were the years when Huntington, the driving force behind the venture, swore he was going to get out of the railroad business once and for all.

Yet the Big Four still managed to push their tracks southward down California's Central Valley. The railroad reached Delano in 1873 and Mojave three years later. In 1877 the Southern Pacific chugged into Fort Yuma. Now the only thing that separated Arizona from a railroad was the Colorado River. The heyday of the steamer and the Murphy wagon was about to end.

* * *   ### The Battle of the Railroads

Before the Southern Pacific could bridge the Colorado, however, it had to cut another competitor off at the knees. That company was the Texas and Pacific Railroad, which had inherited the right to build a transcontinental line from Texas to San Diego. Like so many other speculative ventures, the company also received a grant of twenty sections of land per mile across Arizona and New Mexico and ten sections across California from the federal government. But the Texas and Pacific was chronically short of funds, so it petitioned Congress to guarantee its first-mortgage bonds. Huntington and his colleagues knew that if they could prevent this from happening, they could stall their rival in Texas. Huntington therefore launched his Washington offensive, labeling Texas and Pacific president Tom Scott a "communist" and arguing that private capital, not the federal government, should finance the southern route.

The dour old tycoon also entered Arizona politics with a vengeance. In 1872, Congress passed a law allowing territorial legislatures to charter railroad companies. Most Arizonans favored the Texas and Pacific, but Huntington realized that they would quickly turn to the Southern Pacific if Scott's company could not do the job. Huntington's business philosophy was as calculating as it was simple. "If a man has the power to do great evil, and won't do right unless he is bribed to do it," he wrote an associate, "I think the time spent will be gained, when it is a man's duty, to go up and bribe the judge."

Apparently, that's exactly what he did. In Huntington's own words, "I am inclined to believe that if you could get the right man on that line in Arizona to work with the few papers they have there, to agitate the question in the territory, asking that some arrangement be made with the S.P., at the same time offer the S.P. a charter in the territory that would free the road from taxation, and one that would not allow for any interference with rates until ten per cent interest was declared on the common stock, I believe the Legislature could be called together by *the people* for $5,000 and such a charter granted."

Some historians believe that the "right man" Huntington was referring to was California promoter Phineas Banning, who put together a strong Southern Pacific lobby in Tucson, Arizona's territorial capital at the time. Others claim it was Governor Anson P. K. Safford. According to a letter written by Safford himself, Huntington gave the governor $25,000 to "fix" the legislature in 1877, his last year in office. Safford returned $20,000 of that sum, noting dryly that Huntington had overestimated the legislature's price. Whatever happened, the ninth legislative assembly granted Southern Pacific's charter on February 7 after promising legislators from northern Arizona a line along the thirty-fifth parallel as well. Ironically, the sponsor of the successful bill was none other than wagon freighter Estevan Ochoa.

Scott bitterly protested Huntington's tactics. The Texas and Pacific even tried to prevent the Southern Pacific from securing a right-of-way across the military reservation at Fort Yuma. But Huntington barreled onward, sweeping aside anything or anyone who got in his way. The last confrontation occurred on September 30, 1877, the evening after Southern Pacific crews had completed their bridge across the Colorado. Major Thomas Dunn, commander at Fort Yuma, forbade them to lay any rails across the bridge itself. He even posted a sentry to guard the span. When all seemed quiet, however, he relieved the sentry. Within an hour, Southern Pacific workers were quietly hammering the rails into place.

Nothing happened until 2 A.M., when a rail slipped and clanged against the bridge. The major awoke in a fury, ordering his entire garrison—a sergeant, a private, and a prisoner—to fix their bayonets and march to the bridge. Confronting the workers, Dunn ordered them to lay down their tools. At first the Southern Pacific men complied. Then, out of the darkness, a carload of rails slowly rolled across the bridge, shoving the major and his puny detachment aside.

By sunrise, Engine No. 31 had steamed onto Arizona soil. By 7 A.M. it was blowing its whistle in Yuma as crews laid tracks down Madison Avenue. Angry telegrams flew back and forth between Major Dunn and his superiors in San Francisco, but most of the local citizens quickly joined in the celebration. Soon, even the military realized the absurdity of the situation. Huntington had outmaneuvered the army just as he had outfoxed and outbribed his competitors. The industrial age in Arizona had finally arrived.

* * * Laying Tracks Across the Desert

What followed was a struggle with sun and land, not rival tycoons. Tracklaying began on November 18, 1878. From the start, Chinese dominated the labor force. They received a dollar a day, fifty cents less than Anglo workers demanded. They also had to provide for their own board. Despite such low wages, however, more than 1,100 Chinese graders were building trackbed across the desert by the end of the first month alone.

Desert heat was the official justification for the use of Chinese labor. With temperatures reaching 92 degrees by late February, Southern Pacific officials argued that Anglos could not put in a day's work under such conditions. But the real reason for the importation of the Chinese was that they could be paid lower wages. Charles Crocker had pioneered the exploitation of Chinese labor when the Big Four built the Central Pacific across the Sierra Nevada. A decade later, he and his foreman, James Strobridge, applied the same logic when they pushed their line east across the sun-scorched basin-and-range country of southern Arizona.

And push they did, reaching the gold placers of Gila City by Christmas, Mohawk Summit by February, and Gila Bend by April. The Chinese slapped down tracks at the rate of more than a mile a day while Huntington scoured the east for steel rails. Meanwhile teamsters drove their wagons in from California, Nevada, and Utah to supply the camps. As the crews moved eastward, railhead stations like Adonde and Texas Hill flared and faded in one-month cycles as blacksmiths set up their forges and saloon keepers poured drinks despite Strobridge's campaign against "wet grocers." To keep up with the tracklayers, the federal government even established a portable post office called "Terminus, S.P.R.R." Located in a railroad car, the post office rolled along behind the workers as they trudged toward their rendezvous with the Arizona summer.

That rendezvous came in late May 1879. Strobridge's crews had laid 182 miles of track in 139 working days, but even a hard driver like Crocker realized that the heat of June and July would devastate workers in the low desert. Besides, the supply of ties was dwindling. So twenty-six miles beyond Maricopa—and sixty-five miles from Tucson—Crocker suspended construction at Casa Grande. The Southern Pacific shipped most of the Chinese back to California. Those who remained drifted away to look for work in the mines.

For the next seven months the railhead at Casa Grande became a tent city while freighters and merchants waited anxiously for work to resume. Crocker busily stockpiled ties and pleaded with Huntington to send him more rails.

Huntington fought off challenges to his monopoly over rail traffic in California and sold shares of the Central Pacific in order to finance the Southern Pacific's next surge. Meanwhile, the tents of Casa Grande continued to flap in the wind as the Southern Pacific offices remained on railroad cars, waiting for the next move.

Construction finally resumed on January 24, 1880, when J. H. Strobridge and 300 Chinese workers returned to Casa Grande and headed for Tucson. The terrain was flat. The weather, with the exception of a freak snowstorm in January, was benign. The only thing that slowed the crews was a chronic shortage of rails. During 1879 and 1880, 11,000 miles of railroad were built in the United States. That meant that the Southern Pacific had to compete with everyone else for the steel spilling out of the nation's mills. On February 10, Strobridge asked, "How is Steel coming along?" Two weeks later, he telegraphed Huntington, "End of track Ariz. 26. Out of steel."

As always, however, Huntington found the steel, and the Chinese advanced on Tucson like a relentless army. Several hundred graders paraded through town with picks and shovels on their shoulders in February. By early March, 125 tents had sprouted on Tucson's racetrack—half for the Chinese, the other half for Anglos. A special train of dignitaries from San Francisco rolled into town on March 20, and the celebration began.

It was a celebration full of bombast and rhetoric, with Charles Poston, the "Father of Arizona," proclaiming, "The Chariot of Fire has arrived in Tucson on its way across the continent. We welcome the Railroad as the Messiah of civilization, and we welcome the road builders as the benefactors of Mankind." Most of the other toasts were equally florid. But at least one person in attendance realized that the coming of the railroad meant the end of a way of life for men like Estevan Ochoa and himself. When it was his turn to speak, William Oury—former Texas Ranger, Confederate sympathizer, and leader of the Camp Grant Massacre—stood up and asked, "What are you to do with us? The enterprise of such men as now surround me has penetrated every nook and corner of our broad land, and we have no frontier to which the pioneer may flee to avoid the tramp of civilized progress."

The crowd ignored Oury's question. It challenged the prevailing optimism of the day, and no one wanted to put a damper on the party. So toasts continued to be raised and 1,200 people danced until midnight, drunk on progress. A year later the freighting firm of Lord & Williams went bankrupt, followed soon afterward by Tully & Ochoa, William Zeckendorf (1883), Safford, Hudson & Company (1884), and many other smaller firms. With the clang of a hammer on the head of a spike, the Southern Pacific had driven the freighters out of business and now dominated transportation in southern Arizona.

✳ ✳ The Atchison, Topeka & Santa Fe

Huntington's worries were far from over. From the onset, building a railroad across Arizona was simply a dry, desolate means to an end: the control of rail traffic in California. The construction of the Southern Pacific locked up the thirty-second-parallel route, but Whipple's thirty-fifth-parallel survey still glimmered in the eyes of the speculators. President Andrew Johnson had chartered the Atlantic & Pacific Railroad to build a line from Missouri to the Pacific along that route, and Congress had granted the railroad forty alternate sections of land per mile through territories and twenty alternate sections per mile through states to sweeten the pot. Like so many other transcontinental ventures, however, the Atlantic & Pacific was a financial pipe dream. When it defaulted on the interest on its bonds and went into involuntary bankruptcy in 1875, it had built less than 400 miles of track.

Meanwhile, an obscure local line on the Kansas frontier was contradicting the usual grandiose way of doing business by starting small and growing from the inside out. Founded by an antislavery politician named Cyrus Holliday in 1859, the Atchison, Topeka & Santa Fe moved into Texas and wrested the cattle trade away from the Kansas Pacific. Then it penetrated the Rocky Mountains and entered New Mexico. Its evolution into a major rail line accelerated tremendously in January 1880, when the Santa Fe signed the famous Tripartite Agreement with the St. Louis & San Francisco Railway. The Frisco, as the St. Louis & San Francisco was called, had been formed in 1876 to take over the moribund Atlantic & Pacific. The Frisco agreed to sell half its stock in the Atlantic & Pacific to the Santa Fe. In return, the Santa Fe gave the Frisco access to New Mexico and promised to start building track west from Isleta, New Mexico, immediately. The directors of the two companies ratified the agreement on January 31, 1880, establishing a board of three trustees—one from the Santa Fe, one from the Frisco, and one elected jointly—to resolve disputes and to control all Atlantic & Pacific stock. The second transcontinental railroad in Arizona was about to become a reality.

The Southern Pacific had to lay track across one of the hottest, driest deserts in North America, but at least its route through southern Arizona passed through established towns like Yuma and Tucson. The thirty-fifth-parallel route, on the other hand, ran through a region that had never been colonized by

Spaniards or Mexicans. The only Anglo settlements were a few struggling Mormon communities along the Little Colorado River and a scattering of mines in western Mohave County. In a very real sense, then, the Atlantic & Pacific spearheaded the settlement of northern Arizona.

Before construction could begin, however, the engineer, Lewis Kingman, had to carry out the final survey. With his party of five wagons and twenty-one men, Kingman left Albuquerque in early 1880 and fixed a permanent line as far as the juncture of the Puerco and Little Colorado rivers. Then he hurried west to find a way across the Colorado before the intense heat of summer slammed into the creosote flats along the river. By the end of May, Kingman was ready to retrace his path, setting survey stakes every hundred yards over the rest of the route.

In the interim, graders hired by private contractors were already leveling terrain. Laguna Indians tried to slow their progress by pulling up stakes in western New Mexico, and armed Navajos threatened them in Arizona, but the graders kept working, and the tracklayers followed them in June. Within a year the graders had pushed as far as Canyon Diablo west of Brigham City.

Tracklaying was a more strenuous affair. The first winter, heavy snows interrupted construction. The following summer, torrential rains caused more delays, washing out stretches of the road nearly every day. Despite such problems, however, the tracklayers hammered their way across the grasslands of the Puerco and Little Colorado valleys. On December 3 they arrived in Brigham City, which was renamed Winslow in honor of General E. F. Winslow, general manager of the railroad.

Then the real engineering obstacles began. The first was the rocky gash in the Colorado Plateau called Canyon Diablo. For more than six months, tracklaying came to a halt while crews struggled to bridge the 225-foot-deep, 550-foot-wide gorge. The bridge required eleven spans and 1,489 cubic yards of cut-stone masonry carved from Kaibab limestone, the same rock formation as Canyon Diablo itself. As girder after girder rose in the air, the bridge crept across the chasm like a gigantic praying mantis. When crews finished it on July 1, 1882, the railroad fraternity considered it one of the greatest feats of engineering in the West.

More bridges followed as the mesas of northeastern Arizona gave way to more dissected terrain. Because it was so serpentine, Johnson Canyon near Ash Fork required two bridges in less than a mile. Workers also had to bore a 328-foot tunnel through a basalt promontory there. With two hundred quarrymen, stonecutters, and laborers hacking away at it, Johnson Canyon cost $75,000 per mile in contrast to the $10,000 average along the rest of the route.

Nonetheless, crews reached the Colorado River at a narrow canyon known as "the Needles" on June 8, 1883. Now all they had to do was cross the river itself. But the river kept sliding through their grip like liquid mercury, shifting, changing, taunting them with its intractability. The biggest problem was figuring out how to drive enough piles into the Colorado's shifting bottom to support a railroad bridge. First the Atlantic & Pacific built a barge to hold the pile driver. The barge was too small. So the railroad bought another, bigger barge, but it kept drifting with the current. Finally, the pile driver was bolted to a railroad car and driven to the end of the track each day as the bridge slowly materialized over the muddy water. Then a sudden rise in the river swept away more than four hundred feet of the span. Drawing on the snowmelt of the Rockies, the Colorado pulsed once and destroyed a month's work.

But even the Colorado had to recede. On August 3, 1883, crews completed the bridge, and a week later the railroad held the obligatory ceremony at Needles and drove the last spike. Northern Arizona had been girded by steel and tied by iron and coal to the rest of the nation. Nearly every settlement along the line from Kingman to Chambers bore the name of a Santa Fe or Atlantic & Pacific officer or engineer. No other phenomenon reflected the dominance of the railroad so directly.

Nevertheless, the dream of an independent transcontinental railroad had to wait a few more years. While Atlantic & Pacific crews were battling floods and canyons, Collis Huntington was scheming to stop their railroad at the California line. First, he had Crocker's Chinese crews extend the Southern Pacific line from Mojave to Needles. Then he joined forces with his archenemy Jay Gould to purchase nearly half the stock of the Santa Fe's partner, the St. Louis & San Francisco. That coup won both Huntington and Gould seats on the Frisco's board of directors. Gould got what he wanted when the board voted to curtail the Frisco's expansion in Texas, where Gould's Texas and Pacific controlled the Gulf Coast trade. Huntington protected his monopoly of rail traffic in California when the Frisco agreed to halt construction of the Atlantic & Pacific at Needles. With the ground cut out from under him, Santa Fe president William Barstow Strong had no choice but to accept the Southern Pacific's offer to carry Atlantic & Pacific freight from Needles to San Francisco. The Santa Fe and its subsidiary did not yet have their own tracks to the Pacific coast.

Without the California market, the Atlantic & Pacific remained an albatross around the necks of its controlling companies. The vast empty spaces of northern Arizona could not support large volumes of freight, so between 1883 and 1897 the Atlantic & Pacific lost nearly $14,000,000. In the words of one railroad expert, it was a "wretched road, running as it does through an alkaline desert, where even the water for the locomotives has to be transported by rail."

But not even Huntington himself could keep the Santa Fe out of California forever. In 1884 the Southern Pacific agreed to lease its line between Needles and Mojave to the Atlantic & Pacific, with the provision that the lease would become a sale once title to the line was clear. Four years later the Atlantic & Pacific not only owned its own track into San Francisco but had invaded the Southern Pacific's stronghold of Los Angeles as well. The Santa Fe bankrupted itself in the process and had to be reorganized, but it finally broke Huntington's grip on California. That paid big dividends in the years to come.

※　※　※　**The End of the Frontier**

Through all these rail wars, Arizona was little more than an unpleasant obstacle, a losing proposition on the road to riches along the Pacific coast. The giants of the industry drove their crews and dragged their construction cars across the Arizona landscape not because they thought they could make a profit there but because they wanted to suckle in the land of milk and honey on the other side of the Colorado River. A railroad whose line ended at the Arizona border had no future. California was always the prize.

Nevertheless, the intrigues of men like Huntington—and the backbreaking labor of thousands of Chinese, Mexican, and Anglo workers—transformed a region of refuge into an extractive colony of the United States. Before the railroads, territorial Arizona was a handful of Anglo islands in a Native American sea. After the railroads arrived, big business and big government turned Arizona into a place where natural resources were stripped from the ground and shipped someplace else to be transformed into the products of the industrial age. The freighters brought goods into Arizona. The railroads carried them away.

They also buried Arizona's frontier society. As freighter-merchant firms like Lord & Williams and Tully & Ochoa went bankrupt, commercial centers like Tucson plunged into a depression in the 1880s—one that reflected a major reorientation of the Arizona economy. Prior to the railroads, Arizona looked south for much of its business and many of its goods. Guaymas was an important port of entry. Hermosillo controlled much of the commerce between Sonora and southern Arizona. Pesos were as important as dollars whenever currency changed hands.

With the advent of the Southern Pacific, however, the value of the peso plummeted. Merchants with large reserves of 'dobe dollars were forced to buy goods at unfavorable exchange rates. Workers who were paid in pesos saw their purchasing power decline by as much as 25 percent. People could almost hear the axis of money and power shifting from north–south to east–west. With that shift came a temporary decline in the great immigrant surge that had brought so many Mexicans to Arizona in the 1860s and 1870s. Meanwhile, the Southern Pacific continued to rely on Chinese rather than Mexican labor, employing twenty times as many Chinese as Mexicans in its railroad camps—853 vs. 43 in Benson alone, according to the 1880 federal census. Mexican and Anglo workers eventually drove the Chinese off the railroads and out of the mines, but during the 1880s the demand for Mexican labor was not as voracious as it would later become.

As Arizona became more and more tied to the rest of the United States and less to northern Mexico, ethnic tensions between Mexicans and Anglos intensified. The tensions flared most violently in mining camps and agricultural communities, but even in Tucson, where a Mexican middle-class was developing, business partnerships and the rate of intermarriage steadily declined. Prior to the railroad, frontier conditions occasionally obscured differences of race and class. By the turn of the century, however, Mexicans and Anglos lived in different neighborhoods, worked different jobs, and rarely chose one another as husbands or wives. The segregation that characterized Texas and California took root in Arizona as well.

Underlying all these social changes was an enormous expansion in the scale of Arizona's economy. For twenty years, merchants like Ochoa had perched atop the economic pyramid, but that pyramid crumbled under the weight of a much larger pyramid as the railroads and the great copper, timber, and land-and-cattle companies moved into the territory. From now on, the major players in Arizona would be businessmen and bureaucrats who lived in New York, Chicago, or Washington, D.C., not Tucson or Prescott. The era of Arizona's "Three C's"— cattle, copper, and cotton—was arriving. When it did, every aspect of Arizona society—business, labor, ethnic relations, the scale of production—became subordinated to an extractive economy whose markets and centers of power lay far beyond the borders of Arizona itself.

7

❋ ❋ Cattle

When Colin Cameron arrived in Arizona in 1882, he was dressed in
an Eastern suit and carried a walking stick. He had not grown up in
the saddle or cut his teeth fighting Apaches. On the contrary, he was
Pennsylvania born and bred, the well-educated son of a railroad
magnate and the well-connected nephew of Simon Cameron, secretary of war under Lincoln. Cameron had no experience in the range
cattle industry. After a brief stint in college, he had managed several
large dairy farms in Pennsylvania stocked with Guernsey and Jersey
cows.

But even though the Texan and Mexican cowboys may have
snickered behind his back, Cameron represented the future of the
Arizona livestock industry. He was a businessman, not a pioneer,
and he spent a year scouring southern Arizona for the right ranch to
buy. When he found it—the old San Rafael de la Zanja land grant in
the lush San Rafael Valley—he formed the San Rafael Cattle Company and imported sixty young Hereford bulls to improve his stock.

Cameron realized that the growing demand for high-quality beef would drive the longhorn off the range. He also knew that the small rancher was doomed despite "his courage and his gun."

For the next two decades Cameron used lawsuits and intimidation to impose his vision upon the Arizona grasslands. Surveyor General John Wasson had confirmed the San Rafael de la Zanja grant in 1880, but the new title covered only the original four *sitios* (four square leagues, or 17,361 acres). Cameron argued that the San Rafael encompassed "four leagues square" as well as the "overplus" lands grazed by the original grantees. And since the lands Cameron claimed amounted to more than 152,000 acres, San Rafael was an estate worth fighting for.

But establishing uncontested control of the land was harder than filling it up with blooded stock. Cameron tracked down many of the original shareholders (*parcioneros*) and bought them out for eighty dollars apiece. Then the houses of several "squatters" from Missouri mysteriously burned down just south of the international border. The governor of Sonora issued a warrant and a reward for Cameron's arrest. He was indicted for arson but never tried. When a group of men led by George McCarthy ran off one of Cameron's cowboys and fenced the pasture around a San Rafael cienega, Cameron armed his men with Winchesters and secured a warrant for McCarthy's arrest. McCarthy got the message and fled. Nevertheless, the legal battles dragged on and on. Cameron boasted that he controlled most of Pima County's key offices, but Arizona politics was a volatile mixture. In 1887, Judge W. H. Barnes of Tucson ruled that he had illegally fenced public land. Most people in the territory, who considered Cameron a "landgrabber," applauded the decision. But even though Cameron lost that round—and even though San Rafael's ultimate confirmation in 1900 recognized only the original four square leagues—he ran more than 17,000 head of cattle on five times that amount of range for nearly two decades.

He also survived the drought and depression years of the 1890s that brought so many other Arizona ranchers to their knees. When Cameron entered the cattle business, the boom was just beginning. By the time he sold the San Rafael to Colonel William H. Greene for $1,500,000 in 1903, the boom had gone bust and much of southern Arizona was a wasteland, grazed to bare ground. Cameron prospered because he foresaw the future better than his neighbors. He replaced longhorns with Herefords. He reduced his stock to conserve his range at a time when most ranchers were running as many animals as they could. From his headquarters at Lochiel, where he lived like a country gentleman with his fox terriers and his thoroughbreds, Cameron pioneered the modern cattle business and watched the phantoms of the open range flicker and die.

✳   ✳   ✳   Hispanic Ranching in Arizona

Ranching has always been an important part of Arizona mythology, but the first stock raisers in the region were Hopi Indians, not Spanish conquistadores or Texas cowboys. Beginning in 1629, Franciscans from New Mexico established missions at the Hopi pueblos of Awatovi, Shongopovi, and Oraibi. There they introduced Old World plants like wheat and peach trees and Old World animals like goats and sheep. But even though the Hopis participated in the Pueblo Revolt of 1680, killing four missionaries, Padre Francisco Garcés reported flocks of sheep in their fields nearly a century later. The Hopis may have rejected the religion of the Spaniards, but mutton and peaches remained a part of their diet long after the friars were gone.

Stock raising in southern Arizona took root sixty years later when Padre Eusebio Francisco Kino distributed small herds of cattle and horses among the O'odham of the Pimería Alta. About the same time, Spanish ranchers started running their own cattle on Arizona soil. The first was José Romo de Vivar, who established ranches near Cananea, Cocóspera, and the Huachuca Mountains, where the Santa Cruz River originates. His tough, rangy *criollos* may have grazed the San Rafael Valley nearly two decades before Kino brought cattle to the O'odham.

But Spanish ranching in Arizona did not begin in earnest until the Jesuits restaffed their missions of Guevavi and Bac in 1732. Four years later the discovery of the *bolas de plata* (chunks of silver) at Arizonac triggered a temporary mining boom, generating a market for beef. The revival of the missions and the expansion of the mining frontier attracted a growing number of stockmen to settle in the Santa Cruz Valley, pasturing their cattle and planting their crops between the mission communities. By midcentury, the stockmen had even spilled over into the mesquite grasslands of Arivaca, where they mined the surrounding mountains as well.

These families—the Ortegas, Grijalvas, Bohórquezes, and Covarrubias, among others—were the true Euro-American pioneers of the Sonoran Desert. Their horses were small and quick, their cattle lean and long-legged. They gathered their stock together in roundups (*corridas*) and marked ownership with brands. They were heirs to a way of life that had begun in the deserts of northern Mexico two centuries earlier, when their ancestors had confronted arid North America and had created the range cattle industry.

Throughout the colonial period, the Apaches prevented them from moving beyond the Santa Cruz Valley. In 1804 there were 3,500 cattle around Tucson and 1,000 near Tubac, modest figures compared to the great haciendas of Chihuahua or Coahuila, where the Sánchez Navarro family alone controlled 800,000 acres and ran thousands of cattle and sheep. After Mexican independence, on the other hand, Sonoran ranchers were ready to challenge the Apaches for control of the southern Arizona grasslands. Between 1821 and 1843 the Mexican government awarded ten private land grants in southern Arizona. Five were located along the Santa Cruz River or its tributaries: San Ignacio de la Canoa (1821), San José de Sonoita (1825), San Rafael de la Zanja (1825), María Santísima del Carmén (1831), and Los Nogales de Elías (1843). Another four sprawled across the San Pedro watershed: San Ignacio del Babocómari (1827), Tres Alamos (1831), San Rafael del Valle (1832), and San Juan de las Boquillas y Nogales (1833). The tenth and largest—San Bernardino (1822)—covered more than 73,000 acres, but only the northern tip jutted into Arizona east of Douglas.

According to some Arizona historians, these ranches were haciendas as magnificent as those of Alta California. "Livestock abounded on them in great numbers," wrote Bert Haskett. "In many cases the main buildings, like those at San Bernardino, where the *patrón grande* lived in a sort of regal state, were spacious adobe structures surrounded by patios and flowering gardens. About the home grounds luscious fruits such as the orange, lime, pomegranate, fig, grape, apricot, peach, and others were grown by means of irrigation."

Like the myth of Jesuit buried treasure, Haskett's vision of Hispanic Arizona conjures up images as alluring as the Seven Cities of Cíbola. Yet the evidence for such splendor may be as chimerical as the legends that drew Coronado and his men north. One source was Mariana Díaz, an old woman interviewed by the *Tucson Citizen* in 1873. According to her, "As long as I can remember the country was covered with horses and cattle, and on many of the trails they were so plentiful that it was quite inconvenient to get through the immense herds." Another was boundary surveyor John Russell Bartlett, who visited the headquarters of the San Bernardino ranch in 1851. A Rhode Island bookseller who spent more time sightseeing than surveying, Bartlett reported that San Bernardino alone ran 100,000 cattle, 10,000 horses, and 5,000 mules before Apaches drove the Mexicans away.

To be fair to Bartlett and his contemporaries, large numbers of feral cattle did roam certain parts of southern Arizona in the late 1840s. Nonetheless, a careful evaluation of the evidence suggests that Bartlett and others greatly overestimated the size of Mexican herds. Most grants were occupied for little more than a decade before the Apaches killed their inhabitants or chased them away. Faced with such relentless pressure, it is hard to envision Haskett's "great plantations" flourishing on Arizona soil. It is also difficult to see how southern Arizona ranges could have supported more than a hundred thousand cattle without suffering serious degradation. The centrifugal windmill was not invented until 1854 and was not widely adopted by Western ranchers until the 1870s. That meant that cattle from the Mexican land grants must have clustered around the few springs and streams of the region, which may have given travelers the misleading impression that they were equally abundant away from water. Yet even though observers like Lieutenant-Colonel Philip St. George Cooke noted cattle trails and wallows along the San Pedro River, they also described lush grasslands and a flowing stream with beaver dams and "salmon trout" (possibly squawfish) in "great numbers" up to "three feet long." Such riparian exuberance would not have withstood the hooves and teeth of vast herds.

In all probability, then, the total number of cattle in Mexican Arizona never exceeded twenty to thirty thousand animals. Herd sizes also must have fluctuated considerably. In 1818, before the land grants were awarded, the Tumacacori mission ran 5,000 cattle, while San Xavier possessed 8,797. By 1830, Tumacacori's herd had plummeted to 400. Droughts, Apache raids, and natural predators like wolves, grizzly bears, and mountain lions all took their toll. With no market for cattle except for hides and tallow, the "great plantations" of Mexican Arizona shrivel when confronted with the harsh realities of the time.

❋   ❋   The Early Territorial Livestock Industry

Regardless of their numbers, feral cattle had disappeared in Arizona by the following decade. In 1854, cowboys on two cattle drives from Texas to California kept diaries of their travels, yet neither saw any sign of the fierce bulls that had attacked Cooke and his men. Horses continued to run free, but the cattle had vanished.

During the 1850s and early 1860s, most cattle in Arizona, like most Anglos, were simply passing through on their way to California. The gold rush created a huge market for beef, wool, and mutton, so Texas cattlemen and New Mexico sheepmen trailed their herds to the Pacific coast. It was a long, hot, dangerous gamble. Drover James G. Bell estimated that Apaches ran off 3,000 of the 9,000 head of cattle crossing Arizona in 1854 alone. But longhorns purchased for $5 to $15 a head in Texas sold for $60 to $150 in California, while sheep brought $16 apiece, so the gamble usually paid off.

Once again, California, not Arizona, was the destination, but in the course of those drives, drovers and shepherds could not fail to notice Arizona's enormous stretches of good range. During the 1850s a few pioneer stockmen even tried to make a go of it in Arizona: the Redondo brothers near Yuma, William Kirkland at the Canoa grant north of Tubac, William Oury around Tucson. But Indian depredations and the outbreak of the Civil War brought these early ventures to a standstill. When J. Ross Browne visited Arizona in 1863, he wrote that, because of Apache hostilities, Arizona had no livestock industry. As always, Browne was exaggerating, but not by much.

After the Civil War, however, the Texas cattle industry was a river ready to burst its dam. Four years without a market had left five million longhorns, many of them feral, grazing Texas to a nub. So Texans turned west as well as north during that era of the great trail drives, especially after army posts and Indian reservations provided a growing market for beef. This time, some of the cattlemen saw Arizona's empty ranges and decided to stay. One such individual was Colonel Henry Hooker, who founded the Sierra Bonita Ranch at the north end of the Sulphur Springs Valley. Hooker chose the Sierra Bonita because it was well watered and close to most of the major markets in southern Arizona, including the San Carlos Reservation, the Chiricahua Reservation, Fort Grant, and Fort Bowie. By the mid-1870s, Hooker was running 11,000 cattle on his range.

Most of the other early ranchers grazed much smaller herds. Juan Elías, an Arizona native, ran 600 cattle along Sópori Wash near Arivaca. José María Redondo irrigated wheat, corn, oats, and barley at his San Ysidro Ranch near Yuma and turned his cattle loose to forage among the mesquite bosques of the lower Gila River. Other small ranchers settled near Prescott, Wickenburg, and the new town of Phoenix, which was incorporated in 1875. There they sold beef and dairy products to the miners and merchants of those towns.

But the greatest stimulus to the industry remained the federal government, which purchased thousands of cattle and sheep each year. From 1868 to 1872, Hooker and his partners furnished most of those animals, sometimes by filling the contracts of others. In 1872 alone they drove more than 15,000 head of cattle into Arizona from Sonora, New Mexico, and Texas. By 1873, however, the territory was filling up with competitors. Fiscal year 1875–76 was the last year a single contractor, James Patterson, provided meat for all the soldiers in Arizona. From then on, no one, not even Hooker, monopolized the trade.

Wherever there were forts or Indian reservations, then, stockmen followed. With two army regiments and 4,500 Native Americans to feed, Arizona ranchers still could not produce enough animals as late as 1877. Consequently, prices remained high—10 to 13 cents per pound—and more and more cattlemen drifted into the region. And while many drifted away, victims of drought or a wildly fluctuating market, others remained to found ranching dynasties that endured for three generations or more. The Aguirres west of Tucson, the Riggs in the foothills of the Chiricahuas, and others like them got their start in those early days. A rural way of life—part Mexican, part Texan—was taking shape in the Arizona countryside. It would influence Arizona politics, and Arizona mythology, for many years to come.

❋ ❋ ❋   The Boom of the 1880s

This was the era of the open range, when most cattle roamed unfenced public land. In 1877 the Desert Land Act increased homestead allotments from 160 to 640 acres, but a section of land was still hopelessly inadequate to maintain a successful cow-calf operation in arid country. So as Arizona's ranges began to fill up, the stockmen themselves developed a set of unwritten customs to govern grazing rights. Whoever controlled the water controlled the range. Ranchers patented sections around springs, cienegas, and streams, and then other ranchers and government officials recognized their right to run cattle on the surrounding public lands. During early territorial days, the range must have seemed limitless, and the system made sense. By 1882, however, more than 21,000 acres had been distributed under the Desert Land Act. Soon, every spring, seep, and stream had been pre-empted. The infinite land suddenly became finite; the wilderness was transformed into a gigantic cattle ranch in less than twenty years.

Many of the stockmen were small operators with a homestead, a few hundred cattle, and not much more. These were the people you see in the old photographs—people like the Middletons and the Ellisons, who settled Pleasant Valley and the Tonto Basin in the 1870s and 1880s to build their little shake-roofed cabins in the heart of the Apachería. Part of a westward movement that began in the Appalachians in the late eighteenth century, they were the pioneers of American myth—proud, independent families who leapfrogged from one frontier to another, fighting Indians, killing wolves, mountain lions, and grizzly bears, and living off the land.

But others were investors with ties to Eastern capital and a belief that ranching was big business, not a way of life. Cameron and Hooker were like that. So were Walter Vail and H. R. Hilsop, who started the Empire Ranch with a 160-acre homestead near Fort Crittenden in 1876. For more than a century, Arizona had been a land of fabled mineral wealth. By the 1870s, however, grass had turned to gold as well, and promotional literature sang the praises of the Arizona cattle industry throughout the United States and Europe. According to Patrick Hamilton's *Resources of Arizona,* published in San Francisco in 1883, "Here the climate is almost perpetual spring, and even in the dryest season the feed never fails, and the owner can sit under the shade of his comfortable hacienda and see his herds thrive and increase winter and summer." Suddenly desolate, cactus-ridden Arizona was being touted in the same Biblical terms of abundance formerly reserved for California.

A handful of these investors introduced much-needed innovations into Arizona's breeding-stock industry. Hooker planted alfalfa and grain to supplement the four different types of grama grass that grew on his range, and he was among the first to import purebred shorthorn, Durham, and Devon bulls to improve his stock. He also erected a huge windmill with a 20,000-gallon storage tank and charged his neighbors twenty-five cents per animal to water their cows. Much to their dismay, he fenced his springs and built drift fences along the boundaries of his ranches to keep out strays as well. Hooker knew that the days of the open range were numbered, so he concentrated on improving his herds and his land long before most other ranchers saw the writing on the wall.

Despite the efforts of Hooker and Cameron, however, the battle cry of the boom years was quantity, not quality. In his annual report for 1883, Governor F. A. Tritle boasted that the territory possessed 34 million acres of pasture capable of sustaining 7,680,000 cattle. Two years later, the 1885 annual report listed 652,500 cattle on Arizona ranges. By then, every source of permanent water had been taken and the range was fully stocked, yet cattle continued to pour into the territory from as far away as Maryland. Moreover, large corporations were being formed—the Chiricahua Cattle Company in the lower Sulphur Springs Valley, for example, and the San Simon Cattle Company along San Simon Creek. Cattle fever gripped the territory, shaking every valley and plateau.

If frontiersmen like the Middletons and Ellisons were still scrabbling for survival in isolated areas like the Tonto Basin (Colonel Jesse Ellison later became the largest rancher in the basin), men like Hooker and Cameron, who had access to capital and credit in San Francisco, New York, Philadelphia, and London, fueled the explosion of the cattle industry. Speculation ran rampant. Between 1885 and 1887, 113,178 of the 199,026 acres (57 percent) filed upon under the Desert Land Act belonged to people who did not reside in the territory. In 1870 the federal census reported 5,132 cattle in Arizona Territory. The figure was undoubtedly too low; pioneer stockmen estimated that there were about 38,000 head. By the late 1880s, however, herds had grown to total nearly a million head. As cattleman Will C. Barnes later reminisced, "What a lot of blind men we all were. Nobody wanted to sell a cow for anything. It was numbers and nothing else. We fondly imagined that these wonderful ranges would last forever and couldn't be overstocked."

❋ ❋ ❋   Cattle and the Railroads

Like every major endeavor in the territory, the cattle industry could not have expanded without the railroads. The Southern Pacific and the Santa Fe linked the yucca plains of the Sulphur Springs Valley and the ponderosa meadows of the Mogollon Rim to the stockyards of California or the Midwest. They rumbled through every rancher's life even if the rancher lived hundreds of miles from the nearest railhead. Ironically, however, the major function of the railroads during the early 1880s was to ship cattle into Arizona, not to haul them away.

Prior to the completion of the Southern Pacific in 1881, there were only two large ranches in Arizona—Hooker's Sierra Bonita and Vail and Hilsop's Empire spread. Once the rails were in place, investors shipped stock into Arizona from locations ranging from the Pacific coast to the Mississippi Valley. Texas cattlemen in particular were anxious to find new land because their legislature had passed laws in 1879 and 1883 instituting mandatory grazing fees on state lands. As the open ranges of the Lone Star State filled up—and as politicians had the effrontery to make stockmen pay for the privilege of running their cattle on public land—those ranchers saw freedom and dollars in the deserts of the Southwest.

Until 1885, they sold most of their animals to Arizona and California markets. Army posts and Indian reservations continued to buy thousands of beeves, but newer outlets were arising as well. Tombstone and other mining towns were booming, and railroad construction camps had to feed their hungry workers. As a result, prices steadily rose. In 1881 a three-year-old steer brought fifteen dollars. Two years later the average was thirty to thirty-five dollars a head.

Then the tide began to turn. By 1885 the Arizona market had been glutted and the price of a three-year-old steer plunged to ten dollars. To make matters worse, very little rain fell that summer, and for the first time since the boom had started, overstocking became a problem. As grasses withered and seeds failed to germinate, thousands of cattle died, and ranchers rushed to sell their remaining animals wherever they could. Cameron shipped 600 high-grade shorthorns from Huachuca Station to Kansas, receiving $27.50 a head. Most other stockmen were not so lucky. They sold off all their three- and four-year-olds and were forced to market their yearlings as feeders to California, Montana, and Kansas buyers. Within a year the flow of flesh on the hoof had reversed. Suddenly the railroads were the lifelines of an industry drowning in the results of its own speculation and greed.

Not surprisingly, the railroads were quick to take advantage of the situation. Carload charges for cattle shipped from Ash Fork to Los Angeles rose from $115 to $174, an increase of 51 percent. Willcox's *Southwestern Stockman*—the "Only Paper Devoted Exclusively to the Stock Growing Interests of Arizona"—began complaining about the territorial legislature's failure to regulate the rates of the Southern Pacific. According to the *Stockman,* that failure allowed the Southern Pacific to play the "same game of cinch on the cattle interests that has for years past so retarded mining and agricultural pursuits."

To defy the railroads, then, many ranchers temporarily resorted to that time-tested method of moving cattle—the trail drive. One of the first and biggest drives was organized in November 1889 by George W. Lang, who bought 1,500 steers in Altar, Sonora. Cameron and others joined him in Nogales, and the party headed north to the Salt River Valley. From there they followed the old Gila Trail to Yuma and crossed the Mojave Desert to Los Angeles. The cattle arrived with little loss of weight and an average cost of only $1.25 per animal. The Southern Pacific charged $5.00 per head from Benson to Los Angeles. Soon several of the largest stockmen in southern Arizona, including Walter Vail and Colonel W. C. Land, were hitting the trail to Montana, Kansas, and the West Coast as well.

The future, however, belonged to the railroads. In 1886 the Santa Fe put new livestock cars known as Burton cars on the line from Winslow to Kansas City. The Burton cars were divided into compartments where cattle could be fed and watered. During the journey of nearly 1,200 miles, steers lost an average of only 53 pounds compared to 188 pounds in the older cars. The Southern Pacific quickly followed suit, and enterprising ranchers like Cameron and his brother Brewster were soon singing the praises of the new cars. As markets tightened and the industry grew more competitive, cattlemen had to get their stock to buyers as quickly as possible. Since buyers might be found in Kansas one year and Montana the next, railroads were the only feasible way of exporting the thousands of animals Arizona ranges produced.

❋ ❋ ❋ **The Aztec Land and Cattle Company**

The closest relationship between railroads and cattle, however, materialized in the sparsely populated north. As noted in chapter 6, Congress in 1866 granted the Atlantic & Pacific Railroad forty alternate sections of public land for every mile of track built through territories such as Arizona and New Mexico. And if land within the sections was already claimed, the railroad could select additional sections from ten-mile extensions on either side. In Arizona the grant amounted to more than ten million acres in a corridor encompassing a third of the territory. On paper, the Atlantic & Pacific became the largest private landowner in Arizona history.

For years, the grant existed only on paper. Bankruptcy and construction delays kept the Atlantic & Pacific out of the Southwest for nearly a decade. Even after the railroad reached California, populist opposition led Congress to pass a law restoring much of the grant to the public domain. But most of that land was in California and New Mexico; the Arizona portion remained intact. Nevertheless, northern Arizona's isolation made the real estate business an exercise in frustration, even for a railroad as large as the Atlantic & Pacific and its parent company, the Santa Fe. In 1903, twenty years after the railroad had been completed, the Santa Fe had not adequately surveyed most of the grant and had sold only 1,439,629 acres. By then the Atlantic & Pacific was dead and the Santa Fe had been reorganized. The checkerboard lands did not become a real moneymaker for the railroad until the twentieth century.

Despite these difficulties, however, the Atlantic & Pacific grant had an enormous impact on the development of the cattle industry in northern Arizona. With the exception of the Mexican land grants, stock raisers in the rest of the territory had to piece together ranches by accumulating homesteads and establishing the right to run cattle on surrounding public lands. In the railroad corridor, powerful interests could purchase large tracts directly from the railroad itself. Dr. Edward B. Perrin, who owned both the Babocómari and Baca Float No. Five ranches, bought 258,873 acres around Flagstaff for seventy cents an acre to raise sheep. The Arizona Cattle Company purchased 121,491 acres. Other large buyers included S. G. Little & Company (75,749 acres), the Cebolla Cattle Company (41,592 acres), and Charles Zeiger (11,528 acres). But the first and biggest buyer of them all was the Aztec Land and Cattle Company.

Incorporated in 1884 with a capital stock of $963,100, the Aztec Land and Cattle Company purchased a million acres of Atlantic & Pacific land for fifty cents an acre. That made the new corporation one of the largest land and cattle companies in the Southwest. Its primary stockholders were the Atchison, Topeka & Santa Fe ($215,500), members of the Santa Fe's board of directors ($200,000), J. & W. Seligman & Company ($241,000), and a number of Texas ranchers ($502,400). Since the Seligmans were original investors in the St. Louis & San Francisco Railroad (the Frisco), that meant that interests associated with the Atlantic & Pacific's two parent companies (the Frisco and the Santa Fe) controlled 68 percent of the Aztec stock. Cheap land was one dividend of their investment in the line.

By 1894 only 572,950 acres had been surveyed and formally deeded to the Aztec. Nonetheless, the company soon established a ranch that ran for ninety miles from Flagstaff to Holbrook along the southern edge of the Atlantic & Pacific tracks, and it lost no time stocking that vast range. Aztec cowboys drove 17,000 cattle in from West Texas. Four hundred railcars transported 33,000 more. By 1888 the herd had swelled to 60,000 head. Four years after incorporation, the Aztec Land and Cattle Company was the largest ranch in the territory and the largest ranch anywhere in the West outside Texas.

It quickly became a law unto itself in northern Arizona. Aztec cattle bore a brand shaped like the cookwagon utensil used to chop vegetables, with the straight handle up and the curved blade down. Aztec cowboys therefore became known as the Hashknife outfit, a name that epitomized their rough, slashing ways. Legally, they were only entitled to run cattle on alternate sections of land, but that was impossible in the rugged timber country and juniper grasslands of the Mogollon Plateau. So the Hashknife spread across the entire forty-by-ninety-mile range, taking on everyone else in the region, including rustlers, sheepmen, small ranchers, and Mormon colonists.

Mormons were particularly hard-hit. For more than a decade, small colonies of Latter-day Saints had moved into the region from Utah to "lengthen the cords of Zion." There they attempted to establish cooperative agricultural communities along the Little Colorado River watershed from Brigham City (Winslow) to Snowflake. They also scattered across the Mogollon Rim, eking out a precarious existence and struggling to live up to their religious ideals. But the Atlantic & Pacific and the Aztec considered them just another type of squatter. In 1887, Hashknife cowboys gave the inhabitants of Wilford and Heber ten days to pull up stakes and leave, which they did. Mormons later resettled Heber, but Wilford faded back into the forest, a victim of the perennial struggle between smallholders and big business in the American West.

Isolated small ranchers—both Mormon and gentile—were even more vulnerable. John Paine, the head of a reputed gang of horse thieves, threatened to scalp the Mormon pioneer John Reidhead unless he abandoned his small farm. "I had not harvested my potatoes," Reidhead wrote a friend, "and he said he would kill me if I undertook to dig them." Paine was soon killed in the Pleasant Valley War. About the same time, Special Agent S. B. Bevans of the General Land Office lent official support to the Mormons resisting the Aztec's reign of terror. But the Aztec and the Atlantic & Pacific simply turned to the legal system to evict the Saints or to force them to pay premium prices for the land they held. At Woodruff south of Holbrook, Mormon colonists eventually scraped up $8.00 an acre for railroad land. "When compared to the fifty cents per acre for which the Aztec and other large tracts went," historian Charles Peterson wrote, "it seemed a heavy tax indeed."

✳   ✳   ✳   The Development of the Sheep Industry

Such struggles were common as the frontier disappeared and the era of extraction began. With most of Arizona's Indians removed to reservations, a cross-section of late-nineteenth-century America—speculators and religious visionaries, Eastern capitalists and Texas ranchers—fought for every section of range they could find.

Perhaps the best known and most exaggerated of these conflicts was that staple of Western pulp fiction, the struggle between sheepmen and cattlemen. Some writers even reduce Arizona's bloodiest feud, the Pleasant Valley War, to a battle between the cattle-running Grahams and the sheep-producing Tewksburys. But the reality of the situation was more complex. There were ranchers and cowboys who hated sheep and wanted to drive them off the range. On the other hand, there were cattlemen like E. B. Perrin who ran sheep as well. Western stereotypes seldom captured the complicated nature of capital investment in the Arizona territory.

Nonetheless, conflict did exist, in part because both sheep and cattle numbers skyrocketed during the 1880s. Hopis and Navajos had raised sheep in northern Arizona since the 1600s, but the commercial sheep industry did not really get started until the mid-1860s, when Juan Candelaria and his brothers drove New Mexican flocks into Apache County and settled near what later became the town of Concho. According to a *Special Report of the Sheep Industry,* issued by the Department of Agriculture in 1892, non-Indians in Arizona ran 803 sheep in 1870, 76,524 in 1880, and 698,404 in 1890. These figures were undoubtedly too conservative; in 1879, the *Arizona Star* claimed there were 78,500 sheep in Pima County alone. The development of the sheep industry followed the same basic trajectory as the cattle industry: steady growth during the 1870s succeeded by an explosion the next decade.

There were other similarities as well. The first commercial flocks were hardy little scrubs from New Mexico—big-horned descendants of the sheep introduced by the Spaniards. With the advent of the railroads, however, sheepmen discovered a market for lamb and mutton, so they began importing Merino rams from California and Vermont to improve their herds. Like the cattle industry, the sheep industry had to break away from its Spanish origins to compete in the late nineteenth century.

But there were differences too. Beginning in the 1880s, a characteristic pattern of seasonal movement, or transhumance, developed—one that persisted until the mid twentieth century. During the spring and summer, flocks grazed the grasslands and meadows of the Colorado Plateau. When fall arrived, the shepherds and their quick little dogs pointed the animals south, wintering them in the warm valleys of the Salt and Gila rivers. One of the most important trails dropped off the Mogollon Rim near Strawberry, sliced across the Mazatzal Mountains, and crossed the Verde River north of Cave Creek—a 200- to 300-mile trek through some of the roughest country in the territory. But in spite of the difficulties, the sheep migrations did link the uplands with the desert and helped transform the Salt River Valley into the largest agricultural oasis in Arizona.

Sheep raising was also geographically more restricted than cattle ranching. In 1894 the *Historical and Biographical Record of Arizona* listed 19,000 sheep in Yavapai County, 133,388 in Apache County, and 201,449 in Coconino County. Pima County, by contrast, had 1,620 of the animals, while Cochise County ran only 6,435. Again, those numbers appear far too low, especially for southern Arizona. In 1892 the shipment of 20,000 sheep from Texas to the foothills of the Chiricahua Mountains provoked outrage and resistance among local cattlemen. Nevertheless, the largest and most stable operations continued to be located in the northern part of the territory.

The young town of Flagstaff became a center of Arizona's sheep industry. Early sheepmen in the area included Thomas McMillan, John Clark, and William Henry Ashurst, whose son Henry served as a U.S. senator from Arizona for thirty years. But the biggest producers were the Daggs brothers, who ran as many as 50,000 animals on the Colorado Plateau. The *Tombstone Prospector* of June 6, 1888, reported that the three brothers from Missouri were the "largest wool shippers" in the territory. Their shareholding arrangement with the Tewksburys, who drove several flocks of Daggs sheep into the Tonto Basin, helped trigger the Pleasant Valley War.

A high pocket of grass watered by Cherry Creek, Pleasant Valley remains one of the most isolated spots in Arizona. To the east are the remote northwestern canyons of the San Carlos Reservation. To the south are the Sierra Anchas, where some of the highest black bear and mountain lion populations in the Southwest haunt deep slashes in the mountains with names like Devil's Chasm and Coon Creek. North is the Mogollon Rim, and west is the Tonto Basin. During the 1880s there was no Colin Cameron to dominate the range, and the law was far away. Once the feud ignited, it was hard to put out.

The first of the thirty to fifty casualties was a Ute Indian shepherd employed by the Daggs and Tewksburys, who was murdered in 1887. The last was Tom Graham, who was ambushed in Tempe in 1892. In between there were pitched battles, sneak attacks, and the kind of poisonous vendettas that only arise when neighbors kill neighbors. Perhaps the most gruesome encounter occurred early in the feud, when Tom Graham, enraged by the murder of his younger brother Billy, attacked the Tewksbury ranch along Cherry Creek on September 2, 1887. He and his gunmen killed Frank Jacobs and John Tewksbury. When John's wife Mary Ann ran out to bury the bodies, Graham partisans ringed the corpses with gunfire. For the next three days, feral hogs fed on the bodies while Mary Ann pleaded with Graham to let her bury the dead.

Sheep were certainly one factor in the Pleasant Valley War. Many observers believed that the Daggs brothers financed the Tewksburys, buying them arms and later paying for the legal defense of John Rhodes and Ed Tewksbury, the two men accused of shooting Tom Graham in the back. P. P. Daggs himself wrote, "I ought to know something about the 'Tonto War.' It cost me enough . . . ninety thousand dollars. Gen. Sherman said war is hell. He was right." But to interpret Pleasant Valley as nothing more than a range war would be the worst sort of economic reductionism. Whatever the initial cause, feelings soon ran too high to be fueled by a desire for profit alone. The bloodshed was more primal. As Jim Tewksbury told Deputy Sheriff Joe McKinney after the shootout at the Tewksbury ranch, "No damned man can kill a brother of mine and stand guard over him for the hogs to eat him, and live within a mile and a half of me."

❋ ❋ The Tragedy of the Commons on the Open Range

The Pleasant Valley War was an appalling aberration—a chain of vengeance and death that haunted minds and quieted lips in the Tonto Basin for generations after the last victim was lowered into the ground. But most conflicts between sheep and cattle interests were settled peacefully, even if they went to court. For every Hashknife cowboy like John Paine who pistol-whipped a shepherd, there were cooler heads who worked out compromises or accepted the verdicts of the legal system. Feuds like Pleasant Valley were not only bad for business; they unraveled the social fabric that rural families were working so hard to weave.

Instead of hiring gunmen, many of the biggest ranchers and sheep raisers organized to promote their interests. The sheepmen were the first to do so, meeting in Flagstaff in 1886 to form the Arizona Sheep Breeders and Wool Growers Association. The official purposes of the organization were to encourage selective breeding, organize annual roundups, and fix uniform wages for shepherds and shearers. But pressure from freewheeling cattle outfits like the Hashknife must have frightened or angered many sheep owners into joining as well. Behind this quarrel lurked a much bigger problem, however: the overstocking of Arizona ranges. For two decades, cattlemen and sheepmen alike had followed one overarching principle: Be fruitful and multiply. Promoters, speculators, and pioneers all drove as many animals as they could into every corner of the territory. Whether they bellowed or bleated, the results were the same: there were just too many animals for the land to sustain.

As early as the mid-1880s, a few prescient stockmen saw the future and recoiled. In 1885 the Tres Alamos Association concluded that ranges along the San Pedro were "already stocked to their full capacity." The following year, the Tombstone Stock Growers Association recognized that "a crisis is fast approaching" and called for an end to the importation of any more cattle "without first legitimately securing sufficient grass and water for their herds." Even in the wild heart of the Tonto Basin, an armed band of ranchers halted Colonel Jesse Ellison and his fellow Texans until Henry "Rim Rock" Thompson assured them that Ellison had purchased existing grazing rights. Unfortunately, these crude efforts at regulation were too little and too late to save the range. After five rough early years when they could not afford sugar for their coffee, Ellison and his wife and daughters eventually ran more cattle than the Forest Service later permitted on the 3-million-acre Tonto National Forest. In the words of journalist and historian Don Dedera, "Ultimately, the land fell back from the onslaught in the same way that Ellison had retreated from Sherman. By the vertical yard, the topsoil blew away, slid in sheets, opened cracks miles long, rushed downhill toward the sea, vanished forever."

In 1891 the governor's annual report listed 720,940 cattle and 288,727 sheep in Arizona. Colin Cameron and other astute observers put the real figures for cattle at 1,500,000, or more than twice the official number. That year, stockmen enjoyed the biggest calf crop in the history of the territory, but there was trouble as well. According to Cameron, "When the rainy season had passed and not one-half the usual amount of water had fallen; when it was seen that all the old grass was gone, that the new crop was a failure . . . it began to dawn upon the ranchmen that there was a limit to the number of cattle that the range would feed."

Nonetheless, few ranchers voluntarily limited their own herds. It was an old story in a new setting—the "tragedy of the commons" on the open range. Cameron noted that ranchers "made no effort to sell or remove even a part of their stock, but continued in the even tenor of their way, expecting that the coming year would furnish grass to meet the necessities of the occasion." It did not. Very little rain fell during the summer of 1892, and the following winter and spring were also dry. According to historian Diana Hadley, "By the early summer of 1893, creeks had dried up, cienegas and former springs became mud holes, and the cattle stood around bawling for water, eventually ventured into the mud, and in their weakened condition could not free themselves. Cows and calves fell off to mere skeletons; bulls became too weak to breed; cows aborted or, lacking the necessary vitamin A from green grass, failed to come into heat. The calves died of starvation first, followed by bulls and cows."

It was a disaster of biblical proportions, one in which nature and greed conspired to magnify their individual effects. Cattle died like flies all over the territory, but the losses were greatest in southern Arizona, where 50 to 75 percent of all animals perished. Judge J. C. Hancock recalled San Simon Creek littered with the bodies of cattle and cowboys straining their drinking water through burlap sacks to get rid of the maggots. Rancher Edward Land remembered, "Dead cattle lay everywhere. You could actually throw a rock from one carcass to another." But perhaps the most vivid description of the drought was penned by Forrestine Cooper Hooker, daughter-in-law of Colonel H. C. Hooker and a cattle contractor herself. In Hooker's novel *The Long Dim Trail*, a rancher's wife muses, "She felt the drought was a living, relentless thing, wrapping its coils about them all, men and brutes alike, choking and crushing the very heart of the universe. . . . A gaunt calf stumbled weakly and fell near the fence, making no effort to rise, as though understanding the futility of struggling any longer."

✳ ✳ Changes in the Cattle Industry

Climate undoubtedly contributed to the devastation. The droughts of 1892–93 and 1895 were the most severe, but Hadley argues that the dry period actually began in the summer of 1885 and continued off and on until the early 1900s. During those two decades there were six long stretches when the amount of evapotranspiration (moisture lost through evaporation and transpiration by plants) was greater than the amount of precipitation. Over the same period, however, an unusually high number of El Niño years (1867–68, 1871, 1874, 1877–78, 1880, 1884, 1887–89, 1891, 1896–97, 1899–1900, 1902, 1905, 1907) punctuated the droughts. During those years, warm water surfaced in the equatorial Pacific and triggered a worldwide chain of climatic events. In the Southwest, heavy rains streamed off slopes denuded of vegetation and washed away topsoil. The rainstorms also sent massive floods raging down floodplains that had been channelized and stripped of riparian plants because farmers and speculators had dug canals in the streambeds to intercept groundwater. The floodwaters sliced through the alluvial soil, carving deep arroyos that left floodplain fields high and dry. Human impact upon the environment weakened vegetative cover and provided the perfect matrix for both sheet erosion and gullying.

Most contemporary observers, on the other hand, blamed overstocking for the deterioration of the range. In 1901, botanist D. A. Griffiths distributed a questionnaire to prominent cattlemen in southern Arizona, including H. C. Hooker and C. H. Bayless, who owned a large ranch near Oracle. When asked to compare the abundance of natural feed before the cattle boom with conditions at the turn of the century, Hooker replied, "Fully double," and Bayless responded, "At that time ten animals were kept in good condition where one now barely exists." The questionnaire continued, "Do you attribute the present unproductive condition of the range to overstocking, drought, or to both combined?" Bayless answered, "Droughts are not more frequent now than in the past, but mother earth has been stripped of all grass covering. The very roots have been trampled out by the hungry herds constantly wandering to and fro in search of enough food. . . . Vegetation does not thrive as it once did, not because of drought, but because the seed is gone, the roots are gone, and the soil is gone. This is all the direct result of overstocking and can not be prevented on our open range where the land is not subject to private control."

Photographs of the time support the testimony of Hooker and Bayless. They reveal an almost lunar landscape in places, one that was stripped of grasses, exposed to wind and runoff, and crisscrossed with cattle trails where even the trees have browse lines. And there were other environmental problems as well, particularly the invasion of unpalatable shrubs and weeds such as creosote, acacia, mesquite, senecio, snakeweed, and burroweed. For the last century, scientists have argued whether such changes were caused by overgrazing or climatic change. The most recent evidence suggests that a whole host of factors—overgrazing, channelization, and droughts followed by intense storms—all worked together to devastate Southwestern watersheds and ranges.

Regardless of origin, however, the degradation of the range had an enormous impact on the cattle industry. As the drought worsened, ranchers shipped as many cattle as they could out of the territory, selling them as feeders at rock-bottom prices. In 1892 there were 116,604 cattle in Pima County and 82,122 in Cochise County. Those numbers plummeted to 49,500 (57 percent) and 45,056 (45 percent) the following year. To make matters worse, the national depression of 1893 drove down the price of cattle to an all-time low average of $9.80 a head. Cattlemen were desperate to sell at a time when markets were strangling in the grip of a financial panic. For many ranchers, the malignant intersection of drought and depression proved fatal.

It was a tense and lingering demise. Water control became the key to survival, and confrontations between ranchers erupted across the Arizona countryside. At the north end of the San Simon Valley, Jesse James Benton fought a running battle with the giant San Simon Cattle Company. When Benton fenced off his claim, which contained the only permanent water in the region, several thousand San Simon cattle swarmed around it, "bawling their heads off." When he drove his cattle to market, he was forced to ride through rows of armed San Simon cowboys. Benton stood up to such pressure, but many small stockmen did not. During the 1890s, most of the brand transfers in the Arizona Livestock Board brand registration book recorded the sale of ranches from smaller owners to larger ones. The scale of ranching was shifting upward as cattlemen and sheepmen alike realized that stock raising took money and plenty of it.

But small ranchers were not the only casualties. In 1899 the Babbitt brothers—four enterprising merchants from Cincinnati who had moved to Flagstaff in the 1880s—purchased the Arizona Cattle Company, the second-largest ranch in northern Arizona. Two years later they bought the legendary Aztec Land and Cattle Company as well. According to Hashknife cowboy George Hennessey, "The Hashknife troubles started in 1894, when they had one dry year after another. The company lost a lot of money, and in 1901, most of the cattle were sold."

Hennessey might have added an epidemic of rustling and a lack of scientific range management to the list of Hashknife woes. The Aztec outfit—too big and unwieldy to meet the challenges of ranching in the twentieth century—was as much a creature of the open range as were the small saddle-and-rope operations scattered across the territory. A number of successful cattlemen like Hooker, in fact, sold off outlying spreads to concentrate on their home ranches. Herds had to be improved through selective breeding, and that meant fences in addition to purebred bulls. Ranches had to be consolidated, so land and cattle companies paid "homesteaders" to file claims next to their own in order to transfer those claims to the corporation. Above all, stockmen had to invest in artificial sources of water—windmills, cattle tanks, artesian wells. Both the very large ranches and the very small fell victim to the rising costs of stock raising in Arizona.

The 1890s, then, were the end of one era and the beginning of another. For twenty years, stockmen had binged on Arizona grasses until more than a million cattle and nearly a million sheep were tearing into the range. It was an economy based on the plunder of the public lands, one in which most stock raisers were unwilling or unable to regulate their own herds. Ranching on the open range was a game of chance: livestock poker. When the dry years struck and the national market price for cattle collapsed, many of the players had to fold their hands. Arizona's natural bounty had been exhausted. From now on, successful stock raisers had to be stewards, not scourges.

8

✳ ✳ Silver and Gold

In 1877, Edward Schieffelin drifted into the San Pedro Valley after years of prospecting in the Great Basin and the Pacific Northwest. Because Chiricahua Apaches still inhabited the area, soldiers at Camp Huachuca told Schieffelin that the only thing he would find was his tombstone. "The word lingered in my mind," Schieffelin later recalled, "and when I got into the country where Tombstone is now located, I gave the name to the first location that I made."

It turned out to be the biggest silver strike in Arizona history, producing nearly $30 million between 1879 and 1886. But at first neither Schieffelin nor his ore samples impressed anyone in southern Arizona. "He was about the queerest specimen of humanity ever seen . . . with black curly hair that hung several inches below his shoulders," noted one Tucson resident. "His long untrimmed beard was a mass of unkempt knots and mats. His clothing was worn out and covered with patches of deerskins, corduroy, and flannel, and his old slouch hat, too, was so pieced with rabbit skin that very little of the original felt remained."

Schieffelin therefore sought out his younger brother Albert, whom he finally tracked down at the Signal Mine on the Big Sandy River in Mohave County. Knowing that he was "not of an enthusiastic nature," Schieffelin worked his brother slowly and carefully, like a big fish on a thin line. Albert did not think much of Schieffelin's ore samples either, but he turned them over to an assayer named Richard Gird. Gird examined the chunks of rock and asked Albert where the mine was. Albert replied that he did not know. "Well," Gird told him, "the best thing you can do is to find out where that ore came from, and take me with you and start for the place."

Over the next few months, Schieffelin and his partners found a series of mines that made Western history: the Lucky Cuss, the Tough Nut, the Contention. By 1880, Tombstone was one of the largest communities in the territory, crawling with miners, rustlers, and gamblers. The quintessential lone prospector had spawned the quintessential boomtown. But neither Schieffelin nor his partners stuck around for very long. Al and Ed sold their best claims in the spring of 1880 for about $500,000 apiece. Gird did the same a year later. It was a typical pattern in Arizona silver districts, where companies with the capital to dig shafts, erect mills and smelters, and work lower-grade ores often bought out those who had discovered the mines. But the *Tucson Citizen* of February 4, 1880, predicted just before Schieffelin left Tombstone that the town's founding father would "never rest contented until he finds another district to rival the one to which he gave the sepulchral name." During the next two decades, Schieffelin wandered as far north as Alaska before dying of a heart attack in a miner's shack near Canyonville, Oregon. A few months before he died, he wrote, "I am getting restless here in Oregon and wish to go somewhere that has wealth, for the digging of it. I like the excitement of being right up against the earth, trying to coax her gold away and scatter it."

His friends brought his body back to southern Arizona and laid him "right up against the earth" near his greatest strike. They also built a twenty-five-foot-high monument shaped like a claim marker over his grave. The monument became a historical curiosity, just like the town Schieffelin helped to found. By the turn of the century, less than a thousand people remained in Tombstone. The mines had flooded, the saloons were boarded up, and the bank had closed. The "town too tough to die" slumbered for decades before resurrecting itself as a tourist attraction in the 1950s. Copper became the new king of the Arizona mining industry.

✳   ✳   ✳   Placer Mining on the Arizona Frontier

Before railroads and technological innovations allowed the extraction of low-grade copper ore, however, silver and gold made Arizona shimmer in the dreams of prospectors and speculators for 150 years. In a world where most of the good things in life were scarce, the promise of precious metals exercised a peculiarly powerful hold on the imagination. Europeans in the seventeenth and eighteenth centuries came to the Americas from a continent where periodic famines still stalked the peasantry and where necessary resources like land, water, firewood, and wild game were often controlled by aristocratic elites. Some of these constraints loosened in the New World, but most of the empire builders tried to recreate the social hierarchies of their homelands. Frederick Jackson Turner and Walter Prescott Webb to the contrary, the North American frontier did not impel democracy upon the newcomers.

Prospecting, on the other hand, offered a glimmer of the great escape. Silver drew the Spaniards northward from Mesoamerica, and they leapfrogged from strike to strike, creating great mining centers like Zacatecas, Guanajuato, Parral, and Alamos. And when a Yaqui Indian discovered the *planchas de plata* (slabs of silver) at Arizonac southwest of modern Nogales in 1736, silver gave Arizona both its name and its legend for fabulous mineral wealth. That legend burrowed into the pages of colonial reports and sprouted like mushrooms in the promotions of nineteenth-century speculators like Charles Poston and Sylvester Mowry. In 1859, Mowry addressed the American Statistical and Geographical Society in New York, invoking a Spanish Arizona "of more than forty towns and villages" that "teemed with an agricultural and mining population." It was pure fantasy. Spaniards and Mexicans worked a handful of gold and silver mines in the Santa Rita Mountains, but none of those enterprises rivaled Sonoran operations such as the gold placers of Cieneguilla south of Altar or the great silver mines of Alamos. Then as now, promoters were selling an Arizona that never was.

But even if the reality of Spanish mining never matched the legend, the Spaniards gave Arizona miners not only a body of lore but also a repertoire of techniques perfected over four centuries in the deserts of northern Mexico. Placer mining (mining surface deposits rather than veins), dry washing (winnowing gold from heavier sand and gravel by blowing on it or tossing it in the air), and the *patio* process (separating or "reducing" silver ore from other minerals by mixing it with mercury in round arenas where animals or people trampled the sludge) all were skills the Spaniards brought to the Arizona frontier. Mining in the region, like stock raising, developed from a colonial base.

During the early territorial period, these simple and flexible methods satisfied the needs of most miners. A few rich deposits attracted investors with enough capital to undertake hardrock mining, but most prospectors during the 1860s drifted from placer boom to placer boom across the dry and broken landscape. Many of these early *placeros* (placer miners) were Sonorans who had left their homes for the California goldfields a decade earlier. Placer mining was a part of their heritage, a set of skills they absorbed along with farming and ranching as they grew up on the northern frontier. For generations, Sonoran miners had moved from strike to strike in northwestern Mexico—Soyopa, Saracachi, Cieneguilla. The lower Colorado Valley was simply an extension of that pattern, no different in climate, geology, or water supply from placer districts farther south in the Sonoran Desert.

The important commercial center of La Paz started as just such a placer strike. During the winter of 1861–62, mountain man Pauline Weaver discovered gold dust east of the Colorado River about six miles north of where modern Interstate 10 crosses the river to Blythe. Weaver hid the dust in a goose quill until he could show it to José María Redondo, the head of a mining party from Sonora working placers near Yuma Crossing. Redondo prospected the new strike, found a two-ounce nugget, and quickly moved his operation there. Soon more than 400 Mexican miners and their families threw up brush huts along the easternmost slough of the Colorado River, about three miles from the main channel. By October 1862 a peaceful Mexican community had taken shape there, with the miners replacing the mesquite "bough houses" with adobe dwellings and buying corn, beans, and melons from the Mohave Indians. The residents even formed a municipal government. All the officials except one were Mexicans.

Working in family groups, the placeros dry-washed gravel in Farrar Gulch, Goodman Wash, and La Paz Arroyo because it cost too much to haul water from the Colorado. When those drainages filled up with prospectors, newcomers established the "middle diggings" east of the Dome Rock Mountains. By the end of 1862, some miners were scratching the western slopes of the Plomosa Mountains thirty miles east of the Colorado, where they had to build *arrastras* (primitive crushers) to smash the gold loose from ore cemented with calcium carbonate.

All this activity soon caught the attention of hundreds of Anglo miners in California, who trudged from well to muddy well across the Mojave Desert to reach the strike. "Gold, the great magician of all ages has been at work," trumpeted one report. "New diggings have been discovered, placers of untold wealth!" During the winter of 1862–63, La Paz swelled to 1,500 people, most of them single men who overwhelmed the Mexican families and turned the community into a typical boomtown of boardinghouses and saloons. Gunmen dry-gulched miners to steal their gold. One Confederate sympathizer nicknamed Frog shot down three unarmed Union soldiers on a La Paz street. And while a few prospectors found big nuggets or dry-washed good dust, most barely recovered enough gold to live on.

In the end, it was merchants like Manuel Ravena and "Big Mike" Goldwater who kept La Paz alive after the placers played out in 1864. That year, the federal census revealed seventeen "merchants" in the desert town, many of them Jews from central Europe and only two of them natives of the United States. For the next two years, La Paz flourished by transforming itself into a supply center for the new mining districts of central Arizona along the headwaters of the Hassayampa River. In 1864 La Paz even became the seat of Yuma County after Arizona Territory was created. If the Colorado had not changed course in 1866, leaving the slough that served La Paz landlocked, the community might have flourished until the railroads arrived.

❋ ❋ Early Hardrock Mining

By the beginning of the 1870s, however, La Paz was almost a ghost town. Most of the merchants had moved several miles downriver to the new community of Ehrenberg, prompting one callous journalist to observe, "We fear that the occupation of La Paz—waylaying travelers—is gone, never to return." By its very nature, placer mining was an ephemeral activity. The flakes of gold that eroded from veins in the mountains and washed down arroyos and streams, where prospectors separated the heavier gold particles from alluvial gravels and sand, were exhausted in most diggings by 1867. From then on, miners had to employ more expensive and sophisticated methods to extract both gold and silver from subsurface lodes and veins.

Prospectors therefore probed deeper and deeper into Arizona's interior, where they found the minerals they were looking for in a rugged wedge of terrain known as the Central Mountain Province. Stretching from the Grand Wash Cliffs north of the Grand Canyon to the Mogollon Mountains of western New Mexico, the Central Mountain Province separates the high mesas of the Colorado Plateau from the low ranges and broad alluvial valleys of the Basin and Range country. Thrust upward during the Early Precambrian Mazatzal Orogeny (1.8 to 1.7 billion years ago), the mountains of the province twisted, buckled, eroded, and were thrust up again. In the process, veins and pockets of minerals crystallized as the crust of the earth shuddered. We call these ancient mountains the Cerbats, Hualapais, Bradshaws, Black Hills, Mazatzals, Sierra Anchas, and Pinals. The Yavapais and Apaches gave them other names. Their antiquity mocks all designations. But in that tumbled maze, miners searched for and found silver and gold.

One of the first and most famous of these discoveries was the Vulture Mine, which was located about fifteen miles south of Wickenburg in the Vulture Mountains. Henry Wickenburg, a native of Austria, discovered a gold-bearing quartz outcrop in November 1863 and returned with a few companions six months later to register and work the claim. By October 1864, nine arrastras were crushing ore and yielding about $700 worth of gold a day at a place called the "pumpkin patch" along the Hassayampa. A year later, there were forty arrastras and a new five-stamp mill. The pumpkin patch was awarded a post office and changed its name to Wickenburg, but Wickenburg himself did little to develop his find. Instead, he let others do the backbreaking work, charging them $15 a ton to hack out ore that consistently produced $75 a ton.

In November 1866, Wickenburg sold the mill and most of his claim to a New Yorker named Behtchuel Phelps for $50,000. Like Schieffelin, Wickenburg was a prospector, not a businessman. Phelps and his associates formed the Vulture Mining Company and began pouring money into the operation. By the spring of 1867, the corporation was employing seventy to eighty men, about half of whom were Mexicans. Even though the Vulture was rarely more than one step ahead of its creditors, Governor Richard McCormick called it the "Comstock of Arizona." By 1870 it was yielding half the gold in Arizona.

The costs of extracting that gold were enormous. During the six years they worked it, Phelps and his partners pulled about $2.5 million from the Vulture's craw. But they had to spend $600,000 to haul the ore to the mill and hundreds of thousands of dollars more to sink their shaft, fuel their stamps, and pay their miners and millworkers. "Highgrading"—the theft of rich ore—was common, and miners may have siphoned off 20 to 40 percent of the Vulture's ore. Then in 1872 the shaft began to flood 310 feet underground, and mining had to be suspended. The company searched for the capital to pump the shaft, but the national panic of 1873 dried up credit. After Phelps and his partners failed to pay $1,025 in taxes the following year, Arizona Territory put the Vulture up for sale.

During the next three decades, the "Comstock of Arizona" passed through a series of owners, who drilled wells, built pumping stations, erected new and bigger mills, and dreamed of a branch railroad that would carry their ore to the Southern Pacific line fifty miles to the south. Meanwhile, miners tried to follow the vein, which was severed by at least two major faults. By the early twentieth century, production had all but ceased. Meanwhile, Henry Wickenburg eked out a living on his small farm along the Hassayampa until 1905, when he killed himself at the age of eighty-four. Once touted as the "largest and richest gold mine" in Arizona, the Vulture lived up to its name.

Similar problems plagued other mining operations across the territory. By the 1870s, silver had replaced gold as Arizona's most valuable mineral. It was harder to reduce than gold and only one-sixteenth as valuable, but there was more of it. So most of the great strikes of the 1870s and 1880s were silver strikes. More than 200 prospectors from Nevada descended on the Prescott area, and one of them—Dud Moreland from Kentucky—found the Tiger lode in the Bradshaw Mountains in January 1871. Other strikes followed as newcomers and "Hassayampers" (veterans of the 1860s placer rushes) scoured the Bradshaws and other mountains along drainages like Black Canyon, Humbug Creek, Big Bug Creek, and the Agua Fria River. Mines such as the Peck and the Tip Top, often financed by Prescott merchants, attracted hundreds of prospectors who started out searching for their own bonanzas and ended up working for wages in the mines and mills. Prospectors could pick away at outcrops, but most silver deposits required more capital than individual miners could muster. The days of the *placero* with his blanket (for winnowing) and *batea* (wooden bowl for panning) were gone.

Mexican miners were less and less welcome as well. From the very beginning of the placer boom, Anglo prospectors in central Arizona tried to turn their diggings into "white-men's camps." In the Walker District along Lynx Creek, a miners' meeting passed a resolution to exclude "Asiatics & Sonoranians . . . from working this district" as early as July 12, 1863. Similar resolutions forced Mexicans out of placers in Wickenburg, the Bradshaw Mountains, and Walnut Grove. Mexican *gambucinos* (prospectors) continued to fan out across western and central Arizona, but ethnic tensions were rising. In 1880, for example, a Mexican named Jesús Carrillo entered a saloon in Tip Top and ordered a drink. The bartender threw him out, and then a group of Anglo miners beat him, looped a rope around his neck, and dragged him out of town. Prescott and its satellite communities were Anglo outposts on the Arizona frontier, with no established Mexican presence to temper the racism of the newcomers.

Similar changes affected the relatively few women on the central Arizona mining frontier. According to the federal census of 1864, there were only forty women in the area, thirty-one of whom were Mexican. Seventeen (55 percent) of the Mexican women were living with men without benefit of matrimony; the census taker, the Reverend Hiram Walter Read, described them disparagingly as "mistresses" even though common-law unions were customary among working-class people. And while most of them had formed unions with Mexican men, a few shared bed and board with Anglos. That made them targets for charges of sexual promiscuity, even in the rough-and-tumble mining towns. In 1866 an Anglo man living with a Mexican woman in Prescott was pointedly not invited to a dance sponsored by the Masons. As communities like Prescott took on the trappings of "civilization," Victorian sexual standards and double standards, as well as racism, began to be enforced. By 1870 there were 170 women in central Arizona, yet only 4 percent of them lived with men to whom they were not married.

There were exceptions who flouted racial and sexual mores. One Anglo woman, Mary DeCrow, arrived in the mining districts with a black Texan called "Negro Brown." By 1864 she was living with a Mexican blacksmith named Cornelius Ramos. Another woman, Mary Sawyer, became a legend in the mining camps by wearing men's clothes, drinking as hard as her male companions, and working her claims as well and as profanely as any of the "boys." But Prescott society accepted, or at least tolerated, Mary DeCrow after she married Ramos and started a boardinghouse. She went on to win a reputation for generosity that earned her the nickname "Virgin Mary." A Yavapai County judge, in contrast, declared Mary Sawyer insane in 1877 and sent her to the nearest asylum, in Stockton, California. She died in the Phoenix insane asylum in 1902. Boundaries of gender as well as ethnicity were being strengthened as placer boomtowns gave way to more established communities.

✳ ✳ ✳ The Tombstone Boom

By 1876, prospectors had recorded 11,605 claims in Arizona Territory, most of them in a few established mining regions: Yuma and Mohave counties along the Colorado River, the Prescott area, and the rugged Globe-Superior country, where the Silver King Mine reigned supreme. Because of the Chiricahua presence, however, southeastern Arizona still seemed too dangerous to explore. Then Ed Schieffelin arrived.

During the first phase of Tombstone's development, a handful of prospectors located the mines that generated the Tombstone legend. The first was the Lucky Cuss, which Schieffelin found on March 15, 1878. Its ore was so rich in places that Schieffelin could sink his pick-head up to its handle in outcrops and impress half-dollars into the nearly pure silver. Schieffelin's partner Richard Gird said it was the best sample he had ever assayed in his life.

A week later Schieffelin discovered the Tough Nut, which proved to be even richer. Then he helped his partners move camp or he would have found the Grand Central, which another prospector, Hank Williams, located on March 27.

At first, Williams failed to notify the Schieffelins and Gird about his claim even though Gird had agreed to assay Williams's samples in return for splitting any discovery he found. That evening, Gird and Williams "contended about the agreement," with Williams finally offering to cut from fifty to a hundred feet from the Grand Central and give it to the three partners. Gird and the Schieffelins accepted. They called their last big claim the Contention.

Tombstone history now moved into its second stage as Gird and the Schieffelin brothers searched for the capital to develop the mines. Another group of prospectors from San Francisco, not as lucky but better financed, tried to buy the Tough Nut and the Contention. In May 1878, Josiah H. White and his associates bought the Contention for $10,000. By 1886 the Contention had become the richest mine in Arizona, employing 110 men and yielding more than $5 million worth of silver for its owners.

Gird and the Schieffelins then entered into a complicated series of partnerships with John Vosberg, the Corbin brothers from Connecticut, and Governor A.P.K. Safford. Their first venture was the Tombstone Gold and Silver Mill and Mining Company, which financed the construction of a ten-stamp quartz mill along the San Pedro River. Other financiers organized the Grand Central Mining Company and the Contention Consolidated Mining Company. Corporate mining had come to Tombstone, and by the end of the year, the boom had begun.

As in most booms, chaos reigned. The first settlement sprang up around the nearest water, but that ramshackle little community, known as Watervale or Gouge-eye, was three miles away from the mines themselves. Most miners grew weary of the walk, so they threw up their shacks at a place called Richmond or Hog-em and paid someone to haul their water to them. But Richmond, perched on a narrow ridge among the slag heaps, quickly ran out of room. A group of entrepreneurs then formed the Tombstone Townsite Company, surveying a 320-acre site known as Goose Flats. When the townsite claim was filed on April 19, 1879, the town that has spawned a century of pulp fiction was born.

From the very beginning, violence and fraud characterized the community. The townsite company, headed by a speculator with a shady past named James Clark, never took the necessary measures to secure its patent. As a result, most early settlers ignored its claims and built wherever they wanted. People jumped one another's lots with abandon, causing both fistfights and gunplay. In September 1879, Charley Calhoun defended his lot with a "rather emphatic address" punctuated by two pistol shots. The deputy sheriff arrested him, reassuring his neighbors that "a little too much stimulants was the only trouble." Other incidents were not so comic. In late October 1880, Curly Bill Brocius shot Marshal

Fred White. Brocius was one of the "Texas Cowboys" loosely allied with the townsite company and opposed by the Earp brothers and John Clum, the *Tombstone Epitaph* editor and former agent at the San Carlos Reservation. From then on, violence escalated into the famous gunfight at the O.K. Corral between the Earps and the Clantons in October 1881, the ambush of Virgil Earp two months later, and the murder of Morgan Earp in March 1882. By May of that year, lawlessness had grown so flagrant that President Chester A. Arthur threatened to impose martial law. Mythologized beyond recognition, the sordid little saga of Tombstone unfolded in a haze of black powder, mysterious "suicides," and alcoholic fumes.

Despite the obsessive public interest in that saga, however, its underlying political and economic forces are difficult to untangle. In 1878, Tombstone was a gleam in Ed Schieffelin's eye. Two years later, it was a town of ten to twelve thousand people. According to Wells Spicer, the lawyer who conducted the inquest on the fatalities at the O.K. Corral shootout, there were "two dance houses, a dozen gambling places, over twenty saloons, and more than five hundred gamblers" in town. What Tombstone lacked was an established judicial system and a traditional set of social norms. Conflicting laws and uncertain claims fueled an already incendiary mixture of miners, speculators, cowboys, rustlers, and gamblers. Republicans squared off against Democrats, Northerners against Southerners. Men used any excuse they could come up with to justify a grudge.

The result was no Western morality play, with good triumphing over evil. Like most such boomtowns, Tombstone made itself up as it went along, propelled by silver and pummeled by factions who fought each other in the courts, the newspapers, and the streets. Legal proceedings were often little more than cloaks for the machinations of the power hungry, and lawmen were little more than gunmen. An ambivalent case in point was Wyatt Earp, the most famous "shootist" of them all. Clum considered Earp "quite my ideal of the strong, manly, serious and capable peace officer." Others, like Earp's sister-in-law Allie, thought he was a bully and a compulsive gambler who forced a showdown with the Clantons because Earp and the Clantons had robbed a stage together. Half a decade earlier, when Earp and Bat Masterson were deputies in Dodge City, cowboys called them the "Fighting Pimps" because of their fondness for whorehouses. Depending upon which of his contemporaries you believed, Earp was either a hero or a thug.

The truth was probably somewhere in between. Earp was a product of his times, drifting from one violent town to another in search of good cards and the backing of powerful men. He and his brothers found more than they bargained for in Tombstone, which turned Wyatt into a legend, Virgil into a cripple, and Morgan into a corpse. It was a high price to pay, but not a surprising one. Places like Tombstone epitomized the frontier at its worst: a rootless community where people risked everything—their lives, their fortunes, the land itself—for short-term gain.

❋ ❋ The Tombstone Mines

The short-term gain was indeed spectacular, at least for a time. Obscured by the notoriety of the Earps and the Hollidays, the real business of Tombstone was silver, not six-guns. During Tombstone's heyday, from 1879 to 1886, at least fifty mines were burrowed into the parched hills. Those mines produced $20 to $30 million in silver—the equivalent of about $230 to $350 million today. Miners blasted ore from tunnels, and twelve steam hoists lifted it to the surface. Then 150 stamps rising and falling in seven mills crushed it along the San Pedro River. Those mills, which begot satellite communities like Contention City, Fairbank, Emery City, Millville, and Charleston, chewed up nearly 400,000 tons of ore and consumed 47,260 cords of fuel wood in the process. The mines therefore employed hundreds of teamsters, woodcutters, and millworkers as well as miners. Tombstone's tentacles extended far beyond its dark tunnels and dusty streets.

The lives of the miners themselves were anything but glamorous. During the early years they received four dollars a day for a ten-hour shift, good wages for that era. But hardrock mining was a dirty, often terrifying way to make a living. Miners descended the shafts in rattletrap cages that plunged at the rate of eight hundred feet a minute. When they arrived at the digging face, they wedged candles into the tunnel walls and hammered blasting holes into the rock in two-man teams. The process was known as "double-jacking," with one man holding and turning the drill while the other pounded away at it with a four-pound sledge. "More difficult than I imagined to hold drills properly," miner George Parsons noted in his journal. "One little slip and one's hands, arms, or legs might be smashed to a jelly." Setting the blasting charges was even more perilous. Paper cartridges filled with dynamite were inserted into the holes and tamped with damp clay. The "giant powder . . . has to be handled carefully," Parsons observed wryly, or the "cap explodes and one is likely to go flying out of the shaft."

Work on the surface was just as grueling. Teamsters hauled the ore to the stamp mills in enormous wagons pulled by sixteen to twenty mules. Millworkers then shoveled it into rockbreakers powered by water funneled through flumes from the San Pedro. Batteries pounded the powder until it was fine enough to fall through forty-mesh screens and settle in pans, where it was mixed with mercury. Retorts then heated the resulting amalgam until the mercury vaporized, leaving a residue of silver behind.

The process was an exhausting and dangerous one. Young Sam Aaron recalled that after his first day of shoveling ore, he could not unclench his hands. But when he was offered a better-paying job as furnaceman, he turned it down. Laboring in the reduction works exposed furnacemen to arsenic, lead, and mercury poisoning, a slow and gruesome way to die. In order to sleep, many furnacemen had to loop a rope around their neck and legs to keep themselves from twitching. "The first opportunity I had . . . I started to be a faro-dealer," Aaron wrote.

Despite these dangers, most of the miners and millworkers were Anglo Americans or Europeans rather than Mexicans. Tombstone was one of the first places in Arizona where new, highly mechanized technologies were utilized to extract and reduce ore. As a result, mine owners brought in experienced miners, many of them Cornishmen ("Cousin Jacks") from England, to perform specialized tasks. Spanish colonial techniques, which had dominated Arizona during the early territorial period, disappeared from the big camps. The mining industry in Arizona was changing, even in a frontier town like Tombstone.

Nevertheless, Mexicans performed many other jobs that kept the mines and mills operating. Some were teamsters, transporting ore to the mills. Others were woodcutters, scouring the countryside for the oak and mesquite that fueled the machinery itself. Those woodcutters quickly cut down the mesquite bosques near the mills along the San Pedro and denuded the hills around Tombstone. Then they spread into the foothills of the Whetstone, Huachuca, and Dragoon Mountains, where they often came in conflict with ranchers. "The mesa tracts of southern Pima and eastern Cochise counties are being literally stripped of trees, so that shelter of stock will soon be unknown in these sections," said the *Arizona Daily Star* on April 23, 1884. The ranchers responded by unsuccessfully pressuring the government to prohibit woodcutting on the public lands. By 1885 the mines were importing wood from Sonora.

The impact upon the surrounding vegetation was immense. Geographers Conrad Bahre and Charles Hutchinson estimate that during the boom years Tombstone consumed 31,000 cords of wood for cooking and heating, 47,260 cords for milling ore, and at least that many cords for running the hoists and pumps, roasting the ore, and retorting the amalgam. In other words, Tombstone alone sucked 120,000 to 130,000 cords of wood into its maw between 1879 and 1886—enough wood, stacked four feet high in four-foot lengths, to stretch nearly 200 miles. Similar denudation occurred around other mining districts in southern Arizona, such as Greaterville, Harshaw, Silver Bell, Galeyville, Dragoon, Pearce, Duquesne, Washington Camp, Courtland, Evansville, Helvetia, Gleeson, Dos Cabezas, Turquoise, Middlemarch, Paradise, Russelville, Black Diamond, Mammoth, Oracle, Total Wreck, Winkelman, and Hilltop. With hundreds of thousands of cattle stripping away the grasses and woodcutters cutting down the trees, no wonder the landscape looked so blighted in places by the turn of the century.

❋ ❋ ❋ The Tombstone Bust

Nature exacted its own revenge. Outwardly, Tombstone seemed to be thriving. The Bird Cage offered bawdy variety shows, and Schieffelin Hall presented operas, musicals, and plays performed by touring theater companies. There were also literary societies, amateur bands, and fraternal organizations such as the Knights of Columbus, the Masons, and the Independent Order of Odd Fellows. The town even had four permanent churches—Catholic, Episcopalian, Presbyterian, and Methodist. On the surface, Tombstone seemed to be developing into a town of substance and civic virtue.

Below ground, however, all was not well. In March 1881 miners struck water 500 feet down in the Sulphuret Mine. At first the discovery thrilled most residents. Mills could be erected nearby and operated with water from the mines themselves, saving the cost of transporting ore to the San Pedro at $3.50 per ton. But as the shafts sank deeper, investment skyrocketed. Steam pumps that lifted 500,000 gallons every twenty-four hours could not keep the Grand Central Company's tunnels from flooding, so the owners spent $200,000 for Cornish pumps that could suck three times as much water from the ground in a day. It was a contest between technology and the water table—an ironic contest for a community located in a desert grassland. Tombstone had to pipe its drinking water from reservoirs in the Dragoon and Huachuca Mountains while five hundred feet below the surface, miners burrowed deeper into a world that threatened to submerge them.

There were other problems as well. National monetary policy vacillated in response to pro-silver and anti-silver proponents. In 1873, Congress abolished the silver dollar, causing outrage among mining interests in the West, who called it the Crime of '73. Five years later, they retaliated with the Bland-Allison Act, which mandated the purchase of $2 to $4 million of silver bullion each month to be coined at a ratio of sixteen to one with gold. After passage of the act, the price of silver rose to $1.29 an ounce, but by the mid-1880s enormous new discoveries like those at Tombstone dropped the price below a dollar, and many mines had to close.

In response, mine owners in Tombstone slashed wages from four dollars a day to three. The four-dollar day was the pride of Western hardrock miners, a tradition they had fought for and won as early as the 1860s in the Comstock mines of Nevada. But mine owners began chipping away at the tradition in the early 1880s as the price of precious metals declined, complaining that the wage was "extravagant" and left many mines idle. Miners compromised in the Comstock by agreeing to work longer hours. But in 1884 the conflict in Tombstone developed into a bitter war of attrition. No novelist or film director has ever depicted that struggle, but Tombstone became the site of the first major confrontation between labor and management in Arizona and one of the first big camps in the West where the four-dollar day tottered and fell.

The battle began auspiciously for the strikers. On May 1, more than 300 miners—about three-fourths of the total—organized the Tombstone Miners' Union to protest the wage cut. The owners retaliated by closing down the Grand Central, Contention, and Tough Nut, the three largest mines in the district. At first, most residents supported the miners; on May 5 local businessmen even gave the strikers a thousand cigars and three barrels of beer as they paraded through the streets.

As the strike dragged on, however, parades and beer gave way to boycotts and bank closures. Strikers struggled to survive on contributions from unions in Bisbee, Globe, and Virginia City, and business in the stores and saloons dried up. By the end of June, most merchants were calling on the miners to swallow their pride and take the dollar a day drop in pay. "There is not one in ten of us who can last a month longer," the editor of the *Tombstone Epitaph* concluded on June 21, 1884. "The day has passed when even a compromise at $3.50 could be effected; now the only salvation for the Tombstone camp seems to be to accept the situation, hard as it is to bear."

That summer, resistance degenerated into violence and despair. The Grand Central imported sixty scabs from as far away as Pittsburgh. Deputy sheriffs barricaded the mines and squared off against the strikers. On August 8 a drunken striker resisted arrest and got his skull crushed by a revolver butt. The same night, a striker and a scab opened fire on each other, and the sheriff put the scab in jail for his own safety. At three the next morning, desperate miners marched on the Grand Central hoisting works, and more gunfire erupted. No one was wounded, but Tombstone's last embers of sympathy for the strikers flickered and died.

Three days later, on August 12, acting governor H. M. Van Arman requested that two companies of federal troops from Fort Huachuca be stationed in the divided town. The troops marched in to keep order, which meant protecting the mines. With the community against them and the sheriff and the army out in force, even the most die-hard strikers realized that the war was over and they had lost. Many miners moved away. The rest accepted the three-dollar-a-day wage. Their union collapsed, distributing what was left of the strike fund to sick or injured colleagues. After four months of struggle, the longest strike in the West up to that time had come to an end.

The *Arizona Star* of August 29, 1884, labeled the strike "a deplorable failure" and argued that "no one has been benefited and the miners, the mine owners, the merchants and the entire county of Cochise has suffered great injury." The *Engineering and Mining Journal* of August 30, on the other hand, could barely conceal its glee. "Tombstone has taken the lead that more than one mining camp will be forced to follow," it proclaimed, and its prediction quickly came true. Later that year, unions in Bisbee and Globe accepted the wage cut with little more than a whimper. In 1885, mining camps across the rest of the West followed suit. Tombstone became the first of many victories for the mine owners— a role far more significant for Western history than any shootout on its mean streets.

But the victory was a Pyrrhic one for the district itself. In 1882, at the peak of the bonanza, miners blasted $5,202,876 in silver from Tombstone's mine shafts. By 1884, production had dropped to $1,380,788, a decline of 73 percent. Most of the mines shut down during the strike, and many of the smaller ones never reopened. The boom was going bust, though the larger mining companies held on for two more years.

The beginning of the end came on May 12, 1886. "We heard the fire whistles early one morning and hurried out of the house," Mrs. J. H. Macia recalled. "I remember how the draft from the shaft blew a column of flame and smoke high in the air. You could hear it roar." That roar came from the fire engulfing the hoists and pumps of the Grand Central Mine, the largest in the district. Worth $350,000, those pumps had kept the water table at bay. Soon they were a twisted wreckage.

Ironically, the mine owners themselves were responsible for the disaster that followed. The pumps of the Contention Mine still functioned. They might have held the water level down throughout all the mines until the Grand Central came back into operation. But the two companies squabbled so much about costs that the owners of the Contention finally shut down their own pumps to keep the Grand Central from extracting ore at their expense. As a result, the water began to rise, seeping from one tunnel to another. In the end, two of the four natural elements—fire and water—conspired with human greed to destroy the richest silver mines in Arizona. There would be other silver strikes, but by the end of the century, Arizona had shed its frontier skin and become an extractive colony of industrial America. Industry needed vast deposits of copper more than elusive veins of silver or gold.

9

＊ ＊ Copper

More than any other figure of his era, George Wiley Paul Hunt embodied all the contradictions of Arizona in his walruslike frame. His enemies in the business community sneered at his poor grammar and his uncouth table manners, but Hunt understood Arizona politics better than anyone else in the early twentieth century. When labor was riding high, Hunt railed against the copper companies and played the populist. When labor's star fell, he emphasized his business background as a rancher in the Tonto Basin and a former president of the Old Dominion Bank in Globe. Voters elected him governor of the state seven times between 1912 and 1932.

There were no contradictions in Walter Douglas. The son of Dr. James Douglas, the Canadian metallurgist who built the Phelps Dodge empire in Arizona, Walter became manager of the Copper Queen Mine in Douglas at age thirty-one. Unlike Hunt, he had a passion for anonymity; his name hardly ever appeared in the newspapers, even those he owned. Douglas dominated Arizona by moving behind the scenes. By the time he retired in 1930, he was chairman of the board of the Southern Pacific Railroad as well as president of Phelps Dodge.

The two men were bitter enemies who squared off against one another as Arizona made the transition from territory to state in 1912. Hunt spearheaded a coalition of miners, railroad workers, farmers, and small businessmen that ramrodded a progressive state constitution down the throats of a Republican administration in Washington. Douglas picked the coalition apart and restored Arizona's corporate colonial order during World War I. Hunt won the votes, but Douglas won the war, leading the business interests that forced Arizona to don the "copper collar" in 1917. He made sure that Arizona remained a colony of the extractive industries—the railroads, cotton farms, ranches, and, above all, the copper companies—until the state was transformed by World War II.

❋   ❋   ❋   The Early Copper Industry

Unlike gold or silver, copper never fueled the expansion of empire or underwrote the currency of any modern nation. Used primarily to make kitchen utensils or roofs, most of the world's supply came from a handful of mines in Cornwall, England, and Andalucía, Spain. Antonio Espejo may have discovered copper deposits near modern Jerome as early as 1582. In 1854 a group of miners including Frederick Ronstadt and Peter Brady stumbled across skeletons with ore bags moldering at the bottom of a shaft near modern Ajo. Because the "ruby" ore was so rich, their Arizona Mining & Trading Company even began freighting the copper across the desert to Yuma, where it was transported by ship to Swansea, Wales, and sold for $360 a ton. But when the ruby ore petered out, all but a few desert rats like Tom Childs and Rube Daniells abandoned the Ajo area. Most of Arizona's ore remained in the ground until the Industrial Revolution and the Electrical Age made copper an essential element of the modern world.

The first significant operation sprang up along Chase Creek in the upper Gila River drainage. In 1864 a prospector named Henry Clifton rediscovered veins of copper ore that Mexican prospectors had found in the early nineteenth century. Clifton never filed on the deposits because the area was too dangerous to mine, but six years later Robert Metcalf staked claims to the outcrops of copper carbonate there. Metcalf then sold controlling interest in the claims to the merchants Henry and Charles Lesinsky, who formed the Longfellow Copper Mining Company in Las Cruces, New Mexico.

The first thing the Lesinskys did was to recruit Mexican miners who knew how to smelt copper in the traditional fashion. Then they set up a camp called

Clifton in a canyon where Chase Creek and the San Francisco River came together. During those early years, Clifton was a "rawhide" operation that made do with the materials on hand. Burros carried the ore from the Longfellow Mine five miles down the side of a mountain to the smelter, which was built of adobe and fueled by mesquite charcoal. Then freight wagons hauled the copper 1,200 miles across New Mexico and the Great Plains to Kansas City, Missouri along the Santa Fe Trail. "Sometimes teamsters left Clifton with their loads of copper, and were never heard of again," wrote Scottish mining engineer James Colquhoun. "A few dead bodies, and the wreck of a plundered wagon, told the tale to the teamsters who followed."

But even though isolation and Apache raids plagued the Longfellow, Clifton developed into the largest mining community in Arizona during the 1870s. "They employ some 200 men at the mine and works, principally Mexicans, and a considerable number of freighters and coalburners in the mountains adjacent," reported the *Arizona Star* on April 25, 1878. The workers received two dollars a day, usually in promissory notes "printed on stout red cloth, and payable entirely in merchandise at the company's store in Clifton" or Lesinsky's emporium in Silver City. "Often the company lost money on the copper they shipped, but these losses were more than offset by the profits on the stores," Colquhoun recalled. "Had it not been for the stores the enterprise could not have existed."

During the late 1870s, a few small copper mines opened in other parts of the territory. M. A. Ruffner and the McKinnon brothers worked the Eureka and Wade Hampton claims in Jerome east of Prescott. Silver miners dabbled in copper near Globe, Superior, and Ray—areas which, like Clifton, had originally been included within the first enormous Apache reservation and then withdrawn. But the richest discoveries were made in the Mule Mountains just north of the international border, where the community of Bisbee developed. Bisbee's mines yielded more gold and silver than any other Arizona mining district, but their most important product was copper—nearly eight billion pounds of it—making Bisbee one of the leading copper producers in the world. The discoveries became the foundation of a corporate empire that dominated Arizona politics until World War II.

Bisbee's beginnings, on the other hand, were anything but corporate. In 1877 government scout Jack Dunn and Lieutenant J. A. Rucker staked a gold and silver claim in a manzanita-choked canyon called Mule Gulch. The two military men then grubstaked prospector George Warren to work the mine and to look for other mines as well. The deal they struck was simple. In return for bankrolling Warren, Dunn was supposed to have his name included on every claim. But

Warren, who was often drunk, conveniently forgot to list his backer on any of the new discoveries, including the north side of an outcrop that soon became known as Copper Queen Hill. Not that Warren made a fortune off the Copper Queen either. In 1878 the prospector bet a drinking buddy his share of the Copper Queen that he could outrace a horse in a two-hundred-yard dash. Warren lost, the Copper Queen passed into other hands, and Bisbee took shape in a cloud of double-dealing and booze.

Clearer heads and deeper pockets soon made drifters like Warren little more than footnotes in Bisbee history. A Pennsylvania investor named Edward Reilly purchased the Copper Queen and another claim for $15,000. He then sold 70 percent of the mine to a group of San Francisco investors, who founded the Copper Queen Mining Company and built a smelter in Mule Gulch. By 1880 more than 200 mining claims had been filed in the area. Named after DeWitt Bisbee, the attorney of the Copper Queen owners, the young settlement soon had a population of 500 people served by a post office, a restaurant, a mercantile store, a brewery, and four saloons.

During the early years, Bisbee suffered the same fears as other frontier settlements. Children in the first school learned "the Indian drill," taking refuge in the tunnel of the Copper Queen Mine whenever the whistle of its hoisting works blew four blasts to signal the approach of Apache raiders. But the discovery of a immense body of ore on Copper Queen Hill—sixty feet in diameter and four hundred feet deep—kept money and miners flowing into the hilly little community. The high-grade carbonate even captured the attention of James Douglas, who was managing the plant in Pennsylvania that refined the copper. In 1881 the metal importing firm of Phelps, Dodge & Company asked Douglas whether it should build a copper smelter in Long Island Sound. Douglas told them instead about the Copper Queen. The conservative company took a chance and commissioned Douglas to investigate mines in southern Arizona, including those at Bisbee and Clifton-Morenci.

One of Douglas's first recommendations was to buy the Detroit Copper Company of Morenci, which Phelps Dodge did in 1881. A year later the company purchased the Atlanta mine in Bisbee next to the Copper Queen. For the next two years, Douglas sank shafts and dug tunnels that did nothing but suck up Phelps Dodge funds. By the summer of 1884 the company was ready to abandon the venture. Even the great ore body of the Copper Queen was pinching out. For a time it looked as if Bisbee was going to follow in the footsteps of its silver sister, Tombstone.

Then both Phelps Dodge and the Copper Queen tapped right into a large vein. Douglas reached it from above, and the Copper Queen drifted in from the west. At first, conflicting claims and uncertain mining laws threatened to pit the two companies against each other and squander the resources of both in expensive litigation. After months of negotiations, however, Phelps Dodge bought out the major owners of the Copper Queen and merged the two firms. Douglas became president of the new Copper Queen Consolidated Mining Company and proceeded to buy up most of the contiguous claims. The first link in Arizona's copper collar was being forged.

*   *   *   ### The Expansion of the Copper Industry

In the years that followed, Bisbee set the pattern for the copper industry in Arizona. Phelps Dodge weathered a depression in copper prices and discovered the huge Atlanta ore body in 1886. In 1887 the Copper Queen built a new smelter with four furnaces and produced nine million pounds of copper the following year. But that was only the beginning. As the grade of the ore decreased, Douglas enlarged his furnaces. As the mines burrowed deeper and the carbonate ores changed to sulphides, he introduced the Bessemer converting process pioneered in Montana. Between 1885 and 1908, the Copper Queen yielded more than 730 million pounds of copper and 30 million dollars in dividends. That made it one of the richest copper mines in the world.

An article in the *Bisbee Daily Review* in 1903 conveys the immensity of the operation. "Think of the distance between Chicago and St. Louis! Or two and a half times the distance between New York and Philadelphia and you have nearly the underground workings of the Copper Queen mine. Over one hundred and fifty miles of track are down there, and a hundred miles more in which there is no track at all, all lighted by electricity, and hundreds of men are to be found in every nook and crevice of the workings every hour of the day in the year."

Until the early twentieth century, Phelps Dodge was the only game in town. One of the few claims Douglas failed to purchase was the Irish Mag, which later spawned the Calumet and Arizona Mining Company, another of Arizona's leading copper producers. During the 1890s, however, title to the Irish Mag bounced from common-law wife to saloon keeper after its owner, a drunken brawler named James Daly, murdered a constable and fled to Mexico. For nearly two decades, then, Douglas—refined, well-educated, and trained as a Presbyterian minister—put his paternalistic stamp on the town.

Other personalities dominated other copper colonies. One of the most ruthless was William A. Clark of Butte, Montana. Clark spent most of his career fighting the "War of the Copper Kings" with Augustus Heinze and Marcus Daly to control Butte. He also poured millions of dollars into Montana politics, eventually bribing enough members of the state legislature to buy himself a U.S. senatorship in the days when state legislatures still elected senators. But ore samples from the United Verde Copper Company in Jerome impressed Clark at the New Orleans exposition in 1884. Three years later he sent his superintendent, Joseph Giroux, to examine the mine. When Giroux arrived, Phelps Dodge had already taken an option on the property, but then the sellers suddenly raised their price by $300,000. Phelps Dodge dropped their option, and Clark immediately picked it up, buying 70 percent of the stock. By the time he died in 1925, the calculating little ex-schoolteacher and his family owned 95 percent of the United Verde.

The key to his success was securing enough capital to build the transportation network the United Verde needed in order to survive. The company's original investors went broke because it cost them twenty dollars a ton to haul their ore sixty miles from Jerome to Ash Fork, the nearest station along the Santa Fe Railroad. In 1893, however, the Santa Fe, Prescott and Phoenix Railway connected the Santa Fe with Prescott and the new territorial capital of Phoenix, so Clark built his narrow-gauge United Verde & Pacific Railway between Jerome and Prescott the following year. On Christmas Day in 1896 the *Arizona Republican* dubbed it "the crookedest line in the world," and travelers joked about being able to converse with the engineer from the rear coach as the train swung around curves. Yet that curvy line destroyed the tyranny of the freight wagon and allowed Jerome to develop into one of the major copper towns in the West.

In the process, Clark amassed immense wealth—more than 100 million dollars from United Verde copper alone. Mining historian Thomas Rickard called the United Verde "the richest mine ever owned by an individual" because Clark never sold any of its shares on any stock exchange in the country. Unlike Douglas, Clark was a copper baron, not a company man.

But if Phelps Dodge was the prototype of the powerful corporation and Clark of the swashbuckling tycoon, other copper colonies found their own mix of investment and management. The Clifton-Morenci district boasted three major operations by the turn of the century. Phelps Dodge owned the Detroit Copper Company in Morenci. The Shannon Consolidated Copper Company ran Metcalf. Meanwhile, the Arizona Copper Company controlled Clifton, the oldest copper town in Arizona, producing 870 million pounds of copper between 1873 and 1921.

Perhaps no firm better reflected the importance of rail transport to the copper industry than Arizona Copper, which was owned by a group of investors based in Edinburgh, Scotland. The new owners purchased Henry Lesinsky's Longfellow Mining Company from a speculator named Frank Underwood in 1882. Their first project was to construct a 36-inch narrow-gauge railway between Clifton and Lordsburg, New Mexico, on the Southern Pacific line. It was an enormously expensive undertaking—$1,542,275 for seventy-one miles— but when the Arizona and New Mexico Railway reached Clifton in 1884, the railway could carry twenty tons of copper bullion and thirty-two tons of coke each day.

Rail transport became even more important as richer ores disappeared, leaving ore that was only 3 or 4 percent metal. James Colquhoun, who took over as general manager of Arizona Copper in 1892, introduced new ways of concentrating lower-grade ores. By 1901, according to Clifton historian James Patton, "the Arizona Copper Company was producing almost ten thousand tons of copper a year from copper ore which a few years before had been thought useless." Soon other copper companies were plunging into the railroad business themselves.

Phelps Dodge jumped in the deepest, taking on both the Southern Pacific and the Santa Fe. In 1889, Phelps Dodge financed the Arizona and South Eastern Rail Road, which connected Bisbee with the Santa Fe's New Mexico and Arizona Railroad at Fairbanks on the San Pedro River. Five years later it built a parallel line from Fairbanks to Benson after the Santa Fe raised its rates and sneered that it was not running its railroad "for the benefit of the Copper Queen." The new Phelps Dodge line quickly captured most of the Santa Fe's business in southern Arizona and northern Sonora, making the Santa Fe subsidiary obsolete. Copper companies may have depended upon the railroads, but the railroads needed to haul copper in order to turn a profit. Railroad men would learn and relearn that lesson in the years to come.

When they did not learn it fast enough, Phelps Dodge played railroad showdown once again. In 1900 the Southern Pacific refused its request to build a line to its new smelter town of Douglas on the Arizona-Sonora border, so Phelps Dodge created the El Paso & Southwestern Railroad to transport its ore directly to El Paso, the major smelting center in the Southwest. The Southern Pacific raised tariffs and blocked the tracks, but Phelps Dodge retaliated by locking Southern Pacific crews in boxcars and pushing its line east. "They [the Southern

Pacific] may put us to some expense," James Douglas informed his board of directors, "but the day will come, verily, when they will have to return principal and interest—all they have cost us—or they will not get one pound of freight." Douglas made good on his threat two years later when he forced E. H. Harriman, Huntington's successor at the Southern Pacific, to pay compensation for the cost of building the El Paso & Southwestern line. The war of nerves continued for another two decades until the Southern Pacific finally purchased the El Paso & Southwestern in 1924.

Between 1880 and 1920—the period of greatest railroad building—at least forty-six roads radiated like blood vessels from the two transcontinental arteries. Clark's United Verde & Pacific chugged from Prescott to Jerome in 1894. The Gila Valley, Globe & Northern Railway joined the Old Dominion and other Globe-Miami mines to the Southern Pacific at Bowie between 1894 and 1898. In the decades that followed, railroads chewed into the terrain like giant earthworms wherever new deposits of copper were found: the Twin Buttes Railroad Company southwest of Tucson in 1906, the central Arizona lines of Ray & Gila Valley Railroad in 1910 and Magma Arizona Railroad in 1914, the Tucson, Cornelia & Gila Bend Railroad from Ajo to Gila Bend in 1916. Arizona had 1,678 miles of track by 1912, the year it became a state, and 2,524 miles by 1930, when the Depression began. Most of those tracks led to mines, and most of the mines extracted copper. The copper collar was fastened with iron chains.

✳   ✳   ✳   Labor in the Mines

Railroads were only one side of the industrial equation. Along with transportation networks and expensive machinery, copper mining required a skilled and stable workforce—an essential factor of production that was in short supply along the Arizona frontier. So if copper brought Scottish financiers and Canadian metallurgists to some of the remotest corners of the territory, its working men and women came from even more exotic locales. Native-born Anglo Americans dominated the workforce at first, but immigrants from established mining areas in Germany, Scotland, Ireland, and Cornwall soon moved into the towns sprouting on hillsides above the tunnels. Then, as technological innovations like the pneumatic drill reduced the need for traditional hardrock mining skills, southern and eastern Europeans—Italians, Spaniards, Czechs, Serbs, Montenegrans, and Bohemians—flocked to communities like Bisbee and Jerome. Surrounded by a vast and sparsely populated landscape, the copper towns were miniature models of industrial America, tiny colonies where the immigrant surge from Europe swirled into the Arizona territory. The rest of

Arizona might speak English, Spanish, or Apache, but in Bisbee or Globe the Babel that was then reshaping cities like Cleveland and Chicago could often be heard.

The copper towns were also ethnic battlegrounds. During the early years, most copper mines—like most other businesses in Arizona—depended on Mexican labor. By the late 1870s, for example, most of the several hundred men working in Clifton's mines and smelters were Mexican. Because of Apache hostilities, however, it was difficult to attract laborers to the district, so Henry Lesinsky finally took his cue from the Southern Pacific and imported Chinese laborers. By 1883, 100 of the 400 miners in Clifton were Chinese. According to James Colquhoun, "if occasionally a few were killed no questions were asked, and the work went on as usual."

Such callousness was common among employers of the Chinese. To Mexican and Anglo workers, on the other hand, the Chinese were intolerable rather than expendable. L. C. Hughes, editor of the *Arizona Weekly Star,* expressed the sentiments of many Anglos on July 24, 1879, when he called the Chinese "an ignorant, filthy, leperous horde." On August 4, 1894, *El Fronterizo,* Tucson's largest Spanish-language newspaper, declared that "the Chinaman is a fungus that lives in isolation, sucking the sap of the other plants." With racism fueling the already bitter competition for jobs, violence was inevitable. In railroad camps like Calabasas, Anglo and Mexican workers attacked the Chinese, stealing their money and burning their tents. In Clifton there was so much terrorism and sabotage that Colquhoun and other supervisors were forced to dismiss the Chinese and hire Mexicans and Anglos in their place. Many Chinese remained in Arizona, taking up truck farming or opening small businesses such as laundries, restaurants, and grocery stores. But in the early 1880s, Anglos and Mexicans joined together to drive the Chinese off the railroads and out of the mines.

They then spent the next fifty years fighting one another. During the late nineteenth and early twentieth centuries, ethnic conflict crippled the organized-labor movement in Arizona as divide-and-conquer became a favorite tactic in the war against effective unionization. As Mexican immigration swelled during the reign of Porfirio Díaz and the Mexican Revolution, conflict intensified. Between 1900 and 1910 the Mexican-born population of Arizona more than doubled from 14,172 to 29,452. The decade of the Revolution sent even more *mexicanos* across the border; in Tucson, the number of Hispanics born outside the United States rose from 2,441 to 4,261, an increase of almost 75 percent.

The migrants were part of a great movement northward as peasants lost their traditional communal lands during the Porfiriato and headed for the United States to escape debt peonage or the revolutionary carnage that followed. Labor recruiters known as *enganchadores* "hooked" many of these people and delivered them to U.S. employers. Some came as temporary farm laborers, toiling in the fields until the harvest was over and they were sent back to Mexico. Others were shipped to mining camps across the West. Companies frequently employed Mexicans to break strikes, including the bitter struggle in the Colorado coalfields organized by the Western Federation of Miners in 1903 and 1904. The presence of Mexican scabs infuriated Anglo workers, hardening their attitudes toward people they already mistrusted and misunderstood. Many labor organizers therefore ignored Mexican miners or turned them into scapegoats to win the support of Anglo workers.

By the late nineteenth century, two other responses to Mexican labor had evolved as well. One was the segregation of mining communities into "white men's" and "Mexican" camps. There were relatively few Mexican miners in the Globe-Miami mining district. Clifton-Morenci, in contrast, retained its predominantly Mexican labor force. The copper towns may have been ethnic melting pots for Europeans, but the boundaries between Anglos and Mexicans remained strong.

The other response was a differential wage scale for Anglo and Mexican miners. During the 1890s, the lowest wage in the Old Dominion and other Globe-Miami mines was $3.00 a day. In Clifton-Morenci, Mexicans received $1.75 to $2.00 for a ten-hour shift. The difference in wages only increased after the turn of the century. By 1910, Anglo miners were making $4.00 a day or more in most Arizona copper towns, but Mexican wages leveled out at $2.00 a day and stayed there for several decades. No other figure reveals more dramatically the systematic subordination of Mexican labor.

What was happening was brutally clear: Arizona was creating an economic pecking order organized largely along ethnic lines. At the top were the owners and managers of the railroads, copper mines, and land-and-cattle companies, all of whom were Anglo Americans or Northern Europeans. In the middle were businessmen, ranchers, and farmers, mostly Anglo but also a few prominent Mexicans such as the Aguirre brothers and Leopoldo Carrillo. At the bottom were people who had only their own labor to sell. Anglos dominated most skilled-labor positions in the mines and on the railroads. Mexicans laid track, ran cattle, picked cotton, and hauled ore. Between 1900 and 1920 in Tucson, the percentage of white-collar workers in the Anglo workforce rose from 44.6 percent to 61.5 percent. Among Mexicans, in contrast, the proportion of white-collar workers climbed from only 22 to 28 percent. Meanwhile, Mexicans constituted 68 percent of Tucson's so-called "unskilled" labor force even though Anglos composed 63 percent of the city's population. During the first two decades of the twentieth century, boundaries of race and class became rigid on all levels of Arizona's economic hierarchy.

✳   ✳   ✳   Early Labor Struggles

A major confrontation between labor and management occurred in 1896, when the owners of the Old Dominion mine in Globe tried to weaken those boundaries by lowering Anglo wages to Mexican levels. The conflict began when S. A. Parnell, the new supervisor of the Old Dominion, hired a foreman from Morenci named Alexander McClain. McClain was known as a good "Mexican pusher"—a boss who could use Mexican labor effectively. First, McClain and his supervisor dropped wages for shovelers and car men from $3.00 a day to $2.25. Then they began replacing Anglo workers with Mexican nationals. Soon afterward, 200 miners held a meeting in the Globe courthouse and vowed to keep the community a "white man's town." They marched to the home of Parnell and hauled him out into the street at gunpoint, throwing a rope over his head. Parnell fired McClain and his Mexican workers the next day. He himself resigned shortly thereafter.

Flushed with this initial victory, the miners also voted to join the Western Federation of Miners (WFM), the largest and strongest union in the West. It was the first WFM local in the territory, so Globe quickly won the reputation as the stronghold of labor unrest in Arizona. But the victory of the Anglo miners was not complete. The day after the vote, the owners of the Old Dominion shut down the mine and locked out the pro-union workers. They also pressured the territorial governor to declare martial law. The strikers weathered the lockout and eventually forced the owners to restore wages to former levels. Nevertheless, the Globe strike set two ugly precedents—the coalition between mine owners and law enforcement, and the antagonism between Anglo and Mexican miners—that plagued the Arizona labor movement during the early twentieth century.

Mexican miners carried out the next major strike in Arizona despite being ignored by the WFM and other unions. In 1903 the twenty-second territorial legislature passed an act reducing the workday for underground miners from ten to eight hours with no cut in pay. The law went into effect on June 1. The next day, mine owners in Clifton-Morenci complied by shortening shifts but only agreed to pay their miners for nine hours of work. The result was a 10 percent drop in the daily wage.

Colquhoun and other managers in the district must have reasoned that since most of their workers were Mexicans or recent Italian immigrants, they would docilely accept the pay cut just as they had accepted the differential wage scale. But to the surprise of nearly everyone, several thousand Mexican and Italian miners immediately went on strike. Because the wFM and other labor organizations refused to admit them, they coordinated the strike through their *mutualistas,* or mutual-aid societies. They blocked tunnels, prevented ore from being loaded onto railroad cars, and brought one of Arizona's largest mining districts to a complete halt. By June 3, Clifton-Morenci's mines and smelters had shut down, throwing 3,500 men out of work. Contrary to the stereotype, Mexican miners, not the Western Federation of Miners, carried out the most significant strike in the Arizona territory before World War I.

But nature and Arizona's power structure conspired against them. On June 6, Governor Alexander Brodie called out the Arizona Rangers, a paramilitary organization that had been created in 1901 to patrol the border and prevent cattle rustling. Three days later, 2,000 miners defied the rangers and paraded through Morenci in a torrential downpour, many of them armed with rifles, pistols, or knives. The determination of the strikers terrified the sheriff of Graham County, who pleaded with Brodie for more help. Brodie asked President Theodore Roosevelt for federal troops, so six companies of the National Guard marched into town. It was the largest military force assembled in Arizona since the Apache campaigns of the 1880s. By June 12, Clifton-Morenci had become occupied territory under martial law.

It was also nearly under water. Early June is usually one of the driest times of the year in Arizona, but in 1903 the summer monsoons arrived early, as if they, too, worked for the copper companies. On June 9, soon after the miners' protest parade, floodwaters surged down Chase Creek and the San Francisco River. Retaining dams broke. Houses and businesses washed away. As many as fifty people died. With their relatives missing and their town buried in mud, the defiant euphoria of the strikers quickly suffocated as well. When the federal troops arrived, the miners surrendered their weapons and watched sullenly as the National Guard arrested their leaders. Ten Mexicans and Italians were later convicted of rioting and sentenced to the Yuma territorial prison even though no riot took place.

At the height of the strike, the wFM president, Charles Moyer, proclaimed, "The men of Morenci have the full support of the Western Federation of Miners," but those words were the only assistance the strikers received. The grudging admiration of the wFM soon fell victim to internal conflicts within the union itself, where "inclusionists," who favored organizing Mexican and southern European miners, quarreled with "exclusionists," who wanted to halt the recruitment of Mexican, Spanish, Italian, and Slavic immigrants. And since copper companies imported Mexican scabs to break Anglo strikes and Anglo scabs to break Mexican strikes, ethnic hostility escalated. In the town of Christmas, a small mining community near Ray, 300 Mexican miners grabbed their guns and tried to capture an Anglo deputy sheriff after he had shot and killed a Mexican miner. Anglo miners defended the sheriff, and a "bloody race war" almost erupted (*Bisbee Daily Review,* April 14, 1907). By the end of the decade, exclusionists dominated wfm locals in Jerome and Globe, where they fought to end the employment of Mexicans and southern Europeans. Such divisiveness played into the hands of the copper companies. Strike after strike sputtered and died.

✳ ✳ Labor and the Fight for Statehood

If outright confrontation often failed, however, labor pursued other strategies to attain its goals. Competition for skilled labor forced most of the copper companies to increase wages for underground miners, mechanics, and engineers. As a result, skilled and semiskilled workers in nonunion Bisbee usually made as much as their counterparts in union Globe-Miami. It was the unskilled laborers who suffered because they could be easily replaced.

Organized labor also entered the political arena. During most of the territorial period, large corporations dominated Arizona politics, and bribery was a common practice. George W. P. Hunt, the most successful politician of the era, stated that a governor's veto could be purchased for $2,000, and railroads and copper companies employed early prototypes of professional lobbyists disguised as administrators to manipulate territorial legislatures. One of the most colorful was Henry J. Allen, who worked for William Clark and the United Verde Copper Company. Once, in the late 1890s, someone apparently marked the money Allen used to bribe representatives during a legislative assembly. As the marked bills began to surface, Allen claimed that he had spent the money to buy mules for the United Verde. Thereafter, the session was known as the "mule legislature."

The foremost goal of the corporations was to keep their taxes down—a goal they pursued with great success. At the turn of the century, mines worth an estimated $100 million were officially valued at only $2 million. Much of the vast domain granted to the Santa Fe Railroad remained untaxed or undervalued, especially the unsurveyed portions, while new railroads were often exempted from taxation for ten years or more. This rankled many Arizonans, especially the small businessmen and property owners who paid the lion's share of the territory's taxes. In January 1899, newly reappointed Governor Nathan O.

Murphy tried to mobilize this resentment by urging tax reform in his opening address to the twentieth legislative assembly, but Allen and his fellow lobbyists easily turned back Murphy's charge. The legislature defeated a bill to reinstate a bullion tax on minerals. It also squashed attempts to regulate the hours of underground miners, to prohibit the issuance of scrip rather than legal tender by any mining company or company store, and to create the office of mine inspector. With the exception of the twenty-second legislative assembly, which established an eight-hour day for underground workers and required the payment of money rather than scrip for labor, territorial legislatures rarely supported the goals of working men and women. Organized labor therefore concluded that no significant reforms would ever be enacted as long as Arizona remained a territory.

The result was a strong but evanescent coalition of populists, progressives, and labor leaders who joined the statehood crusade. The coalition had to defeat many powerful enemies. Many Republicans in the U.S. Senate feared that the predominantly Democratic territory would send two Democratic senators to Washington. Other opponents argued that neither "the desert sands of Arizona" nor "the humble Spanish-speaking people of New Mexico" were ready for statehood. But the pressure for statehood was too great, so Republican Albert J. Beveridge of Indiana, chairman of the Senate committee on territories, proposed an ingenious solution to the dilemma: to admit Arizona and New Mexico as one state, just as they had been one territory until 1863. New Mexico was larger, with a population of 195,310 people compared to Arizona's 122,931. More to the point, it usually voted Republican. By joining the two territories, Republicans hoped to keep control of the Senate by creating one huge state in the Southwest.

Arizonans reacted with an indignation that was as much racist as righteous— an indignation the newspapers controlled by the railroads and copper companies carefully stoked. The majority of New Mexico's population was Hispanic, and an entrenched Hispanic oligarchy wielded considerable power. Arizona, on the other hand, had fewer Hispanics, and they were practically disenfranchised except in a few strongholds like Tucson and Florence. As one senator from South Carolina proclaimed, Arizona's opposition to joint statehood was "a cry of a pure blooded white community against the domination of a mixed breed aggregation of citizens of New Mexico, who are Spaniards, Indians, Greasers, Mexicans, and everything else."

Organized labor shared this racist revulsion to joint statehood and viewed individual statehood as a chance to prohibit "alien" labor in Arizona. In November 1906 the two territories voted on the issue. New Mexicans strongly supported joint statehood by a margin of 26,195 to 14,735. Arizonans overwhelmingly renounced it by an even greater margin of 16,265 to 3,141. Joint statehood died with that vote. From then on, the battle was to shape the kind of state Arizona would inevitably become.

✳ ✳ The Constitutional Convention and the Fight Against Mexican Labor

Labor played a pivotal role in the struggle. On June 20, 1910, after its passage by both houses of Congress, President William Howard Taft signed the Enabling Act to admit Arizona and New Mexico as separate states. Governor Richard E. Sloan immediately set up an election to select fifty-two delegates to a constitutional convention. Republicans, a minority in Arizona, argued that the constitution would have to be conservative in order to secure statehood under a Republican administration in Washington. Other factions wanted to wrest control of Arizona politics from the large corporations and called for a progressive charter that would place as much power as possible in the hands of the voters themselves. An emerging coalition of anticorporation forces therefore championed constitutional provisions guaranteeing the initiative, the referendum, and the recall of all public officials, including judges, who were often controlled by the copper companies and the railroads.

Labor was the strongest element in that coalition, with large and disciplined blocks of voters in Bisbee-Douglas, Globe-Miami, and the mining communities of Yavapai County. Before that coalition solidified, however, union leaders seriously contemplated forming their own labor party. In addition to the initiative, referendum, and recall, they envisioned a whole series of prolabor provisions including an eight-hour day, employer's liability, workmen's compensation, the abolition of child labor, and an anti-injunction law. Engineers, machinists, carpenters, blacksmiths, and miners all met in Phoenix in July 1910 to hammer out their platform.

Democrats viewed the creation of a third party with great alarm. "The labor party formed here," argued the *Arizona Daily Star* on July 15, 1910, "bears the ear marks of a ruse put forward by the republican bosses to take away strength from the democratic party in the territory and at the same time insure the defeat of those measures which the workingmen are contending for." Democratic leaders like George W. P. Hunt of Globe therefore made a deal with the unions: The labor party would back Democratic candidates if the Democrats incorporated labor provisions into their own platform. The result was the most successful progressive alliance in Arizona politics.

Progressives won their first victory when it was determined that delegates would be elected by county rather than at-large. That allowed Democrats to sweep the race, electing forty-one of the fifty-two delegates. Yavapai, Gila, and Cochise counties sent staunch unionists to the convention, where they were joined by nine progressive merchants and lawyers from Maricopa County who were jealous of the copper companies' stranglehold on territorial politics. Democrats won every county except rural Coconino (which was controlled by Flagstaff businessmen and ranchers) and Pima (which was dominated by the Southern Pacific). The Democrats then elected George W. P. Hunt president of the convention, who promptly appointed Democrats as chairmen of all twenty-four standing committees. The corpulent politician also wheeled and dealed behind the scenes while presiding over the sessions "in the manner of a stoic, benign Buddha—if one can picture Buddha with a splendid handlebar moustache," observed fellow Gila County delegate Jacob Weinberger. And when Hunt was busy, vice-president Morris Goldwater of Prescott took over, defusing many volatile arguments with his fairness and sense of humor. Arizona soon had a constitution as liberal as the Oregon and Oklahoma charters upon which it was modeled.

Not surprisingly, labor got much of what it wanted. Article 18 established an eight-hour day and prohibited child labor. It also forbade blacklists or the waiver of employees' rights to seek damages because of injuries on the job. Employers were liable for the protection of workers in hazardous occupations, and workmen's compensation for any occupational injuries became compulsory. Article 19 created the office of state mine inspector. Furthermore, the initiative, referendum, and recall—including the recall of judges, which Taft vowed to veto—all passed by large margins. Union leaders were particularly pleased with this last victory because they believed that judges almost always sided with the corporations in labor-management disputes.

Despite these victories, however, labor lost its fight to legalize picketing and the boycott. More seriously, delegates indefinitely postponed a vote on a provision that would prevent judges from issuing writs of injunction, which were used to halt strikes and other labor protests. Judges therefore continued to have the authority to serve as powerful tools of the copper companies and the railroads.

But labor's greatest failure was the collapse of its crusade to restrict "alien" labor in Arizona. Most union leaders considered Mexican workers the Achilles' heel of the organized labor movement in the Southwest. In their opinion, Mexicans broke strikes, worked for lower wages, and endangered other workers because they did not speak English (a racist assumption with no basis in the accident records of the mines that employed them). And there were always thousands more just across the border, ready to pour into the copper towns whenever the corporations needed to crush the unions. Despite the Clifton-Morenci strike of 1903 and the bloody strike in Cananea, Sonora, three years later, labor leaders insisted that Mexicans could not be organized, so they tried to write a constitution that banned most Mexican labor in Arizona.

The first of these exclusionary measures was Proposition 48, which stated that no one who was not a citizen or had not declared his intention of becoming a citizen could be employed on any public project at the state, county, or municipal level. Mexican road construction workers, whom labor wanted to replace with union men, were the primary targets. John Orme, a farmer from Maricopa County, attacked the proposition by stating, "They [Anglo American workers] won't get down in those holes and work all day in and day out." Michael Cunniff of Yavapai County retorted, "If the right salary is paid, they will get American labor where they are now compelled to take Mexican or Indian." The same arguments had been advanced in the debate over Chinese labor on the railroads in the 1880s, and they would be repeated over and over again during labor-management struggles in the years to come. At the constitutional convention, however, Proposition 48 squeaked through by five votes only after Hunt amended it to allow wards of the state—Native Americans and prisoners—to be employed on public projects as well.

Labor was not as successful during the next two rounds. Cunniff, one of the most radical unionists at the convention, introduced Proposition 89, which prohibited the importation of alien contract laborers. After pointing out that federal laws already restricted such labor, opponents of the measure tabled it indefinitely. Labor then unleashed its ultimate weapon: Proposition 91, which prohibited anyone who could not "speak the English language" from working in "underground or other hazardous occupations." It also forbade any "individual, firm, corporation, or association" from employing "alien labor" as more than 20 percent of its workforce. In other words, Mexicans, Italians, and other non-English-speaking immigrants could not work in the mines or as brakemen or engineers on the railroads. Moreover, Mexican nationals could not constitute more than 20 percent of any ranch's cowboys, any lumber company's mill workers, or any farm's field hands. According to a U.S. Immigration Commission study in 1911, 60 percent of Arizona's smelter workers were Mexicans, half of whom had been in the United States less than five years. There are no reliable figures for the agricultural sector, but the percentage of Mexicans on farms and ranches was undoubtedly higher. Proposition 91 therefore threatened not just Mexican labor but the entire foundation of Arizona's extractive economy.

Not surprisingly, the coalition between labor and its allies quickly weakened. Realizing that their own access to cheap labor would be restricted, farmers and ranchers backed away from the 20 percent clause, while other delegates attacked the "English language" stipulation. Lamar Cobb, a mining engineer from Clifton, pointed out that most mines in his district, the second-largest copper producer in Arizona, would have to shut down because "one-half of the men employed underground cannot speak the English language intelligibly." Proponents backpedaled by arguing that Proposition 91 was a safety measure rather than an anti-Mexican measure. A. F. Tuthill, a physician from Morenci, responded by stating that Clifton-Morenci's "percentage of accidents was lowest in the Territory and we employed Mexicans." Thomas Wills, a rancher from Pinal County, declared his opposition to the measure because cowpunching might be considered a "hazardous occupation." When the roll was finally called, Proposition 91 died by a margin of twenty-six votes to nineteen.

❋   ❋   ❋   Racism, Reaction, and the "Golden Age" of Arizona Labor

The defeat of Proposition 91 revealed the weakness of what historian James Byrkit has called the "labor-bourgeois coalition." Demanding more taxes from corporations or supporting direct-democracy measures such as the initiative and referendum did not affect the running of a small firm, ranch, or farm. But choking off Arizona's supply of cheap labor threatened most businesses regardless of their size. Delegates voted their progressive ideals until their own livelihoods were affected. They also backed away from any provision that would have seriously damaged the copper industry. Even though industry representatives railed against "socialists" and "radicals" at the convention, the Arizona Constitution was a progressive, not a radical document.

Labor pursued its goals with greater success among Arizona voters themselves. Taft vetoed the constitution because it allowed for the recall of judges, so voters dropped the provision and Arizona became the forty-eighth state on February 14, 1912. Nine months later the citizens of the new state flexed their muscles by restoring the recall of judges through a referendum vote of 16,272 to 3,705. In the opinion of the corporations, "red-eyed" radicalism was running rampant.

The "radical" trend—along with the fight to limit Mexican labor—continued for the next few years. In 1909, the year before the constitutional convention, the twenty-fifth territorial legislature severely limited Mexican political power in Arizona by passing a literacy law over the veto of Governor Joseph Kibbey. The law prohibited the registration of any voter who could not read a section of the United States Constitution or write his own name (the new state constitution gave women the right to vote in 1912). Supported by Democrats and labor, the law disenfranchised many Mexicans, who generally voted Republican. As a result, the only Mexican elected to the constitutional convention was Carlos Jácome, a prosperous businessman from Tucson. He and the other four delegates from Pima County were all Republicans.

After statehood, the unions took their fight against Mexican labor to the voters. In 1914 they used the initiative to resuscitate the provision that 80 percent of the employees of any individual or firm had to be "qualified electors or native born citizens of the United States." The copper companies and railroads opposed the initiative, as did hundreds of Mexican miners across the state. In the words of the pro–Southern Pacific *Tucson Citizen* of July 18, 1914, "the proposed eighty per cent law is dangerous and paralyzing to industry and also discriminatory." But most citizens of the state agreed with the *Arizona Labor Journal* of July 3, 1914, which muttered darkly about "an unemployed army ranging into the thousands" and warned that Arizona "cannot assimilate untold hordes of aliens." The initiative passed by an overwhelming margin of 10,694 votes. What labor could not win at the convention it won in the ballot boxes.

Or so it thought. Although the primary goal of the law was to restrict Mexican labor, it affected other noncitizens as well. Both the British and the Italian ambassadors to the United States protested its passage, and in December 1914 an Austrian cook in Bisbee named Mike Raich sued to keep from being fired under the new law. Raich was represented by corporation attorneys from Bisbee and Tucson, who took the case to the U.S. District Court in San Francisco. The court ruled that the law violated the 14th Amendment, and the U.S. Supreme Court upheld the decision on November 1, 1915. That turned out to be the stake driven through the 80-percent law's heart.

Between 1912 and 1916, however, the unions and their allies controlled state politics. They elected Hunt as the first governor of Arizona in 1912 and reelected him two years later. They also controlled both houses of the state legislature, which regulated railroads, mandated workmen's compensation, employer's liability, and mine safety, and created a state tax commission with broad powers to make the copper companies and other corporations pay their fair share of Arizona's taxes. The legislature even approved an anti-injunction law that gave workers the right to assemble and to picket. The U.S. Supreme Court eventually struck down that law, but not until 1921.

The WFM and other unions also organized a round of strikes in 1915—strikes in which, for the first time, Mexican and Anglo workers joined together to achieve common goals. The first broke out in Miami, where a coalition of groups that included WFM Local 70, several American Federation of Labor skilled-trade locals, and the "Comité por Trabajadores en General" (General Workers' Committee) forced the mining companies to adopt the famous "Miami scale," which tied wages to the wholesale price of copper in New York. The second took place in the town of Ray, where Mexicans and Anglos had squared off against one another the year before and as many as sixteen people had died. Mexican workers demanded the Miami scale. The Ray Consolidated Copper Company responded by threatening to hire more Anglos. The Mexican strikers held firm and won a wage increase slightly below the Miami scale. Further, since WFM Local 70 in Miami strongly supported the strike, many Mexicans at Ray joined the WFM and formed their own Local 72.

The third and largest strike erupted in Clifton-Morenci, where miners were tired of making the lowest wages in the state: $1.92 for muckers, $2.39 for Mexican miners, and $2.89 for Anglo miners, compared to $3.50 per shift or more in the other major districts. Mexican mutual-aid societies coordinated the early resistance, and then both Anglo and Mexican miners asked the WFM to organize the district. Flush with its successes in Miami and Ray, the WFM agreed, even though about two-thirds of the workforce were Mexican. Guy Miller and a Spanish-speaking assistant named A. N. Tribolet arrived in July and began talking to small bands of workers at meetings organized by the mutualistas. At one such gathering, the Mexican miners interrupted him, shouting, "We can't understand you! Speak in Spanish!" Intentionally or unintentionally, it was a sardonic commentary on the WFM's long "English only" fight in the mines.

The strike itself started on the night of September 11. Most of the 5,000-man workforce walked off the job, shutting down operations in Clifton, Morenci, and Metcalf. In contrast to earlier confrontations, however, this one had the sympathy of key county and state officials. James Cash, the sheriff of Greenlee County, deputized strikers to protect the mines. Governor Hunt was even more supportive. After mine managers rejected the first proposals of the strikers, Hunt arrived to arrange a compromise. But when the copper companies refused to negotiate, Hunt threw his considerable weight behind the strikers. He appealed to Arizonans to donate money and supplies to the families who were out of work. He called in the National Guard, including forty-seven Apache Indians, to prevent the use of strikebreakers. When the corporations mounted an unsuccessful recall campaign against him, Hunt cranked up his populist rhetoric to a fever pitch. "'Truth crushed to earth shall rise again' despite the scoundrelly connivance of 'foreign capitalists' or the lecherous lying of their prostitute press," he roared in a pamphlet distributed to voters. Meanwhile, behind the scenes Hunt worked tirelessly to bring the two sides together.

When the strike was finally settled after five months in January 1916, labor across the nation hailed it as a major victory. The *Kansas City Post* of February 8, 1916, declared the settlement "a triumph for labor of the greatest importance, demonstrating as it does that labor can win its battles for industrial democracy when the government does its duty and protects the workers." The *Arizona Labor Journal* of February 3, 1916, was more vitriolic. "After a five months' shutdown of their property, after becoming thoroughly convinced that neither Sheriff Cash of Greenlee County nor the Governor would permit them to import thugs and murderers, and after an approximate cost and loss to their property of $15,000 per day," the journal crowed, "the arrogance of the petty would-be satraps had somewhat cooled and they have now most willingly agreed that all the difficulties over which the strike occurred should be adjudicated by arbitration, as well as agreeing to a raise in wages of from 20 to 70 percent."

There was some reason for the euphoria. On January 26, the mines' 5,000 workers went back to work with a sliding scale of wage increases pegged to the price of copper. Unskilled laborers who had made $1.92 a shift in September 1915 were making $3.08 by March. During the same period, the wages of skilled miners rose from $2.89 to $4.08. Moreover, the differential pay scale for Anglo and Mexican workers was abolished. In Miami, Ray, and Clifton-Morenci, the divisions between Anglo and Mexican miners began to weaken.

Nevertheless, the strike was not a complete success. Even though wages rose 39 percent, the price of copper soared 56 percent because of World War I, so profits outstripped wage increases by a considerable margin. The miners also agreed to ban the wfm from the Clifton-Morenci district in return for the right to join any other union. At the height of labor's power, its most successful confrontation with the copper companies was little better than a draw.

✳ ✳ The Bisbee Deportation and the Forging of the Copper Collar

The strike also marked the beginning of a counteroffensive by the copper companies. On September 23, 1915, soon after the strike broke out, two men arrived in Clifton on the same train. One was Charles Moyer, president of the wfm. The other was Walter Douglas, who was soon to become vice-president and then president of Phelps Dodge. By the end of the strike, Moyer and the wfm had been rejected. Douglas, on the other hand, was carefully mapping out a campaign to destroy the power of organized labor in Arizona.

For years the copper companies' deep distrust of one another had kept them from developing a united front. Copper towns were geographically isolated—

little company kingdoms reinforced by company monopolies over commerce through company stores and by company control of local law enforcement agencies, county boards of supervisors, and the territorial judiciary. The absentee nature of corporate ownership aggravated that isolation. Of the three largest copper companies in Clifton-Morenci, Phelps Dodge was headquartered in New York, Shannon Consolidated in Boston, and Arizona Copper in Edinburgh, Scotland. Then there was the maverick William Andrews Clark of Butte, Montana. If proximity was a prerequisite for effective interaction, the copper companies rarely qualified.

Ideological differences also divided many of the owners. Clark threatened to lynch organizers and flood his mines rather than give in to the unions. Jewish investors like the Guggenheims and Lewisohns, on the other hand, sympathized with many worker demands. The Guggenheims controlled the Kennecott and Ray Consolidated mines in central Arizona, while the Lewisohns owned the Miami Copper Company. They were the first to accept the Miami scale and the first to recognize the right of workers to organize independent unions. Because the competition for skilled labor was so intense, their greater tolerance of union demands gave organized labor a wedge in the Arizona copper industry.

The taxation policies of the first Arizona state legislature caused that wedge to strike hard ground. After their success at the constitutional convention, progressives and labor leaders abolished the exemption of "productive" mines from property taxes. The legislators also tripled the assessment of Arizona mines by declaring that assessments were to be based on a mine's "full cash value." In 1913 the mining companies claimed that the value of their mines was $31 million. The new state tax commission assessed them at more than $108 million. According to Byrkit, "No other attack could have created a greater degree of positive mutuality than this slash at their ledgers. Their common enemy had at last made itself dramatically, convincingly manifest."

The result was a multipronged assault on labor and its progressive allies. As World War I drove up the price of copper and created an atmosphere of patriotic hysteria, Walter Douglas and the managers of other copper companies picked apart the "labor-bourgeois coalition." They targeted the Arizona senate and helped elect politicians sympathetic to the corporations. They purchased newspapers or bribed editors to turn public opinion against anticompany forces. By 1915, Phelps Dodge alone controlled Clifton's *Copper Era,* Bisbee's *Daily Review,* Douglas's *International Gazette,* Phoenix's *Arizona Gazette,* and Tucson's *Arizona Daily Star.* They influenced public school curriculums, manipulated lawyers and doctors, and even intervened in church politics to eliminate liberal ministers who stood up to the copper companies. Finally, they attacked Governor Hunt himself. Their recall campaign failed, but wholesale fraud in the 1916 gubernatorial race threw the election to Republican Thomas Campbell by a margin of thirty votes. Hunt demanded a recount, and on December 22, 1917, the Arizona supreme court ruled that Hunt had indeed won the election—by forty-three votes. But by the time Hunt assumed the contested office, the copper companies had already triumphed. The unions were broken. Arizona politics was no longer progressive. The copper collar had been forged.

The decisive battles were fought in the copper towns themselves. The United States and its allies needed copper for shell jackets, cable, wire—all the industrial demands of the war. So the value of Arizona copper production soared, from $40 million in 1910 to $200 million in 1917. Copper, which was selling for 13.4 cents a pound in 1914, was fetching 26.5 cents a pound two years later. Since it cost a company like Phelps Dodge only 9.5 cents a pound to produce the copper, profits were enormous—a staggering $24,030,905 for Phelps Dodge in 1916. These profits gave the corporations tremendous clout.

Even more important was the patriotic fervor sweeping over Arizona and the rest of the nation. When the United States plunged into World War I in the spring of 1917, a fear of industrial sabotage spread across the country. In the mining communities, much of this fear focused upon the Industrial Workers of the World (iww), a loose and anarchic amalgam of miners, loggers, and unskilled laborers better known as the Wobblies. Influenced by socialist and syndicalist doctrines, the iww opposed the war and advocated direct action, including violence and sabotage, in the struggle between labor and management. But the Wobblies' bark was worse than their bite. No member of the iww except Joe Hill was ever convicted of any violent act, and one contemporary student of the organization, Paul Brissenden, concluded, "The Wobblies preach violence without practicing it." Moreover, the iww was easy to infiltrate and was riddled with private detectives acting as *agents provocateurs*. About the only effective role the Wobblies played in the labor movement was a negative one, that of scapegoat for the forces that were trying to destroy unions across the West.

Those forces included Walter Douglas and his colleagues. During the war years, union membership soared throughout the United States. Wartime profits in industries like copper whetted the appetites of many workers for wage increases and better working conditions. When managers refused, strikes broke out with increasing frequency and peaked in 1917, when 4,233 walkouts occurred. Twenty strikes erupted that year in Arizona, most of them in the mining communities. Unfortunately for the miners, however, the Republican Tom Campbell, not George Hunt, was the governor. Copper companies fired many union members even before they went out on strike. When they did, the companies responded with a devastating arsenal of tactics that eviscerated organized labor in Arizona.

The International Union of Mine, Mill, and Smelter Workers (iummsw, the Western Federation of Miners under a new name) called the first strike in Jerome on May 25, 1917. Walkouts followed in Globe, Morenci, and Bisbee in June and July. Company-controlled newspapers attacked the strikes and branded all strikers as seditious Wobblies. Yet card-carrying Wobblies constituted only a small minority of the workers. In Jerome, for example, there were no more than 125 members of the iww among 4,000 miners. Wobblies were little more than specters invoked to inflame old fears.

The copper companies did not stop at sensational journalism. In Bisbee the corporations persuaded Sheriff Henry Wheeler of Cochise County to deputize the Bisbee Citizens' Protective League, which was formed to defend the community against the Wobbly menace. Some 1,600 miners also joined the Workmen's Loyalty League, which vehemently opposed both the iww and the strike. Meanwhile, in Jerome several hundred men, many of whom belonged to the Jerome Miners Union, an affiliate of the iummsw, met in the town's high school on July 9 to take their own action against the Wobblies. At four o'clock the next morning, armed with rifles and pick handles, they scoured the hilly community, seizing 104 suspected members of the iww. Then they held a "trial" on the steps of the United Verde headquarters. A three-man review board headed by the state organizer of the iummsw released thirty-seven men. The rest were herded into two cattle cars provided by the United Verde and shipped to Kingman, more than 160 miles away. None of the "emergency volunteers" who arrested them had been deputized. Due process was not observed. The Jerome police had been notified of the roundup but neither opposed nor participated in it. The Jerome deportation was strictly a vigilante affair.

Vigilante action had official sanction two days later in Bisbee. On July 11, Walter Douglas gave a speech in Globe, where several thousand iummsw strikers had shut down the mines. "There will be no compromise because you cannot compromise with a rattlesnake," Douglas vowed. "That goes for both the International Union and the iww's. . . . I believe the government will be able to show that there is German influence behind this movement. . . . It is up to the individual communities to drive these agitators out as has been done in other communities in the past." Plans for a deportation in Globe were thwarted, however, partly because the unions were much stronger and partly because of the presence of George W. P. Hunt, who was asked by President Woodrow Wilson to act as a "mediator and conciliator" in the strike.

No such mediating presence existed in Bisbee. At 6:30 A.M. on July 12, two thousand "deputies" under the command of Sheriff Wheeler fanned out across town. Wearing white kerchiefs around their arms, just as the vigilantes in Jerome had done, the Loyalty Leaguers and the Protective Leaguers broke down doors and pulled strikers from their beds at gunpoint. Some of those arrested were beaten. Others were robbed. Wives were thrown to the floor and children screamed. One card-carrying Wobbly, James Brew, shot and killed Orson Mc-Crae when he and five deputies burst into Brew's rooming house. Brew died in a hail of gunfire.

An hour later a huge travesty of a parade filed from the Bisbee post office to the ballpark in nearby Warren. Armed guards surrounded the prisoners, who eventually numbered two thousand. Throughout the hot summer morning, line after line of strikers and vigilantes straggled down the road while Sheriff Wheeler spurred them on from an open touring car driven by the local Catholic priest. There was a 7.62 mm Marlin machine gun mounted beside Wheeler. Walter Douglas was nowhere to be seen.

Once inside the ballpark, John Greenway and other mine managers promised the prisoners that they could go back to work if they renounced the strike. More than 800 did so, and they were released. The others jeered as family members shouted at them to "be men with the men" from outside the fence. Then, at about 11 A.M., twenty-three boxcars from the El Paso & Southwestern Railroad pulled into the Warren station, and 1,186 men were jammed into the cars. Only about a third of the deportees actually belonged to the IWW. Nearly 200 vigilantes guarded them from on top of the train.

For the rest of the day and into the evening, the train rolled through the high desert of southeastern Arizona and southwestern New Mexico. The July heat made temperatures inside the cramped boxcars unbearable, but the deportees were only allowed to stretch their legs at Rodeo and Hachita. There were machine guns at the railroad stations and more vigilantes in automobiles on both sides of the track. Walter Douglas had planned his final crackdown well.

The train halted at Hermanas, New Mexico, about twenty miles west of Columbus, where Pancho Villa had staged his famous raid the year before. It was 3 A.M., and most of the deportees had not had a drink of water in fifteen hours. At first the men inside the boxcars heard vigilantes running and shouting on the roofs. Then the sounds disappeared. Slowly the parched and cramped miners staggered out of the cars. Their captors had snatched them from their homes and abandoned them in the middle of the New Mexico desert. They had no food or water, only the clothes on their backs. It was the largest mass kidnapping in Arizona history.

The Bisbee deportation appalled New Mexico and federal officials. President Woodrow Wilson sent the deportees food from El Paso and ordered the army commander at Columbus to set up a camp for them and provide them with rations. For the next two months, most of the deportees remained at Columbus under federal care, where a census revealed that 804 of the 1,003 men in Camp Furlong were foreigners from twenty different nations. Mexicans (268) composed the largest group, followed by Austro-Hungarians (179) and British (149). That made it easier for the vigilantes to convince themselves that they were rounding up alien saboteurs.

For a time it looked like the organizers of the deportation might actually be punished for their actions. The Arizona attorney general and then a federal commission headed by Felix Frankfurter, who later became a justice of the United States Supreme Court, investigated the deportation. The commission condemned it as wholly illegal and recommended that such corporate vigilante action should be recognized as a violation of federal law. On May 15, 1918, the U.S. Department of Justice even indicted twenty-one Bisbee luminaries, including Walter Douglas and Sheriff Wheeler, on charges of conspiracy and kidnapping. Labor leaders and progressives applauded the indictments, but most people in Arizona and across the nation supported the deportation. The Wobbly bogeyman stalked the land, tarring all strikers as traitors.

Meanwhile, Phelps Dodge moved the battle from the streets to the courtroom. Defense attorney E. E. Ellinwood argued that no federal laws had been broken, so the case could only be heard in state courts. Six months later Judge William Morrow of San Francisco agreed, and the U.S. Supreme Court upheld Morrow's decision two years later.

The state of Arizona tried 200 Bisbee residents for kidnapping in 1920, but after three months of testimony, all the defendants were acquitted. "The verdict of the jury is a vindication of the deportation," jury foreman J. O. Calhoun proudly proclaimed. Just like the Camp Grant Massacre, Arizonans supported "frontier justice" even when the frontier was a company town.

A year later, Phelps Dodge created a company union whose constitution could be abrogated by the corporation's board of directors. Other companies quickly followed suit. With a Republican administration back in office in Washington and postwar antibolshevik witch-hunts sweeping the country, the labor-progressive coalition shattered and independent unionism withered and died. The copper kingdom became more of a colonial order than ever before. Even Walter Douglas may have been surprised at how thoroughly he had vanquished his foes.

10

Oases in the Desert

In 1877, Brigham Young, the visionary president of the Church of Jesus Christ of Latter-day Saints, told William Flake to sell everything he owned and take up a mission on the Arizona frontier. With a "sad heart and mental suffering," Flake gave up the prosperous life he had carved for himself in Utah and followed the rugged Mormon wagon road south to the desolate valley of the Little Colorado River. Lucy Hannah Flake, one of his wives, made the trip with him, a trip she was to repeat eight more times before her death in 1900. The journey was long and hard under the best of circumstances, but a diphtheria epidemic that spread from water hole to water hole ravaged that first trek across the Kaibab Plateau. The Flakes' daughters were stricken but survived. Another woman was not so lucky. They found her in a wagon at the base of the Kaibab with a dead baby on her knee. "It had died as she drove the team down the mountain," the Flakes' son Osmer wrote. "Mother prepared the body for burial. Father got a few short boards from the wagons and made a box, the teamsters dug a hole, and we buried her darling in a lonely grave. It looked as though her life too, would go."

There were times when Lucy Flake must have despaired as well. Like the rest of the missionaries called to the Little Colorado, the Flakes belonged to the United Order, a Mormon experiment in communal living. Flake was too much of an individualist to abide life in the United Order communities, however, so he struck out on his own, buying a ranch in the Silver Creek Valley in the White Mountains. The leaders of the mission damned his independence and ostracized the Flakes. The solitude of the frontier would have been even more solitary for Lucy Flake if Apostle Erastus Snow had not taken her husband's side and helped him found the Mormon community of Snowflake.

But even when there were no crises to confront, the relentless activities of daily life wore Lucy down. Between 1878 and 1895 she kept a diary of her life in Arizona. With characteristic terseness, she described her typical routine on the Flakes' spread outside Snowflake. "I will just write my morning chores. Get up turn out my chickens draw a pail of watter, watter hot beds make a fire, put potatoes to cook then brush and sweep half inch of dust off floor and everything, feed three litters of chickens then mix bisquits, get breakfast, milk besides work in the house, and this morning had to go half mile after calves. This is the way of life on the farm."

Tough and unsentimental, Lucy Flake persevered. She took great comfort in the fellowship of other Mormon women, reveling in the "meetings and invited parties" that characterized her life in town during the long, hard winters. She also had a deep faith in God. "I felt depressed in my spirits," she wrote toward the end of her life, "and after I got my ironing done went up to my Dear sister Wests and we talked and then went up stares and poured out our soles in prair we had a glorious feast of prair."

Unlike the agrarian visionaries of her church, however, she found little that was ennobling about life on the farm. Mormon leaders exhorted the Arizona pioneers to find a "little oasis on the desert." But the new land was a harsh one, and little oases were hard to find. Lucy Flake complained about the isolation and the drudgery, yet she was one of the fortunate ones. Her husband was successful, and the Flakes made a permanent home for themselves in the Silver Creek Valley. Other Mormon families spent their lives wandering from one place to another, buffeted by drought and flood.

The Mormons were not the only ones who struggled. During the late nineteenth century, thousands of small farmers tried to wrest a living from the Arizona soil. They brought their religious fervor and their Jeffersonian ideals to Arizona, and Arizona tested them, toyed with them, taught them a thousand ways to fail. The soil was fertile but needed water. The rivers flowed but could not be tamed. Not by Mormons, not by private canal companies, not by Eastern capital or Western pluck. And so those who came looking for Zion found Washington, and those who praised unfettered capitalism ended up in the arms of the federal government. Historian Frederick Jackson Turner wrote, "The pioneer of the arid regions must be both a capitalist and the protegé of the government." That strange and seemingly incongruous hybrid defines Arizona politics in the twentieth century. It took the bitter lessons of the nineteenth century to give it birth.

✳   ✳   ✳   **Early Mormon Pioneers and the Gathering to Zion**

When the first Mormon missionaries settled in Arizona, Native Americans had already been farming the region for nearly 3,000 years. The Hohokam developed the largest irrigation system in precolumbian North America. The Tohono O'odham captured the runoff of desert arroyos in a land where no rivers flowed. Quechan, Mohave, and other Yuman-speaking farmers cultivated squash, corn, tepary beans, devil's claw, and Sonoran panicgrass, a small, golden, milletlike grain, in the fertile mudflats along the Colorado River after the floodwaters of the Southwest's greatest river receded. But perhaps the most ingenious farmers were the Hopis, who live on three spurs of Black Mesa known as First, Second, and Third mesas. In an area where rainfall averages ten to thirteen inches a year, the Hopis learned how to plant their seeds in the mantle of sand that covers much of their land. Sand trapped the runoff and snowmelt of Black Mesa, reducing evaporation and conserving the moisture that allowed the Hopis to survive on the Colorado Plateau.

The Hispanic settlers of the Santa Cruz Valley, on the other hand, clung to their shallow intermittent stream. Nonetheless, they, too, were superb desert farmers, heirs to an agricultural tradition that dated back to Roman and Moorish Spain. Their basic adaptation was the *acequia* system, a simple form of water control consisting of earthen ditches leading from diversion dams in rivers and streams. Joining together in *comunes de agua* (water users' associations), they elected one of their members *juez de agua* (water judge) or *mayordomo* (ditch boss) each year and irrigated in turn. When flow decreased, the juez de agua made sure every farmer got his or her share. It was a system rooted in the community and adapted to scarcity, one designed for subsistence rather than commercial agriculture. As Tucson farmer Francisco Munguía noted in the late nineteenth century, "The custom was, we were always together, one for the other, as comrades and friends to help one another out whoever was in need."

Among both Native Americans and Mexicans, agriculture was more than an economic activity. Farming—and the need for rain—shaped how people worshiped as well as how they lived. The Hopis believe that the spirits of the dead become katsinas, who transform themselves into clouds. Their spiritual essence, or *navala,* falls to earth as rain and produces corn, which becomes the flesh and essence of living people. The continuity between the living and the dead is material as well as spiritual, mediated by rain and corn.

The connections were not quite so direct in Hispanic ritual. Nevertheless, major fiestas, particularly the feast days of San Isidro (May 15) and San Juan (June 24), expressed a deep dependence upon the rain and the land. After holding an all-night vigil (*velorio*), people in communities like Tucson carried the image of San Isidro through their fields, praying to the patron saint of farmers to intercede with God to bless their crops. A month later, those same people rose at dawn and bathed in the river, calling upon St. John the Baptist to ask God to send the summer rains. The cosmology was Catholic, but the needs were local. Faith, rain, and the fruits of the earth were woven together to celebrate a way of life that rested upon the fertility of desert fields.

In the late nineteenth century, another group arrived with a religious ideology just as committed to subsistence agriculture. Unlike the Spaniards, these newcomers, exemplified by the Flakes, came from the north, crossing the canyons of southern Utah to ford the Colorado River. They called themselves the Latter-day Saints (LDS) because they believed they had been chosen by God to prepare the earth for the Second Coming of Christ. Most nonbelievers called them Mormons, a name taken from their sacred text, the Book of Mormon, recorded by their prophet, Joseph Smith. Beginning in the 1870s, the Saints attempted to wrest a living from the Little Colorado River Valley. It was an act of religious faith and an experiment in communal living directed by Mormon authorities in Utah, and like many such experiments, it failed. But the seeds of that failure sprouted in more benign soil such as the White Mountains and the Salt, Gila, and San Pedro river valleys, where Mormon pioneers founded communities from Snowflake to St. David.

Mormon colonization rested upon a number of fundamental religious beliefs, including the concept of the gathering to Zion, where, in the words of Joseph Smith's Articles of Faith, "Christ will reign personally upon the earth." Smith envisioned Zion in northwestern Missouri, where he thought the Garden of Eden had been located. But he was driven out of several Midwestern communities and was murdered in Nauvoo, Illinois. His successor, Brigham Young, decided to redeem the Great American Desert instead. Small wagon trains of Saints trudged across the Great Plains and the Rocky Mountains until they came to the edge of the Great Salt Lake in northern Utah. But even though Utah became the heart of Zion, Young and his followers colonized other areas of the inter-mountain West as well. Mormonism was an aggressive, expansionist religion, imbued with its own sense of divine Manifest Destiny. Young even dreamed of creating a great state called Deseret (the term for honeybee in the Book of Mormon) extending from the Rocky Mountains to the Sierra Nevada. The state never materialized, but by his death in 1877, Young's followers had established communities from Idaho to northern Mexico. This was in response to one of Joseph Smith's last revelations: "The whole of America is Zion itself from north to south."

Most of the Mormon colonies were agrarian settlements far from gentile (non-Mormon) centers of population. The Mormon vision of Zion was not only isolationist but decidedly anti-urban, at least in its early years. Cities were centers of vice and corruption—"Babylons" in the biblical imagery of the time. The Western wilderness, on the other hand, was a place where the Saints could grow their own food and create their own society far from the "soulsickening abominations" of urban life. Part of their zeal rested on a conviction that God would reward their honest labor by transforming the natural world itself. "Many streams have been greatly increased in volume, and in some places new springs have burst forth in the desert," J. H. Ward wrote in the *Millennial Star* (1884). "The rainfall has greatly increased in some localities. A few years ago, it was considered impossible to raise crops without irrigation; now quite a pro-portion of the land under cultivation is tilled without artificial irrigation."

The Mormons were not the only ones who held such fanciful ideas. In late-nineteenth-century America, many people believed that rain followed the plough zone even though the North American climate was actually growing warmer with higher rates of evapotranspiration. If you brought more land under cultivation, more rain would fall. It was a simple equation, one conceived by greedy speculators and desperate pioneers. But even though its aftermath was often cruel—broken dreams and abandoned homesteads from the Dakotas to the Texas Panhandle—it lured many a family into the remotest corners of the West.

Few corners were more remote than northern Arizona. Mormons from the Elk Mountain Mission in southeastern Utah first visited the region in 1854 or 1855. They were followed by a handful of remarkable explorers who blazed the wagon trails and discovered the fords of the Colorado River that allowed later settlers to fan out across Arizona Territory. One of those individuals was Jacob Hamblin, who crisscrossed northern Arizona from 1858 to the 1870s. Like most Saints, Hamblin believed that Native Americans were Lamanites, members of a lost tribe of Israel. They, too, were part of the gathering to Zion, so Hamblin did his best to establish close ties with the Paiutes, Havasupais, Hopis, and Navajos.

Another, more controversial pioneer was John D. Lee, who fought beside Joseph Smith in Missouri and followed Brigham Young to Utah. During the hysteria of 1857, when President James Buchanan sent federal troops to occupy Mormon Utah, Lee reportedly planned the Mountain Meadows Massacre, in which a group of Mormons and Paiutes slaughtered a wagon train of Arkansas and Missouri emigrants on their way to California. Because of the massacre, Lee became a dangerous embarrassment to Brigham Young, who was trying to improve relations with the U.S. government. Young therefore called Lee to mission in 1871 and told him to establish a ferry on the Colorado near its junction with the Paria River. It was a wild and lonely place, with towering sandstone cliffs and spare, windswept vegetation, but it was also a key link in the wagon road the Mormons were building across northern Arizona. Lee ran the ferry until 1874, when U.S. marshals finally tracked him down while he was visiting Utah. He was executed three years later in the valley where the massacre took place.

Young Emma Lee, Lee's seventeenth bride, remained at the mouth of the Paria for five more years, raising her children in a place she called the Lonely Dell. Much of the time she ran the ferry alone, nearly a hundred miles from Kanab and almost two hundred miles from the Mormon communities along the Little Colorado. Once some threatening Navajos camped in her yard, so Emma gathered her children and spread her blankets by their fire and slept there until morning. "When the Navajos rode away they called her a brave woman and said she should be safe in the future," wrote historian Sharlot Hall, who was an Arizona pioneer herself. Emma's spirit epitomized the courage of Mormon women along the frontier.

Because of her tenacity, Lee's Ferry developed into one of the most strategic river crossings in the Southwest. Without a reliable ford on the Colorado, Zion remained a Great Basin kingdom. But once Lee's Ferry was in place, a wagon road stretching more than 700 miles connected Salt Lake City with Arizona and northern Mexico. The route led up the Sevier River Valley to Panguitch, where wagons lumbered over the rim of the Great Basin and dropped down between Bryce and Zion canyons to Kanab. From there the road climbed the escarpment of the Kaibab Plateau and descended into House Rock Valley, following the Vermillion Cliffs to the crossing itself. Wagon trains foundered in the snow during the winter and scrambled for water in the summer. There were only four springs, two of them almost undrinkable, between the Kaibab and the Colorado. Despite such hardships, however, the Mormon wagon road served as both gateway and rite of passage for most of the Saints who settled in Arizona.

They made their first attempt to do so in 1873, when Brigham Young called 250 Mormons to mission and told them to colonize the Little Colorado Valley. At Pipe Springs, the president of the mission, Horton Haight, divided the expedition into groups of ten wagons apiece. The first party crossed at Lee's Ferry in late April. After dawdling at the mission outpost of Moenkopi, the advance group reached the Little Colorado a month later in the teeth of a blinding sandstorm. Mormon scouts had optimistically compared the Little Colorado Valley to the "Illinois Prairie," but Haight's party was not entranced. "It is the seam thing all the way, no plase fit for a human being to dwell upon," wrote one Norwegian missionary in vivid if rough-hewn English. "No rock for bilding, no pine timber within 50 or 75 miles of her. Wher ever you may luck the country is all broken op. The moste desert lukking plase that I ever saw, Amen."

The abortive colony lasted little more than a month before the disgruntled pioneers returned to Utah. Young urged them to remain and vowed to take personal command, but one sharp-tongued veteran of the mission replied that the settlers "would not stay if he [Young] should come with Jesus Christ himself." But Mormon leaders were not about to give up on their dream. In January 1876, the call to colonize the Little Colorado went out again. Mormon stakes (territorial subdivisions under the direction of a president) received missionary quotas that had to be filled from within their ranks. The 200 men chosen then had to sell their property and prepare themselves and their families, if they had families, for the long trek south. Perhaps no other endeavor better reflected the deep faith of the Saints or the power of the General Authorities, as the First President (Brigham Young) and the Twelve Apostles were called. The gathering to Zion was a corporate effort organized from above. No other colonial enterprise since the Jesuit and Franciscan missions of the seventeenth and eighteenth centuries had mobilized as many people in such a sustained or authoritarian fashion.

✳ ✳ The United Order

Only such an enterprise could have kept colonies alive along the lower Little Colorado. Mormon leaders selected the river valley because nobody else wanted it and nobody else was there. As George Cannon, Utah's territorial delegate to Congress, thundered after the failure of 1873, "If there be deserts in Arizona, thank God for the deserts. If there be wilderness there, thank God for the wilderness. . . . When we go hence to extend our borders we must not expect to find a land of orange or lemon groves, a land where walnut trees and hard timber abound; where bees are wild and turkeys can be had for the shooting. It is vain for us to expect to settle in such a land at the present time. But if we find a little oasis in the desert where a few can settle, thank God for the oasis, and thank him for the almost interminable road that lies between that oasis and so-called civilization."

The first missionaries did not have much to be thankful for during their early years. The Saints founded four settlements along the Little Colorado west of its junction with the Rio Puerco: Sunset, St. Joseph, Obed, and Brigham City. It is hard to imagine four more unlikely oases. All were located on the high, wind-wracked desert of the Colorado Plateau, and all averaged less than sixteen inches of rain a year. From April through June, a critical time in the agricultural cycle, the Little Colorado and its tributaries often dried up. Late summer or winter storms, on the other hand, sent floods roaring down the drainages. Between 1876 and 1884 the dam at St. Joseph had to be rebuilt five times at a cost of 9,000 man-days and 3,000 team-days of labor.

To overcome such natural obstacles, the settlers adopted a communal form of organization known as the United Order. The United Order movement was the Mormon church's most ambitious effort at utopian social engineering. There were actually four types of orders, ranging from limited cooperatives to communal families in which members shared everything, including property, labor, and proceeds. The first four Little Colorado communities were family orders. Religious communalism had come to the Arizona frontier.

The experiment was not very successful, either from a social or an ecological point of view. Most of the early missionaries were young and poor. Many were unmarried. They brought little personal property with them, and they squatted on unsurveyed public land. Even with this relative lack of class distinction, however, dissension wracked the United Order villages. As soon as they arrived, members pooled all of their possessions. A board of directors then assigned individual tasks. Some men with special skills plied their trades, but others were shifted from job to job. They dug ditches. They taught school. They planted crops. One member of the St. Joseph Order admitted that "when he was away and had a job to do he would work with a zeal, but when he was dictated by everybody he felt a little rebellious."

These feelings of rebellion surfaced even more strongly over the question of wages and the distribution of goods. At Sunset, where Lot Smith ruled his community with an iron hand, no wages were paid. In theory, each individual performed according to his or her ability, and each received according to his or her needs. In practice, the explosive and abusive Smith insisted on investing all surplus back into the Sunset Order, particularly its livestock herds. As one member complained to Apostle Erastus Snow, "Living is unnecessarily poor & niggardly. . . . if a Sister wants a little Thread, Sheeting, Buttons & etc to use in her Family She is told there is none or if she get it, comes frequently with a lecture on economy."

At St. Joseph, where more individual freedom prevailed, adult males received the same pay regardless of what they did. Skilled laborers protested this uniform wage scale, but it remained in place until 1883, when the community voted to switch to a stewardship plan in which all common property was distributed among individual families. The St. Joseph Order itself was dissolved in 1886. It was the last to collapse.

But even if the orders had succeeded as social institutions, they would have failed as agricultural communities. None of the four settlements cultivated more than 350 acres, yet they continually suffered from an acute shortage of labor. Part of this was due to the large numbers of children; in 1881, nearly 50 percent of St. Joseph's population was under eight years of age. An even greater drain came from the joint enterprises run by the orders, including a dairy, a sawmill, a gristmill, and a tannery. Both the sawmill and the dairy were located in Pleasant Valley, sixty miles southwest of the Little Colorado settlements. In 1878, forty-eight men and forty-one women milked 115 cows. They produced 5,400 pounds of cheese and 442 pounds of butter, but no crops.

Meanwhile, floods washed out the crude dams the Saints threw across the Little Colorado with distressing regularity. Obed failed within a year because of its unhealthy location. Brigham City never had a successful crop and was abandoned in 1881. Sunset had one good year in 1879 followed by three poor ones. The farmers left the community to Lot Smith and his livestock in 1883. Only St. Joseph, whose total population rarely exceeded fifteen to twenty families, survived. And it did so largely because tithes from other Mormon communities subsidized the reconstruction of its dams. Searching in vain for a "little oasis in the desert," many Saints must have agreed with one woman pioneer who called the Little Colorado "dirty, muddy, gurgling, seething, belching, vicious, demon-like, bringing havoc, destruction, and death." Even the Mormons could not build Zion along the alkali bottoms of its lower flanks.

✳   ✳   **Mormon Settlements in the Rest of Arizona**

The Mormons had better luck farther upstream. Beginning in 1878, Mormons began settling along Silver Creek, a major tributary of the Little Colorado draining the White Mountains. Many of the early ranchers and farmers there were Mormons who could not tolerate life in the United Order, including William Flake. Flake and Apostle Erastus Snow founded the town of Snowflake. Each family received one city plot and two farm plots in the new community or in the two other Silver Creek towns of Showlow and Taylor. There was no pooling of property or eating at a common table, as Lot Smith made his followers do in Sunset. Mormons supported one another through tithes and cooperatives, but the experiment in communal living was nearly dead.

That transition from communalism to cooperative individualism accelerated as Mormons streamed into other parts of the territory. In the spring of 1877, an expedition of Saints bound for Mexico stopped for a season in the eastern Salt River Valley. There they cleared away heavy mesquite brush along the river and dug an irrigation canal in the brutal summer heat. The pioneers called the settlement Camp Utah, which later became the town of Lehi.

The expedition's leader was Daniel W. Jones, who had traveled widely in Mexico. After converting to Mormonism, Jones concluded that it was his special mission to work among Native Americans. Numerous Pimas, Tohono O'odham, and Maricopas helped the Saints of Camp Utah dig their ditch, and some even asked to join the community. But when Jones welcomed them and insisted they be treated equally in his little gathering to Zion, other members of the party objected to the presence of "dirty Indians." Jones refused to back down, so most of his companions left for the San Pedro River, where they founded the community of St. David. Missionary zeal was not strong enough to overcome the racial prejudice of the time.

Other Mormon settlements soon flourished in the Salt River Valley. Alma, Nephi, and Tempe grew up downriver of Lehi. Several hundred O'odham converts formed the Papago Ward north of town. The largest community took root on a mesa to the southwest, where a group of Saints from Utah and Idaho cleaned out the ancient channel of a Hohokam canal and began planting their crops in 1878. Five years later they incorporated the town of Mesa, which they surveyed and platted into ten-acre blocks separated by streets 130 feet wide. Spacious and prosperous, Mesa reflected the Mormon genius for town planning in the American West.

Mormons also settled along the Gila River at places like Smithville (Pima) and Thatcher. And they continued to migrate up the Little Colorado watershed, establishing the small mountain villages of Greer, Eagar, Nutrioso, and Alpine. In 1879, Ammon Tenney even purchased the land of Solomon Barth, a German Jew who had founded the town of St. Johns. The Mormons hoped to buy the entire community, but many of its predominantly Mexican inhabitants refused to sell out and leave. St. Johns therefore became a flash point in the conflict between Mormons and gentiles in Apache County, which was carved out of Yavapai County in 1879.

The struggle was usually couched in flamboyant moral or religious terms— the wicked gentiles with their vice-ridden Babylons versus the promiscuous Mormons with their "foul and unscrupulous priesthood." Non-Mormons feared that the "polygamous hordes of Mormonism" had been "sent out from Utah to occupy, control and contaminate our beautiful territory" (St. Johns *Apache Chief*, July 18, 1884). Mormons counterattacked by railing against the "St. Johns Ring," which included merchants like Barth, George McCarter, and Lorenzo Hubbell. During the ensuing struggle, non-Mormons rigged elections, harassed Mormon voters, and threw Mormon leaders like David Udall and William Flake into prison for polygamy. Many enemies of the Saints even advocated violence and vigilante action. "In a year from now the Mormons will have the power here and Gentiles had better leave," warned George McCarter. "Don't let them get it. Desperate diseases need desperate remedies. The Mormon disease is a desperate one and the rope and the shot gun is the only cure" (*Apache Chief*, May 30, 1884).

The Saints made convenient targets during those violent times. They practiced a different religion, and some of the men had more than one wife. Perhaps more important, they often pooled their resources and acted as a group, buying land and setting up businesses in competition with non-Mormon ranchers and farmers. They also moved to Arizona in large numbers during the early 1880s, especially to Apache and Maricopa counties. In 1880 there were about 1,500 Mormons in the territory; by 1885 that number had more than tripled to 5,000. Polygamy may have been the rallying cry, but economic and political fears fueled much of the anti-Mormon sentiment.

The crusade came to a head in 1885, when the Arizona legislature unanimously passed a bill forcing Mormon voters to take an oath that they did not believe in plural marriage—a measure the Idaho territorial legislature had enacted the year before. The vote was designed to disenfranchise the Saints, who constituted about 11 percent of Arizona's population in the late 1880s. With few friends in high places and with cowboys of the Aztec Land and Cattle Company trying to run them off the range, about 10 percent of the Mormons fled to Mexico or back to Utah. It looked like Missouri all over again in Arizona Territory.

But both Mormons and non-Mormons had learned something since those early years. In 1885, Grover Cleveland became president and appointed Conrad Zulick as first Democratic territorial governor of Arizona. Mormons consistently voted Democratic, especially for Marcus Aurelius Smith, the incumbent delegate to Congress and a staunch supporter of the Saints. Zulick led the fight to repeal the test oath law, which was overturned in 1887. Mormons therefore cast about 98 percent of their votes for Smith in 1888, helping him win an overwhelming victory against the Republican candidate. Mormon bloc voting infuriated the Republicans, who continued their attack upon the church. Beneath the rhetoric, however, both Republican and Mormon leaders explored ways to end the feud. LDS officials feared that exclusive support of the Democrats would completely alienate the Republicans, and as long as the Saints could vote, Republicans could no longer afford to antagonize them. So even though fiery anti-Mormon editorials still appeared in Republican newspapers, the increasingly Republican Mormon hierarchy in Utah sent emissaries to Republican party leaders in Arizona and elsewhere. A long and mutually rewarding courtship had begun.

That courtship flowered after September 1890, when President Wilford Woodruff issued his famous Manifesto. The Manifesto ordered Mormons to submit to the laws of the United States and abandon the practice of polygamy—an edict that took on the weight of a revelation from God a year later. Some Mormons continued to engage in plural marriage, but the church publicly condemned such unions. It also encouraged its members to stop voting as blocs. Doctrinal change begat political compromise, allowing the transition to take place from "polygamous hordes" to pillars of the community. By 1894, one formerly anti-Mormon editor in Phoenix announced, "The so-called 'Mormon Question' has become obsolete" (*Arizona Republican,* November 10, 1894). As Mormons and gentiles learned to coexist with one another, the dreams of an exclusive Zion in the wilderness faded as well.

Nonetheless, the agrarian basis of that dream remained strong. Unlike many other Arizona pioneers, the Mormons were not interested in mining. They wanted to build stable, orderly communities, not boomtowns. LDS officials even railed against isolated ranch life because it did not encourage the high degree of social solidarity, and social control, the church wanted to achieve. Agricultural communities, on the other hand, embodied all the virtues Mormons held dear—order, hard work, cooperation, the company of other Saints. These virtues took actual physical shape in the wide streets of Mormon towns and the cottonwood-lined irrigation ditches leading to Mormon fields. In 1884, Snowflake was a ramshackle collection of log cabins. Ten years later, graceful two- and three-story brick homes loomed like Eastern visions of stability and progress in the little northern Arizona town.

For many Mormons, however, it was a vision and little more. Families like the Udalls and the Flakes prospered in northeastern Arizona, but many other

Mormon pioneers, like Jacob Hamblin, wandered from Utah to Mexico without ever finding their oasis in the desert. Political turmoil and the antipolygamy crusade forced some of the moves, but others resulted from the same natural disasters that afflicted other Arizona settlers. Crops failed. Cattle died. Rain did not follow the plough zone, and God did not bless the labor of the Saints. Farming in Arizona in the late nineteenth century was a gamble that often drove its players out of the game.

❋ ❋ Farming in the Salt River Valley

Nowhere was that gamble more seductive than in the Salt River Valley, a vast alluvial plain stretching from the Superstition Mountains to the Sierra Estrella. All of Arizona's major rivers except the San Pedro and the Colorado flow together there, so even though the valley is low, hot desert, the snowmelt and runoff from the White Mountains and the Mogollon Rim surge down the drainages on their way to the Gulf of California. Or at least they did until the building of the dams.

Its rivers made the Salt River Valley the greatest conjunction of arable land and flowing water in the Southwest. The Hohokam built some of their largest cities there, but no non-Indians settled near the junction of the Gila and the Salt until 1865, when the army established Camp McDowell along the Verde River twenty miles to the northeast. The four companies of cavalry and one company of infantry stationed there tried to feed themselves by hacking 200 acres out of the dense mesquite bottomland along the river, but their farm failed. Thereafter, civilians, particularly those who settled in the Salt River Valley, supplied the 473 soldiers and their horses. The U.S. military gave birth to Phoenix just as the Spanish military begat Tucson nearly a century before.

One of those civilians was a Confederate deserter named Jack Swilling. Swilling was a morphine addict and a violent drunk who died in Yuma prison in 1878 after being accused of robbing a stage. In 1867, however, he persuaded a group of Wickenburg miners to help him organize the Swilling Irrigation and Canal Company, which dug out a Hohokam canal on the north bank of the Salt River and called it Swilling Ditch. By 1871 the ditch was carrying 200 cubic feet of water per second and could irrigate 4,000 acres. It later became the Salt River Valley Canal, which ran right through the center of Phoenix.

Swilling's Ditch also served as the prototype for the other joint-stock canal companies proliferating across the valley. In contrast to Mormon irrigation ventures, the canal companies were business propositions, not communal endeavors. Investors joined together to form the companies because they did not have enough capital to build dams and ditches on their own. But what share-holders did with their portion of the water was up to them. Some actually farmed their own fields. Many others leased their water and sold their land. Speculators were present in the Salt River Valley from the very beginning. They wanted profit, not Zion.

By 1872, farmers were cultivating 8,000 acres of barley and wheat along with corn, beans, and sweet potatoes, and tending grape vines and fruit trees, The Salt River Valley was developing into the most important agricultural region in Arizona, supplying not only the military but many of the mines as well. Every so often, however, the river slapped the farmers around. Swilling and his associates got a scare from the beast they were trying to tame in September 1868, when heavy summer rains sent a huge flood roaring down the Salt. Six years later, in January 1874, the river ransacked the valley for three days, carrying away the Swilling headgates and destroying William Parker's granary, which was filled with ten tons of wheat. Sodden farmers sought refuge in the school and court-house as their adobe homes collapsed. Religious services were held in a saloon. The Salt could not be forded for more than two weeks, and farmers and promot-ers realized that nature was not yet their handmaiden, at least not in central Arizona. They had to relearn that lesson many times in the years to come.

Nevertheless, farmers and speculators continued to pour into the valley, beguiled by the long growing season and the fertile soil. In 1870 they dug the Maricopa Canal. Eight years later they added the Grand Canal, which snaked all the way to New River. The Desert Land Act of 1877 boosted the size of a home-stead from 160 acres to 640, so even more people arrived. Despite the floods, the Salt River Valley was becoming the "Garden of the Territory" and the "Grain Emporium of Arizona."

The most ambitious project was the Arizona Canal Company, chartered in 1882. Unlike the other major ditches, the Arizona Canal did not follow Hoho-kam blueprints. Instead, it tapped into the Salt more than forty miles upriver, flowing along the northern edge of the Salt River Valley, where no one, not even the Hohokam, had ever farmed. Financed through the sale of bonds from San Francisco to New York, the canal was fifty-eight feet wide on top and thirty-six feet wide on the bottom. When it was finished in 1885, promoters claimed that 100,000 acres of "unproductive desert of no value for any purpose" would blos-som under its waters.

By 1890 there were 11,000 people in the valley. The Arizona, Salt River Valley, Maricopa, and Grand canals irrigated 50,000 acres north of the Salt River. Mor-mon farmers and gentile speculators like Alexander Chandler were busy digging ditches to the south. Wheat, barley, and alfalfa dominated the fields, but farmers were experimenting with other crops as well, including citrus trees. And while some of the produce was locally consumed, much of it was shipped by rail to markets outside the valley and even out of the territory. On July 4, 1887, the Maricopa and Phoenix Railroad crossed the Salt River just northwest of Tempe and chugged into Phoenix, linking the Salt River Valley with the Southern Pacific Railroad at Maricopa, thirty miles to the south. A sandstorm drowned out the official orations, but nobody except the speakers cared. Nothing symbolized progress better than a railroad. The Salt River Valley was on the move.

✳ ✳ ✳ The Disastrous 1890s

The territorial legislature reinforced those feelings of pride in 1889, when it made Phoenix the capital of Arizona. But the decade that followed mocked the dreams of the young communities sprawling across the valley. In February 1890 an early spring storm melted snow in the Salt River watershed. Floodwaters swept away the telegraph line and 200 feet of trestle on the west end of the new railroad bridge that spanned the river at Tempe. The flood also washed out 150 feet of bank and came within three feet of the track itself.

A year later another storm appeared in mid-February. On Wednesday afternoon, February 18, the sky seemed to clear, but that night the rain returned "harder and hoarser than ever." By one o'clock that morning, floodwaters were roaring sixteen feet above the diversion dam of the Arizona Canal, which jutted across the Salt thirty miles northeast of Phoenix. That was four feet higher than the crest of the 1890 flood, so the engineer at the dam telegraphed a warning to the Phoenix fire department about the water roaring their way. Horsemen quickly spread the word, and people grabbed what they could and scrambled for higher ground. But the rain kept falling and the Salt kept rising, carrying driftwood that looked like "black phantoms on grey steeds as they were hurled on the top of a foam-crested wave." When the sun rose on February 19, a scene of utter devastation greeted the cold, wet refugees. In Mesa, "white people and Indians" stranded above the floodwaters looked down to see dams destroyed and bridges crumpled. In Phoenix, adobe buildings south of Washington Street "melted like snow drifts before an April sun." And in Tempe, at 8:05 that morning, onlookers watched helplessly as the trunk of a huge cottonwood rammed into the north end of the railroad bridge, which was already swaying with the waves. For five minutes, the bridge quivered and shuddered, and then its three spans tumbled into the current and bobbed downstream.

By the time a new bridge was completed in August, farmers were caught in another bind. During the summer of 1891, the monsoons dumped only about half their average rains on central and southern Arizona. Soon there was not enough water in the channel to irrigate everyone's crops. It was an old problem, but now there were more farmers and more canals. There were also more canal companies wheeling and dealing rights to a resource in short supply. Tensions rose. Lawsuits proliferated. In 1892, Joseph Kibbey, the chief justice of the territorial supreme court, tried to resolve the disputes by handing down a landmark decision in the case of *Wormser v. Salt River Valley Canal Company*. Kibbey ruled that water belonged to the land, not to any particular canal company, and could not be sold as a separate commodity. He also affirmed the doctrine of prior appropriation. In other words, those who had used the water first had prior rights over those who came later. The "Kibbey Decision" served as a model for water legislation across the arid West. Judge Edward Kent, presiding over the Third Judicial District of the Territory of Arizona, confirmed it in 1910 when he handed down his decision in the case of *Hurley v. Abbott,* which determined the prior rights of all acreage to Salt River water and classified land in the Salt River Valley according to when it was first cultivated.

Despite its legal precedence, however, Kibbey's decision did not immediately stop the canal companies from speculating in water rights or luring more farmers onto their lands. Corporations like the Arizona Canal Company were desperately trying to stay solvent, so W. J. Murphy and other promoters scoured the country for buyers, boasting about the endless sunshine and claiming that the Salt had enough water to irrigate 500,000 acres of land. One group who fell for the pitch were German Reformed Baptists, members of a Pennsylvania Dutch sect also known as the Dunkards. The Dunkards were "plain folk," abstemious and hardworking, and by 1896 about seventy families were trying to make a living along the Arizona Canal near the new townsite of Glendale.

But neither legislation nor promotion could solve the valley's most pressing problem, which was drought. The dry years began in 1891 and continued, with little relief, until 1905. The early part of the drought coincided with a national depression in 1893. The economy recovered, but the drought intensified, reaching its peak in the late 1890s. Young Carl Hayden remembered standing beside his mother as she guarded their allotment of water with a shotgun while her husband was out of town. Such vigils were common in the Salt River Valley at the end of the nineteenth century.

As a result, many farmers abandoned the "Garden of the Territory." One report estimated that there were 127,512 acres in cultivation in 1896 and 96,863 acres nine years later, a decline of 24 percent. Other, more sweeping figures claimed that one-third of the 200,000 acres being farmed went out of production. One casualty was the Arizona Canal Company, which was placed in receivership in 1894. Another was the Dunkard community, most of whom were gone by 1900. Vineyards wilted and fruit trees died. Banks failed and pioneer merchants like Charles Hayden nearly went broke. Those who survived realized that the Salt River had to have a real dam, one that could hold back the floods and store water against a drought. They also realized that private capital could never get the job done. The marriage between farmers and the federal government was at hand.

11

* * # Water and Cotton

Born in 1877 in the little adobe community of Hayden's Ferry (re-named Tempe a year later), Carl Hayden grew up on the cusp, watching Arizona change from a frontier to an extractive colony dominated by outside investors. Hayden loved his parents, but he wanted no part of their hard lives. In 1898, at the height of a drought, his aging father, Arizona pioneer Charles Trumball Hayden, asked him to leave Stanford University and return home to run the family flour mill along the Salt River in Tempe. Hayden refused. "Did I live under conditions prevalent fifty or sixty years ago I might take the business and make a comfortable success of it. But our competitors today are not J.Y.T. Smith of Phoenix or the store up the street," Hayden wrote his father. "The corporation owned mills of Kansas and Minnesota fix the price of our flour. To sell meat we must bow to an Armour or Cudahy. We pay for coal at what a Rockefeller asks and if we oppose him he blasts us with his wrath. C. P. Huntington charges all the traffic will bear and leaves no profit for me."

Nevertheless, Charles Hayden's death in 1900 brought Carl's college career to an end. He returned to Tempe to take care of his mother and two sisters and to pay his father's debts, but he did not remain a struggling businessman for very long. In another letter to his father, Hayden had confided, "I am not of the merchant cast. I was born a lawyer, a politician, a statesman. I have always dreamed of power and the good I could do." So as quickly as he could, he sold off the general store, rented out the flour mill, and entered politics, winning election to the Tempe City Council the year he came home.

It was the beginning of the longest, most successful political career in Arizona history. Hayden fell in love with Washington, D.C., during his first trip there in 1903. So, after serving as sheriff of Maricopa County for three two-year terms, he won election to the U.S. House of Representatives as soon as Arizona became a state in 1912. Hayden kept getting reelected, first to the House, then to the Senate, until he retired fifty-six years later as chairman of the Senate Appropriations Committee. He became the consummate Washington insider, winning highways, air bases, and defense plants for his native state.

But Hayden's consuming interest was water and how to get more of it for Arizona cities and farms. His greatest triumph was the Central Arizona Project, which took him a lifetime to get through Congress. When he finally signed the bill in 1968, the frail old man must have thought of the boy who had watched his parents nearly go broke during the 1890s. Like most Arizonans of that era, Hayden remembered a time when wild rivers were enemies and farmers dreamed of a web of dams and canals to make the desert green.

*   *   *   The Struggle Over Water Control in the Salt River Valley

In Arizona that dream first became a reality in the Salt River Valley when the federal Reclamation Service completed Roosevelt Dam in 1911. Before that happened, however, enormous political and physical obstacles had to be overcome. John Wesley Powell, who became head of the United States Geological Survey (USGS) in 1881, passionately believed that the federal government should use its money and power to establish Jeffersonian communities of small farmers in Western irrigation districts. Many others, such as Republican Senator William Stewart of Nevada, chair of the Senate Subcommittee on Irrigation, favored federal development of water projects but wanted them to serve private capital. Still others wanted private companies, states, or territories to control water in the West. Unlike the conflict between developers and environmentalists a century later, few questioned the need to tame Western rivers. Even Powell, the most famous river runner of them all, wrote that "all the waters of all the arid lands will eventually be taken from their natural channels" because the West needed irrigation to make an agricultural civilization bloom. The battle was over who would benefit from the dams once they were built. The struggle for the soul of the modern West had begun.

The issue of water in the Salt River Valley manifested all of these contradictory tendencies. Everyone agreed that the Salt had to be dammed. The best location for the reservoir had even been discovered in 1889, when the Maricopa County Board of Supervisors sponsored a surveying expedition to the Salt and Verde watersheds. The expedition found what they were looking for about seventy miles northeast of Phoenix in a "wing-shaped double valley" where Tonto Creek flowed into the Salt River. The valley was broad, the canyon steep and narrow and carved out of hard rock. In 1897, Arthur Davis, one of the leading USGS engineers, said, "It would probably be impossible to find anywhere in the arid region a storage project in which all conditions are as favorable as this one."

Before the engineers could go to work, however, the farmers themselves had to be persuaded to accept federal intervention, and that meant another decade of delay while private interests tried and failed to harness the Salt themselves. In 1893 the Hudson Reservoir and Canal Company claimed the site where the Salt and the Tonto came together. Owned by Eastern investors, the company surveyed canal routes and drew up plans for a 225-foot-high masonry dam. It could never raise the three million dollars it needed to build the system, however. Like so many other private water projects in the West, Hudson discovered that reclamation was too expensive for private capital alone.

The company also ran into resistance from Salt River Valley farmers, who formed the Old Settlers Protective Association in 1898. Defending their established water rights, the farmers believed that the company was more interested in bringing new lands into production than insuring their water supply. For the next several years, debate raged between farmers and speculators, between small farmers and large landowners like Dwight Heard and Alexander Chandler, between those who favored federal involvement and those who wanted Maricopa County or Arizona Territory to take control.

Another cause of delay was competition from farmers in the Gila Valley. During the 1870s, Anglos and Mexicans founded Florence and Safford and diverted water that had once flowed onto the fields of the Akimel O'odham. By the 1890s, the O'odham canals were dry and the Indians were pleading with the federal government to intervene. One solution was to take the water away from white settlers and give it back to the Pimas. Another was to build a storage dam on the Gila and increase the water supply. In 1896, Frederick Newell, a hydrologist with the USGS, wrote that "it would be the height of injustice to deprive the present occupants of the water which they have been using for many years." He added, "Several acres well-tilled by white men would be destroyed for the benefit of one acre poorly worked by Indians." That would have violated the "gospel of efficiency" that drove Newell and his colleagues in the reclamation movement, so in 1898 they called for the construction of a dam near San Carlos on the Apache reservation.

By then, however, momentum for a federal dam was building in the Salt River Valley, and plans for the Gila dam were shelved for thirty years. The worst drought in memory was withering crops, and even the most hardheaded farmers were realizing that rugged independence meant the freedom to go broke. There was still resistance to federal intervention, but that resistance weakened under the leadership of Benjamin Fowler, a retired book publisher from Chicago who moved to the Salt River Valley because of his health. Fowler, who invested in cattle and farmland and became president of the Arizona Agricultural Association, developed close friendships with George Maxwell, director of the National Irrigation Association, and Newell, who had become chief hydrologist of the USGS. Maxwell and Newell were spearheading the national crusade to "reclaim" the arid lands of the West through irrigation, and Fowler was swept up by their vision. Through them, he realized that only the federal government had the capital to build a water control project massive enough to tame the Salt, and only it could spread the enormous risks of such a project among millions of taxpayers rather than a few thousand stockholders. It was a strategy Arizona leaders like Carl Hayden were to develop into a political art form in the years to come.

The reclamation vision became legislative reality on June 17, 1902, when Congress passed the National Reclamation Act. The act created a federal reclamation fund supported by the sale of public lands in sixteen Western states and territories, including Arizona. And while the original bill restricted federal support to the reclamation of public lands, Fowler and Maxwell persuaded President Theodore Roosevelt to eliminate that restriction. Soon afterward, Secretary of the Interior Ethan Hitchcock created a new agency within the USGS called the Reclamation Service and appointed Newell its chief engineer. Fowler and Newell met often during the summer of 1902, refining their vision of water control in the Salt River Valley. The federal parts of the puzzle were falling into place.

Fowler then had to talk his fellow farmers into hammering out a plan the government would approve. The biggest challenge was to find a compromise between local and federal control. The National Reclamation Act limited the amount of land within a federal reclamation project to 160 acres per landowner. It also placed great power over the projects in the hands of the secretary of the interior. Many large landowners in the Salt River Valley objected to both propositions. Dwight Heard, a community leader who owned more than 7,500 acres south of Phoenix, argued that individual canal companies should be allowed to regulate the distribution of water along their own ditches. He also contended that established water rights should be respected even if the individuals who held them irrigated more than the Jeffersonian 160 acres. Heard fought to protect the interests of big farmers and canal companies under the doctrines of prior appropriation and local autonomy. Fowler and Maxwell envisioned a centralized authority distributing water to small farmers. They therefore called for the creation of a single association encompassing all landowners in the valley. Members would receive shares in the new water-storage system, but the water rights would be "perpetually and inseparably" tied to the land. Farmers, not speculators, would dominate the organization. Canal companies would be eliminated.

By the end of 1902, farmers who owned about 150,000 acres had subscribed to Fowler and Maxwell's plan. Judge Joseph Kibbey, who had handed down the landmark *Wormser v. Salt River Valley Canal Company* decision a decade earlier, drafted the articles of incorporation for the Salt River Valley Water Users Association, which would administer the storage and distribution system "subject to the approval of the Secretary of the Interior." Pledging their land as collateral for the government's investment, members would be assessed $12.50 per acre of irrigated land in addition to an initial subscription fee, payable over a ten-year period. Heard and other large landowners objected to many of the provisions, but they were voted down by a two-thirds margin. On February 9, 1903, the organization officially incorporated under Arizona law. A month later Newell recommended the association as one of the Reclamation Service's first five projects, and the secretary of the interior quickly agreed. Heard continued to snipe away, but the Salt River Project was about to turn the Salt River Valley into the largest agricultural center in the Southwest.

✳   ✳   The Building of Roosevelt Dam

It was a colossal endeavor. The site of the Tonto Dam, as it was originally called, was sixty miles northeast of Mesa and forty miles northwest of the mining community of Globe. And those were tire-blowing, leg-slashing, hoof-bruising miles across some of the roughest country in Arizona. The Sierra Anchas loomed to the north, and the Mazatzal Mountains curved away to the northwest. To the south brooded the Superstitions. There were no nearby settlements where workers could live, and only one road twisted through the mountains to Globe. Everything else was rock and thorn and desert heat. Thirty years before, General Crook had pursued the Southeastern Yavapais and Tonto Apaches across the basin. Now, Apaches from the nearby San Carlos Reservation made up many of the work crews who would build this monument to Anglo progress.

The first order of business was to connect the dam site to the outside world. The government blasted a new road to Globe and then began construction of the Apache Trail to give it access to the two rail lines in Mesa. The road was an engineer's nightmare and a worker's grave. It wound along the river. It clung to steep cliffs. It ascended and descended mountains like Fish Creek Hill in 10 percent grades. Road builders had to use lifelines to hack twenty- to seventy-foot-deep cuts through solid rock.

The second challenge was to reduce the cost of supplies. Stonecutters quarried the masonry blocks of the dam from nearby sandstone cliffs, but project engineers figured that the cost of buying and freighting cement to mortar the blocks together would be an astronomical nine dollars a barrel. Instead, they searched out deposits of limestone and clay north of the Salt River and produced their own cement for three dollars a barrel despite the protests of the cement trust. After private contractors failed to meet their quotas, they also took over a private sawmill in the Sierra Anchas and raised production from 119,500 board feet per month to 214,000. Led by Louis Hill, a thirty-eight-year-old professor from the Colorado School of Mines, the engineers were visionary technocrats reclaiming the Great American Desert through technology. The "gospel of efficiency" was being proclaimed from the Tonto Basin.

Construction of the dam itself began in 1905, the wettest year in memory. While floods wreaked havoc in the Salt River Valley, J. M. O'Rourke and Company built a camp for the workers, set up a machine shop, quarried stone, and drove piles to erect two temporary dams to divert the Salt while the permanent structure was being built. Then the river played its last wild card. On November 26 a warm rain melted snow in the mountains, and the river rose thirty feet in fifteen hours. Roaring down the narrow canyon at the rate of 130,000 cubic feet per second, it ripped piles out of the river bottom and swept away the diversion dams and flumes. More floods that winter prevented construction from resuming until March 1906.

As soon as the flow subsided, however, O'Rourke and his crews returned. Men toiled like trolls in the riverbed, hacking away at the earth with picks and shovels and sledgehammers because the engineers had concluded that too many explosives would weaken the rocks. Then crews used wooden derricks to hoist stones that weighed up to ten tons, filling the joints with concrete that had to be kept wet for six days to prevent it from cracking. Slowly, block by enormous block, the structure took shape, curving upward between the cliffs like an extension of the mountains themselves. By the time the next floods surged down the channel in the spring of 1908, the south end of the dam was high enough to force the water over the northern end. Flood control in the Salt River Valley was about to become a reality.

Masons laid the last block on February 5, 1911. The finished structure rose 284 feet from the bed of the river. It was 184 feet thick on the bottom and 16 feet wide on top, and it arched a thousand feet from canyon wall to canyon wall in a great concave bow. Behind it the Salt and Tonto spread across the basin floor as tongues of water probed arroyos of the Mazatzals and Sierra Anchas. The dam inundated more than 16,000 acres, making it the largest artificial lake in the world at that time. It was nearly four years behind schedule and had cost more than ten million dollars, triple the original estimate, but the Reclamation Service still hailed it as a "monumental triumph of the skill and genius of [its] scientist creators." With its massive, rough-hewn wall and its three towers, the dam looked like a medieval castle bent to keep the waters at bay.

Its dedication took place a month later. On March 18, former president Theodore Roosevelt led a caravan of twenty-three cars up the Apache Trail from Phoenix. More than 200 other cars joined them from the Salt River Valley and Globe, even though a stagecoach had plunged off Fish Creek Hill and killed a woman passenger the day before. Late that afternoon, Roosevelt addressed the crowd on the causeway. He said that the structure, which was officially christened Roosevelt Dam in his honor, was one of the "two great achievements of his administration," the other being the Panama Canal. He predicted that the Salt River Valley would become "one of the richest agricultural areas in the world." Then he pushed a button that raised three huge iron gates. Water spouted from the dam and headed for the fields sixty miles downstream. Modern Arizona had just been delivered from the Tonto Basin's loins.

❋ ❋ World War I and the Cotton Boom

The completion of Roosevelt Dam did not end conflict in the Salt River Valley. Many members of the Salt River Valley Water Users Association believed that the Reclamation Service had spent too much money, so they demanded an investigation of the agency and a ten-year extension on the loan. Congress granted the extension in 1914. It also forced a Reclamation Service board of inquiry to investigate the agency, which most farmers considered autocratic. The board discovered a whole series of inequities within the project. Forty percent of the land was being farmed by tenants because it was too expensive to purchase. Ditches were being built to irrigate new fields even though old fields were not receiving the water they were entitled to. Nearly 47,000 acres belonged to water users who owned more than 160 acres of land. The Jeffersonian crusade to limit federal reclamation had not prevailed.

Despite such controversies, however, membership in the association continued to grow. In 1912, 3,048 farmers belonged. The number rose to 5,051 by 1919. Those farmers cultivated 205,000 acres of land, with an additional 45,000 acres outside project boundaries. In addition, revenues from the sale of hydroelectric power were beginning to pour in. With their canals flowing and their coffers filling, members of the association voted to take control of the project in 1917 after the secretary of the interior offered to turn it over to them. They also agreed to repay the government $60 an acre over twenty years. The original estimate had been $12.50.

The biggest reason for their optimism was World War I, which disrupted shipping and sent the prices of domestic agricultural products soaring. Just about every crop made money, and at the beginning of the war, diversity characterized Salt River Valley agriculture. Alfalfa covered about half of the land, but farmers cultivated thousands of acres of wheat, barley, vegetables, melons, citrus, and other crops as well. And even though much of the forage was exported, large herds of cattle and sheep wintered on valley fields, and a local dairy industry flourished. "Alfalfa was King, Cotton was Queen, and every Dairy Cow was a Princess," the *Arizona Republican* of August 19, 1917, proclaimed.

The queen soon consumed her children and staged a ferocious palace coup. Extra-long-staple cotton yielded a fiber with greater tensile strength than fiber from varieties with shorter staples, which made it attractive as an industrial fabric, particularly for tires. But long-staple cotton required a longer growing season than the humid Cotton Belt of the southern United States could provide, so most of the world's crop came from Egypt and the Sudan, where it had been developed by British capital. When World War I broke out, however, Great Britain slapped an embargo on the export of long-staple cotton to other countries in order to insure its own supply. Tire companies in the United States were suddenly cut off from their source at a time when the War Department had just ordered thousands of airplanes, which needed cotton fiber for their tires and the fabric covering their wings. Arizona's "long-staple cotton craze" was about to begin.

In 1916, at the beginning of the boom, farmers in the Salt River Valley were growing 7,300 acres of extra-long-staple cotton. Then Goodyear Tire & Rubber Company of Akron, Ohio, bought 24,000 acres of undeveloped land southwest of Phoenix and rushed 1,500 acres into production in 1917. Goodyear also contracted with other farmers to buy more than $3 million worth of their cotton. When other tire companies like Firestone and Dunlop joined Goodyear in the valley, production jumped from 29,000 acres in 1917 to 69,000 the following year. Yuma farmers grew an additional 3,000 to 4,000 acres. Total Arizona acreage increased to 82,000 acres in 1919.

Then, in 1920, cotton production went through the roof. Between 1916 and 1919, prices rose from $233 to $406 a bale, with Goodyear paying as much as $625 ($1.25 a pound). Everyone was convinced that the price would soon leap to $1.50 a pound, so acreage in Arizona and California tripled from 88,500 acres to 243,000 acres. Most of those acres (200,000) were in Arizona, with 180,000 in the Salt River Valley alone. The valley became a vast, uniform grid as farmers plowed under their other crops and sold off at least 30,000 of their 50,000 dairy cattle. "The milk producer and the land owner have yielded to the siren song of cotton and much good dairy stock has gone to the block," observed the *Arizona State Magazine* of March 1919.

With irrigated land increasing in price by as much as 800 percent, dairying and alfalfa production became losing propositions for established farmers and astronomically expensive ones for those looking to buy land. The patchwork of grainfields, date orchards, and citrus groves disappeared as monoculture spread across the Salt River Valley. Cotton joined Cattle and Copper as the three C's driving Arizona's economy. Along the way, Queen Cotton had a sex change, and King Cotton reigned.

✳   ✳   **The Cotton Bust**

The cotton craze extended beyond the valley as well. Cultivation in Yuma County increased from 11,000 acres in 1917 to 27,000 in 1920. In Pinal County the rise was even more rapid, with acreage more than tripling from 2,500 acres in 1919 to 9,000 acres the following year. The fever for "white gold" even swept through the Santa Cruz Valley. "They came—they are still coming— from the cotton lands of Oklahoma; from the Imperial Valley," gushed Richard Wells in a national agricultural magazine called *The Country Gentleman* of April 17, 1920. "Men who never saw cotton grow in their lives . . . brought their bankroll, their youngsters and their household goods down to find the foot of the rainbow."

But then the rainbow evaporated as the war ended and the military canceled many of its contracts. During the fall of 1920, when the bumper crop was ready to be harvested, 450,000 bales of Egyptian cotton flooded the U.S. market. Instead of the $1.50 a pound they expected, Arizona cotton growers were lucky to sell their product for 28 cents a pound. And since it cost 65 cents a pound to grow the crop, many farmers went broke. According to the overheated reports of the time, "white gold" quickly became a "white elephant," the "roulette and faro" crop "that led Salt River Valley up the easy grade to the very top and then kicked it over the edge on the steep side."

The bust did more than bankrupt farmers. Many businesses related to cotton also went broke, banks failed, and even large corporations like Goodyear teetered on the verge of insolvency. Ranchers paid "dizzy prices" for the little alfalfa that was available, and big farmers took over smaller farmers by assuming their loans and taxes. All these ripple effects led to the most basic effect of all. The farm population of Arizona declined by 20 percent, from 90,560 in 1920 to 71,954 in 1925. King Cotton turned out to be a tyrant who drove many of his subjects away.

The people hardest hit, however, were not the farmers or the bankers but the laborers who picked the scratchy, dusty crop. Before the cotton boom, the demand for seasonal labor in Arizona was limited. Many of the farms were small and family-operated, and thus supplied most of their own labor. But the rapid shift to cotton led to much larger operations as well as expanded production. Instead of many different crops with different schedules of cultivation, 200,000 acres of cotton had to be planted and harvested at the same time. Moreover, the tremendous increase in demand coincided with World War I and the draft, so the shortage of labor in the Salt River Valley and other agricultural centers became intense. At first, Arizona cotton growers recruited nearby Pima and Tohono O'odham Indians. Then they advertised for cotton pickers in New Mexico, Texas, Oklahoma, Arkansas, Missouri, and Louisiana. But there were not enough Indians to harvest the crop, and many of the Cotton Belt migrants slipped away to find better jobs. So the growers did what Western mining companies, railroads, and agribusinesses had been doing for decades. They turned to Mexico. Once again, Mexican labor became the foundation of Arizona's economic growth.

It required considerable political maneuvering to secure that labor. In the throes of wartime xenophobia, Congress had just passed the 1917 Immigration Act, which established a head tax and a literacy requirement for all aliens entering the United States. Along with other Western legislators, the members of Arizona's congressional delegation fought to repeal the law. They were not successful, but they did manage to win a temporary admission program for

Mexican workers. More than 72,000 Mexicans legally entered the country to work in Western industries between 1917 and 1922. The number of undocumented immigrants was much larger.

In Arizona, thousands of those workers ended up in the cotton fields. The Arizona Cotton Growers Association assessed its members $1.50 a bale to send labor recruiters to Mexico. In 1919 and 1920 alone the association spent $125,000 to find pickers and transport them to the Salt River Valley. The following year the cost rose to $295,826. The expense was enormous, but one official of the organization later estimated that it saved farmers "who stayed in line" $2,800,000 because it allowed the growers to fix wages and eliminate bidding wars for labor.

If you were a grower, not a picker, those accomplishments were impressive. Between 1918 and 1921 the association provided its members with perhaps as many as 30,000 Mexican workers, including Yaqui Indians from Sonora. Unions generally opposed Mexican immigration, but after an investigation in 1920, two Labor Department officials with strong union ties concluded that Mexican workers were not taking Anglo jobs. The officials also pointed out why few Anglos wanted to work in the cotton fields. Most pickers lived in camps unfit for animals. They slept in tents or overcrowded shacks. They drank from canals. There were no showers, no laundry facilities, and no electricity. Some camps did not even have running water or outhouses. The pickers were paid 1½ to 2 cents a pound, and an entire family was lucky to make $18 a week, half of which was withheld to defray transportation costs, while the other half evaporated as repayments for the debts the workers accumulated in company commissaries that charged exorbitant prices. To make matters worse, growers occasionally refused to pay their pickers at all and routinely reneged on their contractual obligation to pay their way back to Mexico. No wonder the unions were never able to mount much of a challenge to Mexican labor in the cotton fields.

Mexican farm workers, like Mexican miners, resisted the exploitation. In June 1920, 4,000 of them demanded better wages and full compliance with their contracts. The growers responded by declaring that the workers were engaged in an illegal strike. The leaders of the protest were arrested and many were deported, often by employees of the cotton companies themselves. This, after all, was the era of the Jerome and Bisbee deportations, when public officials condoned corporate vigilante action.

But the real crisis arose in the winter of 1920–21, after the cotton had been harvested. Ten thousand Mexican migrants were stranded with no jobs, no money, and no return tickets to Mexico. Unions and charities did what they could, but it was never enough. The Arizona State Federation of Labor set up soup kitchens and fed a single meal a day to 900 people. The Mexican consul wrested $17,000 from his revolution-weary government to provide food and clothing for the castaways. Despite those efforts, however, thousands swelled the relief rolls of Salt River Valley communities, causing community officials to bitterly denounce the growers and demand the return of the workers to Mexico. The city manager of Phoenix even rounded up several hundred indigent families and dumped them in front of the headquarters of the Arizona Cotton Growers Association in Tempe. The growers grudgingly responded by hauling a few hundred hungry individuals to Nogales in the back of big trucks. They were the lucky ones. Most of their compatriots had to fend for themselves.

*   *   *   Agriculture During the 1920s

Like drunks lining up to take the pledge, the first reaction of the farmers was to renounce long-staple cotton. Between 1920 and 1924, production dropped from 200,000 acres to 9,000. Some farmers returned to wheat, barley, and alfalfa, while others planted citrus groves along the Arizona Canal north of Phoenix. The advent of railroad cars allowed farmers to grow more melons and produce, especially lettuce. Meanwhile, livestock once again spent the cold months in the Salt River Valley, and a thriving feedlot industry gave rise to Edward Tovrea's Arizona Packing Company, which according to the *Arizona Republican* of December 30, 1928, was the "largest and most modern equipped packing plant between Fort Worth, Texas, and the Pacific Coast."

Nonetheless, cotton remained Arizona's most important crop as the cultivation of short-staple upland varieties increased from 30,000 acres to 169,000. That meant that the demand for seasonal labor remained enormous. At the same time, however, the postwar depression triggered another wave of xenophobia that led to passage of the Quota Act of 1924—which imposed on immigrants a ten-dollar visa requirement on top of the eight-dollar head tax of the act of 1917—and the creation of the Border Patrol a year later. Farmers vociferously complained about its roundups of Mexican workers, and Border Patrol officials were often told to "go easy" until the cotton harvest had ended. But the new agency's vigilance made farm work ever more uncertain for Mexican workers across the Southwest.

To get around Bureau of Immigration restrictions, Arizona growers lured more than 6,000 Puerto Ricans to their cotton fields in 1926, promising them "suitable living quarters" as well as free movies and electric lights. When the Puerto Ricans arrived and found that the "suitable living quarters" were shacks or leaky tents, they went on strike. The strike was broken, the Puerto Ricans picked cotton for a season, but no more islanders arrived the following year and the first group drifted away.

By the late 1920s, however, paved highways had been built to link Arizona with the cotton states of Texas, Oklahoma, and Arkansas. Growers began recruiting workers there as early as 1924, and by the end of the decade, pickers from the Southern Plains were Arizona's most important source of farm labor. This was due in part to the crackdown on Mexican immigration, which escalated into the repatriation movement of the early 1930s. Another factor was the environmental degradation of the Cotton Belt itself, which turned the Southern Plains into the Dust Bowl. Thousands of farmers and farm workers were forced to hit the road, stopping off in Arizona for a season or two on their way to California. Some were blacks, but most were Anglos. The gaunt and weary white faces captured by photographer Dorothea Lange now dominated Arizona cotton camps.

✳ ✳ ✳ The San Carlos Project

Farmers not only had to find new sources of labor but new sources of water as well. Because the Salt overflowed Roosevelt Dam four times during the dam's first eight years, the Salt River Valley Water Users Association built three new dams downstream from Roosevelt during the 1920s: Mormon Flat Dam (1923–1925), which formed Canyon Lake; Horse Mesa Dam (1924–1927), which created Apache Lake; and Stewart Mountain Dam (1928–1930), which produced Saguaro Lake. The major purposes of those dams were to control floods and to generate hydroelectric power so that the association could sell electricity in order to repay the federal government for the cost of building the dams. Yet the water impounded by Mormon Flat Dam also brought about 34,000 acres into cultivation southeast of Chandler during the late 1920s.

Along the Gila River, on the other hand, water remained a scarce and contested resource. After winning election to the House of Representatives in 1912, Carl Hayden lobbied incessantly for the government to resurrect its plan to build a storage dam near San Carlos. Hayden opposed all attempts to restore Pima water by taking it away from upstream farmers. Instead, he argued that the future of the Akimel O'odham rested on the construction of another reclamation project, not a battle over Indian water rights. World War I delayed his legislative maneuvers, but in the early 1920s, Hayden resumed the struggle, finding a powerful ally in Dirk Lay, a Presbyterian missionary to the Pimas. Lay personally contacted 5,000 Presbyterian ministers, who showered their congressional delegations with letters and telegrams in support of the San Carlos Project. The result was the San Carlos Project Bill, which was approved in 1924.

From the beginning, the project was a flawed compromise. Because of pressure from non-Indian interests, the legislation established an irrigation district of 100,000 acres. Half of those acres fell within the reservation, but the other half belonged to farmers between Florence and Casa Grande, who irrigated about 35,000 acres of cotton with water from the Gila. Farther west, in the Casa Grande Valley, 140 wells pumped groundwater to 18,000 acres of cotton and several thousand acres of other crops, particularly lettuce. The Pimas with their government allotments of ten acres could not compete with the big growers. In the words of one government farmer who worked on the reservation, "The change came with the tractors. They [the O'odham] saw the white man sitting up there on top of the tractor and doing in one day what it took them a week to do with horses. It took the heart out of them."

The construction of Coolidge Dam was supposed to change that bleak picture. Engineers designed the strange, bulging, dome-shaped structure to fill a reservoir with 1,300,000 acre-feet of water. They based that capacity on an average runoff of 460,000 acre-feet per year—a projection developed during the abnormally wet years of 1899–1928. Unfortunately for the Pimas, however, the decades of man-made drought caused by upstream diversion were followed by a regional drying trend that reduced runoff to an average 215,000 acre-feet a year. At the dam's dedication on March 4, 1930, humorist Will Rogers looked out across the swampy reservoir and quipped, "If this was my lake, I'd mow it." Everyone in the audience laughed, but the joke was on them. It took San Carlos Lake more than fifty years to reach its capacity. Most of the rest of the time the reservoir was less than two-thirds full.

But even though Coolidge Dam was not much good at trapping water for irrigation, it did control floods, and once floodwaters no longer surged down the Gila to replenish alluvial aquifers, seeps dried up, trees died, and at least twenty-nine species of birds flew away and never returned. Cultivated land on the reservation rose from 12,000 to 30,000 acres during the 1930s, but most of it was leased by non-Indian farmers and irrigated by pump-powered wells. Thousands of Akimel O'odham, in contrast, hired themselves out as field hands in the cotton fields spreading across central Arizona. Engineers with good intentions had destroyed what was left of the lower Gila and had driven the last nail into the coffin of Pima agriculture.

Meanwhile, the area south of the reservation flourished. During the 1920s and 1930s, groundwater, not rivers, primed Arizona agriculture. This was true around the margins of the Salt River Project in Maricopa County, and it was true in the Santa Cruz Valley from Marana to Sahuarita. But the largest region of agricultural development was Pinal County, where new communities like Coolidge and Eloy took root in the creosote flats and dust. Pumping accounted for about 40 percent (96,224 acre-feet) of the San Carlos Project's average annual irrigation budget, climbing to as high as 69 percent when the reservoir was low. Outside project boundaries, pumps sucked twice as much water (more than 200,000 acre-feet) out of the ground each year. By 1942 there were 130,000 acres of nonreservation land under production. Casa Grande, Coolidge, and Eloy became boomtowns mining Pleistocene aquifers rather than copper ore.

* * * The Colorado River Compact and the Anti-Compact Crusade

The biggest prize of all was the Colorado River, which ran like a drug through the dreams of Arizonans for most of the twentieth century. By the 1920s the Salt had been tamed and the Gila was being broken and maimed. The San Pedro, Santa Cruz, and Little Colorado rivers had never amounted to much in the first place. The Colorado, on the other hand, taunted Arizona farmers as it roared down out of the Rockies on its 1,440-mile journey to the Gulf of California. The river deposited 140,000 acre-feet of silt a year in an enormous delta where real jaguars and mythical alligators stalked the fantasies of the few explorers who ventured there. It also poured millions of acre-feet of runoff into an arm of the ocean that belonged to Mexico. Arizona farmers and politicians figured that there had to be a way to channel that water onto the desert and make it bloom.

That put Arizona on a collision course with California, which had already been diverting the Colorado for a generation to irrigate a hallucination called the Imperial Valley. In 1849 a heat-crazed physician named Oliver Wozencraft fell off his horse in the Mojave Desert on his way to the California goldfields. Crawling to the edge of the Alamo Barranca, he stared into the Salton Sink, a vast shimmering depression 300 feet below sea level. It was one of the hottest, most desolate areas in North America, but what Wozencraft saw there were not sand dunes and salt flats but an oasis of green fields and flowing water. He spent the rest of his life trying to convince others of his vision, dying in 1887 after a congressional committee dismissed it as the "fantastic folly of an old man."

Ten years later, however, engineer Charles Rockwood and investor George Chaffey formed the California Development Company (CDC) and turned folly into profit, at least for a time. In a land where sandstorms lashed across the desert in blinding sheets, Rockwood dug the sixty-mile-long Alamo Canal from the Colorado to the Salton Sink while Chaffey changed its name to the Imperial Valley. "Water Is King: Here Is Its Kingdom," he proclaimed, and people believed him. By 1904, more than 7,000 people were growing 75,000 acres of alfalfa and barley in the sink's rich alluvial soil. Wozencraft's hallucination had become real.

The vision became a nightmare the following year. When their first canal silted up, Rockwood and Chaffey breached the Colorado's banks and dug another one. But the partners had no money to put a headgate on it, so they gambled that the Colorado would remain as tranquil as it had been during their development's first four years. They were wrong, not just on a human but on a geologic scale. The first floods surged out of the mountains in March 1905, driving an uprooted oak tree into the mouth of the intake and creating a whirlpool that sucked floodwater into the canal. Within days the channel was sixty feet wide, and the floods kept seething off and on for the next sixteen months. By the time they subsided, the Salton Sink had been transformed into the Salton Sea, a briny lake that was seventy-two feet deep in places and that spread across 150 square miles. Thirty thousand acres of new farmland drowned, and many farmers went broke and moved away. The California Development Company itself folded under tons of water and silt.

Then the Colorado began to backtrack like a predator stalking its hunter. Because the sink was below sea level, the floodwaters of the Colorado plunged nearly 300 feet in elevation as they rushed down the steep grade of the CDC canal. So, after filling the Salton Sink, the river backcut through the loose alluvial soil, creating a small waterfall that grew larger and larger as it chewed its way upstream. By 1907 the waterfall was 100 feet tall. If the Southern Pacific Railroad, which took over the CDC, had not spent three million dollars to throw a rock dam across the intake, the waterfall would have created a channel so deep that the Colorado never could have flowed back into the Gulf of California. Through greed and blunders, Rockwood and Chaffey almost reshaped the topography of the lower Colorado River Basin.

The farmers of the Imperial Valley spent the next two decades erecting a series of levees to keep the Colorado at bay, but the levees were only a temporary barricade. The Reclamation Service, under Arthur Davis, John Wesley Powell's nephew, decided to tame the river once and for all. As a young engineer, Davis had worked out a plan to develop the entire Colorado River drainage from Wyoming to the Gulf of California. In 1917, when California interests went to Washington to win support for their proposed All-American Canal, Davis shot down the proposal. He was not opposed to the canal itself, but he envisioned it as part of a much more sweeping program, one controlled and financed by the federal government, not private corporations. Irrigation, flood control, water storage, the generation of hydroelectric power—Davis wanted it all. But the cornerstone of his scheme was the construction of the biggest dam in the world "at or near Boulder Canyon" between Nevada and Arizona. The "Great Pyramid of the American Desert" had been conceived.

Before that pyramid could be built, however, the waters of the Colorado had to be divided among the seven states it drained. Those states—Wyoming, Colorado, Utah, New Mexico, Nevada, Arizona, and California—had very different economies with very different needs. Moreover, the political ecology of the Colorado Basin bore little resemblance to the flow of its rivers and streams. Most of the runoff originated in the Upper Basin states, yet the greatest water demand and political power resided in southern California, which contributed next to nothing to the river. The parties involved realized that the apportionment of the Colorado was the biggest pie they were ever going to cut up. None of them could foresee all the implications of their decisions, but they knew those decisions would shape their industries and their states for generations to come.

The single most powerful coalition that emerged was between California and the Reclamation Service. After initial resistance, the Californians realized that they had to buy Davis's whole package to get their ditch. They therefore submitted a series of bills to construct both the dam and the All American Canal. The other states, in contrast, opposed the legislation at first because they believed that Boulder Dam would only benefit California. They also advanced their own schemes to utilize the river, with Colorado arguing that it had the right to all water arising within its boundaries. The fight was long, intense, and complicated, and for several years it seemed that no consensus would be achieved.

But then the U.S. Supreme Court upheld the doctrine of prior appropriation in *Wyoming v. Colorado* (1922), dismissing Colorado's contention. That decision caused Upper Basin leaders to reassess their opposition to Boulder Dam. Delph Carpenter of Colorado came up with the compromise that eventually prevailed. He proposed that the Colorado River Basin be cut in two at Lee's Ferry, with half the river's flow (7.5 million acre-feet a year) going to the Upper Basin (Wyoming, Colorado, and parts of Utah, New Mexico, and Arizona) and half to the Lower Basin (California, Nevada, and parts of Arizona, Utah, and New Mexico). After months of debate presided over by Secretary of the Interior Herbert Hoover, Carpenter's proposal was accepted. The water commissioners of all seven states signed the Colorado River Compact in Santa Fe, New Mexico, on November 25, 1922.

Now they had to persuade their state legislatures to ratify the agreement.

Bitter battles broke out in all the states, but the bitterest of them all took place in Arizona, which would have to compete with California for the Lower Basin allotment. Many Arizona leaders, including Representative Carl Hayden, initially supported the compact. Hayden did not believe that the Upper Basin states would ever use their share of the water and figured there would be plenty of the Colorado left over for Arizona. But George W. P. Hunt did not see it that way. Re-elected to his fourth term as governor two days before the compact was signed, Hunt believed that Arizona was entitled to the lion's share of the Colorado because the river flowed through or along the state for almost half its length (580 miles). "Arizona cannot afford to give away her greatest natural resource, with millions of acres awaiting development, and she cannot afford to plunge blindly into a contract that may be unfair to her," he warned the Arizona legislature in his inaugural address in January 1923. Hunt went on to say that Arizona's economy could not depend on copper forever. Colorado River water for irrigation and hydroelectric power was the lifeblood of Arizona's future prosperity.

Over the next few years, Hunt's opposition to the compact hardened, and as it did, his flamboyant rhetoric heated up. In a jab against Mexico's rights to the river, he muttered about "Asiatic colonies in Mexico just across our border," referring to the 840,000 acres in northwestern Mexico rented to Japanese, Chinese, and Mexican farmers by American speculators like Harry Chandler, publisher of the *Los Angeles Times,* who headed a syndicate of such landowners. Anti-Oriental and anti-Mexican racism was the subtext—and a powerful rallying cry—for opponents of the compact.

Because of his rhetorical excesses and enormous size, Hunt was as easy to caricature as he was to criticize. Hoover dismissed him as that "blunderbuss of a governor in Arizona, who knew nothing of engineering." Arizonans joked that while Jesus may have walked on water, their state had a governor who ran on the Colorado River. But Hunt touched a chord that reverberated not only among his populist followers but also among some of his worst enemies. State representative Lewis Douglas, the son of James S. Douglas of the Phelps Dodge and United Verde copper companies, led the fight to amend the compact in the Arizona legislature. Douglas asserted that Colorado River water was a resource that belonged to the state of Arizona, not the federal government, and that Arizona had the right to levy a tax on power generated by its hydroelectric plants. He did so because the copper companies believed that royalties from the sale of power would reduce their own state tax burden. Douglas later attacked Hunt on other issues, but the two men and their supporters made state control of the Colorado the canon that dominated Arizona politics for the next two decades.

Other Arizona leaders like Carl Hayden quickly came around, especially after William Mulholland, the man who seized the water of the Owens Valley for Los Angeles, announced that his city wanted 1,500 second-feet (1,500 cubic feet per second) of Colorado water for its domestic supply. Arizona now had a new villain, Los Angeles, "the West's most notorious water hustler" according to historian Norris Hundley. The anticompact coalition soon included the copper companies, the private utilities, and the Salt River Valley Water Users Association, which derived most of its revenue from the sale of hydroelectric power. California was stealing Arizona's river with the full support of the federal government, and that made Arizonans mad.

Because of such opposition, ratification died in the Arizona legislature. The battle then shifted to Washington, where Arizona's congressional delegation led the fight to block the Boulder Canyon Dam bill, which was reintroduced for the fourth time in 1926 by Representative Phil Swing and Senator Hiram Johnson of California. Under both the bill and the compact, California would receive 4.4 million acre-feet of the Colorado, while Arizona's share would only be 2.8 million acre-feet (Nevada received the remaining 300,000 acre-feet). An amendment granted Arizona exclusive rights to the Gila River and stipulated that those rights "shall never be subject to any diminution whatever" by any treaty with Mexico. But by then, anti-California sentiment was so strong that compromise would have been political suicide for any Arizona politician.

By 1928, however, California's support had overwhelmed Arizona's opposition. In May the House passed the Swing-Johnson bill, which was still called the Boulder Canyon Project Act even though the dam site had been shifted to Black Canyon twenty miles downstream. Hayden and Henry Ashurst, Arizona's senior senator, led a filibuster that stalled it in the Senate that spring, but at the opening of the second session the Senate invoked cloture and passed an amended bill on December 14. The margin was overwhelming—64 to 11. By the following spring, six of the seven states had ratified the Colorado River Compact, and President Herbert Hoover, one of the pact's architects, declared that both it and the Boulder Canyon Project would now take effect. Two years later the construction of Boulder, then Hoover, then Boulder, then Hoover Dam—the name changed back and forth for seventeen years—began.

✳ ✳ ✳   The Beginnings of the Central Arizona Project

To the rest of the United States, Hoover Dam symbolized the mastery of man over nature at a time when many men and women did not have steady jobs or enough to eat. White concrete against black rock, the structure curved upward for 726 feet, making it the highest dam in the world. It was the New West's most ambitious sculpture, public art that prevented floods and produced hydroelectric power. More than 5,000 workers braved heat, isolation, and death to build it, and it was the first major stage in the transformation of the Colorado from a wild river to a tame ditch.

Depression-era writers fell all over one another rhapsodizing about the dam. Frank Waters called it a "visual symphony written in steel and concrete . . . inexpressibly beautiful of line, magnificently original, strong, simple, and majestic as the greatest works of art of all time and all people." Many Arizonans were not as captivated. To them the dam was a bitter symbol of defeat, a monument to Arizona's powerlessness and California's greed. The state's water politics therefore became increasingly defiant during the 1930s.

That defiance reached its comic-opera climax in 1934, when Governor Benjamin Moeur called out the Arizona National Guard to prevent the construction of Parker Dam 150 miles downstream from the "American Pyramid." Parker Dam was the much more prosaic of the two—a utilitarian structure designed to divert Colorado River water into an aqueduct leading to Los Angeles. It was not going to make another oasis like the Imperial Valley bloom in the desert; it was simply going to water the lawns and wash down the throats of Arizona's insatiable urban neighbor on the Pacific coast. So Moeur summoned about a hundred of his troops and marched them off to the heat-scorched, dust-tormented dam site eighteen miles from Parker, Arizona. There the guardsmen commandeered a ferryboat, which became Arizona's "navy," and one of them caught pneumonia and died.

The press treated the whole affair as a joke, and in most respects it was. Moeur's proclamation "To Repel An Invasion," his declaration of martial law, the very idea of one state taking up arms to halt a construction project all smacked of lunacy. But the stunt did delay the dam for more than a year, and Moeur did wring approval of the Gila Irrigation Project east of Yuma out of the Department of the Interior in return for recalling his "machine-gunners" and "infantrymen." Meanwhile, Arizona lost a series of Colorado water cases in the U.S. Supreme Court and did not ratify the Santa Fe Compact until 1944.

What the state adopted in place of pragmatism or compromise was to embark on a quest for its own Holy Grail. The grail, of course, was water—Colorado River water impounded by a huge dam and transported from 300 to 500 miles to the farmland of central and southern Arizona. In the 1940s the grail became known as the Central Arizona Project, but in the 1920s it was called everything from the "Arizona High Line Canal" to a "madman's dream." Regardless of how quixotic it was, however, the quest burrowed deep into Arizona's collective political psyche. When Congressman Morris Udall was fighting President Jimmy Carter to keep the Central Arizona Project from being abolished fifty years later, he said, "The Central Arizona Project is a very old dream. I first heard it from my grandfather."

One of the first of the dream spinners was George Maxwell, founder and executive secretary of the National Reclamation Association. Maxwell had been involved in Arizona water politics since the 1890s, when he proclaimed the virtues of the Salt River Project across the nation. After that project became a reality, he turned his attention to the Colorado, arguing that a dam should be built in Boulder or Black Canyon to divert water to irrigate 2.5 million acres in Arizona. W. S. Norviel, Arizona's water commissioner, appointed a former member of the U.S. Geological Survey named Harry Blake to study the proposal. "Diverting and carrying water across a hot, arid country without crossing any large bodies of irrigable land until a point 470 miles south of its diversion is reached, would be a very precarious undertaking," Blake concluded. "In fact, it could not be considered feasible unless these lands under irrigation were of such value that cost could not be considered. This is not the case . . . in Arizona."

Other experts, including Arthur Davis, agreed with Blake's assessment, but Maxwell was not deterred. He called for another study to investigate a "high-line canal" leading from a 700-foot-high rock-fill dam at Glen Canyon upriver from Lee's Ferry. Davis retorted that the route would wind through mountainous terrain for much of its 400- to 450-mile course and would be "a waste of our money and time." G.E.P. Smith, a professor at the University of Arizona, concurred, dismissing the canal as an "absurdity." When asked to comment on a rock-fill Glen Canyon Dam, he could only mutter, "My engineering instincts rebel when I try to contemplate it."

But Maxwell's real obsession became the "Asiatic" menace swelling like a tick on Arizona water just south of the border. After the Santa Fe Compact was signed, he ranted to President Harding that the agreement was "a carefully camouflaged effort to hamstring Arizona and . . . to establish a great Asiatic city and state in [the] Colorado River delta." He went on to say that the compact would inevitably result "in a war with Asia in which Arizona and California would be the shock country as was Belgium in the World War." With his white beard and ruddy face, the great crusader for reclamation had become a racist crackpot.

Another, more influential knight of the quest was Fred T. Colter, a rancher and state senator from Apache County. In 1923, Colter founded the Arizona Highline Reclamation Association to champion Maxwell's scheme. Then, in behalf of the state, he filed on all Colorado River water that flowed through Arizona, proposing a series of forty projects to dam, pump, and channel that water to the Salt River Valley and Pinal County. More than anyone else, Colter kept the dream alive in the 1920s and 1930s. He organized public meetings. He ground out propaganda. He published maps showing the routes of his improbable canals. And even though Colter himself failed to win the governorship on several tries, he terrorized any candidate or elected official who dared to suggest that Arizona ratify the compact. That did not happen until after Colter's death in January 1944.

For more than two decades, then, Arizona went its contrary way, fighting and losing in Congress, in the Supreme Court, in just about every political arena except its own voting booths. Farmers expanded their acreage by pumping groundwater aquifers, not by diverting the Colorado. Beneath the grandiose schemes and grotesque racism, however, the greatest irony of all lurked in the pages of the hydrological reports. The Colorado River Compact was based on the assumption that the average annual flow of the river was 16.4 million acre-feet at Lee's Ferry, the dividing line between the upper and lower basins. Hydrologists derived that figure from Reclamation Service measurements made at a gauging station at Laguna Dam just north of Yuma between 1899 and 1920. The dam was hundreds of miles south of Lee's Ferry, but the agency figured that losses from evaporation were offset by the flow of tributaries in between. Furthermore, the measurements did not include discharge from the Gila, which emptied its waters—supposedly 1.07 million acre-feet a year—into the Colorado below Laguna Dam. Under pressure from the politicians, the engineers made the Colorado swell.

Their calculations turned out to be scientific wishful thinking, a bad case of hydrological myopia based upon two of the wettest decades on record. During the drought years of the 1930s, the average annual flow of the Colorado was 11.8 million acre-feet. That average was nearly 5 million acre-feet shy of the 7.5 million acre-feet apiece promised to the upper and lower basins and the 1.5 million acre-feet ceded to Mexico under an international treaty signed in 1944. A number of scientists suspected as much in the 1920s when the compact was being debated. In 1928, Major General William L. Sibert's Colorado River Board of geologists and hydrologists issued a report that recommended the construction of Boulder Dam but concluded that the flow of the Colorado was probably about 15 million acre-feet a year—a figure supported by the average flow of 14.8 million acre-feet between 1896 and 1968.

By then, however, the die was cast. Arizona wanted the grail even if the grail was tarnished and the Colorado was not quite the river the commissioners thought it was back in 1922. Science took a backseat to politics, and men like Carl Hayden spent the rest of their careers fighting for their state's fair share of a pipe dream. They saw the state change. They saw the old extractive order recede into the countryside as a new urban order arose. But the cities needed water to grow, and the competition with California intensified as Arizona attracted its own urban industry and commerce. Besides, Hayden and others remembered and feared the bad years—the floods, the droughts—and wanted to guarantee a future for Arizona free of those fears.

A Hopi family at the Grand Canyon in about
1960. (Courtesy of the Arizona Historical
Foundation, Hayden Library, Arizona State
University)

III TRANSFORMATION

12

❋ ❋ Climate

In the late spring of 1898, a forty-two-year-old art critic from Rutgers University wandered into the Mojave Desert with a horse and a fox terrier for company. He carried a .30-30 rifle for large game and a Chicopee .22-caliber pistol for smaller prey. The rest of his outfit consisted of two light blankets, a shovel, a hatchet, a few pans, a couple of tin cups, and shot sacks stuffed with beans, chocolate, coffee, parched corn, and venison jerky. A later writer called him one of those "desert maniacs" who chose solitude over his own kind.

At the time, John C. Van Dyke was not very sure of his sanity himself. Like many other immigrants to the Southwest, he was sick, his lungs clenched with asthma. But Van Dyke did not take up residence in one of the "lunger camps," as tuberculosis (TB) tent sanatoriums were called. Instead, he and his two animal companions drifted across California, Arizona, and Sonora in a bizarre dance with beauty and death.

What an odd and haunting dance it was. Rather than fleeing the desert, Van Dyke embraced it, reversing the paths of the forty-niners by leaving southern California and heading east across the Mojave and Sonoran deserts. At night he watched the "misshapen orange-hued desert moon" rise in the immense and fathomless sky. During the day, he huddled in whatever shade he could find and scribbled down his precise yet shimmering impressions. The author of several treatises on art, Van Dyke was obsessed with color and light. He left no account of where he went or whom he encountered, but he did leave an incomparable record of such things as the sunset on Baboquivari Peak, which transformed the "tower-like shaft . . . from blue to topaz and from topaz to glowing red in the course of half an hour."

Van Dyke's manuscript, mailed to his publisher, Charles Scribner's Sons, from Del Rio, Texas, in 1901, was a love poem to the desert from a radical aesthete. Like his contemporaries in the art world, Van Dyke spurned realism. "You cannot always dissect a taste or a passion. Nor can you pin Nature to a board and chart her beauties with square and compasses," he wrote in his preface to the manuscript, which was published as *The Desert* in 1903. "Perhaps I can tell you something of what I have seen in these two years of wandering; but I shall never be able to tell you the grandeur of these mountains, nor the glory of color that wraps the burning sands at their feet. We shoot arrows at the sun in vain; yet still we shoot."

Those arrows penetrated the very heart of the matter about how people viewed the desert and Arizona. At a time when promoters were diverting the Colorado into the Imperial Valley, Van Dyke seized on the seemingly perverse notion that the desert should be left alone. He did not believe that rain followed the plow line. He did not want to mine copper or plant cotton or run cattle. He despised the commercialism of the Gilded Age. "The deserts should never be reclaimed," he argued. "They are the breathing spaces of the west and should be preserved forever." It was an idea that would resonate with greater force—and greater conflict—in the years to come.

✳ ✳ ✳   The Health Seekers

Van Dyke was using the term "breathing spaces" metaphorically, but thousands of other health seekers hoped that the metaphor was real. During the nineteenth century, respiratory ailments increased dramatically in the overcrowded cities of industrial America. The biggest killer was tuberculosis, which was known as phthisis, consumption, or the white plague. Physicians estimated that the disease was responsible for 12 out of every 100 deaths in the United

States during the late 1800s, infecting 10 percent of the population. A German scientist discovered the tubercule bacillus in 1882, but by the end of the century, doctors still had not developed an effective treatment for the disease. At an international convention in 1900, TB experts concluded that "there is no known medical specific for this fatal and increasing malady, and . . . the only hope of cure, in its curable stages, is the climatic cure."

The result, in the words of historian Billy M. Jones, was a steady westward streaming of "lungers, consumptives, phthisics, coughers, hackers, invalids, valetudinarians, sanitarians, asthmatics, rheumatics, white plaguers, pukers, and walking death." Colorado was their first major destination, followed by California, but Arizona, New Mexico, and southwestern Texas attracted their share of health seekers as well. Jones estimates that 20 to 25 percent of all immigrants to the Southwest during the nineteenth century came to the region to recover their health. The reason they chose the Southwest was because of their faith in the healing properties of warm, dry air.

That faith was fueled by the "miasmatic concept of contagion," which dominated nineteenth-century medical thought. Before the germ theory of disease began to prevail in the early 1900s, most physicians thought that illnesses were caused by unbalanced natural forces, particularly fogs, vapors, and the effluvia of rotting vegetable and animal matter. They believed that swamps and low-lying river valleys were particularly dangerous sources of "miasmata," a perception reinforced by the experiences of American pioneers in the Mississippi Valley, where malaria and dysentery stalked the settlers. "There appears to be in the great plan of Providence a scale in which the advantages and disadvantages of human condition are balanced," wrote one early-nineteenth-century historian. "Where the lands are extremely fertile . . . they are generally sickly."

With medical theory reinforcing folk beliefs in a balance between good and evil, it is easy to understand why the deserts of the Southwest came to be viewed as God's own sanatoriums. They were hot and dry, so they generated very little "miasmata." They were also agriculturally unproductive, at least under the technology of the time. Therefore, they had to be healthy. J. Ross Browne and other early Anglo travelers had taken great pleasure in disparaging Arizona's climate. Arizona was so hot that a "wicked soldier" who died there sent off for his blankets because he couldn't stand the "rigors of the climate" in hell. But to the blood-spitting, oxygen-starved refugees from the East, the hellish weather seemed heaven sent.

Before the 1880s, Arizona was too isolated and dangerous to attract many tuberculars. Nonetheless, a few, like John H. "Doc" Holliday, the whiskey swigging dentist who fought alongside Wyatt Earp, drifted into the territory to dry out their lungs. Other, more respectable health seekers included Governor A.P.K. Safford, businessman Sam Hughes, and promoter Hiram Hodge. After the arrival of the railroads, however, a modest boom in consumptives began. Individuals like Whitelaw Reid, owner and editor of the *New York Times,* and Harold Bell Wright, a novelist and playwright, spread the word that Arizona was a good place to recuperate from respiratory ailments. As a result, resorts like the Desert Inn Sanatorium east of Phoenix and even entire communities like Arcadia in the northern foothills of the Catalina Mountains sprang up to cater to wealthy invalids.

The majority of the health seekers, in contrast, could not afford to get well or die in comfort. Instead, they camped out in wagons or wandered across the desert as "burro tourists." They also crowded into the tent cities that sprouted like diseased mushrooms on the outskirts of larger towns. One such canvas slum was Sunnyslope, north of Phoenix. It grew up after a 1903 law forbade tents within the city limits. Another, Tentville, stretched along Park Avenue north of the University of Arizona in Tucson. Tentville was typical of Arizona's tubercular ghettos—a miserable conglomeration of several hundred people coughing and dying along a maze of dusty streets. Some of the better tents had steel roofs, raised wooden floors, and wooden wall panels to anchor the canvas. Most did not. There were no sewers, no streetlights, no transportation services. In the early 1900s, there were not even any nearby medical facilities. According to Dick Hall, who came there when he was nine with his brother and his consumptive mother, "The desert with so little vegetation seemed forlorn in contrast with the green fields and tall trees of Kansas or Iowa. The invalids were too sick to work. The nights were heartbreaking, and as one walked along the dark streets, he heard coughing from every tent. It was truly a place of lost souls and lingering death."

Isolation compounded the physical miseries of those souls. Hall remembered reading to his mother from the foot of her bed in their canvas-and-wood tent. That was as close as the little boy got. "She never dared hug or kiss any of us," Hall wrote. "In her mind it would have been tragic madness to do so." Consumptives were warned to keep three or four feet away from other people to avoid transmitting their disease. As a result, families split apart, mothers were afraid to nurse their babies, and many tuberculars wasted away or took their own lives because they had no one to nurse them or even keep them company. They were pariahs in a strange land.

Despite the widespread fear of infection, however, a number of individuals and organizations rose to the challenge. The Catholic Church operated St. Joseph's Hospital in Phoenix and St. Mary's Hospital in Tucson, which began treating TB patients as early as 1880. The Episcopalians founded St. Luke's Home in Phoenix in 1907 and St. Luke's-in-the-Desert in Tucson ten years later. The Southern Methodists built Whitwell Hospital on North First Avenue near Tentville in 1906. And then there were people like Christianna Gilchrist, head of the Associated Charities in Phoenix, and Oliver Comstock, a Baptist minister who ran the Adams Street Mission in Tentville. Hall recalled the minister—small and lean with huge muttonchop sideburns—pedaling from tent to tent with a kettle of soup fastened to the handlebars of his bicycle. That soup was all that some of the residents of Tentville had to eat.

After World War I even the federal government joined the fight. In 1918 a group of consumptive veterans squatted in an abandoned beer garden named Pastime Park four miles northwest of Tucson. When city officials complained about the squatters, the local chapter of the Red Cross persuaded the Public Health Service to open a hospital there. Pastime Park soon was caring for 275 patients, who received a variety of treatments popular at the time. Some had snake venom injected into their veins. Others had sterile air pumped into their chest cavities. Still others were exposed to high-intensity ultraviolet rays, which supposedly killed the tubercule bacillus. Not surprisingly, three or four veterans died each week, leading the patients to dub the hospital "Passaway Park."

Many Tucsonans would have been happy to see the hospital pass away as well. Relations between local residents and the veterans revealed the ambivalence Arizonans felt toward the tuberculars. Tucson businessmen and public officials saw the hospital as a source of federal funds for a depressed economy. Other Tucsonans wanted the "dope fiends" and "rum hounds" run out of town. Some of the servicemen found jobs or took classes at the university, but others squandered their disability checks on liquor in Nogales or marijuana and cocaine supplied by Tucson taxi drivers. The lungers were not the only ones in town who drank or used drugs, but their visibility—and the fear their disease aroused—made them convenient scapegoats in a community that had struggled with the invasion of invalids for more than twenty years.

Nonetheless, the servicemen were there to stay, and in 1928 a new veterans' hospital was built south of Tucson on land donated by businessman Albert Steinfeld. It was a large, graceful pink stucco building with 280 beds, and it symbolized the lasting impact health seekers had on communities such as Phoenix and Tucson. Long after places like Tentville disappeared, hospitals and sanatoriums erected to care for people with lung problems became the foundation of institutionalized health care in Arizona. Thousands of patients died in the desert, but many others survived, remaining in Arizona to found businesses, raise families, and help make the nation realize that the state had more to offer than cattle, copper, and cotton. There was health—and money—in sunshine, and more and more promoters were beginning to appreciate its lure.

✳ ✳ ✳ The Grand Canyon

They were also starting to realize that Arizona had another commodity to sell: natural beauty. In the late nineteenth century, few people shared Van Dyke's love of the desert, but an increasing number of tourists were visiting spectacular natural attractions like Yellowstone and Yosemite. Arizona had the greatest natural wonder of them all—the Grand Canyon of the Colorado—but it was lost in the vastness of the Coconino Plateau. The first Anglo surveyors and military scouts to visit the canyon in the nineteenth century considered it "altogether valueless" and were chilled by its immensity. "It seems intended by nature that the Colorado River, along the greater portion of its lonely and majestic way, shall be forever unvisited and undisturbed," wrote Lieutenant Joseph Ives in 1858. Tourists wanted Italian gardens, not geologic wastelands.

The enormous, brooding gorge did not begin to carve its way into the consciousness of the nation until Major John Wesley Powell ran the river in 1869. Powell was a veteran of the Civil War who had lost his right arm at the Battle of Shiloh. He was also a self-taught geologist, ethnologist, and natural historian with a probing mind and a genius for self-promotion. The fame he won as the leader of the first expedition down the Colorado helped him persuade Congress to fund a systematic survey of the Colorado Plateau known as the Powell Survey. Powell published the results of the survey four years later in an immense treatise entitled *Exploration of the Colorado River of the West and Its Tributaries, Explored in 1869, 1870, 1871 and 1872, under the Direction of the Secretary of the Smithsonian Institution*. The report contained lengthy descriptions of the region's geography, geology, and hydrology. But it was the first part of the report—Powell's diary of his wild boat trip "down the Great Unknown"—that fired the imagination of the American public in the nineteenth century and that became the bible of river runners a century later.

The diary was high adventure in the pursuit of science, and its publication solidified Powell's reputation as the "conqueror of the Colorado" and the "greatest explorer-hero since the days of Frémont," according to historian William Goetzmann. Wedding meticulous scientific inquiry to a narrative about dangerous rapids and daring rescues, Powell's *Exploration of the Colorado River of the West* filled in one of the last remaining blank spots on the map of the American West. Seven years later, geologist Clarence Dutton, one of Powell's assistants, published his poetic *Tertiary History of the Grand Canyon District*

(1882), graced with the elegant drawings of William Holmes. Government officials and the general public could now wallow in the geography and geologic history of the region.

Even after the reports brought the Grand Canyon to their readers, however, few visitors ventured there except in their imaginations. "All the scenic features of this cañon land are on a giant scale, strange and weird," Powell observed. "The streams run at depths almost inaccessible; lashing the rocks which beset their channels; rolling in rapids, and plunging in falls, and making a wild music which but adds to the gloom of the solitude." It was not a description calculated to lure the blank, fleshy, apathetic hordes John Muir despised at Yosemite. A few prospectors like John Hance and Louis Boucher worked asbestos and copper deposits below the South Rim. In 1889, engineer Robert Stanton and Frank Mason Brown, president of the Denver, Colorado, Canyon & Pacific Railroad, even retraced Powell's route in an ill-fated attempt to survey a railroad line along the Colorado. But the "wild music" of the Colorado did not work its magic on many people during the late nineteenth century. Those who heard it were often glad to escape with their lives.

Then the Santa Fe Railroad and the Fred Harvey Company orchestrated the Grand Canyon's rendezvous with the world. Before the advent of the automobile, mass tourism meant railroad tourism. As long as the canyon was a twenty-dollar, all-day, sixty-five-mile stage trip from Flagstaff, few tourists were willing to climb aboard. In 1901, however, the Santa Fe created a subsidiary, the Grand Canyon Railway Company, and built a spur line from Williams to the South Rim just east of Bright Angel Trail. The journey took three hours and cost $3.95. Suddenly a visit to the Grand Canyon no longer had to be a wilderness experience.

The arrival of the railroad triggered a tourist boom that eventually made Arizona the "Grand Canyon State." It also ignited more than two decades of struggle to control tourism at the canyon itself. On one side was the Santa Fe, the major economic power in northern Arizona. On the other were a handful of small entrepreneurs like Ralph Cameron, who filed numerous mining claims in the canyon and constructed the Bright Angel Trail. Like other fights over Arizona's natural resources, the battle ultimately resulted in the triumph of an alliance between big business and the federal government. For twenty years, however, Cameron littered the courts with convoluted lawsuits and the canyon with bogus mines.

The first stage of the contest was a struggle over the canyon rim. In the 1890s, Cameron built a two-story frame hotel at the head of Bright Angel Trail. A decade later the Santa Fe drove him out of the hotel business by building a much bigger and better establishment called El Tovar, a model of rustic elegance constructed of logs and native stone. To run it, the railroad brought in the Fred Harvey Company, which had managed Santa Fe Railroad hotels and restaurants since the 1870s. With their crisp "Harvey Girl" waitresses and their Spanish Revival and Indian Pueblo architecture—much of it designed by architect Mary Elizabeth Jane Colter—the Harvey enterprises defined railroad tourism in the Southwest during the early 1900s. Local entrepreneurs like Cameron could not compete with their capital or their expertise.

Cameron countered by trying to control access to the interior of the canyon itself. He ran Bright Angel Trail as a toll road. He turned Indian Gardens, the only spot with shade and water along the trail, into a dilapidated tourist camp where his employees occasionally made moonshine. He filed hundreds of mining claims and lined up investors to construct two enormous hydroelectric plants within the canyon. And he did his best to keep the Grand Canyon out of public hands, quarreling constantly with the Forest Service, which administered the forest reserve on both sides of the canyon set aside by President Benjamin Harrison in 1893, and fighting every plan to establish Grand Canyon National Park, which finally became a reality in 1919. Cameron was the prototype of that all-too-common character in the twentieth century West: the "rugged individual," who thumped his chest and railed against big business and big government in order to promote his own deals on public lands. The Sagebrush Rebellion of the 1970s echoed many of Cameron's cries.

In the end, Cameron lost the war. Even though he built a political career by portraying himself as a small businessman fighting the federal government and the Santa Fe Railroad, winning election to the U.S. Senate in 1920, the courts eventually declared his mining claims to be nonmineral, and the government shut down his typhoid-ridden tourist camp at Indian Gardens. The final blow came in 1926 when a six-part series in the *Los Angeles Times* disclosed all of his shady canyon schemes. Carl Hayden trounced him by a margin of three to two in the U.S. Senate race, and Cameron left Arizona for Philadelphia.

As self-serving as he was, however, Cameron was at least partly right. The Santa Fe Railroad and the federal government did indeed work together to turn the Grand Canyon into Arizona's premier tourist attraction. By 1923 more than 100,000 visitors a year were coming to the canyon to gawk at the vistas and to buy curios in shops that resembled Hopi pueblos. Most of the tourists rode the Santa Fe spur, and most stayed in Harvey-run hotels like El Tovar or the Bright Angel Lodge. The Colorado River may have created the Grand Canyon, but the Santa Fe Railroad made it famous. The railroad had tried and failed to make a fortune from its vast landholdings in northern Arizona. It found that fortune in sandstone and sunlight on the edge of the South Rim.

*   *   *   Tourism in the 1920s

          Tourism in Arizona flourished during the 1920s. Elegant resorts were built, dude ranching became popular, and cities as well as railroads advertised themselves. The tourist industry also became more democratic, attracting large numbers of the middle class as well as the rich. You no longer had to be wealthy or desperately ill to enjoy Arizona's climate and scenery.

One reason for the surge was a revolution in transportation. At the Grand Canyon, the number of tourists rose from 56,335 in 1920 to 162,715 nine years later, an increase of 289 percent. The number of tourists arriving by rail also grew, reaching a peak of 70,279 in 1927. But those 70,279 people represented only 47.6 percent of the total visitors to the South Rim that year. For the first time in the history of canyon tourism, automobiles brought more people than the Santa Fe Railroad. The supremacy of the car had begun.

That led to the proliferation of gas stations, "auto lodges" (motels), campgrounds, cafes, curio shops, and other facilities designed for tourists who traveled in their own vehicles. It also stimulated highway construction, much of it built with convict labor, and enabled tourism to free itself from the monopoly of the railroad companies. In 1927, the year the Arizona State Highway Commission was established, there were 1,988 miles of road in the state system. Only 219 miles were paved, but 869 were graveled and 758 were graded, allowing access to much of Arizona. The major north–south road, which became Highway 89, ran from Ash Fork to Nogales through Prescott, Wickenburg, Phoenix, Florence, and Tucson. With the completion of the Navajo Bridge near Lee's Ferry two years later, the route was extended from Flagstaff to Fredonia at the Arizona-Utah border. Two roads crossed the state from east to west. The northern route was the fabled Route 66, John Steinbeck's "mother road." Designated a national highway in 1926 even though paving was not completed across Arizona until a decade later, it paralleled the Santa Fe Railroad line through Holbrook, Winslow, Flagstaff, and Kingman. The southern road wound through Safford, Globe, Phoenix, Gila Bend, and Yuma. A third was added in 1928, when the highway from Phoenix to Los Angeles via Blythe was paved. By the end of the decade, the only major region with tourism potential that had been left out of the system was the Mogollon Rim country northeast of Phoenix. That rugged area did not boom until urbanization after World War II turned it into a Phoenix playground.

The proliferation of the postcard in Arizona reflected the expansion of tourism during this transition. According to historian Gerald Thompson, "By the 1920s almost every hotel or auto court in the state offered postcards as a form of advertising." And while most of the postcards printed between 1900 and the 1920s featured the Grand Canyon, auto tourism generated a demand for more images of the state. "Prehistoric ruins, mountain roads, and picturesque towns became common sights," Thompson observes. "Desert scenes filled with blooming cactus remained popular, with the cactus flowers often exaggerated in size to make the desert appear even more wondrous." The Grand Canyon still symbolized Arizona in most people's minds, but cliff dwellings and the saguaro cactus were beginning to penetrate their consciousnesses as well.

More and more women also took the wheel and rattled down Arizona roads. A few traveled alone or with female companions, challenging entrenched perceptions of the automobile as a masculine domain. But most women accompanied their families, carrying all their domestic responsibilities along with them as they prepared meals, washed clothes, and tried to entertain whiny children in campgrounds or auto courts. "The difference between the men I have camped with and myself, generally speaking, has been this," writer Mary Roberts Rinehart wryly noted, "they have called it sport; I have known it was work."

Local civic and business groups quickly took advantage of the new mobility by aggressively promoting their cities. The Phoenix-Arizona Club, founded in 1919, conducted a national advertising campaign to lure tourists to the Salt River Valley. Along with other booster organizations in Phoenix, it placed ads in magazines like *American Golfer, Better Homes and Gardens, Time,* and the *Atlantic Monthly* to tout their city as the "winter playground of the Southwest." To make Phoenix more attractive to the newcomers, the Valley Beautiful Committee even mounted a "Let's Do Away With the Desert" campaign in 1926. Residents were urged to "grow grass and plant flowers" so that Phoenix would rival Pasadena for the "quality, size, fragrance, and variety of roses." Then as now, developers saw California as the model for what they wanted Arizona to become.

Similar patterns prevailed in Tucson. In 1922, local businessmen formed the Tucson Sunshine-Climate Club which advertised Tucson's glories in national magazines and newspapers. At first those publications included the *Journal of the American Medical Association, Hygea,* and *Physical Culture.* "Children of the Sun live here," one ad announced. "Brown, sturdy, rosy-cheeked—growing into robust, vigorous youths." The club also reprinted Harold Bell Wright's *Why I Did Not Die,* which described the famous author's recovery from tuberculosis. In the early and mid twenties, business leaders still felt there was money to be made off the lungers. By the end of the decade, however, the consumptives were no longer welcome. Poor people with infectious diseases were not desirable visitors to cities "where winter never comes." At the bottom of its magazine advertisements, for example, Rancho Linda Vista, a dude ranch (and later an artists' commune) in Oracle, stated, "Absolutely no Tuberculars Accepted."

Instead the boosters targeted tourists with healthy lungs and at least moderate incomes. The late 1920s were the golden age of resorts, especially in the Salt River Valley. The San Carlos and Westward Ho hotels opened in downtown Phoenix in 1928. A year later the Arizona Biltmore rose on 600 acres north of town between Squaw Peak and Camelback Mountain. Designed by a student of Frank Lloyd Wright named Albert McArthur, the Biltmore remained a haven of old money and open desert long after the city grew up to surround it.

Several major resorts also opened in Tucson. The largest was El Conquistador, an imposing Spanish Mission–style building with a sixty-five-foot copper-domed bell tower east of town. But El Conquistador never rivaled the Biltmore's success. During the 1930s Tucson lost the battle for the wealthy tourist to the Biltmore, the Jokake Inn, the Camelback Inn, and the San Marcos Hotel, Alexander Chandler's resort southeast of Phoenix. The Salt River Valley had better highway connections, a bigger airport, less-parochial business leaders, and considerably more greenery to soften its desert vistas. Besides, Tucson had a large and vigorous Mexican community, while Phoenix, in the words of the Chamber of Commerce's 1920 city directory, prided itself on being "a modern town of forty thousand people and the best kind of people, too. A very small percentage of Mexicans, negroes or foreigners."

The only exception was the Arizona Inn, the creation of a remarkable woman named Isabella Greenway. Born on the fringes of wealthy society in Kentucky, Isabella came to the Southwest with her tubercular husband in 1911. After he died, she married John C. Greenway, the general manager of the New Cornelia Copper Company in Ajo. Isabella had been a bridesmaid of Eleanor Roosevelt's, and she served as Arizona's first woman member of Congress during the 1930s. Gracious, confident, and casual, the Arizona Inn reflected her character, embracing the desert with a benign yet regal paternalism that characterized Greenway and her politics as well.

❋ ❋ Cowboys and Indians

Establishments like the Biltmore and the Arizona Inn catered to wealthy winter visitors who demanded elegance as well as warm weather. A growing number of tourists, on the other hand, wanted a vicarious taste of the frontier. As the harsh realities of westward expansion receded from memory, everyone from popular novelists like Zane Grey to professional historians like Frederick Jackson Turner were transmuting the West into the heroic mirror of the nation, an alchemy accelerated by the young Hollywood film industry. The West was a mythical arena where individualism and innovation flourished, where the character of the American people wrote itself large. Many travelers wanted to encounter that myth, to see cowboys and Indians firsthand.

And while most were content to do so from the window of a train or an automobile, others craved adventure in addition to local color. They wanted to ride the high country, to eat steak and beans from a chuckwagon, to rub elbows with the men who chased the wild bovine. Yet few of them were willing to stretch barbed wire or castrate calves. The result was a peculiarly American institution known as the dude ranch, where guests pretended to be workers, and owners walked a fine line between the illusion of authenticity and outright contrivance. "Everyone dressed in western costumes from sombreros to high-heeled boots, and there was much talk of 'wrangling,' 'roping,' and 'rounding up,' despite the fact that there was not a sign of any cattle within fifty miles," wrote Edward Dunn, whose family spent a month on an Arizona dude ranch in the 1920s. Founded in 1924, the Dude Ranchers Association stipulated that its members had to be working outfits, but many operations ran more dudes than cows.

This was particularly true in Arizona, where the line between dude ranches and resorts often blurred. During the 1920s, dude ranches proliferated around Wickenburg, Phoenix, and Tucson. There tourists could ride the range with a real wrangler—or at least a college student pretending to be a wrangler—and bask in the sun at the same time. At some of the fancier establishments, they could also play polo or tennis or dance under the stars. The cattle business was volatile, and many ranchers went broke during droughts or depressions. But dude ranching turned out to be depression-proof, enjoying its greatest expansion during the 1930s. Most of the dudes were well-to-do and wanted certain luxuries after a hard hour or two in the saddle. So even though some ranches, like the Flying V north of Tucson, started out as cattle outfits with a few guest cabins, they soon added amenities like polo fields, tennis courts, and hot and cold running water in all their bungalows. An article in *Progressive Arizona* in September 1925, a magazine published at the height of the tourist boom, captured the contradictions of the profession by observing that dude ranches were born when Easterners came West to "meet nature in her ruggedness and still lead a 'white-man's life.'"

The national infatuation with the West expressed itself in other ways as well.

Singing cowboys and Western music became popular, and some dude ranches employed wranglers who warbled and yodeled as well as cut stock. Rodeos also developed into major tourist attractions, especially Tucson's Fiesta de los Vaqueros, which opened in February 1925. Unlike rodeos in Prescott and Payson, which started in the late nineteenth century as contests among local cowboys, the Fiesta was a full-blown extravaganza from the very beginning. It began with a parade that included a Blackfoot Indian in his grandfather's headdress and ended with a "Cowboy Dance" at the Santa Rita Hotel where "tourists, cowboys, local society members, and Navajo Indians" waltzed to the Tenth Cavalry Band from Fort Huachuca. In between, sell-out crowds watched cowboys from around the country—and cowgirls like Tad Lucas, a bronc rider, and Fox Hastings, a bulldogger—get bucked into the air by writhing horses or stomped into the ground by angry bulls. One cowboy tried to bulldog a longhorn from the running board of a Packard roaring across the arena at forty-five miles an hour. A drunk later attempted the same stunt, landing on his forehead and rolling around in the dust spurting blood. The Fiesta was a shameless mixture of crass hype and genuine rodeo, and the crowd loved it. It showed the rest of the state how to turn rodeos into tourist attractions and make them pay.

Meanwhile, promoters were discovering that Indians could draw crowds as well. Once again the pioneers were Fred Harvey and the Santa Fe Railroad, and they helped bring about the commercialization of Indian arts and crafts. Most visitors were not ready to pretend they were Indians for a few weeks, but they loved to take home an emblem of the exotic from their trip to Arizona. The Fred Harvey Company therefore commissioned Mary Elizabeth Jane Colter to design Hopi House, the recreation of a Hopi pueblo at the Grand Canyon, so that visitors could purchase Hopi and Navajo crafts from the Indians themselves. Other Fred Harvey restaurants and hotels also sold Native American goods along the Santa Fe line in places like Winslow, Holbrook, and Albuquerque.

They were not alone. Beginning in the late nineteenth century, most trading posts on the Navajo Reservation had pawn rooms where everything from saddles to silver jewelry were stored until their owners redeemed them. But if the pawn was not redeemed within six months, it could be sold to buyers from Fred Harvey or marketed by the traders themselves. "Trading posts" soon opened in towns like Flagstaff and Holbrook, and curio shops lined the major highways. In the process, traders encouraged Indian craftspeople to produce items that generated greater demand than utilitarian objects. By the 1890s, traders on the Navajo Reservation were pressuring Navajo women to weave rugs rather than blankets, while Thomas Keams at his Keams Canyon Trading Post was marketing the pottery of Nampeyo, a Hopi-Tewa who shaped and fired stunning revivals of Sikyatki Polychrome and other prehistoric styles. The tourist market became one of the principal ways in which Native Americans entered the cash economy, stimulating a revival of Indian crafts at a time when the availability of commercial blankets and kitchenware was causing a decline in traditional Indian weaving, basketry, and pottery making. Arizona Indians created an artistic renaissance under the patronage—and exploitation—of traders, collectors, and railroad executives.

Fred Harvey also launched anthropological tourism in the Southwest through his "Indian Detours," which bused tourists to Native American communities across northern Arizona and New Mexico. Organized in the 1920s, the Detours were led by young female couriers dressed in Navajo blouses, heavy squash-blossom necklaces, and silver concho belts. The women received crash courses in "Southwestern history, archaeology, and Indian lore" from famous anthropologists like Edgar Hewett and A. V. Kidder. Then they loaded their "Detourists" onto "Harveycoaches" or "Harveycars" and bounced them into Canyon de Chelly or the Petrified Forest. One of the most popular Detours climbed from Winslow to the Hopi Mesas, where the tourists camped in tents and attended the Hopi Snake Dance. For many of them, it was the ultimate encounter with the Other—painted dancers scooping up rattlesnakes with their hands and dangling them from their mouths. The Snake Dance became the most publicized and written-about Native American ritual in the Southwest as the Detours introduced a generation of tourists to a region that seemed as exotic to most Americans as Africa.

Boosters of Arizona's cities liked to throw some Indian ceremonies into their spectacles as well. Indian dancers became frequent participants in rodeo parades, civic events, and county fairs. When the El Conquistador opened in 1928, Yaqui deer and pascola dancers performed at the banquet. Native Americans also organized their own celebrations, such as tribal fairs and the Flagstaff Pow-Wow, where they showcased their cultures and their arts. The involution became complete when All-Indian rodeos were formed.

But the strangest appropriation of Native American ritual took place in Prescott on the second Sunday of June each year. Beginning in 1921, 300 local Anglo businessmen and women dressed themselves in Pueblo costumes and performed their version of the Snake Dance and other ceremonies, including the "Devil Dance" of the Apaches, the "Call of the Children" of the Pawnees, and the "Clolowishkya" or "Corn Grinding Ceremony" of the Zunis. They called themselves the Smoki People, and even though the name was a play on Hopi or Moqui, an earlier name for the Hopi, the Smokis took themselves dead seriously. They created elaborate costumes, they practiced for months under "chiefs" and "snake priests" like "Towa," they tatooed dots on their left hands to indicate status, and they chanted and shuffled across their very own dance plaza with live snakes in their mouths in front of thousands of tourists.

Ever since Lewis Henry Morgan had founded the Gordian Knot, a secret society that developed into the Grand Order of the Iroquois in the mid nineteenth century, Anglos had expressed their fascination with Native American cultures by selectively aping them. This was part of a larger phenomenon: a growing if often unconscious dissatisfaction with American society during the Industrial Age that spawned dude ranches, Indian Detours, and a host of fraternal orders with mystic rites and pseudo-esoteric lore. Riding the range as a wild, free buckaroo was one response. Pretending to be a Pueblo Indian was quite another. The latter fantasy spoke to the need for social cohesion, religious ritual, and a reverence for the earth. It did not matter that the Smoki dances were torn out of cultural context or were viewed by Native Americans with outrage and contempt. Playing a cowboy or an Indian was a reaction to the mundane materialism of modern life.

In the end, however, materialism is what kept the Smokis going year after year. Articles appeared in newspapers across the country about their "marvelous, weird, fascinating, and spectacular dances," causing thousands of tourists to stream into Prescott to see the show and visit the Smoki Museum, which housed a large collection of Indian artifacts. Typical of the enthusiasm was a June 1936 article in *Arizona Highways,* which already was becoming one of Arizona's major promoters of tourism. "Exquisite workmanship! Harmonious color effects! Yet always weird, inhuman, and grotesque," gushed the writer, whose sense of sentence structure momentarily abandoned her. "Fantastic headdresses! Gorgeous costumes! Sun colors! Bright feathers! Beating Tom-Toms! Haunting chants! Fantastic serpents! Thrilling! Different and exquisite are these remarkable dances!" Whether they were sincere or not, the Smokis were one of Arizona's biggest draws.

✳ ✳ The Scientists

Beneath the sensationalism of the Smokis and the escapism of the dude ranches, however, Arizona was working its magic on another, more serious group of people. Beginning with the military surveys of the mid nineteenth century, biologists, geologists, anthropologists, and other scientists trekked across the region to study its natural and human history. Arizona became one of the most famous areas of fieldwork in the world—a dry, wild, fascinating laboratory where new methods and new sciences like dendrochronology were pioneered.

Anthropologists were among the first to be seduced. During the late nineteenth century, government agencies like the Smithsonian Institution and private benefactors like the Bostonian Mary Hemenway sponsored major archaeological and ethnological expeditions to the Southwest, including Arizona. The region was particularly attractive because living peoples and spectacular ruins existed side by side. The Native American presence had not died out as it had in many other parts of the United States. Scholars could interpret the past by investigating the present, and vice versa. Groups like the Hopi were more than analogues of the Anasazi; they were their cultural and biological descendants. Archaeologists could see katsina iconography from kiva murals or rock art come alive on the Hopi Mesas.

One of the first to arrive was Adolph Bandelier, a Swiss-born refugee from the Illinois banking world who made several trips to Arizona to study Anasazi, Salado, and Hohokam archaeological sites. Another was Bandelier's friend Frank Hamilton Cushing, who in 1882 was commissioned by the Bureau of American Ethnology, a newly formed branch of the Smithsonian Institution directed by John Wesley Powell, to "make as large an ethnological collection as possible at Oraibi," the most important Hopi community on Third Mesa. After he tried to use a kiva as a trading center, the Hopis shouted obscenities at Cushing and told him to leave, threatening him with knives when he refused. He later became more sensitive to Native American beliefs, but Cushing's attempt to grab as much Hopi material as possible regardless of Hopi wishes was all too characteristic of early museum collecting.

Nonetheless, the work of Bandelier, Cushing, and their contemporaries made the Southwest the most intense region of anthropological inquiry in the world. Dozens of other scholars followed them to Arizona, including many women, who found anthropology one of the few scientific disciplines that welcomed their participation even though it often ignored their contributions or restricted their access to grant funds and professorships. Frank Russell lived among the Gila Pimas in 1901 and 1902 and died in Kingman a year later. During the 1920s, Florence Hawley Ellis, Emil Haury, and Clara Lee Tanner honed their archaeological skills under Dean Byron Cummings of the University of Arizona. Grenville Goodwin collected exhaustive information on the Western Apaches while working as a trader's assistant at Bylas on the San Carlos Reservation. Edward and Rosamond Spicer studied Yaqui communities in Sonora and Arizona. Gladys Reichard conducted thirty years of research among the Navajos.

And Ruth Murray Underhill, who abandoned a successful career as a social worker to pursue anthropology under Franz Boas, wrote essential scholarly and popular ethnographies of the Tohono O'odham. In 1979 the Tohono O'odham Nation honored her by naming her Grand Marshal of the Papago Rodeo Parade when she was ninety-six years old.

Like other outsiders, those scientists and their colleagues had their biases and blind spots. In contrast to casual tourists, however, they systematically attempted to overcome those biases by learning Native American languages and struggling to understand Native American cultures on their own terms. Rituals like the Hopi Snake Dance or the Navajo Blessingway were not savage customs but complex expressions of moral and social orders as sophisticated as any system of Western philosophy. That message was as radical in the early twentieth century as Van Dyke's aesthetic appreciation of the desert.

The anthropologists found an unlikely scientific collaborator in Andrew Ellicott Douglass, an astronomer who came to Arizona in 1894 to establish an observatory in Flagstaff funded by Percival Lowell. Lowell was a wealthy amateur convinced that the dark lines some astronomers saw on the planet Mars were enormous irrigation canals built by a Martian civilization. Douglass broke with Lowell after seven years, concluding that he had "a strong literary instinct and no scientific instinct." But as his career as an astronomical archaeologist ended, he developed an interest in the effect of sunspots on the annual growth rings of trees. Douglass observed that in the dry Arizona climate the size of the rings corresponded to the amount of precipitation that fell each year. His ultimate goal was to identify climatic cycles in the tree ring record in order to develop techniques for the long-range forecasting of weather. That goal eluded him, but as he examined more and more cross sections of logs, he put together a tree-ring calendar that extended further and further back in time. After two young archaeologists named Lyndon Hargrave and Emil Haury uncovered the charred end of a roof timber at Whipple Ruin in Showlow in 1929, the calendar stretched back to the seventh century A.D. Suddenly archaeologists could give absolute dates to the great ruins of the Southwest like Mesa Verde, Chaco Canyon, and Betatakin. The astronomer and his new science of dendrochronology revolutionized archaeology.

But scientific breakthroughs required institutional support to become scientific fields. Douglass's own career followed a familiar trajectory in American science during the late nineteenth and early twentieth centuries. He came to Arizona as the protégé of a wealthy but eccentric patron. Then he funded his dendrochronological studies by piecing together grants while working in the physics department at the University of Arizona. But when the Depression curtailed even those limited research activities, Douglass turned to a private organization, the Carnegie Institution, which gave him the money to set up his cherished Laboratory of Tree-Ring Research at the university in 1935.

Few private institutions played a greater role in Arizona than the Carnegie, which had been created by industrialist Andrew Carnegie to advance scientific research. The Carnegie project most intimately associated with the state was the Desert Laboratory, founded in 1903. Located on Tumamoc Hill, the dark volcanic mountain that dominates Tucson's western skyline, the laboratory's mission was to investigate "the methods by which plants perform their functions under the extraordinary conditions existing in deserts. " During the early twentieth century, it was the only desert botanical laboratory in the world. There scientists could step outside their offices and let the object of their studies envelop them. To the northeast were the Santa Catalina Mountains, where elevation arranged plants in zones that mimicked a two-thousand-mile-long botanical journey from the subtropics to the subarctic. To the northwest were the endless basins and ranges of the Papaguería. Built of native basalt, the Desert Laboratory made the desert palpable for two generations of botanists, climatologists, and other scientists who conducted their research on the Hill.

One of those researchers was Forrest Shreve, who arrived in 1908 and spent the rest of his life there. During the long, mild winters, the laboratory often had only a skeleton staff consisting of Shreve and his wife Edith, a plant physiologist, and a few other scientists. During the intense summers, on the other hand, the laboratory became known as Tumamocville as dozens of researchers and their assistants from Europe and North America threw up tent houses on the Hill, pioneering a new discipline called ecology. But while most of the scientists left after a season or two, the desert pulled Shreve deeper and deeper into its dry soul. By the 1930s he was seizing every opportunity he could to load up his high-clearance Willys Knight and explore Sonora or Baja California. The result was his masterful synthesis, *Vegetation of the Sonoran Desert*, which was published in 1951, the year after he died.

✳   ✳   ✳   Preservation and Conservation

Fifty years before, John Van Dyke had attempted to capture the poetic essence of the desert. Scientists like Shreve, in contrast, carefully measured, plotted, and dissected the natural phenomena of the region. Yet the more they scrutinized, the closer they came to Van Dyke's passionate belief in the desert's integrity and the need to preserve it. Shreve fought to protect cacti and other desert vegetation from disreputable collectors who were devastating them. He served as president of the Tucson Natural History Association and lobbied for the creation of desert preserves like Saguaro National Monument (1933) and Organ Pipe Cactus National Monument (1937). He wrote that the desert was "a breathing space for those who are fortunate to be able to get away, either permanently or temporarily, from the crowded centers of population." The words may not have burned with Van Dyke's intensity, but the thoughts were the same.

The attitudes of Van Dyke, Shreve, and agronomist Robert Forbes, who pioneered the study of traditional Native American agriculture in the Southwest, represented the first stages of a major transformation in the way people perceived Arizona. By the 1930s the state's economy and society were in transition. The major extractive industries—ranching, mining, and agriculture—still held sway, but for the first time since the establishment of the Jesuit missions more than two hundred years earlier, large numbers of people were coming to Arizona for its climate, beauty, or cultural heritage rather than for what they could rip out of the ground. The landscape was acquiring a utility beyond what it yielded to the pick, rope, or plow.

One result was an increase in national forests, monuments, and parks. The first forest reserve was created on the North Rim of the Grand Canyon in 1893. It was followed by the San Francisco, Black Mesa, and Prescott reserves five years later. Teddy Roosevelt, an avid hunter and conservationist who had made many trips to Arizona, issued presidential proclamations setting aside numerous other stretches of timber, including the Tonto Reserve below the Mogollon Rim and most of the mountain islands like the Catalinas, Santa Ritas, and Pinaleños in the southern part of the territory. In 1908 those reserves were consolidated into seventeen national forests encompassing 13,163,710 acres. Indian reservations reclaimed several million acres in 1912, but Roosevelt and his predecessors managed to protect about 73 percent of Arizona's timber and woodlands from the unrestricted exploitation that decimated privately owned forests across the nation.

Roosevelt also established several of Arizona's national monuments, including Petrified Forest (1906), Montezuma Castle (1906), Tonto (1907), Grand Canyon (1908), and Tumacacori (1908). In contrast to the national forests, most of the early monuments were designed to protect cultural resources, particularly archaeological sites. That process began in 1892, when Congress allocated 480 acres for the preservation of the ruins of Casa Grande, the first federally protected prehistoric site in the country. By the end of the 1930s there were sixteen national monuments in Arizona, ranging from Pipe Spring near the Utah border to Organ Pipe on the international boundary with Sonora. Ranchers, loggers, and miners bitterly opposed most of these sanctuaries, particularly the national forests. They wanted to graze or log the land as they saw fit, and they harassed forest rangers, pressured members of Congress, and lobbied strenuously against the reserves. Most farmers, on the other hand, supported the national forests because they wanted to protect their watersheds against erosion. The exploitation of the various resources created various constituencies with various needs.

But another constituency had come into being, loose and amorphous yet increasingly powerful. As thousands of tourists stared at a sunset over the Grand Canyon or hiked down switchbacks to see the stunning cliff dwelling of Betatakin, they came to feel that Arizona belonged to them. Its dry and rugged beauty overwhelmed them and its Indian heritage intrigued them, so they demanded the protection of that beauty and heritage against the ravages of miners, stock raisers, and loggers. Their instrument was the federal government, which began to exercise more and more control over enormous chunks of the state. From the Indian wars to the reclamation of the Salt River Valley, the government had played a significant role in Arizona's political and economic life. Beginning in the 1930s, however, that role expanded and diversified at an ever-accelerating rate. The copper companies, ranchers, and farmers still dominated the state legislature, but more and more of the critical decisions shaping Arizona were being made in Washington, D.C.

13

The Depression and the New Deal

✹ ✹

In 1909, Walter Packard, the son of a suffragist and a wealthy Chicago lawyer, came West to work as an extension agent in the Imperial Valley. There, amid the green fields and squalid labor camps, Packard embarked on an intellectual odyssey that was common during the first half of the twentieth century. He started out as a progressive reformer and a protégé of Elwood Mead, who believed that federal reclamation projects could create commonwealths of small farmers in the Great American Desert. He ended up as a leftist technocrat who wanted big agriculture without the evils of agribusiness. Packard never joined the Communist Party, but he did become a true believer in agricultural collectives. He spent most of his career fighting for that ideal in California's Central Valley, where he envisioned farmers organized into work brigades "with the normal democratic machinery for protest."

But Arizona was the only place Packard ever had a chance to put his ideas into action. In 1936, at the height of the New Deal, he became the director of the federal Resettlement Administration in central Arizona. There he designed the 3,200-acre Casa Grande Valley Farms Project—one of only four agricultural collectives developed by the Resettlement Administration across the country. Packard and his colleagues selected the first seventeen families in 1937. All were Arizona residents and many had lost their land during the Depression. The government built sturdy, three-bedroom adobe houses for them and provided them with seed, fertilizer, machinery, irrigation water, and a monthly advance on expected annual profits. "We did a swell job," one of the original settlers recalled. "We really pitched in and worked. . . . Some of us have had more and want more. We're all failures or we wouldn't be here, but we try to do better."

The following year, however, thirty-nine more families from Oklahoma, Texas, and Arkansas moved into the project, and the first group took an immediate dislike to them. "There are two classes of people here," the same Arizona settler continued. "The other type are the ones who never made much in their lives before and they're satisfied if they have their bellies full and can lie around on Sunday and booze." For the next five years, the two factions sniped at each other as the nation made the transition from depression to war. And even though they ran their enterprise as productively as their private neighbors, their infighting played into the hands of enemies of the collectives in Congress and the Roosevelt administration. In 1944 the Farm Security Administration put the collective up for sale. Six of the original settlers stayed on the land, but the rest left to work in the defense plants of California. Packard's dream of a democratic collective was dead.

That was the end of New Deal experimentation in Arizona. Despite the intentions of Packard and others, the New Deal did not transform agribusinesses into collectives or bring about a renaissance of small farmers and ranchers across the state. On the contrary, the federal programs of the 1930s contributed to the growing scale of the agricultural economy, which was driving small producers out of business. Ranches and farms grew larger and more capital-intensive, while the Big Three copper companies—Anaconda, Kennecott, and Phelps Dodge—gobbled up their competitors, producing 80 percent of Arizona's copper in 1940 compared to 40 percent ten years before. The New Deal may have provided temporary relief for the destitute, work projects for the unemployed, and loans and grants for businessmen and municipal governments, but the structure of the extractive economy—and the policies of the federal government—continued to place more of Arizona's land, water, and mineral wealth into fewer and fewer hands.

* * * The Depression and the New Deal

The late 1920s were boom years for Arizona's extractive industries, particularly copper mining. The New Cornelia Copper Company built a leaching plant in Ajo in 1917 and followed with a concentrator seven years later. By 1930 the plant had transformed the little desert community into one of the most important mining districts in the state. Production also intensified in established areas such as Bisbee, Jerome, Superior, and Morenci. The boom peaked in 1929, when 16,000 miners blasted more than $155 million worth of copper and its by-products from Arizona ground. Arizona became the largest copper producer in the United States, supplying 50 percent of U.S. demand.

The ranchers were not quite as prosperous. A severe drought from 1918 to 1921 dried up springs and forced many ranchers to shoot their calves. Many stock raisers went broke and sold their ranches. By 1928, however, the rains had returned and yearlings were selling for $45 a head. Cotton farmers also recovered, planting 153,000 acres of short-staple varieties and 67,000 acres of long-staple Pima cotton in 1929. Production had not yet returned to 1920 levels, but cotton remained Arizona's number-one crop, generating an income of $64 million a year.

Then the New York stock market crashed on October 24, 1929, and the global economy, which consumed Arizona's commodities, contracted with frightening rapidity. Copper prices went into free fall, plunging from 18.1 cents per pound in 1929 to 5.6 cents three years later. Mines at Ray, Inspiration, Miami, and Ajo closed down completely. Even the mammoth Phelps Dodge operations in Bisbee and Morenci shuddered and shrank. In 1933—the year the U.S. economy hit bottom—Arizona sold only $10 million worth of copper, a decline of 94 percent. The labor force also plummeted to 3,300 miners, a drop of nearly 80 percent. The cramped, fractious copper communities almost became ghost towns like the gold and silver communities before them.

It was not much better in the countryside. Ranchers watched the price of yearlings fall to $15 a head. To add natural insult to economic injury, drought seared the range again in 1933 and 1934, forcing more stock raisers off the land. Many unemployed mining and ranching families sought work in the cotton fields, but prices there were tumbling from 11 cents per pound to 4 cents. In 1932 farmers planted only 113,000 acres of cotton, and incomes dropped to $24 million. The Three C's were reeling, and that affected just about every other aspect of Arizona society as well. Banks closed. Relief rolls swelled. Arizona's population growth reversed itself, with the state losing 50,000 people between 1932 and 1936.

Not all the exodus was voluntary. As national unemployment rose from 4 percent to 25 percent between 1929 and 1933, employers across the nation fired Mexican workers and replaced them with American citizens. This nativist reaction quickly developed into the repatriation movement, a crusade that deported more than 500,000 Mexicans between 1930 and 1935. A decade before, powerful agricultural, railroad, and mining interests had fought to keep Mexicans from being included in the Quota Act of 1924 by arguing that they were the backbone of Southwestern industries. During the Depression, that backbone was cut out and tossed away as mines closed, railroads laid off workers, and cotton growers turned to "Okies" and "Arkies" fleeing the Southern Plains.

Those who stayed sought help from private charities or state and county welfare boards. But those agencies soon ran out of money, especially after the Dust Bowl refugees joined the lines. In the summer of 1933, 27 percent of all Arizonans (104,565 of 391,847) received aid from the Federal Emergency Relief Administration. Of all the surrounding states, only New Mexico had a higher proportion of people on welfare (32 percent). At the same time, however, the assessed value of Arizona property plunged from more than $700 million to $43 million, slashing state revenues, which came largely from property taxes. By then, all but the most conservative businessmen were ready to admit that Arizona desperately needed federal assistance.

That assistance came in many forms, but the most immediate was the program of massive public works projects sponsored by Franklin Roosevelt's New Deal. The first and largest was the Civilian Conservation Corps (ccc), which recruited single males between the ages of seventeen and twenty-four whose parents were on relief. The ccc established twenty-eight camps in Arizona— eleven in national forests, four in national parks, five on federal grazing lands, three on soil erosion control demonstration areas, three in city or county parks, and two on federal reclamation projects. Organized in quasi-military fashion, cccers fenced off grazing allotments, built 400,000 erosion-control check dams, dug 3,000 wells and reservoirs, fought hundreds of forest fires, and even excavated archaeological sites. Between 1933 and 1939, the federal government spent nearly $44 million on the ccc in Arizona, and about 15,000 young men, including many Mexicans, blacks, and Indians, joined the corps.

Other agencies provided work for a broader segment of the population. The Bureau of Public Roads employed from 1,200 to 3,000 individuals each year and spent $22 million to improve 1,218 miles of state highways and secondary roads. The Public Works Administration (pwa) provided loans and grants of more than $20 million to build federal, state, and county facilities across the state, including substantial additions to the campuses of the University of Arizona and the Arizona State Teacher's College (now Arizona State University). It also spent $38 million on the construction of Hoover Dam, which employed 4,877 people at its height. Finally, the federal government funneled more than $24 million through the Works Progress Administration (WPA), which employed about 16,000 Arizonans. In cooperation with local communities, the WPA constructed 163 new public buildings, improved municipal water supplies, built parks and other recreational facilities, and produced *Arizona: A State Guide* under the editorship of cowboy author Ross Santee.

Even the business community came to rely on the federal government. Walter Bimson, who had worked for the federal Reconstruction Finance Corporation before becoming president of Valley National Bank (VNB), enthusiastically supported the passage of the Federal Housing Act of 1934, which underwrote nearly 200,000 VNB loans during the next ten years. Contractors like Del Webb also made their fortunes on New Deal money, erecting everything from homes to hospitals. "Construction is no longer a private enterprise but rather a subsidiary of the federal government," Webb said. The Big Six who built Hoover Dam—Utah Construction and Mining, Morrison Knudsen, J. F. Shea, Pacific Bridge, MacDonald & Kahn, and Bechtel-Kaiser Warren Brothers—probably would have agreed with him, at least in private. Historian Lawrence Arlington estimates that Arizona received about $342 million in federal assistance between 1933 and 1939 while paying only about $16 million in federal taxes. Once again the federal government played a major role in Arizona's economic development.

But while the New Deal could blunt some of the Depression's blows, the volatile nature of the state's extractive economy exposed thousands of people to the starkest forms of poverty and unemployment, especially in the mining towns and farming communities. The worst period was the winter of 1937–38, when the copper industry collapsed for the second time in less than a decade. Meanwhile, Arizona growers had planted nearly 300,000 acres of cotton and had mounted an extraordinary recruiting campaign across New Mexico, Texas, Oklahoma, Missouri, and Arkansas to make sure there were more than enough workers for the harvest. By the end of November, more than 25,000 pickers and their families had crowded into growers' camps or squatters' settlements on the edges of the cotton fields. The number swelled to 37,000 by the time the harvest was over. Most of these people were not full-time migrant workers but victims of drought, foreclosure, and the growing mechanization of agriculture on the Southern Plains. *The Grapes of Wrath* to the contrary, these Okies and Arkies headed west because of the Arizona Farm Labor Service's advertising campaign. Arizona, not California, was their immediate destination.

Even when the migrants tried to move on to California, however, heavy floods in the San Joaquin and Sacramento valleys destroyed crops and drove them back across the Colorado River. That winter, smallpox, typhoid, whooping cough, and infant diarrhea swept through the camps, where few of the pickers had running water and many had only open pits or abandoned car bodies as toilets. And even though there was more cotton to pick than ever before, the Farm Labor Service had recruited 17,000 excess laborers, so work was irregular and earnings were low, averaging $1.20 to 1.50 per day. Families soon had to sell everything, even their jalopies, to buy food. They also scavenged beet tops and other refuse from the few fields that grew anything besides cotton. "I have five in my family," one picker told Governor Rawghlie C. Stanford. "I now have $1.50 and my two babies are sick. We are living exactly like hogs."

In desperation, many of the migrants demanded better conditions in the lettuce fields, sheep-shearing camps, and cotton districts across the Salt River Valley. A group of farm workers even joined the United Cannery, Agricultural, Packing and Allied Workers of America, which was affiliated with the Congress of Industrial Organizations (CIO), and clamored for food outside Maricopa County's relief warehouse in March 1938. Arizona growers responded to this "Communist" threat by organizing the anti-union Associated Farmers of Arizona. President Kemper Marley, a local cattleman, addressed a mass meeting at Phoenix's Union High School and growled, "If we have 20,000 members and show we mean business, we have nothing to fear. But I warn you now, if you don't believe in our organization, you'd better not join."

Marley's tough words quickly translated into action. Later that month the Teamsters Union tried to organize truck drivers employed by the Hurley Meat Company. To force drivers to join the union, the Teamsters set up a roadblock at the intersection of Buckeye Road and 15th Avenue in southwest Phoenix. The next morning, the Associated Farmers sent sixty to seventy-five members to patrol the intersection after accusing the Teamsters of assaulting one driver and threatening to kill another. Similarly, when the CIO organized a strike in the strawberry fields, Sheriff Roy Merrill deputized 300 Associated Farmers and descended on the strikers, seizing their weapons and tearing down their banners. Once again the alliance between business and law enforcement broke unions in Arizona.

Even without intimidation, it proved nearly impossible to organize migrant farm workers in the late 1930s. As soon as the Farm Security Administration gave $50,000 in relief to about 16,000 stranded pickers, most left the state. During the next three years, growers planted considerably less cotton, and when production boomed again during World War II, the government admitted thousands of Mexican *braceros* to meet wartime needs. Unions of farm workers remained little more than a radical dream.

In the copper towns, on the other hand, independent unionism slowly resurfaced. During the New Deal, the National Recovery Administration (NRA) established industrial codes of conduct that included minimum wages and an eight-hour workday, and the National Labor Relations Act (1935) legalized collective bargaining. For the first time in nearly two decades, labor had allies rather than enemies in the federal government. Open union activity remained dangerous in Arizona, but determined organizers slipped back into the copper communities, often at night, to hold clandestine meetings with miners. Most of these organizers belonged to the International Union of Mine, Mill, and Smelter Workers (IUMMSW), which evolved out of the Western Federation of Miners. Moreover, many of them—like Humberto Sílex, Leo Ortiz, and Arturo Mata— were Mexicans or Mexican Americans. Mata, in fact, had been deported from Morenci as a child because his father led strikes there during World War I. By the late 1930s, unions had finally realized that they needed Mexican miners to throw off the copper collar. The alliance blossomed during World War II.

✱　✱　✱　The Rise of Agribusiness

The rebirth of the unions reflected another goal of the New Deal: the struggle to regulate American industries and make them more responsive to the public welfare. In Arizona that struggle succeeded in some industries and failed in others. It also had consequences government planners never intended or foresaw.

The biggest disjunction occurred in agriculture. The New Deal's first major legislative accomplishment, the Agricultural Adjustment Act of 1933, had two major objectives. One was to control the production of commodities in order to stabilize prices. The other was to prevent the soil erosion that was ravaging the Great Plains. The Agricultural Adjustment Administration (AAA) therefore paid farmers to adopt conservation techniques and to shift part of their acreage from soil-depleting plants to pasturage or even fallow. In Arizona that meant reducing the cultivation of cotton. Between 1933 and 1936, cotton growers received 4,905 of the 5,777 crop adjustment contracts in the state (85 percent), and AAA benefits totaled nearly $3 million. During the same period, however, farmers converted nearly 30,000 acres of wheat, barley, and alfalfa into cotton even though AAA benefit payments were supposedly encouraging them to grow other crops. But alfalfa and wheat did not yield the profits that cotton did, while lettuce was plagued by crop failures and citrus trees took four years to mature.

The goal of agricultural diversity eluded New Deal planners. By 1937, farmers were growing nearly 300,000 acres of cotton, exceeding 1920 levels of production for the first time.

New Deal programs also expanded the scale of Arizona agriculture. During the early years of the Depression, many small farmers went broke while larger farmers weathered the low prices and used AAA benefits to drill wells and buy tractors, thereby increasing their water supply and decreasing their labor costs. When the Supreme Court declared the AAA programs unconstitutional in 1936, Congress passed a series of other measures to subsidize farmers. The Agricultural Adjustment Act of 1938 gave cotton growers "parity payments" when prices fell below certain levels. The Farm Credit Association loaned $16.4 million to Arizona farmers between 1933 and 1939. And even though the Farm Security Administration provided poor rural families with several million dollars, most of the $52,309,639 appropriated for Arizona agriculture—$18,561,972 in grants, $33,747,667 in loans—went to commercial farmers.

As a result, land tenure became more and more skewed. In Pima County, two growers cultivated nearly half the land. Within the Salt River Project, the 160-acre limit was still halfheartedly enforced, but west of Phoenix, corporations and big growers controlled most of the cotton fields from Buckeye to Peoria. In Pinal County—the cutting edge of the cotton frontier—the amount of cropland more than doubled (from 34,001 acres to 79,159 acres, with an additional 26,000 acres of irrigated pasture), yet the number of farms increased by only 30 percent (from 1,008 to 1,309). About 8 percent of the farmers owned 430 acres or more and controlled 41 percent of all cropland in the county. When leased land was taken into account, the trend was even more pronounced: the amount of acreage in units equal to or exceeding 430 acres rose to two-thirds. Many growers also expanded their operations by using AAA benefits to lease state land for a dollar an acre or less. By the end of the decade, 162,000 of the 200,000 acres of state land in Pinal County had been rented, and the rest was in the process of being sold. Big farms grew bigger on federal subsidies and cheap state land.

Meanwhile, the number of owner-operators was shrinking. In 1930, landowners ran most of the farms. Nine years later, owners operated only 101 of the 419 actual farming operations in Pinal County (24 percent), while 237 operators (57 percent) were tenants. Many of the absentee landlords were not even Arizonans; nearly half the private land belonged to nonresidents, particularly Californians. The Jeffersonian ideal of the small farmer had become an anachronism, an economic and ecological impossibility in an industry lashed by fluctuating markets and addicted to enormous investments in water control. Populist rhetoric notwithstanding, the New Deal ended up subsidizing Arizona agribusiness, especially the cotton industry.

✳ ✳ ✳   The End of the Open Range

The Depression and the New Deal changed the landscape of the cattle kingdom as well. Ever since the great die-off of the 1890s, ranchers who could afford to do so had fenced their land—or at least their water sources—to keep out the livestock of their neighbors. This led to bitter conflict between small and large stock raisers, but consensus was growing—among large ranchers, at least—that the federal government needed to restrict grazing on public lands. Beginning in 1907, the Arizona Cattle Growers Association lobbied for national legislation that would extend regulations adopted for the national forests to all federal lands. Led by progressives like Phoenician Dwight Heard, the association believed that the free-for-all of the open range had to give way to well-capitalized operations that could erect fences and windmills, develop springs, practice selective breeding, and prevent overgrazing. Just like the alliance between the Salt River Valley Water Users Association and the Reclamation Service, or the Santa Fe Railroad and the National Park Service, an alliance was developing between large producers and the federal government.

That alliance took a long time to mature. Before 1934 most federal land laws were totally unsuited to the arid and semi-arid West. No rancher could survive on the 160 acres available under the Homestead Act of 1862 or the 640 acres allotted by the Desert Land Act of 1875. On most Arizona ranges, a section (640 acres) could only sustain twenty head of cattle or less, and most ranchers believed that they needed to run at least 100 head to make a decent living. Neither the laws nor traditional use-rights effectively regulated grazing, and Arizona ranges continued to deteriorate during the early twentieth century.

The only exceptions were the national forests, which became the first battleground in the struggle to impose federal control. After a presidential proclamation created the San Francisco Mountain and Black Mesa Forest Reserves in 1896, pressure mounted to remove all livestock, especially sheep, from reserve lands. Two groups behind the movement were Salt River Valley farmers, who believed that grazing on the Mogollon Rim caused flooding and erosion down below, and preservationists like John Muir, who wanted to return the reserves to their pristine natural state. The farmers and the preservationists found staunch antigrazing allies in the Department of the Interior, which managed the reserves at that time. In the summer of 1896, Muir traveled with the Forest Committee, which had been appointed by the National Academy of Sciences at the request of the secretary of the interior to make recommendations about how the reserves were to be administered. The committee listened closely to Muir and called for the elimination of grazing on the reserves.

Sheep and cattle growers reacted with outrage fueled by a bitter sense of betrayal. The stock raisers, one observer noted, "had come into the country, made the Indians 'good' and the country fit to live in; the government had invited them to come in when land was free, to make their homes and develop the country. Now, after years of hardships incident to pioneer life, the government stepped in and took away their free range and timber, and put them on a reservation the same as Indians."

At first the stock raisers turned their anger against the forest rangers, who were cursed and shunned. One newspaper in Williams even blustered that the best way to fight the reserves was "to hang these U.S. tree agents to the trees that they had come to save." After some skirmishes, however, cooler heads prevailed and the stock raisers, especially the Arizona Wool Growers Association, devoted their attention to lobbying rather than intimidation. In 1900 the association persuaded Gifford Pinchot, chief forester of the U.S. Department of Agriculture (USDA) and a member of the 1896 Forest Committee, to conduct a study of the impact of grazing on Arizona reserves before expelling the animals. Pinchot and his colleague Fredrick Colville, a USDA botanist, visited the reserves and concluded that properly managed grazing did not harm the forests.

Within the Interior Department, preservationist sentiment still ran high, and Secretary of the Interior Ethan Hitchcock suppressed the report. In 1902 he also ordered all livestock off the reserves. But Pinchot convinced his friend President Teddy Roosevelt to rescind the expulsion and declare that "The fundamental idea of forestry is the perpetuation of forests by use." Three years later, Roosevelt turned over the reserves to the Department of Agriculture's new Bureau of Forestry, which Pinchot headed. Soon afterward, Pinchot and Colville's recommendations became the basis for a system of grazing allotments and per-head fees that regulated grazing within the national forests. Pinchot's desire to conserve natural resources and rationalize their use prevailed over Muir's desire to preserve the wilderness of the American West. The concept of multiple use was being forged.

It took three more decades to extend the regulations to the rest of the public domain. The Arizona Cattle Growers Association usually supported the regulation of livestock numbers, but stock raisers bitterly opposed any attempts to increase their grazing fees. They also resisted Forest Service supervision and supported measures like the Stanfield Bill, which sought to turn grazing permits into property rights and to make stock raising as important as timber production or watershed management in the national forests. The bill was defeated in 1926, but opposition to regulation grew even more intense during the early years of the Depression, when drought parched the range and sheep and cattle growers demanded a 50 percent decrease in grazing fees. In 1934, however, Congress passed the Taylor Grazing Act, which regulated grazing on all unappropriated federal lands. The act was designed to "stop injury to the public grazing lands by preventing overgrazing and soil deterioration, to provide for their orderly use, improvement, and development, to stabilize the livestock industry dependent upon the public range, and for other uses." After years of stalemate, the specter of the Dust Bowl finally overwhelmed the resistance of the ranchers.

The provisions of the act were not much different from those that applied to national forests. The General Land Office established grazing districts and issued ten-year leases, with preference given to stock raisers with patented land or water rights next to the tract they wanted to rent. The government also levied grazing fees based upon the carrying capacity of the range. In Arizona, that fee was 5 cents per animal unit (cow and calf) per month—a rate that remained in effect from 1935 until 1947. The government returned 25 percent of the revenue to finance range improvements such as fences, stock tanks, and wells.

But if the provisions of the Taylor Grazing Act did not differ much from earlier regulations, they were significant because they affected every rancher who ran his or her animals on federal land. Moreover, most federal officials rigorously enforced its provisions, pressuring Arizona officials to regulate grazing on state land as well. Ranchers preferred working with state inspectors because they were "easy to deal with," that is, more lax than their federal counterparts, but the cattle and sheep growers never again seriously challenged the right of the federal government to control grazing on the public domain.

The result was a transformation of the ranching industry. Mandated by law, fencing became widespread, and the range was divided into smaller and more workable units. Cowboys no longer had to ride for miles searching for strays, and the great communal roundups, which lasted from spring until late summer on spreads like the T-Rail near Klondyke, came to an end. Wild horses and burros were rounded up and sold for tallow, chicken feed, and horse meat. Even the number of cattle on many ranges declined by 25 to 75 percent. As herd size diminished, however, quality improved. Selling cattle by the pound rather than by the head became more common, and ranchers learned to think in terms of weight rather than sheer numbers. Breeds were upgraded. Pastures were rotated. Windmills, stock tanks, and piping from springs to troughs increased the number of water sources and spread stock across broader stretches of the countryside. Large operators like Henry Hooker and Colin Cameron may have pioneered the modern stock industry in the late nineteenth century (as discussed in chapter 7), but the Taylor Grazing Act extended their innovations to the public domain. After more than sixty years of abuse, the range finally had a chance to restore itself. The era of the open range had come to an end.

When it did, most small stock raisers disappeared as well. Government agents tried to give all the ranchers in an area a chance to lease nearby land, but ranchers with larger amounts of patented land generally received larger leases. As their fences went up, many smaller cattlemen sold out because they no longer had access to enough land to run their herds. Cowboys working for many of the big outfits, particularly Mexican *vaqueros* who did not speak English or understand the procedures for filing on land, also found themselves being squeezed out of the industry. When the range was unfenced, ranchers needed more cowboys to watch over the stock and often allowed trusted employees to run a few of their own animals with company herds. "They settled in the country near a water source, put up a little house, worked for a ranch, and made a nice life for themselves," recalled Aravaipa rancher Martín Ramírez. But many of the cowboys "became landless, cattleless, and unemployed within months of the application of the Taylor Act," according to historian Diana Hadley, who interviewed Ramírez in 1990. Once again, New Deal regulations favored larger producers over smaller ones.

✳ ✳ ✳ Arizona on the Eve of World War II

Gerald Nash, the preeminent economic historian of the modern West, argues that the region "changed masters" during the Depression, substituting the federal government for Eastern capital. Yet Arizona had relied on the government ever since the territorial period, when the army provided security for Arizona citizens and markets for Arizona produce and livestock. That reliance continued with Roosevelt Dam and the Salt River Project. Even the cotton boom of World War I reflected the military's demand for fiber. The New Deal, then, was not a radical break with the past, but it certainly deepened and broadened Arizona's dependence on federal funding and federal control. By the end of the 1930s, officials in a variety of federal agencies were subsidizing agriculture, supervising enormous irrigation projects, regulating grazing and timber cutting, and dispersing loans, grants, and relief to businesses, communities, and individuals. The federal government spent three times the per capita national average in Western states, including Arizona. And while much of the money poured into Arizona's extractive industries, federal investment in highway construction, recreational facilities, education, and municipal government also expanded the transportation network and enabled the explosive urbanization of Arizona to take place during World War II and the postwar years.

In 1940, however, few Arizonans could have imagined the changes they were about to see. Manufacturing was limited, and Phoenix, the state's largest city, had only 65,414 people. In 1934 a local advertising firm coined the phrase "Valley of the Sun" to lure tourists to the Salt River Valley, and it quickly became the incantation that expressed the yearnings for change among ambitious young business leaders like Barry Goldwater, Frank Snell, and Walter Bimson. But even though 35,000 winter visitors gamboled under the sun in 1939–40, the center of political and economic power remained the Adams Hotel, where farmers, cattlemen, and mining executives continued to buy the votes of legislators and run the state.

Arizona's political culture—a curious mixture of Eastern colonialism, Western individualism, and Southern Jim Crowism—remained rooted in the extractive economy. The state was overwhelmingly Democratic, but most Democrats were Dixiecrats rather than Eleanor Roosevelt liberals like Isabella Greenway, who served in the U.S. House of Representatives from 1933 to 1936. Struggling to survive in the slums of South Phoenix or in farm camps like Randolph in Pinal County, African Americans faced the full force of legal segregation in Arizona. They went to separate schools, lived in separate neighborhoods, and were barred from most hotels, restaurants, or municipal swimming pools. The "progressive" state constitution even banned interracial marriages despite the fact that African American "sporting women . . . catered to some of the richest and most respected white businessmen," according to Madge Copeland, who opened the first Black beauty shop in Phoenix. One of the women told Copeland, "I can pay for my home and take care of my mother in two years. I can be through and then I'm through with the life. I'm going back to teaching."

But worst of all was the grinding poverty of men and women who could only find jobs as domestic workers or farm hands. Emmett McLoughlin, a Franciscan priest who founded St. Monica's Community Center before leaving the Catholic Church, described largely African American southwest Phoenix as a "cesspool of poverty and disease . . . permeated with the odors of a fertilizer plant, an iron foundry, a thousand open privies, and the city sewage-disposal plant." Most people lived in shacks where "babies were born without medical care" and "often died because of the extreme temperatures (up to 118 degrees) in the summer or froze to death in winter." McLoughlin went on to say, "Southwest

Phoenix helped Arizona attain the highest infant death rate in the nation. Officials of the United States government awarded it the distinction of being the worst slum area in the United States."

Phoenix was also a tough town for Mexicans. Many churches, theaters, and schools segregated them as well as blacks. In McLoughlin's own parish of St. Mary's, Mexicans had to attend mass in the basement. "Mexicans abajo!" (Mexicans below!)—the command issued by priests at St. Mary's—captured the brutal and pervasive reality of discrimination in the Salt River Valley. Mexican children could only use municipal swimming pools the day before they were cleaned, and most Mexican families lived in southside barrios like Cuatro Milpas and Little Hollywood, which one observer described as "a foul slum, the like of which can probably not be found elsewhere in the United States."

In Tucson a small but powerful Mexican middle class successfully resisted the overt discrimination found in Phoenix. Tucson also did not attract the floating population of Mexican farm workers who picked crops in the Salt River Valley. Nevertheless, the occupational structure of the city revealed the enduring economic subordination of its Mexican residents. Between 1860 and 1940 the proportion of Anglo blue-collar workers dropped from 67.7 percent to 35.6 percent of the total Anglo workforce, indicating strong upward mobility. The proportion of Mexican blue collar workers, on the other hand, declined only slightly, from 82.6 percent to 74.1 percent, during the same period. In 1940 most Tucsonenses still lived in *barrios,* held low-paying jobs, and sent their children to schools that sought to "Americanize" them by denigrating their culture and punishing them for speaking Spanish on the playground as well as in the classroom. The public school system therefore became an instrument of subordination rather than advancement, tracking Mexicans into vocational classes and discouraging them from preparing for college. As one prominent Tucsonense remembered, "It was a terrible waste of brain power."

One response to such entrenched discrimination was the vigorous *mutualista* (mutual-aid society) movement. Founded in Phoenix in 1914, the Liga Protectora Latina protested discrimination in the workplace and led the fight against capital punishment, which executed more Mexicans and African Americans than Anglos. Other mutual-aid societies, like the Sociedad Mutualista Porfirio Díaz and the Alianza Hispano-Americana, provided sick benefits, sponsored charitable fund-raisers, and struggled against a whole series of measures to exclude Mexicans from certain jobs. By the late 1930s the Alianza, headquartered in Tucson, was the largest Mexican mutual-aid society in the United States. With most conventional avenues to political power and economic advancement closed to them, Mexicans had to create their own organizations to promote their culture and make their voices heard in the Southwest.

The mutualistas and their African American counterparts—the Phoenix Protective League, the Black Masons, and the Knights and Daughters of Tabor, among others—functioned on a more basic level as well, providing food, clothing, and shelter to poor families when the state or federal government could not or would not aid them. The Depression hit African Americans and Mexicans harder than Anglos. In October 1933, 59 percent of the Mexicans and 51 percent of the African Americans in Phoenix were on relief, compared to 11 percent of the Anglos. But as demand for relief grew, Mexican and black families were the first to be dropped. New Deal programs clearly favored Anglos. Few African Americans were allowed to enroll in the CCC or the WPA, and those that did were sent out of state. The CCC and WPA did not admit Mexicans in large numbers until the early 1940s, after the economy had revived and Anglos had found jobs in the copper mines and railroads.

In the final analysis, then, the New Deal programs never confronted institutionalized racism across the state. Arizona's extractive economy continued to rely on cheap labor, and one of the ways Arizona employers kept their labor costs down was by pitting Anglos against Mexicans and Mexicans against African Americans. Racism remained both an instrument and a result of the subordination of the state's workforce. Those who could not find jobs—or who were no longer needed after the work had been done—were deported to Mexico, pushed across the border to California, or channeled into slums like South Phoenix. There, according to Emmett McLoughlin, they became the "rejects of a lusty, sprawling, boasting cow-and-cotton town trying hard to become a city" by "veneering itself with the gloss of a symphony orchestra, a Little Theater, and a necklace of resort hotels."

✳ ✳ Women and the Extractive Economy

The extractive economy severely limited the opportunities of most women in the state as well. Lusty cow-and-cotton towns wanted women as wives, secretaries, and prostitutes, not lawyers, doctors, or business leaders. About the only professions open to women were the low-paying ones of nursing and teaching. Even then, if a woman married, Arizona schools fired her. Male teachers could have wives and children, but female teachers had to be single.

Outside the cities, women worked hard but rarely for wages. On ranches and family farms, they kept house, cared for the children, did the bookkeeping, fed the hands, milked the dairy cattle, raised chickens and pigs, canned hundreds of jars of fruits and vegetables, and helped out with branding, inoculations, and other stock-raising tasks. A few women, mainly widows, also ran family spreads. Mary Moeur, whose husband died when she was thirty-two, sloshed around in her cotton fields at midnight showing the irrigators how to irrigate and once drove a herd of dairy cattle down Broadway to her farm in Tempe. But the large land-and-cattle companies did not hire women to string barbed wire or round up their herds, so most range work on Arizona ranches was performed by men.

Wage work in the mining industry was even more constrained. The copper companies hired a few women as secretaries or clerks, but most women in the copper towns earned their living as laundresses, nurses, or operators of boardinghouses. Many of these occupations were home-based and part-time, and were overlooked by compilers of occupational statistics. In 1910, federal census takers were instructed not to record women who kept boarders unless it was a family's principal means of support.

Commercial agriculture was more democratic. "Anyone could get a job picking cotton," Phoenician Edna Phelps recalled. "It paid five cents a pound that year [1918], which was rather good. We'd work all day and maybe get a dollar." In 1920—the year the cotton boom went bust—3,282 (17.8 percent) of the 18,386 "gainfully employed" Arizona women noted by the federal census worked in the agricultural sector. Stoop labor was not gender exclusive. But in all the extractive industries, the steadiest and best-paying jobs were the exclusive domains of men. In 1930 only 22.2 percent of all Arizona women aged ten or older were listed as employed. Instead, they "did what the day brought," according to Fern Johnson, a schoolteacher who married a Peoria farmer. "Families were families, and there were women and there were men and you just did what you had to do."

Marguerite Noble provides the best description of working-class women's lives in her novel *Filaree,* which is based in part on the life of her own mother. *Filaree* tells the story of Melissa Baker, a ranch wife in the Tonto Basin who is abandoned by her husband after they sell the ranch and move to the Salt River Valley. The novel starkly evokes the isolation and monotony of ranch life, the desolation of unwanted pregnancy, and the anguish at the accidental death of a child. Then it follows Melissa's life as she "became the 'widder' who took in sewing, did housecleaning, and was the town's washerwoman." Melissa struggles to raise young children in a "tent house" at the edge of the cotton fields. She cooks for gold miners in western Arizona. She follows the crops in California. Written in simple, brutally direct language, *Filaree* captures the desperation of a woman trapped by "six children, a husband she did not love, and days of monotonous drudgery, with few escapes for pleasure or change."

The situation of the women in Noble's novel is not hopeless, however, because it also traces the halting upward mobility of the few women who manage to receive an education. Melissa escapes the life of a migrant farm worker by marrying the kindly mine owner she worked for years before. Together they prosper on a cotton farm in Coolidge during the 1930s. Several of her daughters from her first marriage graduate from normal school and become teachers. One, Mary Belle, never marries. She supports herself, travels to places like India, and makes a life for herself in a man's world without a man. Perhaps the biggest change Arizonans in 1940 were about to experience was the sudden flood of women into the workforce. World War II was drawing closer, unleashing forces that turned Arizona into an urban society with a strong manufacturing base. Mining, ranching, and agriculture remained largely masculine, but barriers of gender as well as race began to weaken in cities like Phoenix and Tucson. Economic transformation led to social change, though that change often came slowly, with as many setbacks and unforeseen obstacles as advances.

14

World War II and the
✳ ✳ Postwar Boom

If Horatio Alger had grown up in Arizona, even he would have had a hard time imagining Del Webb. Born in Fresno, California in 1899, Webb quit school at thirteen to work as a carpenter and play semipro baseball, a passion that would become a business later in life. But after typhoid fever consumed his six-foot-four body and dropped his weight from 204 to 99 pounds, Webb moved to Phoenix to recover his health in 1927. There he formed the Del Webb Corporation and hitched his fortune to Arizona's star. By the time he died in 1974, no one had figured out more ways of making money off the explosive surges that propelled Arizona from the Southwest to the Sunbelt during and after World War II.

Webb made his first millions off the New Deal, erecting homes, hospitals, and government offices with federal grants or loans. Then, during World War II, his corporation built every major military installation in Arizona except for Davis-Monthan Air Force Base in Tucson. Business continued to boom during the Cold War, when Webb's close ties with the federal government brought more contracts for veterans' hospitals, air bases, and missile silos. The Del Webb Corporation made Arizona and southern California an integral part of the emerging military-industrial complex.

By then, Webb had branched out into the entertainment industry. In 1945 he and Dan Topping bought the New York Yankees, who won fifteen American League pennants and ten World Series during the two decades that Webb co-owned the team. The following year, Webb took over construction of the Flamingo Hotel, Bugsy Siegel's vision of paradise on the Las Vegas Strip. Webb claimed that he had never heard of Siegel when he took the job, but added, "I sure found out in a hurry." When the New York mobster once boasted that he had killed twelve men and was going to kill another, he reassured Webb by saying, "Don't worry, we only kill each other."

Throughout the glitter of the New York and Las Vegas years, however, Phoenix remained Webb's corporate headquarters, and that was where he made social as well as financial history in 1960. America's postwar population was aging, but many of the elderly were "active seniors" who had plenty of money and wanted to spend it in the sun. They also wanted golf courses, medical facilities, shopping centers, and swimming pools. Webb's response was to build them Sun City, their own community northwest of Phoenix—no children, no slums, just 30,000 acres of tract homes filled with jaunty, beaming retirees.

That vision of the future put Webb on the cover of *Time* magazine in 1962. No one recognized a growth industry faster than Webb, and no one did more to build the boom, transforming Arizona from an extractive colony into a military and recreational one. And Webb's contradictions were Arizona's contradictions during the boom years. Quiet and reserved, he supported the Boy Scouts and the Boys' Clubs and a hundred other good causes. He also may have been doing business with Bugsy Siegel the night before Siegel was gunned down in his mistress's apartment in Beverly Hills. No one ever accused Webb of doing anything dishonest, but there was too much money to be made to have many scruples about one's partners. The important thing was to fuel the boom, and to ride the boom, and to make Arizona grow.

✳ ✳ ✳ ### The Economic Impact of World War II

The boom began as a combustible mixture of sunshine and destruction. In *World War II and the West,* historian Gerald Nash argues that it would have taken forty years of peace to reshape the West as profoundly as four years of war. By 1945, Arizona and the other Western states were no longer "America's

'Third World.'" Instead, they bristled with defense plants, military bases, and research laboratories. In addition to the extractive industries, manufacturing fueled their economies. Their cities were expanding at exponential rates, shedding their small-town pasts like a snake shedding the skin it had outgrown.

Once again the partnership between big government and big business set the transformation in motion. By 1939, Franklin Roosevelt himself was admitting that "Dr. New Deal" was losing ground to "Dr. Win-the-War." As the president and his advisors monitored developments in Europe and the Pacific, they realized that the United States was going to confront Germany and Japan, generating a voracious demand for tanks, planes, and soldiers. Even though many New Dealers like Harold Ickes, Roosevelt's secretary of the interior, wanted to make sure that small businesses received their share of the military pie, the generals in the Pentagon found it easier to deal with a few large enterprises rather than many small ones. The New Deal subsidized agribusiness in the West; World War II did the same for the aircraft, shipbuilding, steel, mining, and oil industries.

Most Arizonans did not mind, however, because the war revitalized the state's economy. Metal prices started to climb in 1939, enabling Arizona mines to recover from their second major collapse of the decade. By 1943 the state was producing more minerals than it had since its peak in 1929. And while copper remained the most important metal, zinc and lead production soared as well, breaking records year after year.

The only limiting factor of production was labor, which was in short supply because of the draft. Mining companies therefore made hiring practices less restrictive and brought more Mexicans into the workforce. Soon even women were toiling in the copper mines. Union activity also intensified. The mining companies responded with red baiting and the arrests of union organizers, but they were never able to engender the level of hysteria achieved during World War I. The International Union of Mine, Mill and Smelter Workers (IUMMSW) even won a series of grievances against Phelps Dodge and other corporations before the National Labor Relations Board and the War Man Power Board. In 1944 injunctions filed against the Miami Copper Company, the Inspiration Consolidated Copper Company, and the International Smelter and Refining Company ended the dual wage system in Miami, where Mexican miners made $1.15 less per shift. After nearly thirty years of domination, the copper collar was corroding.

There was also a short-lived boom in long-staple cotton, but the real growth—the growth that transformed the state—occurred in the service and manufacturing sectors of the economy. Like the Indian wars of the late nineteenth century, the biggest market for services, at least at first, was the U.S. military. In January 1941 the city of Phoenix bought 1,440 acres west of Glendale and leased it to the War Department for a dollar a year to build an advanced aviation training field. Named after Arizona World War I ace Frank Luke, the base churned out more than 13,500 pilots during the war, making it the largest advanced flying school in the world. Luke Air Field also generated an estimated $3.5 million a year for local businesses. Patriotism was not the only motive behind Phoenix's lease of the base.

Promoted by Senator Carl Hayden, Arizona's clear skies and year-round flying weather soon attracted other installations. In the Salt River Valley, Williams Field east of Chandler was a basic and intermediate school, Thunderbird II north of Scottsdale trained cadets, and Litchfield Naval Air Facility tested planes and flew them to their destinations. Meanwhile, Tucson supplied Davis-Monthan, the municipal airport commandeered by the army; Ryan Field to the west; and Marana Air Base to the northwest, which trained 10,000 pilots before it was deactivated in 1945. The army also established three bases in western Arizona—Camps Bouse, Horn, and Hyder—to prepare soldiers for desert warfare. When they went off-duty, those soldiers headed for Phoenix, where, marveled one former mayor, "They'd just walk through town and buy everything there was—meat, cigarettes, and liquor." World War II was an Arizona merchant's dream come true.

Civilians flocked to the state as well. To minimize the danger of attack, the government decided to disperse strategic defense plants across the country. Paul Litchfield, the man who had engineered the cotton boom during World War I, recommended the Salt River Valley to his friends in Washington. "It is well inland and thus protected from any possible air attacks," Litchfield noted. It was also well-connected by air, rail, and highway to the rest of the nation, especially southern California, where many of the aircraft plants were being built. In July 1941 the federal Defense Plant Corporation (DPC) leased land from the Southwest Cotton Company, a subsidiary of the Goodyear Tire and Rubber Company, which Litchfield headed. The DPC then erected a government-owned plant operated by the Goodyear Aircraft Corporation. Phoenix city officials were ecstatic. "The project brings Arizona its first large defense industry and is expected to herald many other major industries for the Phoenix area," they proclaimed. A military-industrial firebird was rising from the cotton fields.

At its peak, the Goodyear plant employed 7,500 people, making it the largest employer in the Salt River Valley. The Alcoa plant in southwest Phoenix, with 3,500 employees, and AiResearch at Sky Harbor Airport, with 2,700, followed in 1942. Since the local labor pool was limited, the plants recruited people from across the country. "We trained cotton pickers galore out of Tennessee, Mississippi, Arkansas, Kentucky," recalled one Goodyear executive. Okies and Arkies had nearly starved in the valley during the winter of 1938 before moving on to California. Now many of them had returned to put planes together. With more than 12,000 defense jobs and thousands of soldiers and pilots passing through town, Phoenix was humming. Tucson, with its huge Consolidated Vultee Aircraft plant employing thousands of workers, was not far behind.

❊ ❊ The Political Impact of World War II

The result was an urban explosion that rearranged the political and economic landscape of the state. In 1940, about half of Arizona's population lived in Phoenix and Tucson. Ten years later, two-thirds did, a direct consequence of federal military policy. In Maricopa County alone, the population rose from 186,000 to 332,000 during the decade. Not since the early territorial period had the U.S. military played such an enormous role in Arizona's destiny.

The immediate problem was housing. Defense plant workers, even former farm laborers, were not about to live in shacks or drink from irrigation ditches anymore, so the federal government spent millions of dollars to construct public housing projects like Alzona Park near Alcoa and Duppa Villa near AiResearch. Meanwhile, the town of Goodyear sprang up to accommodate newcomers west of the city.

Transportation was the next major challenge. Because of wartime shortages, new automobiles and buses could not be purchased, so city employees scoured the country for secondhand buses "in any condition as long as they ran," according to Mayor Newell Stewart. Roads crumbled, rattletrap vehicles rumbled and backfired, but somehow the city managed to get the workers to the plants, which ran three shifts a day. Because the plants never closed, the city did not sleep either. Restaurants, movie houses, and swimming pools stayed open all night. Horse lovers went on moonlit rides. "You would have thought you were in New York City," hotelier George Luhrs recalled. "The traffic of pedestrians was from the buildings to the curb."

Other forms of entertainment flourished as well. At the beginning of the war, Phoenix was a corrupt, wide-open town. Police and city officials had long tolerated gambling and prostitution because "fines" from those businesses provided city revenue and bribes. But Phoenix's old-style politics were on a collision course with the new military commanders, who had to keep their troops free of venereal disease and out of jail until they were ready for war. The conflict came to a head on November 26, 1942, when a black soldier from the 364th

Infantry Regiment at Papago Park was shot while resisting arrest after a brawl. Other African Americans objected, so the military police rounded up about 150 black soldiers. The soldiers panicked and ran, the police cordoned off twenty-eight blocks on the city's southeast side, and armored personnel carriers rolled down the streets, spraying houses with fifty-caliber machine guns whenever the soldiers refused to surrender. By the time the violence was over, 180 soldiers had been arrested and three men had died.

Four days later, Colonel Ross Hoyt of Luke Air Field declared Phoenix off-limits to army personnel. He claimed that his order had nothing to do with the "Thanksgiving night riot" and everything to do with the "venereal disease situation." Rioting blacks, after all, confirmed Anglo stereotypes and reinforced the army's policy of segregation. Machine-gun fire in African American neighborhoods was easily justified in a community with an essentially Southern mentality. But Hoyt and other base commanders were obsessed with sex. "The city will stay out-of-bounds until it has become untenable for prostitutes," Hoyt announced. The venereal disease rate at his base had tripled in four months, and he demanded "an immediate drive on all loose women . . . no matter who it hurts."

The city's aggressive young business community soon answered Hoyt's call. Recognizing that, as one merchant put it, "The army's payrolls constitute one of the community's largest sources of revenue," more than seventy-five business leaders grilled Mayor Newell Stewart and his city commissioners in the card room of the Adams Hotel. After hours of such pressure, most of the exhausted commissioners finally agreed to fire the city manager, clerk, magistrate, and chief of police. Payoffs from pimps, madams, gamblers, and drug dealers were no longer acceptable. Three days later, Colonel Hoyt lifted his ban. Lawyer Frank Snell later said, "It was kind of like a coup, and we called it 'The Card-room Putsch.'"

It was also the beginning of a revolution in Arizona politics. In 1947 many of the same leaders who had met in the Adams Hotel spearheaded the bipartisan Charter Revision Committee, which sponsored the successful drive to revise the city charter and allow a professional city manager to run the government. Two years later the same group formed the Charter Government Committee (CGC) and elected its own slate of candidates to the city council. Established civic leaders like Snell, Walter Bimson, and banker Sherman Hazeltine were powerful forces on the committee. So was Eugene Pulliam, the conservative newspaper publisher who bought both the *Arizona Republic* and the *Phoenix Gazette* in 1946. One of the first CGC council members was a department store owner named Barry Goldwater. The CGC set the tone for the image postwar

Phoenix wanted to convey. Most members were white, male upper-middle-class businessmen and lawyers, and even though Arizona was a predominantly Democratic state, most CGC members were conservative Republicans. They lived in North Phoenix or Paradise Valley and belonged to the Phoenix Country Club. Their wives ran the Junior League. A number of the women, like Sandra Day O'Connor and Margaret Hance, went on to have successful judicial or political careers of their own several decades later. In the late 1940s, however, men like Pulliam, Goldwater, and Harry Rosenzweig were just beginning to put together the Republican insurgence that captured Maricopa County and eventually swept the state.

Their model of government was undoubtedly influenced by the corporate approach to military buildup that characterized World War II. Members of the CGC wanted a clean, efficient city run by a clean, efficient government, and they wanted that government to continue to attract new businesses, particularly aeronautics and electronics firms with strong ties to the Pentagon. To do so, they had to eliminate embarrassing old-style graft and nepotism because military contractors and corporate site-selection teams frowned on such bottlenecks and the image of a corrupt, sluggish past they conveyed. World War II had shown the country how much it could accomplish when big business and big government joined together and took charge. Phoenix had gotten a taste of that transformation. Now it wanted more.

✳ ✳ The Battle Over the "Right to Work"

Before that happened, however, Phoenix and Tucson had to compete with other cities to attract industry, and the best way to do that was to offer low taxes and low wages. Arizona's climate was a considerable draw, but business executives demanded more than sunshine to move their companies to the desert Southwest.

Lowering taxes was relatively noncontroversial. During its first campaign in 1949, the Charter Government Committee sponsored a series of measures to reduce or eliminate many taxes on businesses in Phoenix. Because CGC candidates swept the city elections, most of the proposals passed. That same year Governor Ernest McFarland established the Industrial Development Committee to recommend changes in the state tax code. During the early 1950s, the state legislature adopted all of the committee's recommendations, culminating in the repeal in 1955 of the Arizona sales tax on products manufactured for sale to the federal government.

The battle against organized labor was considerably more bitter. In 1939,

Arizona representatives of the railroad brotherhoods, the American Federation of Labor, and the Congress of Industrial Organizations set aside their differences and formed the Arizona League for Better Government. By the mid-1940s the creation of another prolabor progressive coalition looked possible. The IUMMSW was organizing successful strikes in the copper mines. Sidney ("When I am in the house of labor, I am in the house of friends") Osborn was the wildly popular governor. Democrats remained in control of the legislature, and even though most of the legislators were conservative, their ties to the national party forced them to pay lip service to the heritage of Franklin Roosevelt and the New Deal. Business leaders believed that labor had to be curbed if Arizona was ever going to realize its destiny as a mecca of light industry and high finance.

The assault began in 1945, when a group of Arizona servicemen formed the Veterans' Right to Work Committee. Their leader, Herbert Williams, had started a welding business and had lost a contract because he ran a nonunion shop. Other veterans found themselves out of work because of union seniority rules. Their resentment drove them into the right-to-work camp just as resentment against the dual wage system caused Mexican veterans in Clifton-Morenci to join the IUMMSW and take on Phelps Dodge during the same period.

The strategy of the new committee was bold and brilliant. After the legislature defeated several right-to-work bills, the Veterans' Committee seized that old populist tool of the Arizona constitution, the initiative, and took the battle to the Arizona public. In November 1946 a constitutional amendment guaranteeing open shops appeared on the ballot. That fall, both sides hurled slurs at one another with cynical abandon. The Tucson chapter of the Citizens' Committee Against the Right to Starve distributed a pamphlet whose headline screamed, *"DID YOU ADMIRE HITLER? Of Course Not!* Neither Did Anybody Else Who Believes in the Democratic Way. How Did He Rise to Dictatorship? FIRST HE KILLED THE LABOR UNIONS. THEN HE OUTLAWED THE CHURCH. HE ENFORCED THE 'RIGHT-TO-WORK.' That's the Fascists' Method. *DON'T LET IT HAPPEN HERE!"*

Right-to-work advocates like the Arizona Farm Bureau Federation countered by calling on voters to "Stop the Communists!" after a local Communist paper came out against the amendment. The Veterans' Committee did not twist its propaganda quite that far, but in an open message to union members just before the election, the committee stated, "Good unions . . . have nothing to fear from the 'Right-to-Work' Bill. It is only a few, powerful, self seeking, domineering bosses who need worry. And, of course, the Communists—for they can't hope to bore in and capture control of any outfit where membership is on a free democratic basis. All we ask is that you vote—as a free American."

Not surprisingly, that message appeared in the *Arizona Republic*. Eugene Pulliam detested unions and did everything he could to support the amendment. Since he owned two of the biggest newspapers in the state, his support carried great weight, especially given the mood of the electorate. More strikes broke out in 1946 than in any other year in U.S. history, and by the time November rolled around, voters were sick and tired of the disruptions. The result was a typically schizophrenic Arizona election. The populist Sidney Osborn trounced his Republican opponent by a whopping 73,595 to 48,867. Despite Osborn's opposition to right-to-work, however, the amendment triumphed by the slimmer but still substantial margin of 61,875 to 49,557. Arizonans were not quite ready to turn Republican, but they effectively gutted the unions except in the copper towns.

The controversy also provided a statewide organization that allowed conservative young Republicans in Phoenix to expand their base of power. One member of the Veterans' Committee was a Harvard-trained lawyer named John Rhodes. He won election as Arizona's first Republican congressman in 1952. Another was Barry Goldwater, who became a Republican U.S. senator the same year. Once in Washington, Goldwater's appointment to the Labor and Welfare Committee gave him the national antilabor exposure he needed to turn himself into "Mr. Conservative" and to lead the charge first against the New Deal and later the Great Society. Handsome, charming, and disarmingly candid, Goldwater became the silver-haired knight of Sunbelt Republicanism.

As Republican power grew, unionism as a statewide political force withered and died. By 1958, at the height of the boom, less than 33,000 workers belonged to unions even though Arizona's workforce numbered more than 450,000. Perhaps the movement's epitaph was written in 1965, when the national labor movement tried to repeal Section 14-B of the Taft-Hartley Act, which allowed open shops in businesses operating across state lines. By then, Morris Udall was a U.S. congressman, the most liberal member of Arizona's congressional delegation. In 1946, Morris and his brother Stewart had ardently opposed the right-to-work crusade. Twenty years later Udall felt compelled to support it. Right-to-work, like the Central Arizona Project, had become a sacred cow. The result was an Arizona wage structure that was 10 to 25 percent lower than in the major industrial centers of the country.

It was ironic, then, that unions in the copper mines were finally winning strike after strike against Phelps Dodge and other copper companies. The first and biggest victory came in 1946, the same year that right-to-work triumphed. During the war years, Mexican miners and smelter workers in Clifton-Morenci met in cemeteries and other secret locations to form a chapter of the IUMMSW, which became known as the "Mexican Union." Flush with a War Department contract that called for 45,000 tons of ore a day, Phelps Dodge refused to recognize the chapter. Company executives still acted as if Arizona were the same state it had been in 1917.

After the war ended, however, Mexican veterans returned to Clifton-Morenci, just as they did to hundreds of other communities across the Southwest. They had fought in Europe, North Africa, and the Pacific. Ed Montoya, for example, a tall Marine with the face of a prizefighter, landed on Okinawa on April 13, 1944. At 8 A.M. his company had 186 men. By 5 P.M. only 24 remained alive. After experiences like that, Montoya and other veterans were not about to accept segregation in Clifton restaurants or a dual wage system at Phelps Dodge.

They went on strike on September 22, 1946. "I would say to myself here after I came back in '46, 'Hey, somebody's been lyin' to me all these years!' " Montoya recalled. "How come I went in as a private and I came out as a leader. If that can happen in the army in combat, why can't it happen in the smelter?' " Signs went up stating, "We Want Equality With Other Workers. No More. No Less." Picket lines kept out the scabs. After 104 days of lost income, the mighty Phelps Dodge capitulated, giving Mexican workers equal pay, equal benefits, and an equal chance at promotions. The "Mexican Union" had wrenched off the copper collar, at least for a time.

＊　＊　＊　The Explosive Fifties

But even though the unions won the copper towns, they lost the cities, and that was where Arizona's meteoric growth was taking place. In a sense, during the postwar years Arizona became two states, or a state with two very different sectors. Phoenix and Tucson devoured their flat desert valleys, splattering the maps of the planners with Rorshach blots of urban sprawl. The countryside, in contrast, remained wedded to the old extractive order or locked up in bombing ranges, Indian reservations, and national forests. Miners, ranchers, and farmers continued to wield a disproportionate amount of power in the legislature, but their contributions to Arizona's economy dwindled. Arizona in the 1950s was a very different state from what it had been when Japanese planes sank its namesake at Pearl Harbor.

The cutting edge of change was manufacturing, especially the electronics and aerospace industries, which came to Arizona in two waves. The first began in World War II with the arrival of Goodyear Aircraft, AiResearch, and Alcoa in Phoenix, and Consolidated Vultee in Tucson. When the war ended, some of the plants like Consolidated Vultee closed, but the manufacturing sector survived the postwar recession. In 1939 there were 313 manufacturing firms in Arizona, employing 7,996 people and producing goods with a value-added worth of $31.6 million. By 1947 the number of enterprises had risen to 545, with a workforce of 14,188 and a value-added production of $104 million.

The second and more sustained wave swept across the state during the 1950s, the most explosive decade of growth in Arizona history. It started in 1949, when Motorola established its Military Electronics Division in Phoenix. If one overlooked what its products were designed to do, Motorola seemed to be the epitome of a clean, safe, nonpolluting industry. Unlike the copper companies, it did not take great bites out of the landscape or spew dangerous chemicals into the air. Moreover, its workforce was well-educated but nonunion. "We can run an ad in the trade magazines mentioning three places to work—Phoenix, Chicago and Riverside, in California," said one Motorola manager. "We'll draw 25-to-1 replies for Phoenix compared with other cities. . . . We don't have to pay a premium to get engineers and other skilled employees to live here, either. The premium is free—sunshine." Right-to-work and the sunshine factor were a heady combination for corporate executives bent on expansion.

The only hitch in the plan was heat, and by the 1950s the desert summer no longer haunted Arizona progress. During the Depression, unemployed craftsmen with plenty of time on their hands tinkered with a Rube Goldberg–like succession of evaporative coolers, which came to be known as "swamp boxes" or "swamp coolers" because of the mold and fungi that grew in them. Thrown together out of chicken wire, wallboard, excelsior matting, electric fans, and water sprayers, swamp boxes sprouted like mushrooms on the roofs and in the windows of Arizona buildings. By the end of the 1930s, Phoenix was the "Air Conditioned Capital of the World," and by 1951, five Phoenix companies— Palmer Manufacturing, the Wright Manufacturing Company, the Mountainaire Manufacturing Company, the Polaire Cooler Company, and the International Metal Products Company—were producing half the evaporative coolers made in the United States and were pumping $15 million a year into the local economy.

But the corporate revolution demanded more than swamp boxes. Evaporative coolers, even well-built ones, required regular maintenance. They also lost effectiveness when the summer rains arrived and the weather turned humid. Then came refrigeration cooling, or air-conditioning, which soon cooled most businesses and many homes. "Motorola management feels that refrigeration cooling is the complete solution to the Phoenix summer heat problem," Motorola executive Daniel Noble declared. "Refrigeration cooling has transformed Phoenix into a year-round city of delightful living."

With its laboratories cool and its workforce happy, Motorola pioneered urban Arizona's Cold War boom. By 1960 the company had added a Semi-Conductor Products Division and a Solid Systems Division in Phoenix. Together, the three plants employed 5,000 people, making Motorola the largest employer in the city. During the same period, nearly 700 other firms settled in the Phoenix metropolitan area alone. Most of the enterprises were small, with a workforce of less than twenty people, but giants like General Electric (1957) and Kaiser Aircraft & Electronics (1957) jumped on the bandwagon as well, in part because of the proximity of the U.S. Army Electronics Proving Ground at Fort Huachuca. After a group of local businessmen raised $650,000 in seventy-two hours to buy a plant site and improve the Deer Valley airport, Sperry Rand came too. Tucson was not as assertive but still managed to snag the expansion of Davis-Monthan Air Force Base in the late 1940s and Howard Hughes's enormous missile plant in 1951. Aggressive business leaders and compliant politicians made sure that the end of World War II would not mean the end of the affair between Arizona and the defense industry.

The result was an orgy of economic expansion driven by manufacturing and lubricated by the lending policies of Arizona's financial institutions. Throughout the state, employment in manufacturing rose from 17,000 in 1950 to 49,300 ten years later, an increase of nearly 200 percent. During that same period, the number of jobs in mining increased from 11,300 to 15,200 (35 percent), while those in agriculture barely climbed at all (from 35,100 to 36,200, or 3 percent). At $260 million, the total wages and salaries in manufacturing dwarfed Arizona's agricultural income of $66 million, the lowest-paid sector of Arizona's economy. Not surprisingly, however, the average per capita income of $6,640 in the largely unionized mining industry remained higher than that of manufacturing, with $5,270.

Nevertheless, the pattern was clear. The copper towns might be prospering, but manufacturing employed more than three times as many people. And because 70 percent of the plants were located in Phoenix and 14 percent in Tucson, Arizona's population surged there. In 1940, 499,261 people lived in the state. That number increased by 50 percent (to 749,587) in 1950, and 74 percent (to 1,302,161) in 1960. But the urban growth rate was phenomenal. Tucson's population rose slowly from 36,818 in 1940 to 45,454 in 1950 (a 23 percent increase), but then it soared to 212,892 (a 368 percent increase) a decade later. Phoenix mirrored that trend but on a larger scale: 65,414 in 1940, 106,818 in 1950 (a 63 percent increase), 439,170 in 1960 (a 311 percent increase). Its population boom propelled Phoenix into the top fifty U.S. cities and made it the fastest-growing big city in the country.

Phoenix's satellites were growing as well. At the beginning of World War II,

Glendale, Tempe, Mesa, and Scottsdale were tiny planets orbiting the small Phoenix sun. Twenty years later, citrus groves and cotton fields no longer separated the satellites from the metropolis. Between 1940 and 1960, Tempe's population grew from 2,906 to 24,897, Mesa from 7,224 to 33,772, and Glendale from 4,855 to 15,696. During the same period, Scottsdale—"The West's Most Western Town"—sprouted to ten times its prewar size (from 1,000 to 10,026). In 1977, Edward Abbey described Phoenix as "the blob that is eating Arizona." But the "mad amoeba" was already slithering across the desert in the 1950s.

✳ ✳ ✳ The New Arizona Lifestyle

In the process, a new society emerged, one based on high-tech industry, real estate speculation, and FHA loans. The upper class clung to its enclaves around Encanto Park and the Biltmore, but it marched up North Central and colonized Paradise Valley as well. Meanwhile, the middle class was filling subdivisions from Mesa to Maryvale, where John F. Long introduced the concept of the "planned community" of tract homes. Soon the entire valley was a checkerboard of developments, each with its own architectural "style." While some of the homes reflected Eastern tastes, the ranch-style house—low, rambling, and dominated by a two-car carport—became Phoenix's architectural signature and the symbol of the new "Arizona lifestyle." Nearly every family owned its own home and drove two cars. People planted bermuda grass in the summer and rye grass in the winter and filled their yards with subtropical plants like oleander and bougainvillea that exploded with color against the dark green of their lawns. Meanwhile, the recreational possibilities were endless. People summered at their cabins in Payson, went waterskiing on Saguaro Lake, and swam in their own backyards, where pools glistened like turquoise beads. There were no limits—to water, energy, or easy credit. It was suburbia triumphant, a strange, sun-dazed experiment taking shape on the northern edge of the Sonoran Desert as air-conditioning and flood irrigation kept the desert at bay.

No organization played a more critical role in this transformation than Walter Bimson's Valley National Bank (VNB), the largest financial institution in the state. Soon after the Federal Housing Act (FHA) was passed in 1934, Bimson sent his employees door to door to persuade "the little guy" that borrowing money for home improvements was patriotic. By the end of 1935, only four other banks in the country had made more FHA loans. So when World War II ended and thousands of veterans returned to Arizona with the GI Bill in their pockets, Bimson and the VNB welcomed them with VHA as well as FHA loans. Between 1957 and 1959, 44,000 building permits were issued in Maricopa County alone, most of them for single-family dwellings, and the state's construction industry boomed. The Valley National Bank also loaned money hand over fist to cattle ranchers and cotton farmers, becoming the nation's fifth largest agricultural lender. But Bimson's heart was in the Valley of the Sun, where he backed Motorola and Del Webb and hundreds of other manufacturing firms and real estate developers. "Walter Bimson did more for the Valley than anybody else," said Robert Goldwater, Barry's brother and the businessman in the family. Like Webb, Bimson was one of the architects of the boom.

And the society Bimson, Webb, and others shaped was a society addicted to the automobile. People valued their independence and mobility and wanted to live in the suburbs. In both Phoenix and Tucson, downtown commercial districts shriveled as new emporiums arose: suburban shopping centers like Town and Country (1956), Park Central (1957), Tower Plaza (1958), and Chris Town Mall (1961) in Phoenix, and Park Mall (1957) and El Con Mall (1960) in Tucson. They also ignored mass-transit systems; 95 percent of all personal travel was by car. In 1940 there were 114,216 cars, 711 buses, and 28,445 trucks registered in Arizona. Twenty years later the number of automobiles (488,988) and trucks (133,010) had increased by more than 300 percent, while the number of buses (1,559) barely doubled. The city of Phoenix sold its bus system in 1959 because it was losing so much money, so the differential grew even more pronounced in the 1970s and 1980s. Yet the dependence on cars grew faster than the ability to move them efficiently. By 1960, Phoenix had only seven miles of freeway, carrying less than 10 percent of its traffic. In many respects, the Phoenix and Tucson metropolitan areas were little more than collections of suburbs whose proliferation outraced their road systems.

* * *   Race During the Boom Years

Despite traffic problems and other growth pains, however, most Phoenix and Tucson business leaders were exuberantly optimistic. Magazines like *Arizona Highways* splashed Arizona's scenic glories across its pages, while promotional journals like the First National Bank's *Profile of Arizona* abounded with statistics about business triumphs and photographs that portrayed a clean, confident, modern Arizona on the move. But not all Arizona workers were bankers or engineers. For Arizona's small African American population (3.3 percent in 1960), about all the boom meant was more jobs as laborers and maids. Arizona defense plants refused to hire African Americans during the war years, and those policies continued into the late 1940s and 1950s, when even new companies like Motorola hired whites only. In the words of African American political activist Lincoln Ragsdale, "Phoenix was just like Mississippi. People were just as bigoted. They had segregation. They had signs in many places, 'Mexicans and Negroes not welcome.'"

Nonetheless, a few determined individuals challenged Arizona's entrenched racism. Emmett McLoughlin opened St. Monica's Hospital (now Memorial Hospital) in South Phoenix in 1944 to treat poor African Americans, Mexicans, and Anglos who were often turned away at other medical facilities. That same year the new hospital established the first integrated nursing school in the state. In 1946 the Phoenix branch of the National Association for the Advancement of Colored People (NAACP) denounced Woolworth's Department Store, which refused to serve African Americans at its lunch counter. But the most sustained protests focused on the public schools. In both Phoenix and Tucson, grade schools were segregated. And while African Americans attended Tucson High School, the only high school in the city, Phoenix was large enough to have a "Colored High School" established in 1914. Renamed George Washington Carver High School in 1943, the school was run by W. A. Robinson, who refused to accept cast-off equipment from white schools and pushed hard to make "separate but equal" a reality. To many African Americans, however, the doctrine itself was an abomination, mocking the principles that African American soldiers had fought and died for in segregated regiments during World War II.

In 1947, then, about 300 African Americans and Anglos in Phoenix formed the Greater Phoenix Council for Civic Unity (GPCCU). Together with the Urban League and the NAACP, they began to challenge school segregation in court, in the legislature, and even through an initiative in 1950, which was trounced by a vote of 104,226 to 57,970. The state's Southern heritage ran deep, and many newcomers from the Midwest and East were conservative as well. A decade later, Republicans like attorney William Rehnquist were still trying to remove African Americans from voting rolls or turn them away from polling places if they could not read passages from the Constitution.

In the end, the courts forced desegregation on the state. In 1953, African American attorney H. B. Daniels and Anglo attorneys William Mahoney and Herbert Finn argued against segregated high schools in Maricopa County Superior Court. Declaring that "a half century of intolerance is enough," Judge Fred Struckmeyer handed down the first legal opinion against school segregation in the United States. Judge Charles Bernstein soon followed suit by ruling that segregated grade schools were unconstitutional as well. A year later the U.S. Supreme Court's decision in *Brown v. Board of Education* made school desegregation the law of the land.

Phoenix's small band of activists—African Americans like mortician Lincoln

Ragsdale, beauty shop owner Madge Copeland, teachers and journalists Eugene and Thomasena Grigsby, and clergymen Robert Phillips and George Brooks, and Anglos like attorney William Mahoney, physician Fred Holmes, Rabbi Albert Plotkin, and GPCCU organizer Fran Waldman—also battled discrimination in housing and on the job. To integrate the workforce, they confronted Phoenix businesses with sit-ins, boycotts, and face-to-face meetings. During the 1950s their protests met with little success, but in the early 1960s things began to change. In 1962 the NAACP picketed Woolworth's after it refused to hire African Americans. Afraid of the publicity, the national office ordered the local store to reverse its policy. When Motorola decided to hire local high school graduates, the company made an arrangement with the Arizona Welfare Department to screen only white applicants. Brooks charged into the office of Arizona Attorney General Robert Pickrell and "accused the welfare department and the state employment services of being in collusion with private industry to keep black folks unemployed." After newspapers ran the story, African Americans got jobs at Motorola. Brooks and Ragsdale also teamed up to play good cop–bad cop with James Pattrick, the president of Valley National Bank. According to Brooks, "Lincoln was brash, nasty. . . . He would back him up into a corner and I was the good guy. I would pull him out. . . . That's what you call creative conflict." VNB hired its first African American teller soon after the confrontation.

Mexicans faced fewer legal barriers than African Americans, but their struggle was compounded by Arizona's proximity to Mexico and the continuous influx of Mexican nationals into the state. Many Anglos did not distinguish between Mexican citizens and Mexican immigrants even though some Mexican families had lived in Arizona for six or seven generations. Both were stereotyped as stoop labor, and both were welcomed or feared depending upon the state of the regional economy. Between 1942 and 1964, the official U.S. policy bounced back and forth between legal immigration and deportation. During the war, an executive agreement between the United States and Mexico created the *bracero* program, which allowed nearly 300,000 Mexican nationals to toil in U.S. fields or work on the railroads. The federal government then terminated the program in 1947 only to reactivate it during the Korean War. By the early 1950s, however, the enormous traffic in undocumented workers had summoned up all the old nativist fears, so in 1954 the Border Patrol launched Operation Wetback, the largest deportation drive since the repatriation sweeps of the 1930s. Like those sweeps, Operation Wetback rounded up U.S. citizens as well as Mexican nationals. Being born and raised in the United States was no guarantee of civil liberties when your skin was brown and you spoke Spanish.

And because there were far more Mexicans in Arizona than African Americans, institutionalized discrimination against them blighted many more lives. According to the 1960 federal census, 194,000 "persons of Spanish language or Spanish surname" lived in the state, compared to 43,403 "Negroes." But most scholars agree that the census missed many people of Mexican descent (less than 2 percent of Arizona Hispanics were of Caribbean or Latin American descent). Ten years later, the 1970 census recorded 333,349 Mexicans in Arizona, a rise of 71 percent, which reflected better enumeration as well as immigration and natural increase. Mexicans were clearly Arizona's largest minority group, with 19 percent of its total population (1,770,900).

By then, very few of them were farm laborers who had been born in Mexico. On the contrary, 81 percent of all Mexicans in Arizona lived in cities and towns, and 80 percent had been born in the United States. So the United States was where they fought their political battles. Mexican veterans formed new organizations such as the American GI Forum, which joined established groups like the Alianza Hispano-Americana and the League of United Latin American Citizens (LULAC) to struggle for school desegregation and other causes. In 1950, for example, attorneys Ralph Estrada and Greg García filed an injunction to force Tolleson School District 17 to allow Mexican pupils to attend the Anglo school, which had much better facilities. The "separate but equal" doctrine was not supposed to apply to Mexicans, but towns like Flagstaff, Ajo, Douglas, Miami, Clifton, Superior, Safford, Duncan, Glendale, and Tolleson were still segregating Mexican students in the early 1950s. *Brown v. Board of Education* was therefore a triumph for Mexicans as well as blacks.

Mexicans also fought for equal opportunities in the workplace. Even though many Mexicans worked in defense plants in California during World War II, their employment in Arizona plants was limited. Access improved somewhat after the war, but in 1959, James Officer estimated that only 200 to 250 Mexicans had jobs at Hughes Aircraft in Tucson even though its workforce numbered 3,000. The aircraft and electronics industries may have pioneered modern manufacturing in Arizona, but their commitment to minority hiring was not impressive.

Other large corporations like the Mountain States Telephone and Telegraph Company also discriminated against Mexicans, refusing to hire them as operators because "all Mexican American girls have a language difficulty." But some of the biggest barriers to Mexican employment or upward mobility were the membership practices of many unions, particularly those affiliated with the American Federation of Labor. In 1950 only 125 Mexicans belonged to the Teamsters Union, which had a statewide membership of 2,000. Mexicans composed less than 10 percent of the unionized carpenters in Arizona and an even smaller proportion of the electricians. Mexican workers made considerable progress during the next ten years, and by the end of the decade they represented about 33 percent of all members in thirty-two Tucson unions, including the carpenters, city employees, and various railway associations. But the Railroad Brotherhood of Locomotive Engineers, perhaps the most prestigious union of them all, continued to exclude "Spanish Americans" into the 1960s. Even though the IUMMSW had demonstrated the determination of Mexican copper miners a generation earlier, some unions continued to cling to their racist pasts.

✳   ✳   ✳   Rosie the Riveter vs. the Postwar Cult of Domesticity

Ever since the Mexican War and the Gadsden Purchase, Mexicans had constituted the ultimate reserve labor supply in the Southwest. During times of expansion, mining, ranching, and agricultural interests clamored for Mexican workers. During times of contraction, the border slammed shut and Mexican workers were fired or deported. World War II brought the bracero program, but for the first time Mexican labor could not meet all the demands of a nation at war, so boundaries of gender as well as race had to be breached.

Between 1940 and 1944, the number of women in the U.S. workforce increased by 47 percent to 19 million, and the jobs were in better-paying, nontraditional sectors—a 141 percent increase in manufacturing, a 20 percent decline in domestic service. In other words, there were more Rosie the Riveters and fewer maids. The proportion of women in manufacturing climbed from 22 percent to 32.7 percent, and from 19.4 percent to 38.4 percent in government. Arizona public schools lifted their ban against married women as teachers, and many women even went to work in the copper mines, the best-paying jobs in the state. Elsie McAlister called World War II "a great release" for the women who took over men's jobs in the smelters and mines. For a few short years, the sexual segregation of the workplace collapsed because of wartime industrial expansion and the draft.

More jobs did not mean equal pay, however. Elsie Dunn worked as a saw operator for eighteen months at Goodyear Aircraft, where a majority of the employees were women. Yet men received higher wages for the same tasks. "The man [who] sat [next to me] would take two days, and I would get mine done in eight hours," Dunn remembered. "He got more money than I did per hour, and I said to the boss, I said, 'How come George got to take two days to do this [and] I get it done in one? Why do you bring his [unfinished work back] to me?' He says, 'I know you'll get it done.'" Dunn went on to say that unequal pay was accepted at that time.

After the war, however, there was tremendous pressure on women to leave the workforce. The cancellation of military contracts forced many defense plants to shut down or cut back at a time when veterans were demanding jobs. Women were expected to return to their homes and let the "Cincinnatuses" take their places. By 1947, women held only 1,193 (9 percent) of the 13,186 manufacturing positions in Arizona. They had become the new reserve labor force—called up when they were needed, dismissed when the boys came home from war.

The conservative ideology of postwar America reinforced this trend. The late 1940s and 1950s were the height of the "baby boom"—a time when homes were cheap and family values reigned supreme. The sense of liberation that many women felt when they entered the workforce dissipated as wartime jobs came to be viewed as a temporary aberration—a sacrifice women made until they could resume their proper roles as wives and mothers. "With their stress on manipulative femininity and the importance of purchasing marital harmony at the cost of a woman's individuality," historian Karen Anderson has observed, "the postwar themes resembled closely those of the nineteenth-century cult of domesticity."

Few areas of the country bought into that vision with more vengeance than urban, middle-class Arizona. Most Arizonans were newcomers who had left extended family networks behind. There were fewer mothers, aunts, or sisters to take care of the children if women wanted to work. Moreover, everything from architecture to geographic mobility emphasized the nuclear family. People did not sit on their front porches and visit with their neighbors or congregate in public places like parks. On the contrary, the Arizona lifestyle meant single-family homes with big yards where the kids could play and the family could recreate in private. Suburban sprawl also made the traditional division of labor within families a practical necessity as well as a moral imperative. Mothers were expected to drive their kids to school in the morning, dart all over the city to do the shopping, pick the kids up from school in the afternoon, and ferry them to Girl Scouts or Little League in the evening. Phoenix and Tucson did not have the mass-transit systems or urban densities to allow children to get places on their own. Instead, women had to become chauffeurs as well as cooks, maids, and child-rearers.

Despite the tremendous demands of their families, however, many women also volunteered for civic, political, and charitable organizations. They raised money, staffed museums, and stuffed envelopes. They managed large budgets and kept many vital community services afloat. Volunteer work gave women a chance to get out of the house and use their creative or administrative talents without appearing to abandon their families for the work world. If it was not possible to operate a company or a department of the government, ambitious and capable women could run the Junior League or a hospital auxiliary. For some, those volunteer activities served as the springboard for a business or political career later on.

In 1960, however, the status of women—like that of African Americans and Mexicans—remained subordinate. Women composed 32.2 percent of the civilian workforce in Arizona (140,619 of 453,988), but that was also the ratio of their median income (0.32) compared to men. In other words, working women made a third of what working men were paid. Less than 20 percent of all professionals and less than 10 percent of all office managers, government officials, or business owners were women. Fifteen years after the end of World War II, many wartime gains had disappeared. Rosie the Riveter had not risen through the ranks to run the plant. More likely, she had gone home to raise her family or was working as a secretary.

Nonetheless, the changes triggered by World War II were sea changes, even in the desert. Arizona no longer was an isolated Southwestern state with an extractive colonial order. On the contrary, it was a rising star of the Sunbelt, that new regional constellation reshaping the demography and political character of the nation. The economy had expanded and diversified, particularly in the manufacturing and service sectors, and there were no compelling physical reasons why women could not perform the same jobs as men in offices or electronics plants. Moreover, the growing need for a better-trained work force, coupled with the demand for equality unleashed by the war, led to a growing emphasis on education regardless of race or gender. The Sunbelt spawned its own problems, but urbanism and occupational mobility broke down many of the old ethnic and sexual boundaries. The postwar "cult of domesticity" was not strong enough to contain the rising expectations of middle-class women or to suppress the economic demands of working-class families where women had to work to make ends meet. World War II and the postwar boom created a social and economic order that allowed the civil rights and feminist movements of the 1960s to arise, even in politically conservative Arizona. By the 1980s, Arizona would have a woman governor and Phoenix would be run by a woman mayor.

15

The Other Arizona

In 1871 a Pima war party slipped north of the Salt River and attacked a group of Yavapais below Four Peaks in the Mazatzal Mountains. The Pimas killed most of the adults but took the children captive, including a little boy named Wassaja. They sold him to an Italian photographer named Carlos Gentile for thirty dollars, and Gentile renamed him Carlos Montezuma.

That name encompassed a world of changing meaning for Wassaja and Indian children like him. Gentile gave the boy his first name, but the second was generic Indian, harkening back to an Aztec past that had nothing to do with the Yavapais of central Arizona. Wassaja would never see his immediate family again. His mother was shot by army scouts while searching for her children. His father died on the San Carlos Reservation. His sisters were sold to a man who took them to Mexico. It was a time of diaspora and disintegration, when the Anglo world felt justified in taking Indian children away from their parents in order to "civilize" them. Wassaja grew up in Illinois and New York, far from his kinsmen and the sacred mountains of his people.

When he returned to Arizona thirty years later, Carlos Montezuma was a physician and a leader in the emerging pan-Indian movement. One of the first Native Americans to receive a medical degree, he spent seven years working for the Bureau of Indian Affairs (BIA) on reservations across the West. His experiences gave him an abiding contempt for the BIA and its reservation system. Like Booker T. Washington and other nonwhite reformers of the era, Montezuma believed that Native Americans had to pull themselves up by their bootstraps and "press forward where the Indians ought to be—man among men." He advocated hard work and off-reservation boarding schools. He thought that reservations turned Indians into "idlers, beggars, gamblers, and paupers."

But Montezuma's own homeland began stalking him during the last two decades of his life. He returned to Yavapai territory for the first time in 1901 and met relatives like his first cousins Charles and George Dickens. They drew him into the struggle to create a Yavapai reservation at abandoned Fort McDowell on the Verde River. That battle eventually pitted Montezuma against both the BIA and the Salt River Valley Water Users Association, who wanted Yavapai water rights and who tried to have the Yavapais transferred to the Salt River Reservation, where the Pimas, their ancestral enemies, held sway.

Montezuma never accepted the reservation system and continued to practice medicine in Chicago, but he also fought tirelessly for Indian land and water rights, realizing that without a land base Native American societies would wither and die. He hated the BIA's power over Indian people, and he supported Indians who tried to preserve traditional ceremonies and political authority even though Montezuma, himself a devout Baptist, was profoundly ambivalent about "traditional" Native American culture. Ironically, his closest supporters among the Yavapais, Apaches, and O'odham were the traditionalists, who became known as "Montezumas" in the 1920s and 1930s.

By then, Montezuma himself was dead. In 1922 the combative "cast iron" doctor contracted tuberculosis. He published the last issue of his newsletter, *Wassaja,* in November, ending with an article called "The Indian Bureau—the Slaughter House of the Indian People." Then, in December, he pulled himself onto a train in Chicago and made the long trip home. George Dickens and his family built a brush shelter for him at Fort McDowell, keeping a fire going while Montezuma lay on a mattress on the winter ground. But even though he told them, "I'm cold. I'm going to die of cold in here!" he refused his doctor's request to move to a sanatorium. "I want to die like my ancestors did," he said. And so he did, on January 23, 1923.

The Yavapais buried Montezuma in the Fort McDowell cemetery, where Four Peaks dominates the horizon and the Verde flows through an enormous mesquite bosque nearby. His tombstone reads:

Wassaja

Carlos Montezuma, M.D.

Mohave Apache Indian

Those simple words capture Montezuma's strange, circular odyssey. In the 1980s, when Yavapais turned back yet another attempt to destroy their reservation by halting the construction of Orme Dam, one activist said, "I don't want to see the land where Montezuma is buried covered with water." The tombstone still stands.

❋ ❋ ❋ Reservation Life in Arizona

All the other Native Americans of Arizona endured similar conflicts and contradictions as they made the transition from independence to reservation life. To talk of a "reservation system" itself is to credit U.S. Indian policy with more rationality than it deserves. The creation of Arizona's twenty Indian reservations proceeded sporadically and haphazardly over 119 years. The first was the Gila River Reservation, established in 1859. The last was the Pascua Yaqui Reservation, established in 1978. Reservations today range in size from the enormous Navajo Nation, which covers nearly 16 million acres and is the largest reservation in the United States, to the tiny Tonto Apache Reservation, which occupies 85 acres south of Payson.

After the disastrous attempt to resettle all Western Apaches, Chiricahua Apaches, and Yavapais on the San Carlos Reservation in the 1870s, however, the government did establish most Arizona reservations within the homelands of the people themselves. The huge Tohono O'odham (2,774,390 acres) and Navajo reservations encompassed significant portions of those homelands. Yavapais, on the other hand, received only small enclaves at Fort McDowell, Camp Verde, Middle Verde, Clarkdale, and Prescott. But even when the size of the reservations was substantial, the government often withheld crucial resources from their inhabitants. The Gila River Reservation was enlarged several times until it contained 371,929 acres. But the Akimel O'odham and Maricopas living there have never recovered the water of the Gila that was being diverted upriver. Their lawsuits have ground through U.S. courts for decades, but their lands remain dry.

Even after the boundaries of most reservations had been fixed, the BIA continued to move people around with little regard for cultural or linguistic affinities. A case in point was the Colorado River Reservation, created in 1865. Mohaves comprised most of the inhabitants, but the reservation was also open to other tribes living along the Colorado, including the Chemehuevis, who spoke a Shoshonean rather than a Yuman language. The original reservation embraced about 75,000 acres. It was later enlarged to 268,291 acres, most of which are in Arizona. Because there were less than 1,000 Mohaves and only about 200 Chemehuevis living there, however, the government decided to fill the desert lowlands with other people. The process began during World War II, when nearly 18,000 Japanese American Nisei were interned at a camp named after Charles Poston, the "Father of Arizona." At its height, Poston was the third largest city in Arizona—a boomtown built on wartime fears—until Japanese relocation ended in 1945.

Not long after the Nisei left, the BIA asked the Colorado River Tribal Council to allow Hopis and Navajos to resettle on the reservation because their reservations were running out of good land. Under pressure, the council agreed, and in 1947 seventeen Hopi families arrived to farm alfalfa along the Colorado. More Hopis and Navajos followed until the Mohaves, fearful that they would lose control of the council, denounced the colonization program and called for its termination. It ended in 1957, but fourteen years later Navajos still constituted 8.6 percent and Hopis 7.4 percent of the reservation's population.

Resettlement was just one manifestation of the insensitivity of many BIA programs. Another was the boarding school system. The boarding schools operated according to the principle enunciated by Indian Commissioner Thomas Morgan in 1889: "The Indian must conform to the 'white man's ways,' peacefully if they will, forcibly if they must." With proper Victorian contempt for non-Christian Indian culture, the BIA therefore tore thousands of Native American children away from their families and forced them to attend institutions like the Phoenix Indian School, which was founded in 1890 after Commissioner Morgan persuaded Phoenix residents that it was "cheaper to educate Indians than to kill them." Another incentive was the "outing system," which placed Indian children in local businesses and gave those businesses a steady supply of cheap labor. By the early twentieth century the BIA had given up its goal of complete assimilation and instead was trying to turn off-reservation Indians into a docile working class.

To do so, the Phoenix Indian School combined an emphasis on vocational training with detribalization and rigid military discipline. As soon as they arrived at the school, children were separated from other members of their tribe, forbidden to speak their native language, stripped of their traditional clothes, and organized into military companies where they were subject to corporal punishment. "I worked in the dining room, washing dishes and scrubbing floors," recalled Akimel O'odham Anna Moore Shaw. "If we were not finished when the 8:00 a.m. whistle sounded, the dining room matron would go around strapping us while we were still on our hands and knees. . . . We just dreaded the sore bottoms."

Not surprisingly, many Indian children resisted. Young boys formed tribal gangs and spoke their language whenever they were free from the supervision of boarding school personnel. Others, like the Hopi Edmund Nequatewa, ran away and embarked on their own personal odysseys back to their homelands, odysseys which, in Nequatewa's case, took him up the Verde Valley and across the Mogollon Rim on foot. Historian David Wallace Adams aptly characterized the intent of the boarding schools as "de-Indianization," but Native American children subverted that process in countless ways.

Meanwhile, the government attempted to transform reservation Indians into property-owning farmers by passing the General Allotment Act in 1887. Also known as the Dawes Severalty Act, the law called for the division of reservations into private allotments that would be transferred to individual Indian families. "Surplus" lands could then be sold to non-Indians, a process that cost Native Americans 91 million acres between 1887 and 1934. In Arizona, allotment affected less than 3 percent of reservation land but caused numerous problems on the Yuma, Colorado River, San Carlos, San Xavier, Salt River, Gila River, and Navajo reservations where it was applied. Most tribes fought the act, and in 1978, after decades of protest, the Quechans finally won back 25,000 acres of their original reservation by arguing that they had agreed to allotment only under duress. Nonetheless, the Dawes Act severely weakened the principle of mutual agreement, the covenant between tribes and the federal government that supposedly guided U.S. Indian policy.

The Indian Reorganization Act of 1934 was designed to restore that principle. The act was the brainchild of John Collier, a social worker in New York City who became enchanted with the Pueblo Indians of New Mexico and developed a deep respect for Pueblo communalism, which he saw as an enduring alternative to the alienation of modern capitalism. As executive secretary of the American Indian Defense Association, Collier condemned the BIA for suppressing Pueblo dances and demanded an end to allotment and the restoration of communal lands. When Franklin Roosevelt appointed him commissioner of Indian affairs in 1933, Collier made cultural pluralism and reservation self-determination the goals of his "Indian New Deal."

Despite such good intentions, however, the legacy of the Collier era was mixed. Arizona Indians eventually approved constitutionally based tribal councils that took more active roles in reservation affairs, but the constitutions were written by non-Indians and were based on the U.S. Constitution rather than Native American legal and political traditions. In the case of the Hopis, the tribal council became a vehicle for the "progressives" and eroded traditional clan and village authority. Among the Tohono O'odham, the very notion of tribal organization was an alien concept imposed from above. "The 'tribe' which adopted a constitution in 1937 was really a group of Indians, speaking dialects of a common language, who in 1916 had come to share a common Indian reservation," anthropologist Bernard Fontana observed. "An overall chairman and political districts had been totally foreign to them." Tribal councils allowed Native Americans to exercise some control over education, health care, and economic development on their reservations, but they also factionalized many groups by creating bases of authority that had never existed before. Moreover, most tribal constitutions contained the clause "subject to the approval of the Secretary of the Interior." Not even Collier believed in full-fledged Indian sovereignty. In Fontana's words, "One might argue that IRA constitutions gave Indians the illusion of self-government."

The history of many Native American groups since then has been a struggle to turn that illusion into reality. In the process, issues of self-determination became entangled with issues of cultural identity and economic development. Indians were demanding greater sovereignty at a time when the federal government was exerting greater control over Western resources, including those on reservations. That control drew Native Americans into another struggle—the struggle between the rural and the urban—escalating across Arizona and the West. The Indian wars forcibly incorporated them into an expanding nation-state with a racist ideology of Anglo superiority. BIA policies tried and failed to turn them into dark-skinned reflections of Christian, capitalist Anglo America. Now cities like Phoenix, Los Angeles, and Las Vegas wanted their water and minerals so they could keep on expanding across the desert. Marginalized on isolated reservations for decades, many Indians in postwar Arizona found themselves straddling prime recreation areas or rich deposits of oil and coal. That forced them to make hard choices about how they wanted to live in their homelands. It also made them players in a game to determine the future of the West itself.

✳   ✳   ✳   **Stock Reduction and the Creation of Navajo Dependency**

No group illustrates the complexity of that struggle better than the Diné, or Navajo. After the Long Walk and the disastrous relocation at Bosque

Redondo, the U.S. government allowed the Navajos to return to the Four Corners region in 1868. The government also replaced the herds of sheep and goats that Kit Carson's soldiers had slaughtered in 1863. During the next sixty years, both the Diné and their animals multiplied rapidly as they spread across the Colorado Plateau. By the early 1930s, Navajo herds numbered more than a million head, reducing plant cover and eroding soil within five miles of Navajo fields, where most herds grazed. The traditional response to such localized environmental degradation was to move, but by then Anglo and Mexican stock raisers had leased or homesteaded most of the land around springs and seeps on the checkerboard lands along the Santa Fe Railroad. The BIA tried to enlarge the reservation by consolidating the checkerboard, but Anglo and Hispanic ranchers blocked its efforts. The government therefore decided that if the Navajos could not continue to expand, they had to learn to live within their means on the reservation itself.

That meant a drastic reduction in the size of Navajo herds. BIA officials believed that Navajo herds were three times the size the range could sustain, so they decided to save the Navajos from themselves. Reservation superintendent E. R. Fryer compared the Diné to children who needed sterner rearing. "The youngster will not always understand a dose of castor oil may sometimes be more efficacious than a stick of candy," Fryer intoned. The need for stock reduction may have been evident, at least to government officials, but their arrogance and insensitivity to Navajo values and economic needs made the process a calamity for the Diné. The Long Walk was the first major trauma in Navajo-Anglo relations. Stock reduction was the second. Ironically, the individual who made stock reduction a reality was John Collier, one of the BIA's harshest critics. In the eyes of many Navajos, Collier became the lying white man who, in the words of the Navajo Ben Morris, stepped out of his car in Tuba City dressed in black "like a big, black crow" and destroyed the old, independent Navajo way of life.

The government called stock reduction the Navajo Project, an elemental clash of cultures that revealed how poorly government officials, even sympathetic ones like Collier, understood the people they were trying to help. When the first phase of the program began in 1934, the Dust Bowl was the dominant metaphor for the ills plaguing the western United States. Farmers and ranchers had abused the land, and now the land was blowing away in huge black clouds or flowing out of the mountains and clogging the rivers. Controlling soil erosion became an evangelical crusade—a grand experiment to prove that humans could restore as well as destroy nature—and the new Soil Conservation Service developed its first demonstration project at Mexican Springs in the eastern part of the Navajo Reservation. Soil Conservation Service personnel believed that Navajo grazing practices threatened that new icon of human progress, Boulder Dam. If Boulder Dam silted up, the federal reclamation of the West would be a sham.

But most Diné did not buy the new conservation gospel and refused to believe that their sheep were the cause of the problem. If the soil was eroding, it was because the rains had failed. To the Navajos, stock reduction was unthinkable. Sheep were food, clothing, and the principal form of wealth among the Diné. They were also members of Diné households. "Everything comes from the sheep," said Old Man Hat, who told his daughter that they were her mother and her father. "Stock reduction was self-destruction, likened graphically to cutting off one's arms and legs and head," historian Peter Iverson has observed. In many respects, to be Navajo was to have sheep. Without them, a family was less than whole.

The existence of a bond between the Diné and their herds eluded most government officials. The first reduction took place in 1933 and 1934, when 100,000 sheep were purchased or slaughtered by the BIA. Pressure from wealthy Navajos led to 10 percent across-the-board rather than proportional cuts, which meant that families with big herds dumped their culls while poor Navajos lost vital producing animals. The second reduction was even more devastating. This time the government demanded that the Navajos get rid of 100,000 goats as well as 50,000 sheep. Furthermore, they had to castrate the rest of their billy goats. To the government officials in charge of the project, goats were ravenous pests that destroyed the range. To the Navajos, however, they were sturdy beasts that survived hard winters better than sheep and provided meat and milk. The government was trying to protect an ecosystem and was arguing that stock reduction would improve herds and increase their marketability. The Navajos were trying to feed their families and stay alive.

Since poor Navajos depended on goats more than did rich Navajos, the second reduction decimated many of their herds, forcing them to eat their breeding stock and buy more food from trading posts. Then they had to watch helplessly as the government killed thousands of their beloved animals because there was no market to buy them and not enough water to keep them alive. "Scientific" range management, based on the assumptions of a market economy, collided with Navajo culture, which was rooted in a subsistence economy, not market production. In trying to save Navajo rangeland, the Navajo Project was destroying the livelihoods of many Navajo families without offering them a viable alternative to stock raising. According to Indian Service field representative Walter Woehlke, reduction helped create "a Navajo proletariat" while protecting a "Navajo aristocracy." It also burned memories of rotting carcasses into the minds of the Diné.

The first two mandatory reductions and a third voluntary sell-off failed to bring Navajo herds within the carrying capacity of the reservation. In 1936, 1,269,910 animal units remained on ranges that could sustain only 560,000, so the government called for a further reduction of 56 percent. The BIA divided the enormous reservation into eighteen grazing districts, or Land Management Units, and placed a ceiling on the number of livestock in each unit. This time the goal of the reduction was to level wealth differences among Navajos as well as to reduce the number of animals on their land. As a result, the 1,448 stock raisers who were over-permit lost most of their productive animals and saw their herds dwindle to the size of their poorer neighbors. Since a Navajo family needed about 40 to 50 sheep per member to meet its subsistence needs, commercial stock raising became impossible, and most families could not even eke out a living with their remaining herds. Good science and good intentions on the part of government officials led to economic devastation and social disintegration among the Diné.

Many Navajos fought back, intimidating government officials, hiding their animals, and forming alliances with right-wing Anglo and Hispanic politicians who detested Collier. They also organized themselves into a shifting array of factions that politicized the Diné in a way they had never been politicized before. The most prominent leader of the resistance was Jacob Morgan, a tribal councilman from Farmington who became a Protestant missionary. Like Carlos Montezuma, Morgan believed that Navajos had to educate themselves and assimilate into Anglo society. But while he may have accepted Christianity and boarding schools, he, like Montezuma, did not recognize the BIA's authority to determine the destiny of the Diné. In 1935, Morgan mobilized opposition to Collier's cherished Indian Reorganization Act, which called for the creation of constitutionally mandated tribal councils. Two years later he condemned the commissioner's attempt to create a hand-picked tribal council of traditional leaders from the grazing districts. His political agenda was complex and convoluted, but in the eyes of many of his supporters, he symbolized resistance to stock reduction. That resistance won him the tribal chairmanship in 1938.

✳ ✳ Development and the Creation of the Navajo Nation

Despite the efforts of Morgan and others, reduction continued. Between 1934 and 1946, Navajo herds declined from 1,053,498 sheep units to 449,000, a decrease of 57 percent. Before the 1930s, most of the Diné had led isolated and self-sufficient lives—lives in which the BIA and other government agencies were little more than distant shadows. After reduction, reliance upon wage work and relief increased while self-sufficiency all but disappeared. Many Navajos, no longer able to ignore the federal government or the outside world, survived by working for the Civilian Conservation Corps or another government agency. The old life died with their animals, and many who had lost both sheep and status turned to spiritual sources of support such as peyotism and the Native American Church.

But one positive legacy of reduction was the growing demand for Navajo self-determination. Reduction forced many Navajos to confront the forces that were intruding upon their lives. That intrusion intensified during World War II, when 3,600 Diné, including both men and women, served in the armed forces, and 10,000 to 15,000 others found off-reservation jobs on the railroads, as farm laborers, or in defense plants like the Navajo Ordnance Depot near Flagstaff. Navajos who fought in Europe or the Pacific returned to the reservation with the same mixed emotions of pride and anger felt by other Native American, Mexican, and black veterans. The legendary Navajo Code Talkers, after all, had transformed their complex language into a military code the Japanese were never able to break. Discrimination and paternalism were even harder to swallow after the experience of national service.

When the war ended, however, off-reservation jobs dried up and prosperity collapsed. Between 1944 and 1946, Navajo per capita annual income fell from $200 to $80. The government provided relief to keep Navajos from starving, but more and more Diné were realizing that the tribe itself had to take charge of economic development on the reservation. By the 1950s the tribal council was meeting a hundred days a year rather than four. At a time when the Republican administration in Washington, D.C., was advocating the termination of Indian reservations, the tribal council was administering an ever-expanding bureaucracy that brought clinics, schools, police, and courts to many corners of the reservation. It financed much of the development by leasing land to oil and gas companies, which paid the tribe $378,931 in 1950 and $34.8 million seven years later. The tribe also received substantial income from prospectors and mining companies during the uranium boom earlier in the decade. But the Navajos became more adept at securing federal funds as well, receiving $89 million through the Navajo-Hopi Long Range Rehabilitation Act, which Congress passed in 1950. Those monies built nearly 700 miles of roads on the reservation and increased school enrollment from 14,049 to 32,669 between 1952–53 and 1960–61. They also funded hospitals, water projects, and range improvements. In 1964 the Diné even wrested the Office of Navajo Economic Opportunity

(ONEO) away from the BIA and ran their own preschool program, youth corps, small-business development center, and community development project.

One of the architects of that takeover was Peter MacDonald, the executive director of ONEO. MacDonald had grown up speaking Navajo in the little reservation community of Teec Nos Pos, but during World War II he joined the Marines and served as a Navajo Code Talker. Then he graduated from the University of Oklahoma with a degree in electrical engineering and went to work for Hughes Aircraft in southern California for six years. When he returned to the reservation, MacDonald was bright, young, ambitious, and completely at home in the Anglo world of big business and government bureaucracy. But he was also fiercely committed to Navajo self-government and the creation of the Navajo Nation, which became the tribe's official designation in 1969. The following year MacDonald won the office of tribal chairman. MacDonald urged his fellow Diné to throw off the "bonds of forced dependency," and said, "We must do better. We must do it in our own way. And we must do it now."

By the end of MacDonald's first term, those goals seemed more than political rhetoric. The Navajo Division of Education, established in 1971, extended the lessons of the Rough Rock Demonstration School across the reservation, bringing Navajo community control over other schools and the Navajo Community College. The division also sponsored programs to train Navajo teachers and school administrators. Navajos entered the health care professions, becoming nurses, midwives, medics, technicians, and community health representatives. Medicine men were allowed in hospital rooms, and new medicine men were trained by an innovative program operated by the Rough Rock School.

MacDonald stimulated economic development as well, building upon the achievements of his predecessors. Tribal enterprises like the Navajo Forest Products Industries nearly quadrupled its profits during the early 1970s. Navajos also owned a majority of the retail and wholesale enterprises on the reservation other than trading posts. In addition, while oil and gas revenues declined considerably, the tribe mined and sold its first uranium in 1971 and entered into a joint venture with Exxon to extract more uranium in northwestern New Mexico in 1974. When MacDonald became chairman of the Council of Energy Resources Tribes (CERT), which he called a "domestic OPEC," in 1976, he also became the most powerful Indian leader in the United States. The Diné—more than 130,000 of them—were the largest tribe in North America. Moreover, they controlled some of the largest deposits of coal and natural gas in the United States. Far from being exotic curiosities or members of a marginal culture, the Navajos were central to the future of the American West. Their destinies mirrored the destinies of other rural Westerners, including Arizonans, regardless of their ethnicity.

* * * The Grand Plan

What that mirror of destiny revealed was the enduring power of the city to sacrifice rural interests to urban goals. Despite attempts to diversify the economic base of the Navajo Nation during the 1970s and 1980s, most jobs and tribal revenues still came from the same two major sources of money and power that had dominated the West since the late nineteenth century: the U.S. government and the extractive industries. It was a dilemma shared by rural people across the region, and it exposed the Diné, along with their Anglo and Hispanic neighbors, to a host of physical and psychological hazards most city dwellers did not face.

One of those hazards was the nature of the work itself. Running cattle was a dangerous occupation, fraught with head injuries and broken bones. Working in the mines could be even more perilous, especially if safety precautions were not observed. Fibrous lungs and cancerous tumors were two possible consequences of copper and uranium mining, not to mention cave-ins, explosions, and equipment failure. Miners made good money, at least by Western standards, but they took big risks, and the risks often spilled over into the general population, giving the Diné a higher rate of cancer than the national average, especially in areas near uranium mines, where both miners and non-miners alike risked exposure to radioactive materials.

A second hazard lurked like fool's gold at the end of the rainbow. When properly managed, stock raising was a sustainable enterprise. With rotation and the regulation of livestock numbers, grasses recovered and erosion could be controlled. Once ore bodies had been mined out and oil fields had been depleted, however, the desolation of the bust followed the euphoria of the boom. Vital communities became ghost towns, and skilled miners and oil workers had to move on or settle for low-paying jobs. Extractive industries like coal and uranium mining also degraded the environment, ripping gashes in the landscape and spewing chemicals and particulates into the atmosphere. In 1979, for example, the tailings dam of a uranium mill broke northeast of Gallup and poured a hundred million gallons of radioactive water into the Puerco River. It was the largest radioactive spill in the history of the United States, and it made Puerco water undrinkable for at least a generation. Because of such hazards, the Diné and other rural residents often faced one of the hardest of all choices: to remain in a place they loved, surrounded by friends and family but working at a job that leaves scars, or to abandon their homeland and migrate to the cities like everyone else. Many Navajos and other Westerners chose jobs over the environment, accepting the scars. Meanwhile, the cities continued to glitter and grow.

The fuel for much of that growth came from Navajo coal. In 1957, Utah Construction and Mining, one of the fabled Big Six companies that had built Hoover Dam, leased 25,000 acres in the northeastern portion of the reservation so it could strip-mine coal for fifteen cents a ton. At first, Utah Construction found no buyers, but then Arizona Public Service agreed to purchase the coal for $2.50 a ton. The utility company used it to fire its Four Corners Power Plant near Farmington, New Mexico, which opened in 1962. It was the first stage in what came to be called the Grand Plan—the construction of a huge power grid to supply metropolitan centers from San Diego to Albuquerque.

The energy was to come from two sources. The first were nuclear power plants along the California coast. Because nuclear power was supposedly a clean industry, there would be no pollution and hence no squawking from the urbanites the plants served. The second, and more reliable, were the great coal fields of the Colorado Plateau. In order to finance, construct, and administer that regional power grid, twenty-three public and private utilities from California, Nevada, Utah, Colorado, Arizona, New Mexico, and Texas joined together in 1964 to form the Western Energy Supply and Transmission Association (WEST), which later included federal agencies such as the Bureau of Reclamation. It was a new chapter in an old story—internal colonialism on a colossal scale. But this time the colonialists were not Eastern or European capitalists but Western utility companies—Southern California Edison, El Paso Electric, Arizona Public Service, the Salt River Project, Tucson Gas and Electric, Public Service of New Mexico, and many others. With characteristic Western vision, or hubris, WEST intended to generate three times as much power as the Tennessee Valley Authority. Its job was to keep the water pumping, the defense plants rolling, the cities lit. It was the keeper of the flame. Without energy, the boom would collapse.

The second stage of the Grand Plan began in 1964 and 1966, when the Peabody Coal Company signed leases with the Navajo and Hopi tribal councils. Granted after little or no consultation with tribal members, these leases gave Peabody the right to strip-mine 400 million tons of coal from 40,000 acres of land on the Navajo Nation and 25,000 acres on the Navajo-Hopi joint-use area. The land itself was on Black Mesa, an immense escarpment of piñon and juniper that rises in the north along Highway 160 and extends southward until it breaks into the long, narrow fingers of the Hopi mesas. Sitting on top of the largest coal field in Arizona, this isolated upthrust became the major artery

WEST opened to give the metropolitan West its transfusions of fossil fuel. The first flowed eighty miles north by conveyor belt and electric railroad from the Kayenta Mine to the Navajo Generating Station at Page, Arizona, the boomtown created by the Glen Canyon Dam. The second slid down an eighteen-inch-wide, 274-mile-long pipeline in a slurry of coal and water (3.9 million gallons a day) from the Black Mesa Mine to the Mohave Power Plant on the Colorado River in southern Nevada. Ripped from the ground by enormous draglines, Diné and Hopi coal made the grid surge.

The Navajos received about $2 million annually in revenues from Peabody's leases. Several hundred Diné also worked in the coal mines. In return, the Navajo and Hopi tribes sold their coal at bargain-basement prices (20 to 25 cents a ton in the 1960s; 54 cents by 1980) and gave Peabody the right to pump 38 billion gallons of water from deep Black Mesa aquifers. By the late 1960s, the Four Corners plant alone was spewing 1,032 tons of sulfur dioxide and 383 tons of fly ash a day into the atmosphere, more pollution than New York City produced during a twenty-four-hour period. Astronauts reported seeing the emissions from high in space. Like so many other Western politicians, tribal leaders had struck a Faustian bargain that gave them short-term gains in return for long-term environmental consequences. Peter MacDonald even succumbed to the temptations of power and was convicted of conspiring to defraud the Navajo Nation of more than $7 million by accepting kickbacks from the purchase of the Big Boquillas Ranch. Development meant jobs, but it also meant falling water tables, ravaged landscapes, and corruption. San Diego, Phoenix, and Las Vegas were importing cheap electricity and exporting strip mining, pollution, and a few million dollars in leases and wages. From Black Mesa to Caesar's Palace, that exchange epitomized the enormous inequities of the modern West.

Not all tribal members agreed that the benefits were worth the cost. Many Navajos vehemently protested uranium mines and coal gasification plants, and demanded concessions—more jobs, renegotiated leases, higher revenues, the restoration of strip-mined land and depleted aquifers—from the giant corporations like Peabody, Texaco, Phillips, and Exxon that were extracting their minerals. In 1978 a group of Diné even occupied the largest pump station of the Aneth oil field in southeastern Utah and shut down all drilling for seventeen days. The debate over development bitterly factionalized both tribes. Many tribal leaders believed that coal, oil, and uranium had to be exploited in order to lower the tremendous rates of unemployment on the reservations and to provide desperately needed revenue to run tribal health and social programs. But others, including traditional Hopis, saw energy development as a desecration of Mother Earth and filed a series of unsuccessful lawsuits to shut down the

Peabody coal mines. As the Navajo Ned Yazzie, a Black Mesa miner, told author Steve Trimble, "In the beginning we agreed to everything without knowing what a mine is like. In the future, if it happens in another place, the people should say, 'No.' "

✳ ✳ ✳ Rural Life in Twentieth-Century Arizona

In some respects, the struggles of the Diné during the twentieth century were unique to Native Americans living on reservations. But the struggle to survive in the countryside was one they shared with rural people across the West. Whether a worker was a Diné coal miner on Black Mesa, a Mexican copper miner in Clifton-Morenci, an African American lumber mill worker in McNary, or an Anglo logger in Flagstaff, he or she was performing a hard task for a huge company. Working conditions and job security depended on corporate decisions and global laws of supply and demand, and workers had very little control over either of those two domains.

Even then, the workers were the lucky ones. Many rural inhabitants did not have steady, good-paying jobs. As a result, poverty, out-migration, and high rates of unemployment characterized much of rural Arizona, not just Indian reservations. Yet the commonalities between rural Indians and rural non-Indians were rarely recognized. Instead, most non-Indians continued to stereotype Indians in profoundly ambivalent ways. On the one hand, Indians were enemies to be conquered, savages to be civilized, pagans to be Christianized. On the other, they were natural men (and women), noble primitives living in harmony with Mother Earth. When non-Indians portrayed the Diné, romantic images of proud Navajo sheepherders butted up against meaner images of drunks stumbling across the streets of reservation border towns like Flagstaff and Winslow. Neither image captured the reality of most Diné lives.

When those realities are revealed, however, the lives of rural Navajos and other northern Arizonans do not seem so different. After more than three decades of studying Navajo medical problems, physician Stephen Kunitz and anthropologist Jerrold Levy decided to test the common assumption that the rate of alcoholism was much higher among the Diné than the non-Indian population. To do so, they compared Navajo mortality rates from cirrhosis of the liver, suicide, homicide, and traffic accidents—so called alcohol-related pathologies—with death rates among their non-Indian neighbors in rural Arizona and New Mexico.

What Levy and Kunitz found was a regional rather than an ethnic pattern. In 1987 and 1988, the average annual death rate from cirrhosis was 35.2 per 100,000 among Anglos in the rural Southwest. Among Navajos, it was 22.4 per 100,000. The rate of homicides was 15.9 among Anglos and 14.9 among Navajos, while the suicide rate was 54.5 among Anglos and 29.9 among the Diné. Navajos exceeded Anglos in only one mortality statistic: deaths from motor vehicle accidents, which was 87.1 among Anglos and 129.9 among Navajos. The higher rate among Navajos may have been due to poorer driving conditions, greater distances traveled, and much less access to emergency medical care on the reservation itself. In other words, Navajos were less likely to drink themselves to death, kill themselves, or kill others than non-Indians in the rural Southwest. Being Navajo was not an important factor in those destructive acts.

What was important was the cultural geography of the Southwest itself. To put their study into a national perspective, Kunitz and Levy examined alcohol-related mortality rates in different parts of the country. The South, with an average alcohol-related fatality rate of 57.9 per 100,000, was more dangerous than the North (44.8), but the Western mountain states were even more deadly, with a rate of 65.9. Among the rural populations of the mountain region, the southern states of Arizona and New Mexico outranked the northern states of Colorado, Idaho, Montana, Utah, and Wyoming (25.1 per 100,000 versus 11.6 for cirrhosis, 72.5 versus 44.1 for motor vehicle accidents, 18.0 versus 6.1 for homicides, and 38.9 versus 29.6 for suicides). Regardless of whether they were Indian or non-Indian, people in the rural Southwest were more likely to destroy their livers or die violent deaths than people in other areas of the nation. Comparing Navajos to national norms reinforced the stereotypes of drunkenness and self-destruction, but those stereotypes evaporated when the Diné were viewed alongside their neighbors.

Perhaps the biggest similarity in the lives of rural people, however, was the role of the federal government. During the twentieth century, the government expanded its authority over Indian education, Indian health care, and above all Indian resource use. But non-Indian ranchers, loggers, and other rural inhabitants experienced the same encroachment. The problems were complex, but they rested upon one simple fact. Nearly 71 percent of Arizona (51.4 million acres out of 72.7 million) was controlled by the federal government. Arizona's twenty Indian reservations encompassed nearly 27 percent of the state (19.6 million acres). The state's seven national forests occupied 11.4 million acres (15.7 percent), and its national parks accounted for 2.4 million acres (3.4 percent). The Bureau of Land Management exercised jurisdiction over an additional 12.8 million acres (17.5 percent), with other federal agencies dividing about 1.5 million acres (2 percent) among themselves. Finally, the Department of Defense held 3.6 million acres (5 percent) as military bases, bombing ranges, and prov-

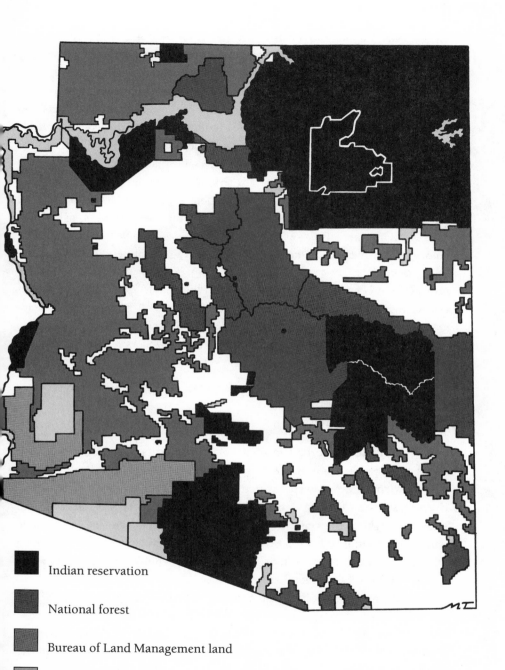

■ Indian reservation

■ National forest

■ Bureau of Land Management land

■ Military land

□ National park, monument, wildlife refuge, or recreation area

Federal Lands in Arizona

ing grounds. Private individuals or corporations, in contrast, owned only 16 percent (11.7 million acres) of Arizona, with the state possessing the remaining 13.2 percent (9.6 million acres), most of which was leased as grazing land.

The federal government was therefore patron, partner, overseer, and antagonist in most rural people's lives. During much of the century, stock raisers and timber companies wielded considerable influence within many federal agencies and the state legislature, but explosive urbanization after World War II produced strong counterforces, which exercised more and more influence over federal resource policies. Ranchers, loggers, and miners no longer had free rein to run cattle, cut trees, build roads, kill predators, or blast holes in the ground. Instead, they had to compete with other constituencies—hunters, fishermen, hikers, environmentalists—who had their own ideas about how to utilize the land. The city dwellers of Phoenix, Tucson, and their satellites did not share the same concerns as rural people, and they competed ever more relentlessly for critical resources, including government funds, business development, and access to federal lands. Whether they were running their homes on electricity generated by Navajo coal or telling government agencies what rural people could and could not do with the countryside, city dwellers were subordinating rural Arizona—the other Arizona—in ways that would have been inconceivable a century before.

✳ ✳ ✳ The Ranchers

Perhaps the best example of this trend is the controversy over ranching on public lands. Ranchers pioneered the Hispanic and Anglo occupation of Arizona. Miners were restricted to their ore bodies, farmers to the few rivers and streams flowing across the state, but stock raisers ran their cattle and sheep throughout the state. In many rural areas, they were the most stable part of the cultural landscape, stringing fences, building windmills, improving springs. They established the most far-flung settlements. There was not a corner of Arizona that escaped their herds.

Ranchers also became the West's most cherished self-image: the rugged individualist who battled wild beasts and wilder country to supply a nation with beef or wool. But there was a contradiction lurking within the symbolism. Because most of their animals ranged across public lands, the freedom of the ranchers was always contingent upon the actions of the government. At the beginning of the century, preservationists fought conservationists to remove cattle and sheep from Forest Reserves. They lost, but ninety years later radical environmentalists were plastering "Stop Welfare Ranching" and "Cattle-Free in '93" bumper stickers on road signs across rural Arizona. Once ranchers and cowboys had been the country's heroes. By the 1990s they were being reviled as environmental scourges. More and more people were talking about removing stock raisers and reintroducing wolves and grizzly bears on public lands.

Like the Diné, the ranchers fought back. Between the passage of the Taylor Grazing Act in 1934 and the battle over raising grazing fees during the early 1990s, federal policy vacillated between cooptation and increased regulation. During the early 1940s, Nevada senator Patrick McCarran, an ally of the ranchers, conducted an investigation of the Forest Service and the Department of the Interior's Grazing Service, the predecessor of the Bureau of Land Management. The investigation drove a wedge between the two agencies and weakened the resolve of many federal administrators to enforce or reduce grazing permits. As World War II intensified, however, Forest Service officials opposed efforts to increase grazing, arguing that unrestricted expansion during World War I had denuded the range and had resulted in a postwar collapse of the livestock industry. They also attempted to initiate new reduction programs even though those programs were resisted by some local Forest Service employees as well as stock raisers. In January 1947 the fiftieth annual convention of the American Livestock Association met in Phoenix and passed a resolution demanding that Forest Service ranges be transferred to the Department of the Interior or sold to private individuals. Ranchers wanted to reverse the policies of the New Deal by transforming grazing permits from privileges granted by the government into legal rights held by the ranchers.

Critics of the livestock industry counterattacked, noting that the Department of the Interior's grazing fees were about one-seventh of those in national forests. In an influential series of articles in *Harper's* magazine, Bernard De Voto exposed the inconsistencies of the stock raisers, who cloaked themselves in the mantle of free enterprise while calling for government-funded range improvements and tariff barriers against foreign beef producers. De Voto was joined by many sportsmen, who were heartened by the recovery of big-game populations during the Depression and World War II and who wanted to ensure that wildlife would continue to flourish on public land. Foresters and farmers concerned with watershed management also opposed the livestock industry. By the 1950s the alliance had become strong enough to defeat several bills that would have weakened federal control of grazing lands even though those measures were supported by the Eisenhower administration. In 1960, Congress even passed the Multiple Use–Sustained Yield Act, which declared that the national forests "shall be administered for outdoor recreation, range, timber, watershed, and wildlife, and fish purposes." National forests became the "Land of Many Uses," not just the preserve of loggers and stockmen.

Nonetheless, overgrazing continued. The number of cattle in Arizona rose from 770,000 in 1930 and 818,000 in 1950 to 1,420,000 in 1973. Not all of those animals were range cattle; during the 1960s, Arizona's feedlot industry expanded at a rapid rate. Moreover, the increase in cattle was offset in part by a corresponding decrease in sheep from 1,080,000 to 502,000 head during the same period. In 1973, however, forester William Hurst of the Forest Service's District 3 (Arizona and New Mexico) contended that only 13.2 million of the 19 million acres distributed in allotments were suitable for grazing and that of those suitable acres, only 1.3 million (10 percent) were in good condition, while 6.6 million (50 percent) were in fair condition and 5.3 million (40 percent) were poor. Six years later, an internal review of range conditions in the Tonto National Forest concluded, "Presently the majority of the forest has serious grazing problems that have been compounded through many years of misuse. The Sonoran Desert and associated grasslands are producing at just a fraction of their former level of productivity. Areas in the Tonto Basin are described by early settlers as producing native grass to cut for hay. These areas are now dominated by thorny shrubs and annuals. Perrenial grasses have been almost completely eliminated over large areas."

The report went on to mention the reasons why the Tonto was in such bad shape. Perhaps the biggest was that quintessential Arizona activity: land speculation. Until the 1950s, most ranches remained in the family and most holders of grazing permits were descendants of original settlers. Ranching was a way of life as well as a business, and ranchers were owner-operators who lived on their spreads and sold cattle rather than real estate. Between 1959 and 1975, however, about 25 percent of the ranches on the Tonto changed ownership each year. Rapid turnover led speculators to resist any reduction in the number of cattle they could run because that lowered the resale value of their ranches. Because they never intended to spend their whole lives on the same spread, speculators had little stake in the conservation of the land. "Rather than accept reduction in livestock numbers, many livestock operators seek political assistance in their behalf," the Tonto report noted dryly. "Under political pressure, the Forest Service either capitulated or increased the intensity and number of studies determined necessary to support anticipated grazing appeals." In other words, the ranching industry was still able to coopt or deflect federal agencies mandated to regulate it.

But as Arizona and the West grew ever more urban, a new environmental movement invigorated and expanded the efforts of older conservation groups. One result was the Federal Land Policy and Management Act of 1976. The act created a fund for range improvements, authorized a new study of the federal grazing-fee structure, and stated clearly and unequivocally that the federal government would retain perpetual control of the public lands. Angry Westerners responded by mounting the so-called Sagebrush Rebellion, which demanded state ownership of the public domain. Outside of a few state legislatures, however, the rebellion was all bark and no bite. By the late 1970s most people lived in cities and supported federal stewardship and multiple use.

Nevertheless, the livestock industry still had clout at the state and national levels. Stock raisers lost the battle to maintain a bounty on the mountain lion, which was declared an Arizona big-game animal rather than a predator in 1971. But they won the fight to keep stock-killer clauses in Arizona game laws, allowing them to trap, shoot, or run down calf-killing lions with dogs. Ranchers also could not halt the creation of the National Wilderness Preservation System in 1964, yet they continued to graze their animals in those protected areas, including the huge Mazatzal Wilderness northeast of Phoenix.

Their biggest victory, however, was a basic economic one. Stock raisers may not have been able to turn grazing permits into private property, but they still managed to defeat or delay any effort to increase their grazing fees. As early as 1966 a joint study of the Forest Service and the Bureau of Land Management recommended a gradual increase in fees until fair market value was achieved. That increase was postponed, as was another in 1977. During the early 1980s, federal fees actually dropped to $1.86 per animal unit. Lease rates on private ranges, in contrast, ranged from around $5.00 in Arizona to $8.83 in lusher climes.

Ranchers defended the low fees by arguing that they had to pay for improvements—stock tanks, fences, windmills—on land that did not belong to them. Their critics countered by charging that American taxpayers were subsidizing the Western livestock industry. As usual in such polemics, exaggerations and half-truths proliferated like flies around a corral. The antiranching lobby rightly zeroed in on ranchers who overgrazed their allotments, illegally killed bears or elk, or used stock raising as a tax dodge to hide land they meant to develop. They never talked about the family ranchers who cleaned up illegal dumps, turned in poachers, developed water sources that benefited wildlife as well as livestock, or ran fewer animal units than their permits allowed because they had made a long-term commitment to the land. Nor did the critics admit that ranching was one of the few extractive industries that could be sustainable over the long haul. The myth of the cattle kingdom was fraying for wrong reasons as well as right. Meanwhile, ranching families struggled to survive changing land ethics and increasing government control on ranges their ancestors had nursed through droughts and national depressions.

✳ ✳ ✳ The Loggers

An even more inconsistent process of conservation and cooptation characterized the relationship between the Forest Service and the logging industry. When the Santa Fe Railroad sliced across northern Arizona in 1880, it paralleled the largest stand of ponderosa pine in the world. Since most of that stand undulated across high plateaus rather than mountainsides, its trees were relatively easy to cut and haul away. During the late nineteenth century, logging therefore became one of Arizona's most important extractive industries. Chicago lumberman Edward Ayer's mill in Flagstaff and smaller mills in Williams and other communities spit out hundreds of thousands of ties to build the transcontinental railroad and the American-owned Mexican Central Railroad. Ayer also shipped millions of board feet to Los Angeles, New Mexico, and the mines of southern Arizona. Between 1882 and 1886, when he sold his sawmill to Denis Riordan, Ayer's company cut nearly 54 million board feet of timber. As with copper and cattle, the railroad was the wood-ribbed key that unlocked the exploitation of Arizona's vast timber resources.

It was slash-and-burn timber cutting in those days. In 1878, Congress passed the Timber Cutting Act, which gave Western pioneers, including Arizonans, the right to "fell and remove timber from the public domain for mining and domestic purposes." That same year the Timber and Stone Act authorized forested land to be sold for $2.50 an acre in 160-acre parcels to homesteaders so that they could have a wood lot in addition to their 160 acres of cultivated land. The laws were ostensibly designed to promote Western settlement, but they actually profited speculators and the owners of big lumber companies, who secured hundreds of thousands of acres through front men and fraud. Companies spread the word that they would buy timberland from "entrymen" who filed for it under the Timber and Stone Act. According to the commissioner of the General Land Office in 1882, "depredations upon the public timber by powerful corporations, wealthy mill-owners, lumber companies and unscrupulous monopolists . . . are still being committed to an alarming extent." Illegal timber cutting was rampant. Loggers often set fire to the younger "blackjack" trees in order to clear their way to the "yellow bellies," or great orange-barked ponderosas. Every tree was toppled even though many were left to rot where they fell.

Federal legislation eventually tried to curb such exploitation by passing the General Revision Act of 1891, which gave the president the power to create national forest reserves. Between 1893 and 1908, Teddy Roosevelt and his predecessors set aside more than 13 million acres, or about 73 percent of Arizona's forest land. Loggers as well as ranchers opposed the reserves, especially smaller operations that relied on the public domain. A few large loggers, on the other hand, initially supported the reserves. A case in point was Denis Riordan and his brothers, who purchased Ayer's sawmill in 1886 and ran the biggest timber company in northern Arizona. "Upon the rational use of our forests will depend the happiness, welfare, and may I say the absolute existence of any large population in the territory," Riordan piously intoned. But even though he sounded like a high-minded Eastern conservationist, Riordan's words cloaked a subtle and calculating business mind. His Arizona Lumber and Timber Company controlled the timber rights on nearly all the land—868 sections, or 556,000 acres—owned by the Santa Fe Railroad. The Riordan brothers also held the option to cut all the timber on 238 sections owned by the Aztec Land and Cattle Company. Because he felled private rather than public timber, Riordan figured that locking up timber on the forest reserves would eliminate much of his competition and increase his monopoly over the logging industry in northern Arizona.

Southwest Forestries, the Fortune 500 giant that dominated Arizona's logging industry after World War II, took Riordan's strategy several steps further and learned how to monopolize the timber on Forest Service lands themselves. Southwest's original base of operations was the White Mountains, the last expanse of virgin timber in the state. During the late nineteenth century, loggers cut the forests along the railroad first. Saginaw and Manistee, a Michigan-owned firm that was Riordan's biggest competitor, rapidly "liquidated the timber resource" of Tusayan National Forest (later renamed Kaibab) around Williams, according to a later Forest Service supervisor. By 1907, when Arizona's national forests ranked fourth in timber production in the country, the vast stands of Coconino National Forest southeast of Flagstaff were providing 50 to 75 percent of the state's yield. But the Forest Service wanted to thin the forests of the White Mountains to encourage new growth, and the agency also realized that expansion of the timber industry was the surest way to increase its own budget and power. In 1912, then, the Forest Service and the Commissioner of Indian Affairs put 600 million board feet up for sale in a region that later would become part of Sitgreaves and Apache National Forests and the Fort Apache Indian Reservation.

It was an enormous contract, and it enraged the Riordan brothers and the executives of Saginaw and Manistee, who hated the thought of more competition and argued that the market was glutted. An early venture failed to raise the necessary capital, but in 1917, Thomas Pollock, a Flagstaff banker and one of Riordan's fiercest competitors, formed the Apache Lumber Company and snared the "Apache" contract. Pollock built a sawmill at the little settlement of Cooley just inside the reservation. Then he constructed a 75-mile narrow-gauge railroad from Holbrook to the mill site so he could ship his lumber out of the mountains. By 1919 both the mill and the railroad were running, but the costs were staggering and the timing was bad. World War I ended and the demand for lumber declined. Pollock's financial empire, like that of the Babbitts and other northern Arizona entrepreneurs, drowned in debt during the postwar depression.

The Cady Lumber Company, a Louisiana operation owned by William Cady and James McNary, resuscitated the White Mountain timber industry in 1923. Cady and McNary subscribed to the "clear cut and clear out" philosophy; they made a fortune in the South but ran out of timber in ten years. As a result, in 1924 they loaded not only their machinery but most of their workers and their families onto railroad cars and moved them from Louisiana to the White Mountains on two long trains. It must have been a strange sight to the few cowboys and Apaches who saw the trains arrive. More than eight hundred men, women, and children—most of them African Americans—suddenly descended on Cooley, turning the little Western logging camp into a Southern segregated community almost overnight. Cooley, renamed McNary, soon had an Anglo neighborhood known as Hilltown and a black neighborhood called Milltown or "the Quarters." The Quarters sprawled around the mill on lowlands where pools of water often collected and stagnated. African Americans had their own school, their own cemetery, even their own Masonic lodge. They also lived in leaky, drafty shacks with no indoor plumbing or running water. Paying a low Southern wage scale and operating according to typical Jim Crow principles, the Cady Lumber Company recreated a little piece of the Old South in the Arizona high country.

For the next two decades, McNary, who soon eased Cady out, wheeled and dealed to keep the company afloat. His efforts failed in 1930, when the company went into receivership, but McNary reorganized the venture five years later with a little help from his friends at the Standard Oil Company of California and the Santa Fe and Southern Pacific Railroads. Even in its new incarnation as Southwest Lumber Mills, Inc., however, McNary made sure his workforce remained Southern in wages if not in origin. During the late 1930s, New Deal reformers in the Forest Service tried to pressure Western logging companies to match the wages of the Pacific Northwest, where common laborers made 42.5 cents per hour. McNary, whose labor force was 25 percent Anglo, 25 percent African

American, 25 percent Mexican, and 25 percent Indian, argued that Arizona labor was similar to Southern labor—less skilled and less efficient than the predominantly Anglo workforce in the Northwest. His argument prevailed, and in the Ninth District of the Forest Service (Arizona, New Mexico, and southern Colorado), timber companies continued to pay the Southern scale of 25 cents an hour.

But even with victories like that one, Southwest might have followed Cady Lumber into bankruptcy if World War II had not driven up the demand for lumber. McNary got his first big break when he secured a loan from the federal Reconstruction Finance Corporation. The loan gave him the funds he needed to build a railroad into the heart of the White Mountains southeast of McNary, where Mount Baldy, the Apaches' sacred peak, towered over a lush forest of pine, spruce, and Douglas fir. McNary began building the railroad in 1944. When it was completed two years later, it ended at a new logging camp called Maverick, which was snowbound for several months each year. By then, Southwest had nearly exhausted its old Apache contract and needed the new timber to keep the McNary mill in operation. Once again, McNary had to cut a complicated deal with the Department of Agriculture and the Department of the Interior to log both national forest and reservation land.

Several years earlier, McNary scored another coup by pressuring Congress to pass the Haugen-McNary Act (named after its cosponsors, Congressman Gilbert N. Haugen of Iowa and Senator McNary), which allowed a few large lumber companies in the United States to corner the contracts to cut timber on "sustained-yield units" in the national forests. Even though most of them were enormous, the contracts were not subject to competitive bidding. The one granted to Southwest in 1949 guaranteed the company 61 million board feet a year for thirty years in the Coconino National Forest. McNary, who parted his wavy hair down the middle, Calvin Coolidge style, had long been active in Republican politics. He also served as president of the National Lumber Manufacturers Association and was a member of the board of directors of the National Association of Manufacturers. Those political and business contacts helped him push the bill and win the contract. Big business had found another way to make a fortune on federal lands in Arizona.

McNary retired as president of Southwest Lumber in 1949 and as chairman of the board a year later. His successors, a group of Texas investors headed by Jim Ben Edens, went him one better. In 1952 they orchestrated the fabled Colorado Plateau Contract, which gave Southwest the exclusive right to cut pulp trees on five national forests in Arizona and New Mexico. The pulp trees were trees too thin to be turned into lumber—trees that had sprouted like weeds after the

Forest Service suppressed the fires that would have naturally thinned the forests. With an estimated yield of 3 billion board feet over thirty years from the "tamed forests," Southwest built a huge pulp mill in Snowflake and paid a dollar a cord until the Western Forest Industries Association cried monopoly and forced the Forest Service to increase the rate. It was the largest federal timber contract outside of Alaska, and it catapulted Southwest into the Fortune 500, where it ranked 412th in 1984.

By then the McNary mill had burned down, but bigger mills in Flagstaff and Eagar turned logs into lumber with sophisticated machinery run by computer. Southwest employed more than 400 Arizonans and 6,000 people nationwide. It also contracted with many independent loggers and truckers, spreading its money and extending its control across eastern and north central Arizona. With its pine-paneled headquarters in Phoenix, Southwest dwarfed Kaibab Industries and other timber companies in Arizona. It ran enterprises in twenty-three other states as well, selling more than a billion dollars worth of lumber, newsprint, and other wood products a year.

Like copper mining, the timber industry favored a few big companies rather than many small ones. Logging, milling, and transportation costs were too high for small enterprises to afford unless they subcontracted with the larger firms. But the huge size of most Forest Service contracts dictated the scale of the industry as well. Like the National Park Service, which encouraged the Santa Fe and Fred Harvey monopoly over tourism at the Grand Canyon, the Forest Service found it easier to deal with a few efficient and reliable giants rather than dozens of small wildcat operations. Political pressure was also a factor: Congress determined the Forest Service's budget, and big companies had clout in Congress. The Forest Service may have established its right to regulate timber cutting on the national forests, but it had to accommodate big timber companies in the process.

In Arizona that process resulted in the most intensively harvested national forests in the United States. According to a study conducted by journalist Ray Ring for the *Arizona Daily Star* in 1984, the rate of timber cutting on Arizona's national forests between 1908 and 1983 was more than twice as high as that in Oregon, the second most voracious logging state. That rate averaged nearly 1 percent of the timber inventory each year, compared to about 0.5 percent in Oregon and 0.4 percent in Montana. Even though its total amount of forest land was much smaller than that in Montana, Idaho, Oregon, Washington, or California, Arizona led the United States in timber production from national forests in 1925 and 1933. Until 1950, in fact, Arizona's national forests yielded more timber than the immense national forests in Montana.

❋ ❋ ❋   The Urbanization of Rural Life After World War II

Lumbering also contributed to the development of rural Arizona. Extractive industries—mining, ranching, logging—gave most rural towns their reason for being until the postwar boom. Mills contributed to and often dominated the economies of Flagstaff, Williams, Snowflake, Eagar, McNary, Fredonia, Payson, and Winslow. Loggers, truck drivers, and mechanics who made their living off the timber industry also lived in these towns, as well as in seasonal camps like Happy Jack and Maverick. Even the Forest Service returned 25 percent of its revenues, most of which came from timber sales, to counties where the trees were cut. Coconino County received $1.7 million in 1983. The revenue return compensated, in part, for the fact that national forests do not pay property taxes. The federal government—and the companies that depended on the resources of government land—shaped the lives and controlled the pocketbooks of most people in the forest towns.

Beginning in the 1950s, however, the economies of those towns began to change. As the populations of Phoenix and Tucson exploded, thousands more city dwellers headed for the mountains to escape the heat. Prescott—prewar Phoenix's traditional playground—attracted some of these desert refugees, but the biggest boom occurred on the Mogollon Rim, which Zane Grey had immortalized more than a generation earlier in novels like *The Last of the Plainsmen, The Light of the Western Stars,* and *Under the Tonto Rim.* A few hardy souls braved the old dirt road from Phoenix to Payson during the 1940s and 1950s, but the trickle became a flood in 1959, when the final paving of Highway 87—the Beeline Highway—was completed. Suddenly, relief from summers in the Valley of the Sun was less than two hours away, and the cabin craze swept across just about every piece of patent land above 5,000 feet. Ranchers sold off homesteads that had been in their families for generations, and subdividers mounted nationwide promotional campaigns to attract the crowds. Soon summer visitors outnumbered old-time residents as the serious business of extraction took a back seat to the more lucrative business of land speculation and recreation.

In the process a fine, wild, close-knit way of life died as thousands of people streamed up the Beeline each weekend in a crowded ritual of escape. Payson became the gateway to the Mogollon Rim and the White Mountains, changing from a sleepy little cowtown to a crowded commercial hub. In 1940 the *Arizona Republic* noted that the town had two saloons, two stores, two cafes, one street, and 750 people. Prohibition was over, but residents still remembered "Payson Whiskey" with great fondness and claimed that at least twenty bootleggers had fired up their stills in the surrounding hills. By 1974, however, 2,885 people lived within the town limits alone, with hundreds more in Star Valley, Beaver Valley, Kohl's Ranch, and other Payson satellites.

The most telling sign of change was the "August Doins," which had started as a local rodeo in 1884. By the 1940s the August Doins had developed into the August Celebration, with slot machines, all-night dances, high-stakes poker games, and legendary horse races down Main Street. Twenty years later, sponsored by the Payson Chamber of Commerce, it became the Payson Rodeo with formal rodeo grounds and professional cowboys rather than "local waddies." Deputy sheriffs still had to break up fights and lob tear gas into bars, but the crowds were outsiders rather than Tonto Basin residents. The rodeo had become a tourist attraction instead of a local celebration of ranching life.

Similar changes were taking place in Pine, Strawberry, Heber, and the communities of the White Mountains such as Show Low, Pinetop, and Greer. Phoenix had engulfed the agricultural communities of the Salt River Valley, and now it was urbanizing the forest towns by turning them into summer extensions of itself. Shopping centers crowded out general stores. Motels, restaurants, and convenience stores proliferated. Summer cattle ranges like Houston Mesa northeast of Payson were sliced into subdivisions like Mesa del Caballo. Even the lumberjacks and ranchers themselves were now considered local color rather than leading citizens.

It was the urbanization of the rural—the latest stage in a process that was shifting the state's political, economic, and ideological center of gravity from the countryside to the city. In 1900, 84.1 percent of Arizona's population dwelled in rural areas. By 1990 the proportion had more than reversed itself, with cities and towns claiming 87.5 percent of all Arizonans (3,206,973), leaving only 12.5 percent (458,255) in the countryside. There were still a few pockets of the old Arizona left, but the rest of the state had become a Sunbelt society—urban, mobile, often rootless. Arizona society was a society in constant flux.

The more the crowds came and went and the faces changed, the more the Other Arizona became the city's metaphorical backyard. Sometimes it was a secret garden, wild and tranquil, where the city could find refuge from itself and enjoy strange plants and animals it had banished from its own space. At other times it was a playground where the city could race its boats across the water or spin its off-road vehicles in the dirt. It was also a place to dump discarded or noxious things and to carry out tasks city dwellers did not want to see or smell. The Other Arizona was by turns recreational, utilitarian, and aesthetic. But it was almost always subordinate to Urban Arizona.

16

From the Southwest to the Sunbelt

Before the 1960s the financial world of Arizona was run by local bankers like Frank Brophy, the flamboyant president and chairman of the board of the Bank of Douglas, and Walter Bimson, the son of a Colorado blacksmith who put down roots in "The Valley" and made the Valley National Bank (VNB) synonymous with Arizona growth. Arizona was a real place to these businessmen, not just a place to make money. Headquartered in Phoenix, they loved the city they were carving out of citrus groves and cotton fields.

The old elite began to lose ground in the 1960s. Californian David Murdock was the prototype of the new Arizona financier, diversifying investments, speculating in real estate, pushing regulations to the limit. Murdock, whose holding company, the Financial Corporation of Arizona, acquired Union Title and Trust, the Pioneer Bank, Home Savings and Loan, and several other companies, never became a community leader like Bimson or Sherman Hazeltine, the president and chairman of the board of the First National Bank, but neither did the executives who succeeded Bimson or Hazeltine. As Gilbert Bradley, chairman of the board of vNB, confided, "I just can't do what Bimson was able to do. The bank has gotten too big, and I'm too tied up with it to spend the same kind of time that Walter did on Phoenix matters."

The plate tectonics of the financial world shifted for good in the 1980s. With inflation spiraling upward, savings and loans were going broke borrowing money at 15 to 20 percent and loaning it out as low-interest mortgages on single-family homes. So Congress decided to turn the industry loose from the restrictions imposed by the Federal Home Loan Bank Board by passing the Garn–St. Germain Depository Institutions Act, which Ronald Reagan signed into law on October 15, 1982. It turned out to be one of the most expensive signatures in the history of the American taxpayer. The federal government still insured deposits, but now the thrifts were free to raise interest rates and invest in just about any speculative venture under the sun, including junk bonds. Arizona had already acquired a reputation as the latest frontier of land fraud, but deregulation created a money machine of unparalleled avarice and complexity. In 1976, after the murder of investigative reporter Don Bolles, a young attorney general named Bruce Babbitt talked about Arizona being up for sale, but no one could have predicted the transition from the real estate scams of confidence men like Ned Warren to the financial sleights-of-hand performed by lawyers like Charles Keating.

The result was a bizarre and artificial world that had nothing to do with the production of value or a sense of place. Savings and loans were bought to be plundered, and by the end of the decade, thrifts were toppling like dominoes and developers like Keating were going to jail. Because the collapse of his Lincoln Savings and Loan cost the taxpayers billions, Keating had to be singled out and demonized, turned into the greedy, arrogant monster who ate the savings of the little people who trusted him. But Keating and the other wheeler-dealers always had plenty of willing accomplices—local businessmen who wanted a piece of the money pie, politicians who wanted campaign contributions, customers who wanted to live on the water in a valley that averaged less than ten inches of rain a year. The world they collaborated in creating was a world where Arizona was rendered down to its abstract capitalistic essence—grids on the desert ground—and where water, that scarcest of all desert resources, was shot out of a fountain 300 feet into the air or poured into artificial lakes surrounded by green grass and homes.

✳ ✳ ✳ Society and Politics in the Sunbelt

Contemporary Arizona is a strange and schizophrenic place. Between 1960 and 1990, the state's population grew from 1.3 million people to 3.6

million, an increase of 181 percent. With a 1990 population of 1 million within its city limits and a total metropolitan population of 2.1 million in Maricopa County, Phoenix is one of the ten largest cities in the country and the largest urban center between Los Angeles and Dallas–Fort Worth. Yet Arizona politics during this period degenerated into comic-opera parody. In 1964, Barry Goldwater accepted the nomination of the Republican party for president of the United States. He lost by a landslide but won a reputation for integrity and humor. Twenty-four years later, in 1988, a Glendale car dealer named Evan Mecham became the first U.S. governor in fifty-nine years to be impeached and the only governor in the history of the republic to be recalled, impeached, and indicted on criminal charges at the same time. Then, in 1991, some of the same Arizona state legislators who had voted for impeachment were themselves indicted for taking bribes from a Las Vegas talk-show host named Joseph Stedino posing as "Tony Vincent," a lobbyist for legalized casino gambling, in a sting operation known as AzScam.

The final blow fell when the National Football League yanked the rug out from under a small army of horrified boosters and told Phoenix it would no longer be the site of the 1993 Super Bowl because the state had refused to ratify a state holiday in honor of Dr. Martin Luther King, Jr. The sleek modern image that Arizona businessmen had worked so hard to cultivate was crumbling under a barrage of scandals that paraded across the front pages of newspapers across the nation and, worse yet, cost the state millions of dollars in convention business. Journalists devoted inch after inch of column space trying to fathom what these developments "said" about Arizona. Part of the explanation was demographic: Arizona was a society of perpetual newcomers who rarely stayed long enough to create a coherent political culture. According to the 1990 census, only 37 percent of Arizona's population had been born in the state. In-migration, not natural increase, accounted for most of Arizona's phenomenal postwar growth. Between 1955 and 1980, for example, the state ranked second in the nation in net migration. A study of newcomers to the Phoenix and Tucson metropolitan areas between 1975 and 1980 (who totaled 357,043 and 117,137 individuals respectively) revealed that more than 93 percent came from outside the state, particularly California (13.6 and 11.3 percent), Illinois (8.3 and 6.1 percent), New York (6.8 and 6.9 percent), and Ohio (5.8 and 4.5 percent).

The 1990 census also determined that 56.9 percent of all Arizonans had resided in a different house five years earlier. For every ten people who settled in Arizona each year during the early 1980s, seven moved away. Between April 1982 and April 1983, Arizona's rate of out-migration (47.8 per 1,000 people) was nearly twice as high as out-migration from the economically depressed Rust Belt state of Michigan (24.3 per 1,000).

Such rapid turnover did not promote the development of neighborhood identity or community cohesion. Most Arizonans simply did not share a long collective memory of the state's political history, much less of the neighborhood or city in which they lived. One of the reasons Evan Mecham was able to beat consummate political insider Burton Barr in the Republican gubernatorial primary in 1986 was that nearly 50 percent of the electorate had not even lived in Arizona in 1980. Most voters were not aware of Barr's twenty-two years of effective service as majority leader of the Arizona house or Mecham's long string of failed candidacies and sensational tabloids. That allowed Mecham to win the votes of enough newcomers to supplement his core constituency of Mormons, senior citizens, and the radical right. Politics became a tawdry sideshow that reinvented itself over and over again as it lurched from election to election.

❋ ❋ ❋ The Rise and Fall of Arizona's Political Elite

Mecham liked to present himself as a populist David taking on Arizona's Goliath, which he perceived as the Phoenix newspapers (especially the *Republic* and the *Gazette*) and the Phoenix Forty, a coalition of business leaders organized in the early 1970s. But Mecham and his supporters did not realize that Arizona's explosive growth and transient population had fractured the state's political power structure, fragmenting it into an unstable collection of interest groups no single body of power brokers could control. The Phoenix Forty of the 1980s was a pale imitation of the early postwar establishment—men like Walter Bimson, Eugene Pulliam, Frank Snell, Sherman Hazeltine, Del Webb, the Goldwater brothers, and jeweler Harry Rosenzweig—who led the Charter Government insurgency that captured Phoenix in the late 1940s. Those businessmen ran Phoenix from 1950 until 1975. During that twenty-five-year period, no Phoenix mayor and only two city council members were elected without the endorsement of the Charter Government Committee. It was a white, male, Republican, upper-middle-class group and it selected largely white, male, Republican, upper-middle-class candidates like John Driggs of Western Savings, who defeated Milton Graham, the incumbent mayor and former Charter Government candidate, in 1969.

Members of the Phoenix elite also used their power base in Maricopa County to extend their control over state politics. At a time when the legislature was still run by rural Democrats led by Senator Howard Giss of Yuma, Republican Paul Fannin won the first of three two-year terms as governor in 1958. Then, in 1964, Harry Rosenzweig, one of the architects of the Charter Government takeover, beat Mecham to become chairman of the state Republican party. Rosenzweig's organizational efforts paid off two years later, when Republicans snared a majority of seats in the Arizona house and elected Burton Barr their majority leader. Barr remained the most powerful member of the state legislature for the next twenty-two years, setting its agenda through persuasion, pressure, and a pragmatic genius for crafting coalitions and making deals.

Perhaps the most visible manifestations of the elite's power, however, were the officials it sent to Washington. In 1952, John Rhodes became the first Republican from Arizona elected to the House of Representatives, where he became minority leader and served until his retirement in 1982. Paul Fannin made the transition from governor to U.S. senator in 1964. The elite's most famous representative, however, was Barry Goldwater, who began his political career as a successful Charter Government candidate for the Phoenix City Council in 1949 and went on to narrowly upset Ernest McFarland to win a U.S. Senate seat in 1952. Goldwater was from an old Arizona family of Jewish-turned-Episcopalian merchants whose roots extended back to "Big Mike" Goldwater and the steamer trade along the Colorado River in the 1850s. He was also a pilot, photographer, and legendary raconteur. Goldwater's conservatism emanated from earlier Western wellsprings, not the get-rich-quick mentality of the postwar years. The only major holdout against this rising tide of Republican power was Pima County, where Democrats elected liberal Democrat Stewart Udall and then his brother Morris to the U.S. House.

The postwar establishment's political power began to wane in the late 1960s, when liberal Democrat Ed Korrick became the first candidate to win a seat on the Phoenix City Council without the support of the Charter Government Committee. Then, in 1975, Charter Government lost four of six city council seats. In that same election, a former CGC city council member named Margaret Hance sought its endorsement for mayor and did not receive it because, in her words, she was a "woman, and therefore couldn't win." So Hance, a conservative Republican and a member of the board of directors of the Valley National Bank, ran as an independent and beat the CGC candidate. She went on to win three more terms, serving until 1983. Phoenix became the largest city in the nation to have a woman mayor, and Charter Government withered and died, the victim of its own atrophied paternalism and the changes in the city itself.

Similar changes occurred at the state level. During the 1960s and early 1970s, Republicans controlled the governor's office except for Sam Goddard's one term from 1964 to 1966, when the term was increased to four years. In 1974, however, the Watergate scandal dominated national politics, and a number of prominent Arizona Republicans, including U.S. Attorney General Richard Kleindienst and Robert Mardian, were indicted for various crimes. Riding the revulsion against the party of Richard Nixon, Democrat Raul Castro won the governorship and Bruce Babbitt, another Democrat, captured the attorney general's office, where he carved a national reputation for himself as a crusader against land fraud and organized crime. Visions of a U.S. Senate race in 1980 or 1982 were dancing in the heads of many Democratic supporters when the improbable happened not once but twice. In 1977, President Jimmy Carter appointed Governor Castro ambassador to Argentina. His successor was Wesley Bolin, Arizona's perennial secretary of state, who promptly died of a heart attack. Suddenly, through two unlikely twists of politics and mortality, Bruce Babbitt was governor of Arizona.

He went on to become both popular and effective, winning re-election in 1978 and 1982. Despite Babbitt's success, however, he hardly represented a new Democratic tide. During his terms in office, Babbitt faced a legislature controlled by Republicans. To survive politically, he portrayed himself as a non-ideological pragmatist who valued competence over party politics or interest groups. Babbitt was a social liberal but a fiscal conservative; an environmentalist who recognized the rights of ranchers, miners, and developers to make a living off the land; an advocate of business as long as business acted responsibly and within the law. He sent in the National Guard during the 1983 copper strike in Clifton-Morenci, and he appointed numerous Republicans to state commissions and boards. In a sense, he was a lucky fluke, as much the product of chance and the Republican coalition's disintegration as any Democratic resurgence.

When he decided not to run again in order to seek the presidential nomination in 1988, Babbitt did not leave behind a powerful Democratic machine to pick his successor. Instead, the Democrats split between businessman Bill Schultz and Superintendent of Public Instruction Carolyn Warner, while what was left of the Republican elite waited complacently for Burton Barr to assume office. Meanwhile Evan Mecham, the spoiler who had run and lost his races for Carl Hayden's Senate seat in 1962 and for the governorship in 1964, 1974, 1978, and 1982, finally captured the governorship with a dirty but effective guerrilla campaign of smear tactics and scattershot rightist proposals. Mecham then unleashed his holy war against Democratic socialists and Republican apostates and left his party—and the state government—in shambles. The state got its revenge in the spring of 1988, when the Arizona house voted 46 to 14 to impeach the governor, and the senate convicted him of two articles of impeachment: obstructing justice and misusing state funds. It took Mecham twenty-two years to win the governorship and fifteen months to lose it. Secretary of State Rose Mofford assumed the governorship and tried to restore some semblance of order and professionalism to state government.

Three years later, Mecham and his followers must have concluded that AzScam was God's judgment upon the wicked. In 1991 the Maricopa County Organized Crime Bureau hired Joseph Stedino, a Mafia associate and FBI informer from Las Vegas, as an undercover agent to investigate sports gambling in Arizona. Stedino called himself Tony Vincent and drifted through the Phoenix gambling scene, where he met a lobbyist with political connections named Gary Bartlett. Bartlett asked what his "game" was. Stedino replied that he represented four mob backers who wanted to legalize casino gambling in Arizona. Bartlett told him that members of the state legislature were up for sale. As a result, the investigation shifted from gambling to state politics as the burly, fast-talking Stedino opened an office in central Phoenix with a walled-off room where police recorded and videotaped "Tony Vincent's" verbal dances with the legislators and lobbyists. Stedino was not allowed to use women or any enticement other than cash (nearly $1 million in confiscated drug money) to win votes, but bribes ranging from $660 to $60,250 led to the conviction of eighteen people, including two state senators, five representatives and one former representative, five lobbyists, two officials of the Democratic party, and one justice of the peace.

Between the Charter Government ascendancy and AzScam, Arizona politics had drifted from the corporate to the surreal. Following the scandals, however, there were some ambivalent signs of reform. The Arizona legislature passed the "gavel-to-gavel law," for example, which prohibited lobbyists from contributing money to legislators or the governor while the legislature was in session, yet citizens continued to vote down every pay increase for legislators, expecting them to run the state and stay clean for $15,000 a year. Meanwhile, Republican moderates fought to keep Mechamites and the Christian fundamentalist right from seizing control of the party the same way they had seized control of the 1989 Republican state convention, when they passed a resolution declaring the United States "a Christian nation, . . . a republic based upon the absolute laws of the Bible, not a democracy." This coalition even targeted Barry Goldwater, the grand old man of the conservative movement, and tried to strip his name from the Republican state headquarters in Phoenix. Among their reasons for doing so were Goldwater's outspoken support for abortion rights—a cause his wife, Peggy, one of the founders of the Phoenix chapter of Planned Parenthood, had long championed—and his staunch defense of other individual matters of conscience, including the right of gays to serve in the military. Goldwater's conservatism was the conservatism of personal freedom from government interference, not religious and sexual intolerance, and the new theocratic right could not abide him. The moderates appeared to be regaining the upper hand, but nothing resembling the power of the postwar establishment emerged on the Arizona scene.

✳ ✳ ✳ Economic Trends

Arizona's economic development reinforced its transitory population and political amnesia. During the 1960s, 1970s, and early 1980s, the economy continued to boom. But many sectors of that economy were extremely volatile, fluctuating dramatically in response to national and global factors over which Arizonans had little control. Between 1960 and 1974, for example, the value of Arizona mineral production rose from $320 million to more than $1.5 billion, 85 to 90 percent of which came from copper. By 1974, Arizona mines and smelters were employing nearly 29,000 people and were providing about 60 percent of the nation's copper, with production peaking at 1.1 million tons in 1981. But plunging copper prices and foreign competition caused output to drop to 747,604 tons two years later. Employment also fell below 10,000 from 1986 until 1989, devastating copper towns like Ajo, Bisbee, and Clifton-Morenci, where businesses and tax bases depended almost entirely upon the copper industry.

The industry began to recover in the late 1980s, and by 1991 production was once again breaking records at 1.27 million tons. Technological innovations, however, required a workforce of only 12,000 to do so. And since miners made the best wages in the state—an average weekly salary of $716 versus $604 in manufacturing, $521 in government, $501 in construction, $427 in services, and $233 in wholesale and retail trade—the loss of 17,000 good-paying jobs left permanent scars.

The scars were most vivid in the mining community of Clifton. In June 1983, as another three-year union contract was about to expire, more than twenty miners' unions approached the major copper companies of the Southwest with their offer for the next contract. Recognizing that the industry was in trouble, they agreed to freeze their wages as long as their cost-of-living protection was retained. Magma, Inspiration, Asarco, and Kennecott accepted the offer. Phelps Dodge refused. So at one minute after midnight on July 1, thousands of miners in Ajo, Bisbee, Douglas, and Clifton-Morenci walked off the job.

It was an old drama in the mining towns, one that none of the strikers expected to last very long. But for the first time since 1959, Phelps Dodge decided to keep its mines and smelters running during the strike. At first the company tried to operate them with foremen, office workers, and nonunion employees. But the confrontation intensified on August 8, when busloads of nonunion recruits rolled up to the huge open-pit Phelps Dodge mine in Morenci. The strikers shut the mine down. Governor Bruce Babbitt ordered a ten-day cooling-off period and then called in the National Guard. "All of a sudden we saw these caravans passing," one Clifton woman told author Barbara Kingsolver. "I said, 'Oh, God, they've betrayed us.'"

Babbitt justified his actions by saying that he was just trying to preserve public order. Two weeks earlier, someone had fired a bullet into the home of an Ajo miner who had crossed the picket line, wounding his sleeping three-year-old daughter. But to the striking miners and their families, the soldiers and agents from the Department of Public Safety (DPS) were like an army of occupation, hovering overhead in their helicopters and pointing rifles at them as they walked the picket lines. Because Phelps Dodge had obtained injunctions limiting the number of picketing strikers, women from Clifton kept the picket lines active, heckling the DPS and carrying hand-painted signs that screamed, "WHO IS GOVERNOR, PHELPS DODGE OR BRUCE SCABITT?" Then, just as it had during the strike of 1903, the San Francisco River rose after a week of rains in late September and raged through Clifton's winding streets, destroying a third of the town's homes. Once again nature seemed to be on the side of Phelps Dodge.

The women, however, especially the Morenci Miners Women's Auxiliary, kept the strike going, walking the line and bolstering the morale of their husbands. "They'll never be rid of us," said Fina Roman, president of the auxiliary. "Do they ask us to forget the elderly being tear-gassed? Do they ask us to forget the beatings and arrests? To forget the past generations who handed down a sacred trust to preserve a dignified way of life won through tremendous sacrifice? Many did not live long enough to benefit from those sacrifices, yet because of them we enjoy those benefits today. Do they ask us to give them up without a fight?"

The most violent incident occurred on the first anniversary of the strike, when two hundred DPS agents in full riot gear broke up a union rally by firing tear gas and wooden bullets into the crowd. The provocations of the DPS won momentary public support for the strikers, but as the strike wore on, some of the miners went back to work, and others moved away. Family members stopped talking to one another. Marriages fell apart. Children of scabs and strikers fought at school. The strikers were bucking an industry with its back against the wall because of falling copper prices and were confronting a nation increasingly indifferent or hostile to organized labor. Phelps Dodge closed its operations in Ajo and Douglas and sold part of its Morenci mine. Workers voted to decertify the unions, and the National Labor Relations Board upheld that vote. As the wife of one striking miner confided to Kingsolver, "I felt defeated, just lost. I think we all felt that way. I have to say our town was raped."

Statistics bore the woman out. At a time when the rest of the state was growing in both population and employment, tiny Greenlee County, where Clifton was located, lost nearly 30 percent of its people and 80 percent of its manufacturing base because of declining copper production. But the rest of the state paid little attention to the plight of the mining communities because decreasing employment in the mines was more than offset by the growth of jobs in the manufacturing sector. In 1960 the manufacturing workforce stood at 49,300. That figure doubled to 99,600 in 1975. A decade later, manufacturing employed 182,800 people, an increase of 84 percent. In addition, while manufacturing ranked fourth in wage and salary employment (with 14.6 percent) behind services (with 23.8 percent), retail trade (with 19.1 percent), and government (with 16.4 percent), its payroll exceeded $4 billion, the largest among the state's economic sectors, because of relatively high-paying jobs in electronics and aerospace. In 1984 Arizona possessed only 0.87 percent of the manufacturing jobs in the United States, but 48 percent of those jobs were in high-tech industries, compared to 15 percent for the nation as a whole. The Arizona manufacturing sector may have been small, but it generated good jobs and little pollution— the kind of industries a Sunbelt state on the move wanted in the brutally competitive global economy of the late twentieth century.

National corporations accounted for much of the growth. In 1985, Motorola, the pioneer of the postwar surge in Arizona's electronics industry, remained the largest manufacturer, with 18,930 employees. But new arrivals such as Honeywell (6,100 employees), McDonnell Douglas Helicopter (5,000), IBM (5,000), and Sperry Rand (3,700) joined established firms like Motorola, the Garrett Corporation (8,300), Hughes Aircraft (5,300), and Goodyear Aerospace (1,500) to make Arizona the third largest center of high-tech electronics and aerospace manufacturing in the eleven Western states. Other national corporations established their headquarters in Arizona as well, including Greyhound, Southwest Forestries, Ramada Inns, American Express, and State Farm Insurance. "Chicago is a good business city, but Phoenix offers us a substantial reduction in expenses—wage, rentals, communications," a Greyhound executive noted in 1971. Once again the old draw of low wages and other costs brought companies to the state.

A positive aspect of these developments was the continued growth of opportunities for women. By 1981, women constituted 41 percent of Arizona's labor force of 1,213,579. Between 1969 and 1981, the percentage of women managers and officials in private industry rose from 12.9 percent to 24.4 percent, while the percentage of women professionals climbed from 24.4 percent to 35 percent. The percentage of women employed in the manufacture of durable goods increased from 30.2 percent in 1975 to 35.7 percent six years later. The number of women in government also rose. In Phoenix, for example, the percentage of female municipal employees rose from 15.5 percent in 1972–73 to 22.8 percent ten years later. During that same decade, the number of women administrators jumped from 2.9 to 12 percent. Levels of education also rose modestly. From 1970 to 1980, the percentage of women who completed high school increased from 34.8 to 38.1 percent, while the proportion of college graduates increased from 9.8 to 13.8 percent. These advances promised better jobs in the future.

Progress was slower when it came to income: full-time working women still made only 59 percent of what full-time working men made. That was a considerable increase since 1960, when the median income of women was 32 percent of male median income, but it masked a more disturbing statistic. In 1970, 29 percent of all Arizona families classified as poor by the U.S. census were headed by women. Ten years later the figure had grown to 34 percent. At a time when divorce rates and inflation were rising and the percentage of female-headed households increased from 9.7 to 11.7 percent, more women with children were falling below the poverty line. The numbers were even worse for African American, Hispanic, and Native American women, who were three to four times more likely to be poor. Despite Arizona's economic growth, the "feminization of poverty" was growing as well.

Similar trends characterized the employment trajectories of Hispanics, African Americans, and Native Americans. In 1981, so-called "minorities" constituted 21.7 percent of the total labor force in private industry but only 10.1 percent of the administrators and 8.4 percent of the professionals. Once again the figures represented an increase since 1969, when only 5 percent were managers and 3.6 percent were professionals, but they still indicated that barriers of race had not collapsed.

Nonetheless, the growth and transformation of Arizona's economy was transforming Arizona society as well. The upward mobility of Hispanics, African Americans, Native Americans, and women was slow but steady, and by the early 1990s a few individuals were even breaking through the glass ceiling and moving into the upper echelons of power as well. Manuel Pacheco was president of the University of Arizona. Karen English and Ed Pastor, a Hispanic, were members of the U.S. House of Representatives. Art Hamilton, an African American, was one of the most powerful figures in the Arizona house. Differences of race, ethnicity, and gender still reinforced differences of class, but the boundaries had weakened in the past fifty years.

Meanwhile, the uncertain impact of the North American Free Trade Agreement loomed on the horizon while more and more southern California firms moved their operations to Arizona as taxes, land values, crime, and smog poisoned the land of milk and honey. In the nineteenth and early twentieth centuries, most people passed through Arizona as quickly as possible to get to California. Now the flow of money, people, and dreams was beginning to reverse itself, culminating in the decision of Hughes Aircraft to consolidate its engineering division in Tucson in 1993. Weapons contracts, pseudo-Mediterranean architectural styles, gangs like the Crips and the Bloods—California's problems as well as its prosperity were entering Arizona (and Oregon, Washington, Nevada, and Utah) during the 1980s and early 1990s. Arizona's boom was not over yet. After making the transition from the Southwest to the Sunbelt, it now stood poised to become a force in Latin America and the Pacific Rim as well.

But much of this growth was almost as much of a crapshoot as was copper mining. Tucson won big with the Hughes consolidation, which promised several thousand more jobs. Before that decision was made, however, employment at the Hughes plant bounced up and down with the vagaries of the Cold War and the procurement of Defense Department contracts. In 1987, 7,500 people worked for Hughes. That figure dropped to 5,200 in 1991, a decline of 30.7 percent—and Hughes was a southern Arizona success story. A grimmer high-tech example was IBM, which built a huge assembly plant and a research and development laboratory on the southeastern outskirts of Tucson in the late 1970s. City officials had leaped around like eager puppies to lure the giant corporation to Tucson. Phoenix might have Motorola and a string of electronics and computer companies along the Black Canyon Freeway in northwest Phoenix, but Tucson had IBM, the prototype of high-tech corporate culture.

Or so it seemed. By the late 1980s the assembly plant had closed and IBM was lumbering around like a dinosaur in a world of small, sleek predators, laying off thousands in the process. The symbol of Tucson's high-tech future employed 5,000 workers in 1987 but only 2,350 in 1991. Competition in the computer industry, like so many other sectors of the global economy, was speeding up at an incomprehensible rate and was making a mockery of long-term economic planning.

✳ ✳ ✳   The Money Game

That did not stop the financial world of Arizona from plunging into an orgy of speculative investment that made the state's earlier boom-and-bust cycles look like balanced growth. Nothing reflects a society more accurately than the sources of its money, and through the 1950s Arizona banking was a tight-knit little universe run by families like the Bimsons, the Brophys, the Hazeltines, and the Douglases. In 1956 there were eight banks and 110 branch banks in Arizona, but the Valley National Bank and the First National Bank alone possessed 72 percent of the state's banking assets. VNB also owned 51 percent of the Bank of Douglas through its holding company, the Arizona Bancorporation, while the Transamerica Corporation, which controlled First National, held 98 percent of the stock of the Southern Arizona Bank and Trust Company. That gave VNB/Arizona Bancorporation and Transamerica 93 percent of all Arizona banking assets. In 1953, Walter Bimson even "loaned" his son Lloyd to the Bank of Douglas for five years because it needed a good vice president. Lloyd remained to became president of the institution in 1960, when it changed its name to the Arizona Bank.

The banking elite was so intertwined, in fact, that in 1956 the Federal Reserve System began an investigation to see if it was violating antitrust laws. Six years later the Justice Department filed an antitrust suit against VNB, charging that it had "substantially lessened and unreasonably restrained" competition by purchasing a controlling interest in the Arizona Bank through the Arizona Bancorporation. The suit was dropped three years later after the VNB agreed to give up control of its holding company. By then, however, new faces were beginning to dominate the business scene.

One of the biggest changes was the penetration of the Arizona economy by regional and national corporations. Giants like Phelps Dodge and the Southern Pacific had stalked Arizona's political and economic landscape since the late nineteenth century, but other domains, such as banking and the savings and loan industry, had been run largely by people within the state. A. P. Giannini's Bank of Italy, which became the Bank of America, acquired First National through Transamerica in the late 1930s. But VNB, the Arizona Bank, the Southern Arizona Bank, First Federal Savings, and Western Savings remained Arizona institutions throughout the first few decades of the postwar boom. Many of these enterprises were family-run operations that reflected the personalities of the men at the top, who often made decisions based on instinct and intuition rather than market research or the advice of subordinates. They were larger than life, the stuff of legends, men like Joe Rice of Western Savings, with his Western-cut suits and martinis, and Frank Brophy of the Bank of Douglas, with his racehorses and far-right politics. They supplied the money that kept Arizona businesses, farms, and ranches afloat during the Depression, and they stoked the postwar boom.

By the late 1960s, however, no single individual, no matter how brilliant or well connected, could navigate Arizona's financial waters by the sheer force of his personality. One institution caught up in the change was the Arizona Bank, run by the acerbic and domineering Lloyd Bimson. At a time when Bimson was in the process of selecting the Morning Kachina logo that would soon give the Arizona Bank massive statewide name recognition, Signal Oil Company of Los Angeles, which also owned the Garrett Corporation and AiResearch, offered to purchase the Arizona Bancorporation in order to gain control of Bimson's bank. Bimson had put his personal stamp on the bank for seven years, but he was dying from a rare and insidious form of melanoma. So attorney Frank Snell—his father's old friend and one of the most powerful members of the postwar Phoenix elite—arranged the merger, which was completed in 1967, the same year Lloyd Bimson died. Perhaps no other conjunction of events symbolized the transition of power in Arizona banking circles so poignantly.

The professional managers who took over the Arizona Bank and other institutions faced a financial universe of cutthroat competition and Byzantine complexity. Prior to the 1970s that universe had been divided into neat little compartments. Banks financed businesses and personal consumption items like automobiles, while savings and loans furnished credit for single-family homes. Interest rates on deposits were tightly controlled, and different types of institutions rarely fought with one another over deposits or loans. But competition accelerated in 1980 when the Depository Institution Deregulation Act removed the ceilings on interest rates, and it exploded in 1982, when the Garn–St. Germain Depository Institutions Act allowed thrifts to invest their money in everything from real estate to junk bonds. Suddenly, savings and loans, banks, credit unions, and brokerage houses were wrestling for assets from the same huge pool of depositors. Meanwhile, thrift executives were speculating in the stock market and plunging into enormous development schemes. Ever since the 1930s the trend had been toward increased state and federal regulation of institutions that gambled with other people's money. Now deregulation had triumphed, and the old rules unraveled with mind-boggling rapidity.

The dark prince of deregulation in Arizona was a tall, rawboned, former champion swimmer named Charles Keating. When Keating moved from Cincinnati to Phoenix in 1978, he parlayed American Continental Homes, a company with assets of $510,000 and debts of $110 million, into the biggest homebuilder in Phoenix and Denver. But the global economy was in a feeding frenzy fueled by petrodollars and inflation, and Keating wanted to do more than build homes, even at the rate of eight a day. So in 1983 he picked up a California thrift called Lincoln Savings and Loan for $51 million, and that bought him a billion dollars' worth of assets, which, under California and federal law, he could invest just about any way he wanted. Suddenly Keating was playing at the same table with Michael Milken, John Connally, and the oil-rich Kuwaitis.

Keating's financial transactions soon transcended any sense of place. He kept nine pilots on call to fly him anywhere in the world, and his secretary always kept her bag packed because she never knew when she and her boss would be jetting off to New York, London, Monaco, or Geneva. In the words of journalists Michael Binstein and Charles Bowden, "For years, Charlie Keating will patiently explain to people that his house happens to be in Phoenix, Arizona, but he is not of Phoenix, Arizona. He belongs to a much larger and increasingly borderless world."

Despite his global ambitions, however, Keating launched two of his most ambitious projects in the Phoenix area. The first was a city of 200,000 people in a valley of the Estrella Mountains west of Phoenix. Del Webb had turned cotton fields into Sun City; Keating wanted to transform a chunk of desert administered by the Bureau of Land Management into a satellite of Los Angeles. Because Keating was a devout Catholic, his Estrella was going to be a shining city at the base of a desert hill, with covenants prohibiting abortions or pornography. It was also going to be a city that denied the desert, one that carefully arranged more than 73,000 lots around an enormous man-made lake designed by Walt Disney Productions. Keating planned to recreate southern California in the Sonoran Desert, complete with windsurfing and sailboating but minus the high labor costs and rioting minorities. As Binstein and Bowden point out, "Charlie Keating in the mid-eighties anticipates what will become a fact by the early nineties—the flight of human beings and jobs from Los Angeles to Nevada, Utah, and Arizona. He senses that he is not stuck in the middle of the desert but located in a new, cheap zone of the booming Pacific Rim."

Keating's other local obsession was the Phoenician, his world-class resort at the foot of Camelback Mountain. In many respects the Phoenician became his monument, a project that grew bigger and bigger as the concrete was being poured. Originally designed for 400 rooms, it swelled to 600 during construction, with Keating adding a 47,000-square-foot golf clubhouse and a 17,000-square-foot health spa as well. The hotel was also supposed to cost $150 million, but the bills soon spiraled above $300 million. The grandiose scale, the obsessive attention to detail, the refusal to let others make any final decisions—every aspect of the resort reflected the driven man who created it.

Keating wanted to be a merchant banker—one who not only made loans to investors but also developed projects himself. For six high-flying years he did just that, buying millions of dollars' worth of junk bonds from Michael Milken, loaning millions to Ivan Boesky, cutting deals with shadowy figures of international high finance like Britain's Sir James Goldsmith and the Kuwaitis. By 1986, however, two billion of Lincoln's three billion dollars in assets were tied up in risky investments that might have taken years, if ever, to yield a return, so federal regulators began nipping at Keating's heels. As the gap between income and expenses ballooned to $10 million a month, Keating and the people who worked for him like right-hand woman Judy Wischer threw themselves into a grinding, relentless scramble for cash. They shuffled electronic money from one paper subsidiary to another, they loaned money to customers who then ploughed the money back into projects with Lincoln (straw buyers making linked transactions that were felonies under the law), and they sold junk bonds in the American Continental Corporation to more than 20,000 buyers right out of the branches of Lincoln itself—bonds that, unlike Lincoln's deposits, were not insured by the federal government. Some people, many of them elderly, invested their life savings after listening to the sales pitch and glancing through the glossy promotional literature.

It was a multibillion dollar juggling act on an international high wire, and federally insured deposits were its only safety net. But even though Keating entertained U.S. senators at his hideaway in the Bahamas and poured thousands into their campaigns, a few tenacious federal officials like Edwin Gray, chairman of the Federal Home Loan Bank Board, slowly put the pieces of the financial puzzle together and were appalled by what they saw. Keating tried to torpedo Gray and stack the board with regulators who would let him keep on juggling, but he failed. In 1989 the balls came tumbling down. On April 13, American Continental filed for Chapter XI bankruptcy. On April 14, federal regulators seized Lincoln Savings. On September 15, special investigator Michael Manning lodged a RICO (Racketeering Influenced and Corrupt Organization) complaint accusing Keating, his family, and his officers of looting Lincoln Savings of more than $1 billion. Two months later, FBI agents and federal regulators staged a predawn raid and took over the Phoenician itself.

It were as if someone had not only cut the high wire but had put a torch to the circus big top as well. American Continental bonds were worthless. Life savings were lost. Lincoln became the biggest thrift failure in U.S. history, with a potential cost to U.S. taxpayers of $3.2 billion. By 1993, Keating had lost numerous civil lawsuits filed by angry bondholders, and then a federal jury convicted him of seventy-three counts of racketeering, fraud, and conspiracy to commit fraud. Nearly seventy, he was sentenced to more than twelve years in federal prison and was ordered to pay $122.4 million in restitution. Driven by a hunger for power and a need to prove to the high rollers that he could play at their level, Keating had finally made it into an exclusive club. Along with Boesky and Milken, he was among the most recognizable symbols of one of the greediest decades in American financial history.

Like most such symbols, he was also a scapegoat. It was tempting for many Arizonans, like people across the nation, to blame the collapse of the savings and loan industry on outsiders—big, bad wolves like Keating and the others who haunted the junk bond Predator's Ball, which was hosted every year by Drexel, the company Michael Milken worked for. But even though Lincoln was the worst example of deregulation run amok, the California thrift had plenty of company. During the first half of 1989—the year the dominoes fell in Keating's empire—Arizona banks won the dubious honor of losing more money than the banks in any other state in the country. MeraBank lost $209 million in 1988 and ceased to make loans in July 1989. Valley National, the largest bank in Arizona, registered losses of $64 million during the first two quarters of 1989 and $72 million during the third. Then it stopped paying dividends on its common stock and plummeted in the market. Six smaller banks failed.

Arizona thrifts did even worse, much worse—$710 million in total losses during the first six months of 1989, and $5.6 million a day thereafter. Three savings and loans closed that year: Southwest, Sun State, and the granddaddy of them all, Western Savings, the largest and oldest savings and loan in the state. By 1992, ten of Arizona's eleven thrifts were in receivership and were being administered by the Resolution Trust Corporation (RTC), one of two entities created out of the Federal Home Loan Bank Board, which had formerly regulated thrifts. But the most shocking collapse of all was the failure of Western Savings. Founded by a prominent Mormon family who had long been active in city and state politics, Western had followed established principles for thrift institutions for most of its sixty-year history, lending 80 percent of its assets to buyers of single-family homes. But in the 1980s even the conservative Driggs family could not resist the temptations of deregulation and speculation. By 1988 only 25 percent of Western's loans were single-family mortgages. The rest of the thrift's assets were used to play the real estate market, including the purchase of the 20,000-acre Banning-Lewis Ranch in Colorado, the largest lemon in Western's growing portfolio of sour deals. When RTC took over Western the following year, it became the third largest bloated body among the 700 corpses littering the savings and loan industry. Federal regulators estimated that Western's demise would eventually cost taxpayers $1.7 billion.

❋ ❋ ❋ The Lay of the Land

Most of the bad deals the thrifts invested in had to do with land. As people poured into Arizona, every subdivision, shopping center, office complex, industrial park, golf course, and resort had to start from the ground up, so land speculation—or land fraud—became Arizona's biggest growth industry. Because the state and federal governments controlled 82 percent of the land, the 18 percent in individual or corporate hands became an exceedingly valuable commodity, especially if it was near Phoenix or Tucson or high enough to offer some relief from the summers in those two cities. Fortunes in postwar Arizona were not made in gold or silver mining but in real estate—in buying the private, or patent, land of a ranch beneath the Mogollon Rim, for example, and subdividing it into lots for summer cabins, in swapping remote private land for state or federal land near the cities or in persuading city councils or county boards of supervisors to grant the needed zoning changes and tax breaks. Arizona became a vast Monopoly board of raw land waiting to be developed. Every once in a while, if the developer was particularly clever, public officials even made the taxpayers pay for water, power lines, and roads.

One of the most audacious developments was the McCulloch Corporation's Lake Havasu City along the Colorado River. In the early 1960s, Robert McCulloch persuaded numerous state officials to arrange the transfer of 13,000 acres of federal land in Mohave County to the state. The state then sold that land at public auction to the McCulloch Corporation for less than $1 million, or about $73 an acre. Critics of the land transfer, particularly the IRE (Investigative Reporters and Editors), a team of thirty-six reporters who wrote a twenty-three-part, 80,000-word series on crime and politics in Arizona for various newspapers, charged that the land could have brought $6.5 million if it had been broken up and sold in smaller parcels. McCulloch countered by saying, "The basic fallacy regarding the purchase is the glib assumption that it was an unethical land grab of undeveloped property for which there was a ready market. Exactly the opposite was true. Nobody wanted it. It was bare, sandy, rocky land mainly of value only in a large quantity to someone who was prepared to risk millions to improve it for habitation."

McCulloch was right about the landscape. It was one of the hottest, driest stretches of desert in North America, where temperatures reached as high as 128 degrees. Regardless of its legal or political proprieties, however, Lake Havasu City became another one of those Arizona developments that exhibited a truly baroque disregard for its natural setting. By 1990, 24,363 people were living in air-conditioned splendor there. They golfed. They drifted down their man-made lake in houseboats. They gambled upriver in the casinos of Laughlin, Nevada. McCulloch, the same entrepreneur who blasted water 300 feet into the sky to advertise Fountain Hills northeast of Phoenix, even provided them with a world-class landmark—London Bridge in Arizona, which was reassembled piece by piece alongside the Colorado River. No dream of the Quechans or Mohaves could have been as fantastic as the new community emerging on the Yumans' ancestral land.

But while developments like Lake Havasu City were grandiose, many promoters did not even bother with basic amenities. Before he was killed by a car bomb in 1976, reporter Don Bolles of the *Arizona Republic* estimated that more than six million lots and $1 billion had changed hands in phony Arizona real estate transactions during the past twenty years. Tales abounded of elderly couples coming out to see their place in the sun and being told that they needed a helicopter to fly them there because there were no access roads. As the nation aged, Arizona became a warm, sunny dream that rippled across billboards, television screens, and the pages of promotional pamphlets. Sometimes those pages were the only place the dream was real.

The names the developers gave their paradises also tripped off the tongue in an exotic poetry that evoked what linguistic anthropologist Jane Hill calls the Nouvelle Southwest. Some of the names, like Ned Warren's Great Southwest Land & Cattle Company or Conley Wolfswinkel's Diamond Bell Ranch Estates, harked back to the Old West. Many others were in Spanish, or what passed for Spanish in the promotional world. Real estate developers in the Tucson Basin indulged in an orgy of Spanish naming that ranged from the ungrammatical to the absurd: San Anna Drive (instead of the correct Santa Ana, or Saint Anne's Drive), Calle de las Albondigas (Meatball Road), or Camino de Esperanto (Esperanto Road; the developers probably meant to say Camino de Esperanza, Road of Hope, though Esperanto, the name of an artificial international language, is strangely appropriate). Like real estate promoters in southern California in the late nineteenth century, Arizona developers wanted to conjure up romantic visions of the Spanish Southwest, pastoral scenes of gracious haciendas and ancient missions that had little to do with Arizona's historical reality or postwar growth. Instead, they often perpetrated the desert equivalent of the Florida swampland frauds.

Growth gobbled up the bits and pieces of private land in Arizona at a voracious rate, generating a land rush that sucked swindlers and mobsters into the state and corrupted local businessmen and public officials. Arizona soon led the nation in land fraud complaints received by the Interstate Land Sales division of the federal Department of Housing and Urban Development. Reminiscing about the mid-1970s, when he became state attorney general, Bruce Babbitt said, "Things were literally out of control. The public had gone to sleep, the press was on the sidelines, law enforcement was demoralized, frustrated. There was an air of indifference in Arizona, sort of a sense that anything goes. I was always reminded of Woody Guthrie's statement that, you know, it's somehow okay to steal as long as you use a fountain pen instead of a gun."

The czar of the fountain pen, the godfather of Arizona land fraud, was a tanned, leathery New Yorker named Ned Warren. Warren moved to Arizona in the early 1960s after serving time for violating federal bankruptcy laws back east. A protégé of Nathan Voloshen, who peddled political influence from the office of Speaker of the House John McCormack in Washington, Warren set up the Thunderbird Land Corporation with some of Voloshen's money. It was the first of Warren's more than three dozen fronts for real estate scams across the state. Through Thunderbird and corporations like the Queen Creek Land & Cattle Company and the Great Southwest Land & Cattle Company, Warren ran a variety of schemes. The simplest was little more than a variation on the cut and run. Salesmen would fan out across the country and take down payments from buyers who never saw the lots they had purchased. When and if they did, they often found a development with no roads, no water, and no electricity. At other times, the lots themselves had been sold more than once, making it almost impossible to determine legal title. By the time enough angry buyers had complained to the authorities, the company had folded and siphoned off its profits into other companies and other schemes.

More sophisticated swindles involved the sale of "paper"—the installment sales contracts that represented future income in the form of monthly payments. Developers could use those contracts as collateral to obtain a bank loan. They could also "package" the contracts and sell them to other investors at a discount. Those techniques were legal—common ways in which developers got the cash they needed to market their projects and put in the necessary utilities and roads. But crooks like Warren generated phony paper by "fenceposting"— signing sales contracts in the names of imaginary individuals or of real people without their knowledge—or by paying people to sign the documents with the agreement that they would never be required to make a down payment. Great Southwest reputedly had a Phoenix bar full of people who regularly scrawled their names on fraudulent contracts. By the time its house of cards collapsed in 1972, Great Southwest alone had swindled nearly 10,000 buyers of both land and paper out of more than $5 million.

Drawing on what he learned from Voloshen, Warren also cultivated and plundered a series of business partnerships with prominent Arizona politicians.

The first was Lee Ackerman, a member of the Democratic National Committee (DNC) and an unsuccessful candidate for governor in 1960. Warren and Ackerman formed the Western Growth Capital Corporation in 1965. Two years later it went bankrupt, and Ackerman accused Warren of fraud and filed a $39 million lawsuit against him. It was settled out of court. Warren then sold another of his enterprises, Prescott Valley, Inc., to Dr. John Kruglick, who became a member of the DNC after Ackerman resigned. But Warren did not confine himself to Democrats. He bought Great Southwest's Lake Montezuma property from G. Robert Herberger, a powerful Republican fund-raiser. He also employed two political allies of Republican state chairman Harry Rosenzweig at Queen Creek. In 1971, Warren even managed to secure a promotional letter signed by Barry Goldwater on official U.S. Senate stationery. The letter touted a company that sold land owned by Jack Ross, a powerful Democrat, to servicemen overseas.

When challenged about the letter, Goldwater replied that he did not know Warren and could not remember who asked him to sign it. No one ever accused Goldwater of profiting from the company itself, but the letter demonstrated how easily someone like Warren could insinuate himself into the highest levels of Arizona society. Arizona had little old money and few old families. The economy was surging, and no one cared who you were twenty years ago because you were only as important as your last deal. Honest businessmen unwittingly formed partnerships with mobsters and got bilked. *Arizona Republic* publisher Darrow "Duke" Tully dressed up as a colonel and regaled admirers with his stories about flying combat missions in Vietnam, which turned out to be complete fabrications. Many people were shedding their past and recreating their present to take advantage of the boom. The cast of characters changed so rapidly that no one could check out every potential business partner, political contributor, or employee, and no one asked too many questions because there was too much money to be made.

❋   ❋   The Underbelly

Association did not necessarily imply guilt, but there were plenty of cases of outright corruption and plenty of evidence that, in some industries at least, organized crime was determined to rake its cut off Arizona's growth. On January 9, 1975, Edward Lazar, Ned Warren's top accountant, testified before a grand jury that Warren and other developers had made monthly payoffs to J. Fred Talley, the aging real estate commissioner of Arizona who had resigned under a cloud and had died of a heart attack in 1974. On February 19, the day before he was to appear before another grand jury, Lazar was shot five times in the chest and head. Meanwhile, Warren was indicted on perjury and bribery charges in two separate cases. Both were dismissed.

A federal court in Seattle eventually convicted Warren of extortion in a case that had nothing to do with Arizona land fraud. Back in the state, however, Lazar was not the only corpse linked to Warren. Eleven other former associates were murdered as well, including Tony Serra, the former sales manager of Great Southwest who had been convicted of land fraud and sentenced to the Arizona State Prison in Florence. Unlike the other victims, who were killed on the outside, Serra was stabbed and beaten to death inside the prison—his ear nearly torn off and a hole bored through his forehead with an electric drill. Another convict, George Warnock, told reporters that Warren and Phoenix attorney Neal Roberts had put out a contract on Serra after Serra implicated several Arizona public officials in Warren's fraudulent empire. Warnock also said that the man who masterminded the murder was Gary Tison, a charming, remorseless trusty who was allowed to wear cowboy boots and live in the medium-security annex at Florence even though he had killed a prison guard ten years earlier.

Tison, an Oklahoma native whose family had made the Dust Bowl–driven trek to California in the early 1940s, went on to win his own notoriety. On July 30, 1978, a year and a half after Serra's death, Tison's three sons broke murderer Randy Greenwalt and him out of the annex. For the next twelve days the five careened across Arizona, New Mexico, and southern Colorado, slaughtering a family and a couple on their honeymoon before Pinal County sheriff's deputies finally blasted their stolen van off a dark road on the immense Tohono O'odham reservation. Tison's oldest son, Donny, was killed in the shootout. Tison himself was found eleven days later, his body bloating next to an ironwood tree where he had died of thirst. It was a sordid ending to a sordid, brutal tale, one that scuttled like a tick through the coarse hairs on Arizona's underbelly—land fraud, prison corruption, the hardscrabble lives of uprooted Okies. Sparring with reporters and bribing public officials from his $250,000 mansion on Camelback Mountain, Warren considered land fraud a grand game. But the game got dirty at times, and some of the players lost their lives.

Nevertheless, men like Serra and Lazar *were* players—crooks killed by crooks—and the public reacted to their murders the same way they responded to gangland slayings back east, with gruesome fascination but little outrage. What happened on June 2, 1976, however, shocked not just Arizonans but the nation. Don Bolles of the *Arizona Republic* was the best investigative reporter in the state. With his pompadour, his leisure suits, and his open face, he looked more like a friendly, small-town insurance salesman than a big-city journalist.

But Bolles was relentless in tracking political corruption, land fraud, and organized crime across the state. He shed light on Ned Warren's tangled web. He listed nearly 200 of the Mafia "newcomers" to Arizona. He exposed extortion and organized crime in the dog-racing industry, which was monopolized by the Emprise Corporation of Buffalo, New York, and the Funk family of Arizona, who co-owned Arizona's six tracks. Finally, he raised disturbing questions about rancher and wholesale liquor distributor Kemper Marley, forcing the tough old cattleman to resign from the state racing commission soon after his appointment in 1976.

By the mid-1970s, many of his friends and fellow reporters thought that Bolles was burned out, tired of writing exposés that never resulted in any concrete reforms. Yet in late May 1976 he met with an alcoholic, Valium-popping hustler named John Adamson, who said he could link Emprise with Sam Steiger, a U.S. congressman and a bitter enemy of Emprise. Bolles asked for proof, and Adamson set up another meeting on June 2 to provide it. The meeting was scheduled for 11:25 A.M. in the lobby of a hotel called the Clarendon House in downtown Phoenix. Bolles kept the meeting, but Adamson called the hotel and canceled, so Bolles climbed back into his new Datsun. A homemade car bomb exploded underneath him at 11:34, blowing out every window on the south side of the hotel. It also nearly severed Bolles's legs. Both had to be amputated along with his right arm during the eleven days he fought for life. He died on June 13, never regaining consciousness after telling the paramedics, "They finally got me. Emprise. The Mafia. John Adamson. Find him."

The resulting investigations, cover-ups, convictions, and overturned convictions were the most disgraceful chapter in recent Arizona history, dwarfing the political circuses of Mecham's impeachment or AzScam, which came later. Adamson was quickly arrested and charged with first-degree murder. Neal Roberts, the lawyer who chartered a plane to fly Adamson to Lake Havasu City after the bombing, hired John Flynn, the best defense attorney in Arizona, and Flynn managed to persuade the prosecution to grant Roberts immunity before he offered any evidence. In return, the prosecution got its guiding theory—that Kemper Marley ordered Bolles killed in an act of "rangeland violence" for articles the reporter had written about him. But Roberts never provided any proof to back up his allegations, and Marley was never indicted. Attorney General Bruce Babbitt, who had not yet taken over the case, called the immunity agreement "disastrous." The investigation of Bolles's death started to unravel before it really got started.

After remaining silent for months, Adamson cut his own deal, fingering contractor Max Dunlap and plumber Jimmy Robison as accomplices in the bombing in return for a twenty-year prison sentence. Dunlap and Robison were convicted of first-degree murder and sentenced to death in 1977, but the Arizona Supreme Court overturned their convictions in 1980. Adamson then announced that he would not testify against them in a retrial unless the state released him from prison. The prosecutors refused, Adamson kept quiet, and charges against Dunlap and Robison were dismissed. That led the state to declare the plea agreement null and void and to prosecute Adamson for first-degree murder. He also got the death penalty, but a federal court of appeals overturned his sentence as well, arguing that the original plea agreement was still valid.

The state retried both Dunlap and Robison in the early 1990s. Juries acquitted Robison but convicted Dunlap, who was sentenced to life imprisonment. Nearly two decades after Bolles's assassination, however, Arizonans still did not know why Don Bolles had been killed or who ordered the killing, even after two-time Pulitzer Prize winner Robert Greene and a shifting cast of thirty-five other reporters launched the IRE group's Arizona Project, a wide-ranging series of investigations into the social and political milieu that produced Bolles's death. The series documented everything from land fraud to the growing drug trade in Arizona, but it never produced any solid evidence that Marley or anyone else had ordered Bolles's murder. The Phoenix *New Times* of June 1986 best summed up the whole sorry episode when it wrote, "Think of a merry-go-round with its colorful horses posed for action. This one is galloping; that one rearing; this one prancing. Everyone realizes that the only *real* action comes from the hidden hub of this giant wheel, with its spokes and gears and juice to make the carousel turn endlessly. The Don Bolles murder case is a lot like that—showy characters forever striking their own poses while the hub that holds them all together stays safely hidden."

✳ ✳ ✳ The Big Canal

Land fraud, political corruption, and collapsing thrifts all had one thing in common. They were parasites of the boom, feeding on a society addicted to constant growth. And while cheap wages, easy zoning, and probusiness tax structures fed that growth, Arizona's development ultimately depended on an old partnership and an ancient need. Without water, the land was worthless and the cities would go dry. Without the federal government, the state could not supply enough water to keep the boom surging. Federal dams and electricity turned the Salt River Valley into an agricultural oasis and the largest urban center between Los Angeles and Dallas–Forth Worth. But Phoenix monopolized the waters of the Salt and Verde rivers, and groundwater was a shrinking resource, so Arizona politicians and developers continued to tie Arizona's future to the Central Arizona Project (CAP). As senators Carl Hayden and Ernest McFarland warned in the late 1940s, "Arizona is doomed to wither away to the point of disaster" unless Washington built the big canal.

The crusade was little more than a gleam in Arizona's eye until the Arizona legislature finally ratified the Colorado River Compact in 1944. Two years later farmers, bankers, utility companies, and urban planners formed the Central Arizona Project Association to lobby for the scheme. Dominated by agricultural interests, the association joined forces with the Bureau of Reclamation and Arizona's congressional delegation to win authorization for the CAP in Congress, where Arizona's two powerful senators—Ernest McFarland and Carl Hayden—introduced a series of bills beginning in 1947. Three years later the Senate approved one of those bills by a substantial margin (55–28). Opposition in the House, on the other hand, was considerably more formidable. Influenced by the enormous California delegation, many representatives agreed with Arthur Carhart, who wrote that the CAP would be a "big, fat handout to those boomers who gambled and mined water and when they had squandered their wealth, turned to Uncle Sugar to perpetuate them in their exploitation."

In the end, the House Committee on Public Lands sidestepped a showdown by delaying action until the U.S. Supreme Court resolved the quarrel over water rights between Arizona and California. Arizona had tried to bring its case to the Court on three different occasions during the 1930s, but the Court dismissed the suits because the state had not ratified the compact. In 1953, however, the Court agreed to hear Arizona's complaint. Because the case was so complex, it also appointed a Special Master to weigh the legal, economic, and hydrological issues presented by the two states. *Arizona v. California* began before Special Master Simon Rifkind on June 14, 1956. It ended on August 28, 1958. During the 132 trial days, Rifkind heard from 105 scientific experts, examined 4,000 exhibits, and plowed through 22,593 pages of testimony. Nearly two years later, he issued his draft report.

Rifkind upheld Article III(a) of the compact, which allocated 2.8 million acre-feet of the Colorado annually to Arizona and limited California to 4.4 million acre-feet per year. If there was not enough flow to meet the allocation of 7.5 million acre-feet to the Lower Basin states, the flow would be apportioned according to allocation percentages: 44/75ths for California, 28/75ths for Arizona, and 3/75ths for Nevada. Rifkind also determined that the tributaries emptying into the river below Lee's Ferry (the dividing line between Upper Basin and Lower Basin states) were not included in the compact. The amount of water Arizona removed from those drainages therefore could not be subtracted from its allocation. On June 3, 1963, the Supreme Court adopted most of Rifkind's recommendations by a vote of 5 to 3. After ten years of courtroom sparring, Arizona had finally triumphed over its archenemy, California.

But legal victory did not ensure congressional appropriations. During the next five years, the fight over CAP degenerated into blatant pork-barrel politics. On one side were Secretary of the Interior Stewart Udall; Arizona's five-member congressional delegation led by Carl Hayden, chairman of the Senate Appropriations Committee; and Hayden's close friend Floyd Dominy, the cigar-chomping, woman-chasing head of the Bureau of Reclamation. On the other side were the forty-two-member California delegation, Congressman Wayne Aspinall (D-Colorado), Senator Henry Jackson (D-Washington), and a growing army of environmentalists marshalled by David Brower and the Sierra Club.

Aspinall, the chairman of the House Committee on Interior and Insular Affairs, wanted to ensure that the Upper Basin states, particularly Colorado, got their share of the compact's allocations. In return for his support, Hayden tacked five water projects in Aspinall's Colorado district onto the CAP bill. Jackson feared that the bill's authorization of studies of transbasin water transfers would eventually siphon water from the Pacific Northwest's Columbia River system, so he received a ten-year moratorium on such research. The environmentalists opposed two dams—Bridge Canyon and Marble Canyon—that would have flooded both ends of the Grand Canyon to provide hydroelectric power to pump CAP water 1,200 feet uphill to Phoenix and 2,100 feet uphill to Tucson. Udall killed both dams and suggested instead that the bureau purchase a share of, and become a partner in, the coal-fired Navajo Generating Station at Page, Arizona. Finally, California demanded the delivery of all of its annual allocation of 4.4 million acre-feet of water even during years of low flow. That was the hardest compromise of all because the Colorado had only averaged 13 million acre-feet of flow since 1930, 7.5 million acre-feet of which had to go to the Upper Basin states. But Arizona finally bit the bullet and accepted the California Guarantee. On September 30, 1968, President Lyndon Johnson signed the CAP authorization bill. Gathering in Phoenix's venerable Westward Ho Hotel, Arizona's movers and shakers celebrated the bill's passage.

Nevertheless, the battle over CAP continued on two fronts. One concerned the route of the system itself, particularly the location of its dams. The 1968 bill authorized more than 300 miles of aqueducts and pipelines, the consumption of 547,000 kilowatts of energy from the Navajo Generating Station, and the construction of four dams to impound CAP flow or the flow of Arizona rivers besides the Colorado. The Buttes Dam was to be located on the middle Gila River, Charleston Dam along the San Pedro, and Hooker Dam along the upper

Gila, where it would have flooded portions of the massive Gila Wilderness, the first wilderness area set aside in the United States. But the dam that generated the most controversy was the Orme Dam at the confluence of the Salt and Verde rivers northeast of Phoenix. Promoted as a flood-control structure, the dam's primary purpose was to store CAP water during the winter so that it could be released during the summer peak demand season in the Salt River Valley. The dam also would have inundated twenty-five miles of floodplain along the Verde, a stretch that contained the nesting grounds of three of the seven pairs of endangered southern bald eagles along the river as well as two-thirds of the Fort McDowell Indian Reservation. Once again, the Yavapais of Fort McDowell were being called upon to sacrifice their reservation so the Salt River Valley could have more water.

Many Yavapais objected. So did the Maricopa Audubon Society and a newly formed group called Citizens Concerned About the Project, which brought environmentalists and Native Americans together to protest the site of the Orme Dam. The federal government tried to splinter the opposition by offering the Fort McDowell Yavapais $30 million for their land, about $70,000 per member. So tribal leaders polled the residents of the reservation and found that 140 opposed the sale, 8 had no opinion, and only 1 supported relocation. The Bureau of Reclamation and the Central Arizona Project Association then sponsored five seminars designed to "educate" the Native Americans and forced a second vote, in which voting age was lowered to eighteen and tribal members living off the reservation were allowed to vote. This time the margin was narrower—144 to 57—but once again the Yavapais turned the government down. Invoking the spirit of Wassaja (Dr. Carlos Montezuma), who, more than five decades earlier, had warned them not to surrender the "sweet waters of the Verde," the Yavapais educated the government, teaching it that land had more than a dollar value and that cost-benefit analysis was not the only worldview. After hearing their testimony, the Carter administration eliminated the funding for Orme Dam in 1977.

Proponents tried to resurrect the structure three years later when huge floods surged down the Salt River and forced the Salt River Project to release massive amounts of water that washed out eleven bridges in Phoenix. "Are you fed up . . . [with] this community playing second fiddle to high-and-dry special pleaders who shed tears over nesting eagles, but can't find compassion for the thousands of families who endured hardship, fear, and ruin as flood waters rampage through the valley?" snarled publisher Pat Murphy of the *Arizona Republic* on February 27, 1980. "I'm mad! I'm mad as hell that high-and-dry Washington bureaucrats have been dilly-dallying for at least ten years over approval of Orme Dam. . . . Now dammit, give us our dam!" But the escalating cost projections for the dam finally doomed the project: $38 million in 1968 had become $350 million in 1981 and a whopping $700 million a year later after geologists revealed that the dam site was on a fault zone subject to earthquakes.

The Bureau of Reclamation came up with its $746 million Plan 6 instead, which called for the strengthening of the Stewart Mountain Dam on Saguaro Lake and the raising of Roosevelt Dam by seventy feet. Plan 6 also proposed two new dams—the relatively noncontroversial New Waddell on the Agua Fria River to enlarge the storage capacity of Lake Pleasant, and the Cliff Dam on the Verde upriver from the Fort McDowell Reservation. Because Cliff Dam would have created a six-mile-long reservoir that would have submerged the sites where two pairs of bald eagles nested, environmentalists and dam builders squared off a second time, and bald eagles once again became a symbol of the resistance. But opponents also charged that the only real reason for the dam was to protect a stretch of the Salt River floodplain through Phoenix where the Rio Salado Project was being planned. The Rio Salado Project—a riverfront development of homes, factories, businesses, and hotels—was the largest real estate scheme in Arizona, one that would have cost Arizona taxpayers at least $600 million. When voters rejected it, the rationale for Cliff Dam disappeared, and the bureau settled for New Waddell and a bigger Roosevelt.

But even though the bureau lost several battles over the route of the CAP, it won the war to fund the project itself, and victory on that second front turned out to be increasingly expensive for CAP beneficiaries as well as the American taxpayers. In 1968 the estimated cost of the CAP was $1.5 billion, which Arizona pledged to repay over a fifty-year period after construction was completed. There was a huge federal subsidy hidden in that repayment schedule, however, because farmers utilizing CAP water were exempt from interest payments, and municipal and industrial water users had to pay interest at a rate of only 3.3 percent. As interest rates soared into double digits a decade later, President Carter put the CAP on his famous hit list of eighteen water projects he wanted to eliminate in 1977. But as author Marc Reisner points out in *Cadillac Desert,* "water projects are the grease gun that lubricates the nation's legislative machinery. Congress without water projects would be like an engine without oil; it would simply seize up." House majority leader Jim Wright called Carter a "laughingstock" and tried to turn opposition to the hit list into a constitutional crusade to protect congressional prerogatives. Morris Udall labeled it the "George Washington's Birthday Massacre" even though he later admitted that "one man's vital water resource project is another man's boondoggle." After both the House and Senate passed bills restoring all but one of the projects, Carter threatened to veto them, but congressional pressure cracked his resolve. CAP and the other water projects survived, and perhaps no other controversy besides the Iran hostage crisis so undermined Carter's presidency on Capitol Hill.

Meanwhile, CAP began to bulldoze its way across the desert, chewing up federal money and threatening the solvency of the people it was supposed to help. Congress appropriated $1.5 billion in 1971, but the Office of Management and Budget impounded those funds until Arizona came up with a workable repayment plan. In response, the state legislature created the Central Arizona Water Conservancy District, consisting of Maricopa, Pinal, and Pima counties. The district was given the power to levy an *ad valorem* property tax to repay the cost of constructing the CAP, but irrigation districts still had to bear the cost of building the canals that would deliver CAP water to individual fields. In 1967—a year before Congress authorized the project—William Martin and Robert Young, two agricultural economists from the University of Arizona, predicted that farmers would never be able to afford CAP water after paying for the delivery systems. They argued instead that farmers should offset the growing costs of groundwater pumping by conserving water and shifting to higher-value crops. Their statements were seen as outright heresy. Arizona agricultural interests denounced Martin and Young as traitors. Politicians and the press raked them over the coals, accusing Martin of being a paid agent of California. The pressure got so intense that Young eventually left the state.

Nevertheless, as CAP costs skyrocketed, Martin and Young's predictions took on the force of prophecy. By 1980, CAP water cost $30 an acre-foot more than groundwater even before the cost of building the distribution system was factored into the equation. When they were, the difference was astronomical. In the Maricopa-Stanfield irrigation district alone, Martin and political scientist Helen Ingram discovered that farmers would have to spend an additional $160 million to channel CAP water onto their crops. That would tack another $100 per acre-foot to the price of CAP water, which exceeded the cost of groundwater pumping ($39 an acre-foot in 1980) by $91. "In 1980," according to Marc Reisner, "about the only crop you could raise with water that cost $130 per acre-foot was marijuana."

The scenario grew even grimmer a decade later. By then the projected cost of the project had swollen to $3.6 billion. In 1991, CAP sold 745,000 acre-feet of water, most of it to farmers. The next year, demand dropped to 421,000 acre-feet, and many irrigation districts contemplated bankruptcy despite the interest-free loans that Congress had been granting them since 1984. By 1992, farmers were planting only 49 percent of the land eligible for CAP water, and since the government expected farmers to buy 60 to 80 percent of the CAP water during the first thirty years of delivery, their inability to afford it threatened the financial viability of the project itself. A study by agricultural economist Paul Wilson of the University of Arizona concluded that property taxes would increase and costs would rise to $150 to $200 an acre-foot if agricultural demand continued to plunge. True to form, in 1992 the Bureau of Reclamation and the Central Arizona Water Conservancy District began to talk about financially restructuring the project.

Former Congressman Sam Steiger had predicted as much seven years earlier. Blunt and colorful, Steiger had voted for the CAP in the 1960s, but after losing a Senate race and becoming a broker who helped cities buy other people's water, the conservative Steiger decided that a free market in water was not such a bad idea after all. With his usual flair, Steiger dissected the CAP for the gigantic federal subsidy that it was. In his words:

> They'll skin the cat twenty ways if they have to, but they're going to make the water affordable. Congress will go along, because it will be goddamned embarrassing for Congress to have authorized a multibillion-dollar water project when there's no demand for the water because no one can afford it. The CAP belongs to a holy order of inevitability. Will Congress bail out the big banks that pushed all those loans on Latin America, when the countries finally default? Of course. Will it make water affordable to Arizona farmers? Of course. The sensible thing would have been for the farmers to move. There are hundreds of thousands of acres of good farmland right along the Colorado River where you'd only have to build short diversion canals and maybe pump the water uphill a few hundred feet. But the farmers got established in the central part of the state because of the Salt River Project. The cities grew up in the middle of the farmland. The real estate interests, the money people—they're all in Phoenix and Scottsdale and Tucson. They didn't want to move. So we're going to move the river to them. At any cost. We think.

✳ ✳ ✳ Water and the Native Americans

One of the biggest ironies of CAP was the decline in agricultural demand. What began as a farmers' vision to make the desert bloom turned out to be more expensive than pumping fossil groundwater. That left Phoenix and Tucson as the biggest markets. By the time the water reached Tucson consumers in 1992, however, its different chemical composition corroded old pipes and poured rust-colored water into more than 1,000 homes. City and county officials began muttering darkly about suspending delivery until the water was fit to flow out of the tap.

An even greater irony threatened to reverse Arizona history by turning the water over to Native Americans. Anglo and Mexican settlers had diverted water in the rivers that had once irrigated Indian crops. They had also pumped groundwater from aquifers beneath Indian reservations, in clear violation of the Winters Doctrine, which evolved out of the Supreme Court decision in *Winters v. United States* (1908) that Indian reservations were entitled to enough water to meet present and future needs. The Winters Doctrine has been ignored more often than enforced, but it has never been revoked.

The Supreme Court decision in *Arizona v. California* (1963), which reaffirmed Arizona's allotment of Colorado River water under the Colorado Compact, was another legal victory for Native Americans. *Arizona v. California* supported *Winters* and extended the reserved-rights principle to other federal lands in addition to Indian reservations. It also demanded quantification of those rights. The result was a formula based on the amount of water necessary for all "practicably irrigable acres" of reservation land. Because of the decision, five tribes along the lower Colorado were granted nearly a million acre-feet of the Lower Basin's 7.5 million acre-feet allotment. Suddenly the fight over the interpretation of the compact and the apportionment of CAP water involved not only farmers, municipalities, and seven state governments but Indian reservations as well. Pork-barrel politics dominated the fight to win authorization for the CAP. Complex legal horse trading characterized the negotiations over Indian water rights that followed.

The horses that got traded the most were CAP allotments. There were two possible ways of providing Indians with the water they were entitled to under law. One was the strategy pursued by Senator Edward Kennedy, who introduced a bill in 1977 to force the federal government to fulfill its obligations under *Winters* and *Arizona v. California* to five reservations in central Arizona: the Ak-Chin, Salt River, Gila River, Fort McDowell, and Papago (now Tohono O'odham) reservations. The bill called for the delivery of 1.2 million acre-feet of water to the Native Americans, primarily by shutting down the Wellton-Mohawk Irrigation District east of Yuma and by purchasing farmland with water rights through eminent domain. When they learned of the bill, Arizona farmers and other non-Indian water users rose up in outrage and swatted it down. Taking water from Anglos and giving it back to Indians had never been popular in the state. The political principle behind the San Carlos Project in the 1920s was to find another source of water for the Gila Pimas, not to seize the water of the Anglo farmers upstream.

That same principle triumphed a year after the Kennedy bill's defeat, when Congress passed the Ak-Chin Act. Ak-Chin is a small (20,000-acre) reservation for Tohono O'odham living around the town of Maricopa. In the 1970s, the Bureau of Indian Affairs (BIA) and the Department of the Interior, acting in behalf of the Ak-Chin community, sued the federal government and the surrounding groundwater pumpers. Instead of plunging into a complex legal wrangle that would have dragged on for years, however, the BIA and the Ak-Chin O'odham agreed to a settlement negotiated by Congress. Congress promised to deliver 85,000 acre-feet of water per year to the Ak-Chin reservation, but that water would not be sucked away from farmers in the Stanfield-Maricopa irrigation district. On the contrary, it would come from the CAP, the pot of liquid gold at the end of Arizona's rainbow.

CAP water became a crucial part of the 1988 Salt River Pima–Maricopa Indian Community Water Rights Settlement Act as well. As part of the much larger stream adjudication of the Gila River system, the federal government was both defendant and plaintiff in a series of suits against water users in the Salt River Valley. As plaintiff, the government contended that the Salt River Reservation was entitled to 190,000 acre-feet annually to irrigate its 29,000 "practically irrigable" acres. The negotiated settlement gave the reservation 122,400 acre-feet—30,000 acre-feet from three nearby irrigation districts through the retirement of farmland, 40,000 acre-feet of stored surface water, 23,000 acre-feet of groundwater, 13,000 acre-feet from the CAP itself, and 20,000 acre-feet of stored Salt River Project water in exchange for an additional 22,000 acre-feet of CAP water purchased from farmers in the Wellton-Mohawk Irrigation District. Once again the CAP, along with groundwater and the shift from an agricultural to urban landscape, enabled the government to avert a possible water war between Indians and non-Indians.

The Salt River Act was a good example of an emerging growth industry in Arizona and the West. Rather than lengthy and expensive lawsuits, water users could turn to America's most cherished economic ideal—the free market—and simply transfer water rights among themselves. Farmers and Indian reservations could sell water to the relentlessly expanding cities, and everyone could swap water subsidized by the federal government. Politics would be reduced to supply and demand, resource use would be "rationalized," and everybody would prosper and be happy.

Implicit in this horse trading, however, was the recognition that the limits were being reached. CAP had danced in the heads of promoters and developers for more than fifty years before any water flowed down the big canal. Yet all but a few dreamers with visions of water flowing from the Columbia or the Yukon realized that CAP might be the last big water project on Arizona's horizon, so the lawyers, farmers, and city planners had to figure out new ways to allocate the existing water rather than finding new sources. The culmination of this realization came in 1980, when the Arizona legislature passed the Groundwater Management Act. At the time, Arizona water users were consuming about 4.8 million acre-feet of water a year, about twice the state's annual renewable supply. Rivers and streams provided 40 percent of that water, but 60 percent had to be pumped from hundreds of feet below the ground. Arizonans were mining Pleistocene aquifers, pumping 2.5 million acre-feet more water out of the ground than was recharged through rainfall and runoff. The federal government therefore threatened to hold up the delivery of Arizona's CAP allotment until the state curbed its profligate ways.

Bruce Babbitt was governor then. A lawyer with an intimate knowledge of water law, Babbitt brought together the representatives of the major interest groups—mines, farmers, cities, and water companies—and coaxed, cajoled, and threatened them through a series of marathon meetings that lasted for more than two years. The result was one of the most comprehensive groundwater codes in the nation. The Groundwater Management Act divided the state into four Active Management Areas (AMAs)—Phoenix, Tucson, Prescott, and Pinal—where 80 percent of the population resided and 70 percent of Arizona's water was being consumed. Within the three urban AMAs of Phoenix, Tucson, and Prescott, "safe-yield" (in which groundwater withdrawals did not exceed recharge) had to be achieved by the year 2025. Water users had to view groundwater as a renewable resource, not a deposit to be plundered.

There was more. Because agriculture swallowed about 89 percent of Arizona's water while producing less than 3 percent of the state's personal income, no new acreage could be irrigated within any of the four AMAs. Moreover, new urban development was banned unless there was an "assured water supply." Before a developer could obtain a license to sell subdivided land from the State Real Estate Department, he or she had to demonstrate that the proposed development had enough water to meet its needs for at least 100 years. What this meant in practice was more horse trading, more competition, and more scrambling for water among farmers, cities, Indian reservations, and mines.

＊   ＊   ＊   Other Voices

Not everyone saw water and the land it irrigated as commodities that could be reduced to dollar values. The Tohono O'odham, like their linguistic relatives the Gila Pimas (Akimel O'odham), had fought a long and desperate battle for water—one littered with broken promises and squandered opportunities by the federal government to protect and preserve their water supply.

By the 1980s about 15,000 members of the Tohono O'odham Nation occupied three reservations in southern Arizona. The largest encompasses 2,774,370 acres. South of the Gila and west of the Santa Cruz, it is a land of arroyos, not rivers. The other two—which are actually districts rather than autonomous jurisdictions of the Tohono O'odham Nation as a whole—straddle once-living rivers. The smallest lies along the Gila north of Gila Bend. The other surrounds Mission San Xavier del Bac. Located on the Santa Cruz River south of Tucson, the San Xavier Reservation is the wedge the O'odham used to force their way into the convoluted water wars of late-twentieth-century Arizona.

For the O'odham the wars began more than a hundred years ago. Back then, the Santa Cruz was what geographers call an intermittent stream. Much of its course was dry except during floods, but wherever geological formations forced underground aquifers to the surface, spring-fed streams trickled through dense *bosques* (forests) of mesquite, cottonwoods and willow. One of those springs was Punta de Agua near San Xavier. For 3,000 years, Archaic, Hohokam, and O'odham farmers had irrigated their crops from its flow.

During the late 1800s, however, non-Indian farmers tried to intensify agriculture along the Santa Cruz by digging large ditches upstream in the channel to intercept more of the water. The strategy underestimated the terrible force of desert floods. When heavy rains fell, runoff roared down the ditches instead of spreading across the floodplain, as it had in the past. The ditches downcut, headcut, and ate away at the loose alluvial soil. By 1912 the Punta de Agua ditch had turned into a massive arroyo two miles long, six to twenty feet deep, and sixty to one hundred feet wide. The Sam Hughes ditch below Tumamoc Hill in Tucson was even more devastating. Between 1889 and 1912 it carved an eighteen-mile-long arroyo, carrying away 150 acres of prime O'odham farmland in the process. The water table dropped and fields were left high and dry. A living river was transformed into a barren chute that carried runoff away rather than slowing it down and allowing it to percolate into the desert soil.

The changes meant the death of O'odham agriculture along the Santa Cruz. The federal government made a feeble attempt to keep the corpse alive for a few years, but the Bureau of Indian Affairs "quit the pumps" in 1917 because they were too expensive. Meanwhile, the city of Tucson was sinking more and more wells into the Upper Santa Cruz Basin aquifer beneath the reservation. By the early 1960s, discharge exceeded recharge by nearly 100,000 acre-feet a year. In the words of one reporter for the *Tucson Citizen* (February 6, 1980), the reservation's water table had been "sucked so low that new wells hit dry bedrock." Once again, the BIA had proved to be a miserable trustee of Indian water rights.

But the O'odham refused to dry up and blow away. In 1975 they pressured the federal government to file suit against the city of Tucson, the corporate farmers, and the copper mines plundering their aquifer. The legal foundation of the suit was the Winters Doctrine, which, as discussed above, proclaimed that Indians "have prior and paramount rights to all water resources which arise upon, border, traverse, or underlie a reservation." The BIA had never tried to enforce the Winters Doctrine until the O'odham forced their hand. "More than a century of government failure to preserve the Papagos' interests assured the tribe of a court victory," an editorial in Tucson's *Arizona Daily Star* of June 14, 1982, observed. "And victory for the Papagos could have meant the permanent shutdown of mines and farms and an end to city growth and development."

That appalling prospect—to developers and bureaucrats, at least—led to an endless series of negotiations to prevent an Armageddon over water in the Tucson Basin. The first stage in the process culminated in 1982 with the passage of the Southern Arizona Water Rights Settlement Act (SAWRSA). The act granted the Tohono O'odham 76,000 acre-feet of water a year from three sources: 10,000 from groundwater pumping; 28,200 from Tucson effluent; and 37,800 from the CAP. The water had to be "suitable for agricultural use" and could be utilized for any purpose, including leasing to non-Indians. But the act also provided funds to "subjugate" reservation land and deliver CAP water to irrigate it. One possibility was the creation of a 10,000-acre commercial farm called the San Xavier Development Project. Another was the transfer of 20,000 acres of nonreservation farmland in the Avra Valley that had been purchased and "retired" by Tucson so that the city could use its water. Both possibilities presented the Tohono O'odham with an uncertain agricultural future that depended on massive investments of capital and continued federal intervention.

Ten years after the act was signed by President Reagan, however, it still had not been implemented. On the contrary, debate raged among the Tohono O'odham about what to do with the water when it arrived. Tohono O'odham leaders in Sells opposed the Avra Valley option and advocated the San Xavier alternative. The San Xavier district council initially supported the farm, but then, in a sense, past generations of O'odham jumped into the controversy and changed the very vocabulary of the debate. In early October 1983 an enormous storm sent floodwaters roaring down the drainages of southern Arizona. At San Xavier those waters exposed a prehistoric burial site and triggered a chain of events that transformed the politics of reservation resource use across the country. In the decade that followed, the disposition of Native American human remains became a burning issue that dominated the lives of archaeologists, museum curators, and government bureaucrats, including those determining what to do with SAWRSA water.

The issue was "not simply a procedural one" about what to do with bones and ash, anthropologist Thomas McGuire observed. On the contrary, it challenged the dominant ideology of resource use by addressing "a fundamental cosmology of the past." In a debate dominated by the "vocabulary . . . of law and economics"—one framed in terms of cost-benefit analyses and environmental impact statements—many O'odham argued that the well-being of the dead had to be assured as well. By 1989 the San Xavier district council had changed its mind about a commercial farm on reservation land. Juliann Ramon, a member of the council, said that if her ancestors were disturbed, her family would be "cursed with pain and disease until the seventh generation." Reservation land was living land that should not be scraped and "subjugated." The past was not to be sacrificed to either the present or the future.

For the Tohono O'odham and all Arizonans, Indian and non-Indian alike, the future remains clouded by water: how to get it back and what to do with it when it comes. More and more, however, the O'odham and other Native Americans are calling for water in their own cultural idiom and not just in the language of lawyers, economists, and hydrologists. The community of the living and the dead has to be preserved. That means preserving the land and the water that gives it life.

Environmentalists are also trying to transform the terms of the debate, arguing that native plants and animals have to be preserved as well. Their rallying cry is biodiversity, and many argue that each species, no matter how small or seemingly insignificant, has a right to survive. Whether it is bald eagles along the Verde or red squirrels on Mount Graham, nonhuman organisms are invoked to halt dams, university telescopes, and other "intrusions" of a relentlessly expanding state. More and more people are entering the negotiation for Arizona—its land, its water, all that lies on and below its ground—with more and more points of view. Not all of the viewpoints fit an economist's equation. There are the Charles Keatings, who was not "of" Phoenix even though he was headquartered there. And then there is Danny Lopez, a Tohono O'odham who spent most of his life off the reservation, first in a Catholic boarding school and then in Tucson, where he worked in a copper mine south of the city.

Lopez returned to the reservation as a middle-aged man to teach O'odham children the language and dances of "The People." One day, he allowed his friend, anthropologist Bernard Fontana, to accompany him to the village of Gu Oidak (Big Fields) on that ongoing journey home.

> Growing near the house where his parents live in Gu Oidak is a mesquite tree. He pointed to a spot on the ground beneath the tree. "That," he said, "is

where I was born." I marvelled. How many of us, I thought to myself, can point to a place on the earth and say with honesty it marks the location where we first emerge into sunlight or starlight? Here was where Danny first breathed the desert air; this is where he uttered his first cries as a human being. Not twenty miles away "somewhere," not even a mile away nor ten feet to the left or right. But here. On this very spot!

Emergence for most of us is a hospital happening, an event surrounded by medical paraphernalia and the studied indifference of our medical sub-culture. Hospitals, like their personnel, come and go. Small wonder that we lack a sense of place, of roots. We are born in Rochester or Phoenix or Denver or New Orleans. But Danny was not born in Gu Oidak. He was born *there,* under that mesquite tree on that piece of ground. Roots and a sense of place? How could it be otherwise?

17

The Political Ecology
* * of a Desert State

In 1976, Arizona business leaders commissioned Herman Kahn's Hudson Institute to peer into its crystal ball and divine Arizona's future. The institute's report, entitled *Arizona Tomorrow,* called Arizona "the development prototype for post-industrial society." During the nineteenth century, it observed, many people perceived Arizona as a desert wasteland on the route to California, hot, parched, and desolate. But in the second half of the twentieth century, the state had managed to redefine "the very term *desert.*" Desert, Arizona style, now meant "an appealing landscape, an attractive place to live, and a new kind of adult playground." According to *Arizona Tomorrow,* "Desert living with air conditioning, water fountains, swimming pools—getting back to nature with a motorized houseboat on Lake Powell (itself a man-made lake), and going for an ocean swim in a man-made ocean are all contemporary examples of the marriage between life-style and technology."

It was a futuristic vision of paradise in an arid land, with technology the handmaiden of lifestyle, and the old extractive order banished by the economic miracle of the Great Transition. Rust Belt industrialism had given way to Sunbelt postindustrialism. There were no undocumented Mexican workers living in citrus groves and drinking from irrigation canals, no striking copper miners forced to take minimum-wage jobs, no unemployed Indians hauling uranium-contaminated water in the back of their old pickup trucks. Instead, everyone was a young, upwardly mobile urban professional with plenty of leisure time to pursue Arizona's beguiling pleasures. Water images permeated this Xanadu. Redefining the desert meant pouring massive amounts of water onto it. A water-rich desert was an oxymoron futurists and their developer patrons promoted without a trace of irony.

Whether the water was used for the old extractive purposes or for creating this bright, new playworld, the vision assumed an endless flow. It also presupposed plenty of cheap energy to run the air-conditioners, fill the swimming pools, power the houseboats, and keep the man-made waves cresting. Water and energy were just two sides of the same coin—the currency that bankrolled the postwar boom and made the down payment on the postindustrial future. One without the other was inconceivable and unusable. Gravity caused runoff from the Rockies to surge down the Colorado River and rainfall from thousands of years of desert storms to percolate through the alluvium to create underground aquifers. Whether with pumps, canals, or dams, Arizona history has been one long reversal of gravity. In the modern West, water flows uphill toward money. Cheap energy makes that astonishing feat of legerdemain possible.

It also gives us the illusion that we have freed ourselves from most environmental constraints. We are living at a time when the relationships between that fundamental cultural dichotomy—culture and nature—are increasingly ambiguous. For most of human history, nature was a collection of forces to be propitiated and feared. Two centuries ago, however, the relationship began to change as Western industrial civilization harnessed steam, electricity, fossil fuels, and vaccines. People boasted about triumphing over nature as distances shrank and the terrifying threats of flood, drought, and pestilence were reduced. Today, we even contemplate the "end of nature," confident of our ability to control natural forces and convert them into commodities. We debate "multiple use" and consciously set aside refuges where nature can be protected from our onslaught. Our understanding of nature—and our ability to transform it—always changes. In that sense, nature is historical and socially constructed, a reflection of our scientific knowledge, technology, and needs. In the words of *Arizona Tomorrow*, we have transformed the desert into an "adult playground," vanquishing heat, aridity, and all the other ancient constraints on endless growth.

Nevertheless, nature has a way of intruding into our consciousness and imprinting itself on us in novel and unexpected ways. As historian William Cronon notes in *Nature's Metropolis,* his history of Chicago and the West, "the boundary between human and nonhuman, natural and unnatural, is profoundly problematic." Cronon goes on to say, "Just as our own lives continue to be embedded in a web of *natural* relationships, nothing in nature remains untouched by the web of *human* relationships that constitutes our common history." Consciously and unconsciously, people have shaped vegetation communities, animal communities, and disease environments from prehistoric times to the present. Now we may even be shaping global climatic patterns. Sometimes those changes benefit human beings; at other times they unleash new plagues. Our social constructions are always partial and incomplete. In the 1920s, when they were forging the Colorado River Compact, engineers and politicians concocted a river that flowed an average of 16.4 million acre-feet a year. The river spent the next seventy years deconstructing that hydrological phantasm. The social construction of nature does not necessarily imply its social control.

In this book I have examined the ways in which the social and the natural have interacted in Arizona over the past 12,000 years. In particular, I have stressed the importance of water and how attempts to control it have shaped the political ecology of human societies in the state. Until the late nineteenth century, Indian and Hispanic farmers engaged in a creative give-and-take with Arizona rivers but never learned to tame them. The Hohokam may have constructed the largest canal systems in precolumbian North America, but they, like the farmers of the Salt River Valley in the 1890s, were vulnerable to both drought and floods.

Beginning in the late nineteenth century, however, farmers and speculators strove to domesticate rivers across Arizona and the Arid West. The development of those irrigation projects, almost without exception, followed an identical trajectory. First came costly and convoluted attempts to finance and construct the projects with private capital. Developers formed canal companies and searched for investors across the United States and Europe. Promotional literature lured thousands of farmers to hallucinatory visions like the Imperial Valley of southern California. If private capital could build transcontinental railroads and open great gold, silver, and copper mines, it could reclaim the Great American Desert.

But nature slapped those dreams down one by one. Between 1890 and 1905 in the Salt River Valley, floods alternated with droughts, ruining farmers and canal companies alike. Anywhere from 24 to 33 percent of the acreage in cultivation was abandoned. Banks failed and merchants went broke. Individuals like Carl

Hayden acquired their near-mystical belief in the power of big water projects while watching their parents struggle to survive those hard times. Big business had the capital and expertise to work the mines, stock the ranges, and plant the cotton, but it could not afford the massive long-term investment to build the waterworks. That enterprise required the federal government, which could spread the costs across millions of taxpayers. Without the federal government, there would have been no Salt River Project, no cotton boom, and no urban explosion. The alliance between big business and the federal government is the foundation of Arizona's economy, the very essence of its political ecology.

But the character of this shifting axis between business and government is easy to misunderstand. The axis revolves around water, and in his provocative book *Rivers of Empire: Water, Aridity, and the Growth of the American West*, historian Donald Worster resurrects Asian scholar Karl Wittfogel's hydraulic hypothesis to explain it. Wittfogel, a German Marxist who became a rabid anticommunist, argued that aridity was the determining factor in the rise of ancient states in China, Egypt, and Mesopotamia. As more and more people congregated along rivers in desert areas, the need to control floods and provide irrigation water led to the creation of immense water-control systems run by bureaucratic elites. It was a simple and powerful equation: the greater the size of the hydraulic system, the more powerful the elite. Oriental despotism rested upon the magnitude of its dams and canals.

Worster argues that the same can be said about the modern West. In his words,

> This American West can best be described as a modern *hydraulic society,* which is to say, a social order based on the intensive, large-scale manipulation of water and its products in an arid setting. That order is not at all what Thoreau had in mind for the region. What he desired was a society of free association, of self-defining and self-managing individuals and communities, more or less equal to one another in power and authority. The hydraulic society of the West, in contrast, is increasingly a coercive, monolithic, and hierarchical system, ruled by a power elite based on the ownership of capital and expertise.

It is a seductive argument, particularly for those who think in terms of conspiracies and monoliths. It also shifts responsibility for what has happened in the West from ordinary people to the bureaucrats and their powerful patrons—the agribusinessmen, ranchers, mining executives, and utility companies. According to Worster, Arizona and the West could have been a Jeffersonian democracy of small ranchers and farmers living in harmony with the land.

Instead, it is a region of dammed rivers and polluting power plants, of water-guzzling corporate farms and gigantic draglines that scrape away Navajo coal. Ordinary citizens are not considered to be responsible for the degradation of the environment or the betrayal of democratic ideals. On the contrary, such degradation is the work of dark forces, of interlocking directorates, of a power elite. In a perversely fatalistic way, Worster's notion is a comfortable one because it absolves most of us of guilt and ignores the messy realities of power.

Other scholars, such as historian Donald Pisani, sharply criticize Worster's model, arguing that it grossly overstates the amount of control exercised by its two-headed elite. Pisani counters by citing an earlier study by political scientist Arthur Maass and economist Raymond Anderson, who examined irrigation projects in Spain and the American West. According to Maass and Anderson, "The most powerful conclusion that emerges from the case studies is the extent to which water users have controlled their own destinies as farmers, the extent to which the farmers of each community, acting collectively, have determined both the procedures for distributing a limited water supply and the resolution of conflicts with other groups over the development of additional supplies. . . . In this realm of public activity—and one wonders in how many others—formal centralization of authority, where it has occurred, has not meant substantial loss of local control *de facto*." A case in point is the Salt River Project, the Reclamation Service's first major experiment of the twentieth century. The federal government built it, but the Salt River Valley Water Users Association bought it back. The farmers who belonged to the association, not federal bureaucrats, ran the organization within seven years of the completion of Roosevelt Dam.

The critique of Worster's monolithic and hierarchical hydraulic society needs to be broadened beyond the institutions directly involved in water projects. Perhaps a better metaphor for the politics of resource control in Arizona would be that of a feudal society of competing warlords held together by a weak king. Copper companies, railroads, ranchers, farmers, loggers, utility companies, real estate developers, and municipal governments all need water to make their enterprises thrive. At one time or another, most of them have turned to the federal government to supply that water, along with many of the other resources they need. But different interest groups have different needs. During the early 1900s the Salt River Valley Water Users Association supported the abolition of grazing within the forest reserves in order to protect its watershed on the Mogollon Rim. Farmers and ranchers were enemies, not allies, in that struggle. Business, big or otherwise, is not always a monolithic force.

Neither is the federal government. Different interest groups have cultivated, manipulated, or co-opted different agencies of the government to pursue their goals. In the process, the agencies have turned against one another to defend their constituents and to grab a greater share of the federal budget. The Corps of Engineers fought the Bureau of Reclamation for the right to build more and more dams. The Bureau of Land Management does not always have the same land-use priorities as the Forest Service, not to mention the Department of Defense. Different agencies of the federal government sue one another over Indian water rights. Finally, there are bitter divisions within agencies themselves. Which of its multiple uses are privileged within the Forest Service— logging, grazing, recreation, wildlife? The answer varies from one administration to the next.

But even the feudal warlord model implies too much concentrated authority and too many conspiracies. In the final analysis, Arizona has been exploited because of consumer demand. People want housing and automobiles, which require lumber and copper. We also want beef, cotton, and citrus, and if we are going to continue to live in desert cities while denying the desert, we need cheap water and cheap energy to keep our lawns green and our buildings cool. The dead rivers and sprawling metropolises are not the result of the conspiracies of a power elite but are rather the product of the individual actions of a monstrous democratic economy of ordinary people who vote with their checkbooks and their feet, cars, and recreational vehicles. As long as people continue to move into Arizona faster than they move out, and as long as they demand inexpensive water and energy once they settle here, utility companies will manipulate government agencies and circumvent existing water rights to provide them. There will be endless negotiations and Byzantine compromises, but no one is going to turn off the tap or pull the plug.

One example is Arizona's Groundwater Management Act. After it was passed in 1980, opponents quickly challenged its constitutionality, but the act was upheld by the Arizona Supreme Court, the United States District Court for Arizona, and the United States Court of Appeals for the Ninth Circuit. In the words of federal district judge Carl Muecke, "Water users have long been on notice that the state would at some time have to intervene to regulate prospective uses of a dwindling resource in the face of increased use. The code does so in a structured, principled manner with the state's general welfare as its talisman."

A decade after the law was passed, however, the vultures were circling, waiting for it to die. The most vocal opponents were developers, who argued that the groundwater code violated that most sacrosanct of Arizona traditions: unrestricted growth. They even challenged the hydrological foundation of the code by citing a report from the state auditor general's office. According to the report, "There is enough water for several hundred years for the Phoenix [area] and for 700 years for Tucson." It went on to say, "The safe-yield goal should be reviewed to determine if it is actually needed, needed by 2025 or later, or if slow depletion of the aquifer is acceptable."

It was yet another example of the water game, that high-stakes contest that pitted the promoters of endless growth against conservationists and, ultimately, the forces of nature. How much water really flowed down the Colorado? How big were the aquifers beneath Phoenix and Tucson, and what was the quality of the water locked within that permeable gravel and sand? The numbers varied depending on the experts consulted and the ends that needed justification. Further, numbers could be inflated, deflated, or denied. This was not a dispassionate exercise in hydrology; billions of dollars rode on the outcome.

What about the role of nature in this struggle? Did the control of Western rivers pose an enormous initial challenge that was overcome once and for all by massive dams and regional water compacts? Or does nature keep intruding upon the ongoing negotiation of water control? One complication among many is the problem of determining the appropriate time frame. In Arizona before the completion of the Salt River Project and the Central Arizona Project, natural events such as floods and droughts had an immediate effect on farmers, ranchers, and even city dwellers. In modern Arizona, on the other hand, technological developments and government subsidies have buffered people against floods, droughts, and other natural disasters. We have subdued the original natural landscape and substituted a cultural landscape of waterworks, transportation networks, capital flows, energy exchanges, and commodity production. That substitution has been so complete that many of us no longer feel that nature is a significant factor in the political and economic development of Arizona or the rest of the West.

Our perception of human omnipotence may be an illusion, or at least an exaggeration. Modern society in the Arid West depends on perpetual maintenance and investment—investment that continually rises even as the costs of that investment are spread among more and more people through taxes and subsidies. Dams must be constructed and repaired, but what happens when they silt up? Canals must be extended for hundreds of miles, but what happens when farmers cannot afford the water they convey? One of the ironies of Arizona history, in fact, is how quickly agrarian dreams have faded, only to be replaced by urban dreams. The Central Arizona Project—that pipe dream of Arizona farmers since the 1920s—now serves Tucson and Phoenix, the latter of which has captured the Salt River Project as well.

In the final analysis, then, modern Arizona society is a fragile and volatile creation—one that can never renew itself. Without ceaseless inputs of energy

and capital from outside the region, it will wither and die. And the more elaborate that society becomes, the more dependent it is on regional, national, and
global forces. With the passage of the North American Free Trade Agreement
(NAFTA) in 1993, Arizona greatly expanded its role as a gateway between Latin
America and the United States. Border cities in Arizona and Sonora will continue to swell, requiring massive investments in transportation systems and
public utilities. Trade with Mexico and South America will increase, and even
more produce, livestock, and manufactured goods will flow back and forth
across the border along Arizona's freeways and railroad tracks. Millions of people will make their way to the border and beyond as Latin America's populations
continue to outpace its capacity to support them. Latin America's problems and
opportunities will become Arizona's problems and opportunities. As people
and industries continue to flee southern California, Arizona will become a
major player on the Pacific Rim as well. Competition for water and energy will
skyrocket.

The ultimate loser in this competition will be Arizona agriculture, which
consumes 85 to 90 percent of the state's water. As Phoenix becomes a new Los
Angeles of five to seven million people, as Tucson turns into a new Phoenix of
one to two million people, and as the border cities of Nogales, Arizona, and
Nogales, Sonora, transform themselves into a new El Paso and a new Juárez,
farmers will face intense pressure to sell their water rights to these urban giants.
Urban growth, in turn, will generate even greater demand for bedroom communities and vacation homes outside the cities. Rising taxes and rising land prices
will tempt more ranchers to sell their private land to subdividers, especially if
urban environmentalists continue to clamor for an end to grazing on public
lands. Fewer and fewer people will make a living directly off the land. For those
of us who love the Other Arizona, this urban future looks grim. For others,
however, it represents jobs, upward mobility, or a chance to make even greater
profits off water, energy, land, and construction.

But how long the cities can continue to grow remains unclear. In the short
run, there will be plenty of water as long as it can be wrested away from the
farmers. In the process, however, much of what attracted people to Arizona will
be destroyed. The Mazatzals and other mountain ranges will still stand, but
there will be more hiking clubs, more Boy Scout troops, less of that piercingly
beautiful sense of wilderness and isolation many of us crave. National forests
will become gigantic city parks like Yosemite, Yellowstone, and the South Rim
of the Grand Canyon.

Will nature rebel? Will the Colorado burst its dams? Will the cost of main-
taining our enormous water and energy networks become prohibitive? Or will

we ourselves rebel for spiritual and aesthetic reasons and put a brake on growth? No one really knows. But if we want to create a society in Arizona that is more than a series of booms and busts, we need to make the fit between nature and culture more like a membrane and less like a life support system. There is too much at stake in this wild, dry land to do otherwise.

Farm workers from Oklahoma, Texas, and Arkansas in the cotton fields north of Palo Verde in central Maricopa County in 1932. (Courtesy of the Arizona Historical Society)

REFERENCE MATERIAL

Bibliographic Essay

✱   ✱   ✱ Introduction

The best way to place Arizona in historical and geographical perspective is to read David Weber's *The Spanish Frontier in North America* (New Haven: Yale University Press, 1992) and his *The Mexican Frontier, 1821–1846: The American Southwest Under Mexico* (Albuquerque: University of New Mexico Press, 1982), followed by Edward Spicer's *Cycles of Conquest: The Impact of Spain, Mexico, and the United States on the Indians of the Southwest, 1533–1960* (Tucson: University of Arizona Press, 1962) and Richard White's *It's Your Misfortune and None of My Own: A History of the American West* (Norman: University of Oklahoma Press, 1991). Lawrence Clark Powell's *Arizona: A Bicentennial History* (New York: W. W. Norton, 1976; reprint, Albuquerque: University of New Mexico Press, 1990) is a short but elegant introduction to the state. Thomas Farish's eight-volume *History of Arizona* (San Francisco: Filmer Brothers Electrotype Company, 1915–18) contains excerpts from many documents and pioneer reminiscences concerning Arizona from the Spanish colonial period to the early twentieth century. Howard Lamar's *The Far Southwest, 1846–1912: A Territorial History* (New York: W. W. Norton, 1970) and Jay Wagoner's *Early Arizona: Prehistory to Civil War* (Tucson: University of Arizona Press, 1975) and *Arizona Territory, 1863–1912: A Political History* (Tucson: University of Arizona Press, 1970) remain critical sources for Arizona prior to statehood. C. L. Sonnichsen's *Tucson: The Life and Times of an American City* (Norman: University of Oklahoma Press, 1982) and Bradford Luckingham's *Phoenix: The History of a Southwestern Metropolis* (Tucson: University of Arizona Press, 1989) are the best histories of Arizona's two largest cities. Henry P. Walker and Don Bufkin's *Historical Atlas of Arizona* (Norman: University of Oklahoma Press, 1979) and Melvin Hecht and Richard Reeves's *The Arizona Atlas* (Tucson: University of Arizona, Office of Arid Lands Studies, 1981) are two indispensable cartographic guides.

Arizona: The Land and the People, edited by Tom Miller (Tucson: University of Arizona Press, 1986), provides a good introduction to the state's physiographic provinces and major ethnic groups. Gregory McNamee's *Named in Stone and Sky: An Arizona Anthology* (Tucson: University of Arizona Press, 1993) excerpts everything from Native American myths to Jack Kerouac's *On the Road* to capture how different writers have felt about the state. James Griffith's *Beliefs and Holy Places: A Spiritual Geography of the Pimería Alta* discusses the O'odham sense of place in the Sonoran Desert. Keith Basso's *Western Apache Language and Culture: Essays in Linguistic Anthropology* (Tucson: University of Arizona Press, 1990) contains a superb essay entitled "'Stalking with Stories': Names, Places, and Moral Narratives Among the Western Apache," which does the same for the Apaches. Charles Bowden dissects the pathologies of a society with no sense of place in *Blue Desert* (Tucson: University of Arizona Press, 1986).

Immanuel Wallerstein's *The Modern World-System I: Capitalist Agriculture and the Origins of the European World-Economy in the Sixteenth Century* (New York: Academic Press, 1974) presents his seminal concept of the world-system. Eric Wolf's *Europe and the People Without History* (Berkeley: University of California Press, 1982) critiques that concept while elaborating on the impact of Europe on Asia, Africa, and the Americas. Thomas Hall's *Social Change in the Southwest, 1350–1880* (Lawrence: University Press of Kansas, 1989) explores the Southwest's incorporation into the modern world-system in great depth.

＊　＊　＊　I. The Native Americans

Southwestern archaeology is in a state of dynamic and creative flux. As new techniques are developed and new evidence is uncovered—much of it the result of federally mandated "contract archaeology"—old conventions crumble. When dealing with potsherds, pollen samples, fragments of bone and stone tools, the interpretations of informed scholars often vary dramatically.

Nonetheless, there are a few places to start. Both Paul Martin and Fred Plog's *The Archaeology of Arizona* (Garden City, N.Y.: Doubleday, 1973) and Linda Cordell's more recent *Prehistory of the Southwest* (San Diego: Academic Press, 1984) provide overviews of Arizona prehistory, though they are written for specialists rather than the general public. A more accessible volume is Robert and Florence Lister's beautifully illustrated *Those Who Came Before: Southwestern Archeology in the National Park System* (Tucson: University of Arizona Press, 1983). Another good introduction is *Emil W. Haury's Prehistory of the American Southwest,* edited by J. Jefferson Reid and David Doyel (Tucson: University of Arizona Press, 1986), which contains a collection of Haury's essays, including his classic "Artifacts with Mammoth Remains, Naco, Arizona: Discovery of the Naco Mammoth and the Associated Projectile Points" (pp. 78–98) and "The Lehner Mammoth Site, Southeastern Arizona," which Haury co-authored with E. B. Sayles and William Wasley (pp. 99–145). Randall McGuire and Michael Schiffer's *Hohokam and Patayan: Prehistory of Southwestern Arizona* (San Diego: Academic Press, 1982) synthesizes what archaeologists know about the prehistory of the driest part of the Sonoran Desert. The book includes appendixes by Julian Hayden ("Ground Figures of the Sierra Pinacate, Sonora, Mexico") and by Elaine Maryse Solari and Boma Johnson ("Intaglios: A Synthesis of Known Information and Recommendations for Management"). Hayden's own "Pre-Altithermal Archaeology in the Sierra Pinacate, Sonora, Mexico" (*American Antiquity* 41 [1976]: 274–89) advances his controversial theories about the antiquity of humans in the Sonoran Desert.

Quaternary Extinctions: A Prehistoric Revolution, edited by Paul Martin and Richard Klein (Tucson: University of Arizona Press, 1984) presents the arguments for and against Martin's "Pleistocene overkill" hypothesis. Technical discussions of changing climate and vegetation from the late Pleistocene to the present (late Holocene), based largely on the analysis of packrat middens are found in Thomas Van Devender and W. G. Spaulding's "Development of Vegetation and Climate in the Southwestern United States" (*Science* 204 [4394] [1979]: 701–10) and Van Devender's "Holocene Vegetation and Climate in the Puerto Blanco Mountains, Southwestern Arizona" (*Quaternary Research* 27 [1987]: 51–72).

Two recent works that focus on the introduction of agriculture in the Southwest are Wirt Wills's *Early Prehistoric Agriculture in the American Southwest* (Santa Fe: School of American Research Press, 1988) and R. G. Matson's *The Origins of Southwestern Agriculture* (Tucson: University of Arizona Press, 1991). Bruce Huckell's unpublished "Agriculture and Late Archaic Settlements in the River Valleys of Southeastern Arizona," presented at the 1987 Hohokam Symposium, is a clear and comprehensive overview of the groundbreaking archaeological research conducted there. A clear summary of radiocarbon dating with an accelerator mass spectrometer, and other dating techniques applied to archaeological material, can be found in David Hurst Thomas's *Archaeology* (Fort Worth: Holt, Rinehart and Winston, 1989).

Good but technical discussions of the Western Anasazi include "The Colorado Plateaus: Cultural Dynamics and Paleoenvironment," by Robert Euler et al. (*Science* 205 [4411] [1979]: 1089–1101), "Human Behavior, Demography, and Paleoenvironment on the Colorado Plateaus," by Jeffrey Dean et al. (*American Antiquity* 50 [1985]: 537–54), and George Gumerman and Jeffrey Dean's "Prehistoric Cooperation and Competition in the Western Anasazi Area" in *Dynamics of Southwest Prehistory*, edited by Linda Cordell and George Gumerman, 99–148 (Washington, D.C.: Smithsonian Institution Press, 1989). *Chronological Analysis of Tsegi Phase Sites in Northeastern Arizona* (Tucson: University of Arizona, 1969) is Jeff Dean's classic dendrochronological study of Betatakin and other sites in Tsegi Canyon.

The archaeological literature on Chaco Canyon is enormous, but some recent summaries include W. James Judge's "Chaco Canyon–San Juan Basin" in Cordell and Gumerman, *Dynamics of Southwest Prehistory*; Patricia Crown and W. James Judge's *Chaco & Hohokam: Prehistoric Regional Systems in the American Southwest* (Santa Fe: School of American Research Press, 1991); and R. Gwinn Vivian's *The Chacoan Prehistory of the San Juan Basin* (San Diego: Academic Press, 1990). Julio Betancourt and Thomas Van Devender document the deforestation of Chaco Canyon through the analysis of packrat middens in "Holocene Vegetation in Chaco Canyon, New Mexico" (*Science* 214 [1981]: 656–58).

During the last twenty years, largely because of archaeological contract research, the amount of literature on the Hohokam has skyrocketed. Emil Haury's *The Hohokam: Desert Farmers and Craftsmen* (Tucson: University of Arizona Press, 1976) remains a good introduction, but Haury's chronology and many of his observations about the Hohokam have been challenged. *Exploring the Hohokam: Prehistoric Desert Peoples of the American Southwest,* edited by George Gumerman (Albuquerque: University of New Mexico Press, 1991), and Crown and Judge's *Chaco and Hohokam* summarize much of the more recent scholarship, as does Paul Fish's "The Hohokam: 1,000 Years of Prehistory in the Sonoran Desert," in Cordell and Gumerman's *Dynamics of Southwest Prehistory*. David Wilcox's "The Mesoamerican Ballgame in the American Southwest" in *The Mesoamerican Ballgame*, edited by Vernon Scarborough and David Wilcox, 101–25 (Tucson: University of Arizona Press, 1991), analyzes the distribution and possible functions of ballcourts among the Hohokam. David Gregory's "Form and Variation in Hohokam Settlement Patterns," in Crown and Judge's *Chaco and Hohokam,* discusses the spread of platform mounds. *The Marana Community in the Hohokam World,* edited by Suzanne Fish, Paul Fish, and John Madsen (Tucson: University of Arizona Press, 1992), describes the cultivation of agave by a Hohokam community in the northern Tucson Basin.

Steven LeBlanc's "Cultural Dynamics in the Southern Mogollon Area," in Cordell and Gumerman's *Dynamics of Southwest Prehistory,* and his essay "Development of Archaeological Thought on the Mimbres Mogollon," in *Emil W. Haury's Prehistory of the American Southwest,* provide overviews of the Mogollon through time. Roger Anyon and Steven LeBlanc's *The Galaz Ruin: A Mimbres Valley in Southwestern New Mexico* (Albuquerque: University of New Mexico Press, 1984) is the most detailed monograph on a Southern Mogollon site, while Emil Haury's *Mogollon Culture in the Forestdale Valley* (Tucson: University of Arizona Press, 1985) and Paul S. Martin's "The SU Site: Excavations at a Mogollon Village, Western New Mexico" (Field Museum of Natural History Anthropological Series, 32 (1) [1939] and 32 (2) [1943], Chicago) describe Northern Mogollon sites in Arizona and New Mexico. Le Blanc's *The Mimbres People: Ancient Painters of the Southwest* (London: Thames and Hudson, 1983) and John Brody's *Mimbres Painted Pottery* (Albuquerque: University of New Mexico Press, 1977) focus on the Classic Mimbres florescence.

Key volumes debating the connections between Mesoamerica and the Southwest include *Across the Chichimec Sea: Papers in Honor of J. Charles Kelley,* edited by Carroll Riley and Basil Hendrick (Carbondale: Southern Illinois University Press, 1978), and *Ripples in the Chichimec Sea,* edited by Frances Mathien and Randall McGuire (Carbondale: Southern Illinois University Press, 1986). One of the best introductions to the late prehistoric and protohistoric periods is *Perspectives on Southwestern Prehistory,* edited by Paul Minnis and Charles Redman (Boulder, Colo.: Westview Press, 1990). Steadman Upham's *Polities and Power: An Economic and Political History of the Western Pueblos* (New York: Academic Press, 1984) presents his interpretations concerning the social complexity of the Anasazi. For contrasting views, see J. Jefferson Reid's "A Grasshopper Perspective on the Mogollon of the Arizona Mountains" in Cordell and Gumerman's *Dynamics of Southwest Prehistory,* and Reid and Stephanie Whittlesey's "The Complicated and the Complex: Observations on the Archaeological Record of Large Pueblos," in Minnis and Redman, *Perspectives on Southwestern Prehistory.* E. Charles Adams's *The Origin and Development of the Pueblo Katsina Cult* (Tucson: University of Arizona Press, 1991) discusses when, where, and why the katsina "cult" spread across the Pueblo world of Arizona and New Mexico.

✳ ✳ 2. The Arrival of the Europeans

Anthropologist Frank Russell, who lived among the Akimel O'odham (Gila Pimas) in 1901 and 1902, noted that the Pimas possessed five surviving calendar sticks. In his ethnography *The Pima Indians* (Tucson: University of Arizona Press, 1975), Russell states, "Dots or shallow circular pits and short notches are the most common symbols on the sticks. These have no distinctive meaning, and are used for recording a great variety of events. The human figure is freely used, and may signify that a man killed Apaches or was killed by them, that he was bitten by a rattlesnake, killed by lightning, or, in short, any event relating to a man in any manner may be denoted by this symbol. The date of building railways was recorded by an ideogram, representing rails and ties."

Historian Alfred Crosby's *The Columbian Exchange: Biological and Cultural Consequences of 1492* (Westport: Greenwood Press, 1972) discusses how the exchange of plants, animals, and diseases affected people on both sides of the Atlantic. His *Ecological Imperialism: The Biological Expansion of Europe, 900–1900* (Cambridge: Cambridge University Press, 1986) explores some of the biological and ecological reasons why Europeans achieved dominion over most of the temperate regions of the world. Paul Ezell's *The Hispanic Acculturation of the Gila River Pimas* (Menasha, Wis.: American Anthropological Association, 1961) and Thomas Sheridan's "Kino's Unforeseen Legacy: The Material Consequences of Missionization Among the Northern Piman Indians of Arizona and Sonora" (*The Smoke Signal* [Tucson Corral of Westerners] nos. 49 and 50 [1988]) examine the impact of the Columbian Exchange on the O'odham.

Both Henry Dobyns (*From Fire to Flood: Historic Human Destruction of Sonoran Desert Riverine Oases* [Socorro, N.M.: Ballena Press, 1981]) and Daniel Reff (*Disease, Depopulation, and Culture Change in Northwestern New Spain, 1518–1764* [Salt Lake City: University of Utah Press, 1991]) argue that epidemics of Old World diseases devastated the Indians of the Greater Southwest during the sixteenth century. Most archaeologists, on the other hand, believe that civilizations like the Hohokam collapsed before 1492. For a critique of the disease hypothesis, see David Doyel's "The Transition to History in Northern Pimería Alta" (pp. 139–58) and Randall McGuire and María Elisa Villalpando's "Prehistory and the Making of History in Sonora," in *Columbian Consequences*, vol. 1: *Archaeological and Historical Perspectives on the Spanish Borderlands West*, edited by David Hurst Thomas, 159–77 (Washington: Smithsonian Institution Press, 1989). Jeffrey Dean's "Thoughts on Hohokam Chronology" in Gumerman's *Exploring the Hohokam* surveys the problems in dating Hohokam remains.

The debate over the Hohokam-Pima continuum has sputtered along for decades. For various points of view, see Paul Ezell's "Is There a Hohokam-Pima Cultural Continuum?" (*American Antiquity* 29 [1963]: 61–66); Julian Hayden's "Of Hohokam Origins and Other Matters" (*American Antiquity* 35 [1970]: 87–93);

Emil Haury's *The Hohokam*; Charles DiPeso's "Prehistory: O'otam" (*Handbook of North American Indians,* vol. 9: *Southwest* [1979]); David Wilcox's "The Tepiman Connection: A Model of Mesoamerican-Southwestern Interaction," in Mathien and McGuire.

David Weber's *The Spanish Frontier in North America* (New Haven, Conn.: Yale University Press, 1992) summarizes early exploration by the Spaniards and the controversies over their routes. Daniel Reff provides a highly speculative reconstruction of Fray Marcos de Niza's journey to Cíbola in "Anthropological Analysis of Exploration Texts: Cultural Discourse and the Ethnological Import of Fray Marcos de Niza's Journey to Cibola" (*American Anthropologist* 93 [1991]: 636–49). Herbert Eugene Bolton's classic *Coronado: Knight of Pueblos and Plains* (Albuquerque: University of New Mexico Press, 1949) remains the best summary of the Coronado expedition. George Hammond and Agapito Rey's *Narratives of the Coronado Expedition, 1540–1542* (Albuquerque: University of New Mexico Press, 1940) contains English translations of the expedition chronicles. Hammond and Rey also published an English translation of Farfán's account in their *Don Juan de Oñate: Colonizer of New Mexico, 1598–1628* (Albuquerque: University of New Mexico Press, 1953).

David Wilcox's "The Entry of Athapaskans into the American Southwest: The Problem Today," in *The Protohistoric Period in the North American Southwest, AD 1540–1700,* edited by David Wilcox and Bruce Masse, 213–56 (Anthropological Research Papers, no. 24; Tempe: Arizona State University, 1981), and James Gunnerson's "Southern Athapaskan Archeology" (*Handbook of North American Indians,* vol. 9: *Southwest*) summarize what we know about the arrival of the Athapaskans in the Southwest. Numerous articles in the *Handbook of North American Indians,* vol. 10: *Southwest,* edited by Alfonso Ortiz (Washington: Smithsonian Institution, 1983), discuss the cultural diversification of the Athapaskans once they reached the region, including David Brugge's "Navajo Prehistory and History to 1850" (pp. 489–501) and Morris Opler's "The Apachean Culture Pattern and Its Origins" (pp. 368–92).

Bolton's *Rim of Christendom* (Tucson: University of Arizona Press, 1984) often reads like a historical novel, with Padre Eusebio Francisco Kino as the hero, but it does present a detailed account of Kino's missionary efforts in the Pimería Alta. Ernest Burrus's heavily annotated *Kino and Manje: Explorers of Sonora and Arizona* (Rome: Jesuit Historical Institute, 1971) contains both Spanish transcriptions and English translations of Kino and Manje's journals of their expeditions. Kieran McCarty's *Desert Documentary: The Spanish Years, 1767–1821* (Tucson: Arizona Historical Society, 1976) offers a glimpse of Spanish-Pima relations on the Arizona frontier.

James Officer's *Hispanic Arizona, 1536–1856* (Tucson: University of Arizona Press, 1987) is the finest summary of Arizona under the flags of Spain and Mexico. Officer discusses Hispanic missionization, mining, ranching, and Indian affairs, puncturing a number of myths about Hispanic Arizona in the process. Henry Dobyns's *Spanish Colonial Tucson: A Demographic History* (Tucson: University of Arizona Press, 1976) traces the rise of Hispanic Tucson and the decline of surrounding Pima populations due to Old World diseases. Other key works include two histories by John Kessell: *Mission of Sorrows: Jesuit Guevavi and the Pimas, 1691–1767* (Tucson: University of Arizona Press, 1970), and *Friars, Soldiers, and Reformers: Hispanic Arizona and the Sonora Mission Frontier, 1767–1856* (Tucson: University of Arizona Press, 1976). Both are written with Kessell's inimitable flair.

The critical works on Western Apache society and culture are Grenville Goodwin's classic *The Social Organization of the Western Apache* (Tucson: University of Arizona Press, 1969) and his *Western Apache Raiding and Warfare,* edited by Keith Basso (Tucson: University of Arizona Press, 1971). Basso, the leading contemporary ethnographer of the Western Apache, explores Apache language, religion, and philosophy with great skill in his *Western Apache Language and Culture: Essays in Linguistic Anthropology* (Tucson: University of Arizona Press, 1990).

✱ ✱ ✱ 3. Mexican Arizona and the Anglo Frontier

David Weber's *The Mexican Frontier, 1821–1846: The American Southwest Under Mexico* (Albuquerque: University of New Mexico Press, 1982) surveys the entire Southwest, including Arizona, from Mexican independence to the Mexican War. The key source for Mexican Arizona itself is Officer's *Hispanic Arizona,* supplemented by Wagoner's *Early Arizona* and Kessell's *Friars, Soldiers, and Reformers.* The statement by Ignacio Pacheco in the text comes from Pacheco's letter to Governor Gaxiola of Sonora, written in Tucson on November 4, 1826. Kieran McCarty supplied the translation.

Weber's *The Taos Trappers: The Fur Trade in the Far Southwest, 1540–1846* (Norman: University of Oklahoma Press, 1971) is the finest summary of trapping in the Southwest. William Goetzmann's *Exploration & Empire: The Explorer and the Scientist in the Winning of the American West* (New York: W. W. Norton, 1966) and Ray Allen Billington's *The Far Western Frontier, 1830–1860* (New York: Harper & Row, 1956) also contain considerable information on trappers, government surveyors, and other early Anglo American explorers. Richard Batman's *James Pattie's West: The Dream and the Reality* (Norman: University of Oklahoma

Press, 1984) takes a critical look at the veracity of *The Personal Narrative of James O. Pattie,* which has been republished many times since its original appearance in 1831.

In *From Fire to Flood,* Henry Dobyns argues that trappers decimated beaver populations, triggering a process that led to an increase in both arroyo cutting and downstream flooding. It is an intriguing hypothesis, yet the accounts of soldiers who accompanied Colonel Stephen Watts Kearny and Captain Philip St. George Cooke through Arizona in the late 1840s describe healthy beaver populations and clear streams supporting lush riparian vegetation. According to Goode P. Davis, Jr., who wrote *Man and Wildlife in Arizona: The American Exploration Period, 1824–1865* (Scottsdale: Arizona Game and Fish Department, 1982), "The trappers who worked the rivers of Arizona had no permanent impact on the land. They doubtless suppressed beaver populations in parts of Arizona for a time, but their activities were sporadic and short lived" (p. 24).

In addition to the works by Officer, Wagoner, and Kessell described above, information on the fate of individual Spanish and Mexican land grants can be found in Ray Mattison's "The Tangled Web: The Controversy Over the Tumacacori and Baca Land Grants" (*Journal of Arizona History* 8 [1967]: 70–91) and Jane Wayland Brewster's "The San Rafael Cattle Company: A Pennsylvania Enterprise in Arizona" (*Arizona and the West* 8 [1966]: 133–55).

Michael Meyer and William Sherman's *The Course of Mexican History* (New York: Oxford University Press, 1979) provides an excellent survey of Mexican history, including Mexico's ambivalent relations with the United States. Richard Griswold del Castillo's *The Treaty of Guadalupe Hidalgo: A Legacy of Conflict* (Norman: University of Oklahoma Press, 1990) explores how the treaty ending the war with Mexico was interpreted, implemented, ignored, or subverted during the 140 years since its passage.

Brief summaries of U.S. military expeditions during the Mexican War and of the forty-niners after the war can be found in Officer's *Hispanic Arizona,* Sonnichsen's *Tucson,* and Thomas Sheridan's *Los Tucsonenses: The Mexican Community of Tucson, 1854–1941* (Tucson: University of Arizona Press, 1986). Firsthand accounts of individual expeditions include Philip St. George Cooke's "Cooke's Journal of the March of the Mormon Battalion," in Ralph Bieber and Averam Bender's *Exploring Southwestern Trails, 1846–1854,* vol. 7 (Glendale, Calif.: Arthur H. Clarke Co., 1938) and Cave Johnson Couts's *Hepah, California! The Journal of Cave Johnson Couts from Monterrey, Nuevo León, Mexico, to Los Angeles During the Years 1848–49,* edited by Henry F. Dobyns (Tucson: Arizona Pioneers Historical Society, 1961).

Cormac McCarthy's *Blood Meridian; or, The Evening Redness in the West* (New

York: Ecco Press, 1985) is to the historical novel what the Book of Job is to moral parable—a masterpiece that explodes the genre. Despite the exalted language, philosophical speculations, and unrelenting bloodshed, however, it also serves as a vivid introduction to the Southwest at perhaps the most chaotic time in its history. William Griffen's *Apaches at War & Peace: The Janos Presidio, 1750–1858* (Albuquerque: University of New Mexico Press, 1988) and *Utmost Good Faith: Patterns of Apache-Mexican Hostilities in Northern Chihuahua Border Warfare, 1821–1848* (Albuquerque: University of New Mexico Press, 1988) provide the most detailed accounts of Apache-Mexican relations during the first half of the nineteenth century.

* * * 4. Early Anglo Settlement and the Beginning of the Indian Wars

The literature on the Chiricahua Apaches is immense and uneven. Morris Opler's *An Apache Lifeway: The Economic, Social, and Religious Institutions of the Chiricahua Indians* (New York: Cooper Square Publishers, 1965) is the standard ethnography. Dan Thrapp's *The Conquest of Apacheria* (Norman: University of Oklahoma Press, 1967) remains the single best source on warfare between the Apaches and the Anglos. It also provides a good introduction to campaigns against the Hualapais and Yavapais, who were frequently misidentified as Apaches. John C. Cremony's *Life Among the Apaches* (San Francisco: A. Roman & Company, 1868; reprint, Glorieta, N.M.: Rio Grande Press, 1970) is a colorful account of the Apaches during the mid nineteenth century by a member of Bartlett's Boundary Commission. It makes great reading but should be taken with many grains of salt. Perhaps the best book is Edwin Sweeney's *Cochise: Chiricahua Apache Chief* (Norman: University of Oklahoma Press, 1991). Unlike most historians of the Apache wars, Sweeney thoroughly researched Mexican as well as U.S. sources, including newspapers and archives. He also mastered the anthropological literature, thereby avoiding many of the misunderstandings of Apache society embedded in earlier works.

Early accounts of Anglo Arizona include J. Ross Browne's *Adventures in Apache Country: A Tour Through Arizona and Sonora, 1864* (Tucson: University of Arizona Press, 1974) and Martha Summerhayes's *Vanished Arizona: Recollections of the Army Life of a New England Woman* (Tucson: Arizona Silhouettes, 1960). Wagoner's *Early Arizona* provides a good overview of railroad surveys across Arizona and transportation on the Colorado River during the 1850s. *Samuel Peter Heintzelman and the Sonora Exploring & Mining Company,* by Diane North

(Tucson: University of Arizona Press, 1980), examines corporate capitalism's first venture into mining on the Arizona frontier. Joseph Park's invaluable master's thesis, "The History of Mexican Labor in Arizona During the Territorial Period" (University of Arizona, 1961) describes the exploitation of Mexican labor.

Boyd Finch's "Sherod Hunter and the Confederates in Arizona" (*Journal of Arizona History* 10 [1969]: 137–206) discusses the brief Confederate occupation of Tucson. A firsthand account of the Walker Party, which also discusses Wolsey's massacre of the Apaches, is Daniel Ellis Conner's *Joseph Reddeford Walker and the Arizona Adventure* (Norman: University of Oklahoma Press, 1956). Howard Lamar's *The Far Southwest, 1846–1912: A Territorial History* (New York: W. W. Norton, 1970) puts Arizona in broader regional perspective as it made the transition from a contested outpost of Sonora to a territory of the United States.

The best source for warfare between the Navajos and the Spaniards, Mexicans, and early Anglo Americans who tried to conquer them up to Kit Carson's campaign is Frank McNitt's *Navajo Wars: Military Campaigns, Slave Raids, and Reprisals* (Albuquerque: University of New Mexico Press, 1972). Gerald Thompson's *The Army and the Navajo: The Bosque Redondo Reservation Experiment, 1863–1868* (Tucson: University of Arizona Press, 1976) is a careful study of that bleak episode in Navajo history. Tiana Bighorse's *Bighorse the Warrior,* edited by Noël Bennett (Tucson: University of Arizona Press, 1990) presents a Navajo account of the war and subsequent Navajo history through the stories of Gus Bighorse. Peter Iverson's *The Navajo Nation* (Albuquerque: University of New Mexico Press, 1981) and Garrick Bailey and Roberta Glenn Bailey's *A History of the Navajos: The Reservation Years* (Santa Fe: School of American Research Press, 1986) both concentrate on the Navajos after Bosque Redondo but briefly survey earlier Diné history.

Clara Woody's "The Woolsey Expeditions of 1864" (*Arizona and the West* 4 [1962]: 157–76) presents firsthand accounts of King Woolsey's expeditions against the Yavapais and Apaches. Lonnie Edward Underhill's "A History of the First Arizona Volunteer Infantry, 1865–1866" (master's thesis, University of Arizona, 1979) describes the formation and operations of the Arizona Volunteers. The best ethnography of the Hualapai, which contains information on the Hualapai War, is Henry Dobyns and Robert Euler's *Wauba Yuma's People: The Comparative Socio-Political Structure of the Pai Indians of Arizona* (Prescott: Prescott College Press, 1970). Darlis Miller's *Soldiers and Settlers: Military Supply in the Southwest, 1861–1885* is an indispensable overview of U.S. military affairs in the Southwest, including Arizona.

❋ ❋ ❋   5. The Military Conquest of Indian Arizona

Robert Utley's *The Indian Frontier of the American West, 1846–1890* (Albuquerque: University of New Mexico Press, 1984) is a concise and balanced overview of the ways in which the United States attempted to conquer Native Americans in the West and incorporate them into U.S. society. First published in 1940, Ralph Ogle's *Federal Control of the Western Apaches, 1848–1886* (Albuquerque: University of New Mexico Press, 1970) remains a useful work. See also Edward Spicer's magisterial *Cycles of Conquest: The Impact of Spain, Mexico, and the United States on the Indians of the Southwest, 1533–1960* (Tucson: University of Arizona Press, 1962).

Key sources on General George Crook's campaigns in Arizona include Captain John G. Bourke's *On the Border with Crook* (1891; reprint, Lincoln: University of Nebraska Press, 1971) and *General George Crook: His Autobiography,* edited by Martin Schmitt (Norman: University of Oklahoma Press, 1946). The best synthesis of the Apache wars remains Thrapp's *The Conquest of Apacheria,* supplemented by his *Al Sieber: Chief of Scouts* (Norman: University of Oklahoma Press, 1964) and *Victorio and the Mimbres Apaches* (Norman: University of Oklahoma Press, 1974). One of Thrapp's weaknesses, however, is his treatment of the Yavapais. Most discussions of the battle at Skeleton Cave, for example, refer to the Indians cornered and killed there as Apaches. In their chapter on the Yavapai in the *Handbook of North American Indians,* vol. 10: *Southwest,* Sigrid Khera and Patricia Mariella state that the Indians belonged to the Kewevkapaya, or Southeastern Yavapais. The ethnic boundaries between Kewevkapayas and Tonto Apaches often blurred because both groups ranged through the Mazatzal and Superstition Mountains and the Tonto Basin. Yavapais and Apaches undoubtedly intermarried, and anthropologist Grenville Goodwin notes that two Tonto Apache clans on the western slopes of the Mazatzals were absorbed by the Yavapais.

Because Goodwin's interpretation of Western Apache political organization and territorial range in *The Social Organization of the Western Apache* (Tucson: University of Arizona Press, 1969) was based on information supplied by Western Apaches themselves, many of whom were alive during the Apache wars, I believe it is more accurate than the accounts of U.S. Army officers who could not speak Apache and were not trained ethnographers. For a perceptive account of how those officers and their wives viewed the Apaches and other Indians, see Sherry Smith's *The View from Officers' Row: Army Perceptions of Western Indians* (Tucson: University of Arizona Press, 1990), which contains an excellent chapter on Indian women.

The most complete account of the Camp Grant Massacre is Don Schellie's *Vast Domain of Blood: The Story of the Camp Grant Massacre* (Los Angeles: Westernlore Press, 1968). Schellie's reconstruction of the massacre is solid and well written, but he himself admits that he has embellished the "structure of the narrative" by inventing certain details and conversations. See also Elliot Arnold's *The Camp Grant Massacre* (New York: Simon and Schuster, 1976) and James Hastings's "The Tragedy of Camp Grant in 1871" (*Arizona and the West* 1 [1959]: 146–60).

There is no full-length study of the San Carlos Reservation or the disastrous experiment in relocation there. John Clum's son Woodworth penned a highly favorable portrait of his father entitled *Apache Agent* (Boston: Houghton Mifflin, 1936). Asa Daklugie left his own acerbic opinions of both Clum and San Carlos—as well as favorable impressions of Cochise, Victorio, Geronimo, and his own father, Juh—in Eve Ball's *Indeh: An Apache Odyssey* (Provo, Utah: Brigham Young University Press, 1980). The oral histories of other Chiricahuas who accompanied Victorio, Geronimo, and other Chiricahua leaders are recorded in Ball's *In the Days of Victorio: Recollections of a Warm Springs Apache* (Tucson: University of Arizona Press, 1970). The indispensable source on Cochise is Sweeney's *Cochise*. C. L. Sonnichsen's "Who Was Tom Jeffords?" (*Journal of Arizona History* 23 [1982]: 381–406) attempts to answer that question with Sonnichsen's usual wit and skill, while his "Tom Jeffords and the Editors" (*Journal of Arizona History* 29 [1986]: 117–30) reprints some of the vituperative editorial exchanges concerning Jeffords's management, or mismanagement, of the short-lived Chiricahua reservation.

Geronimo inspired a vast and uneven literature, but the finest study is Angie Debo's *Geronimo: The Man, His Time, His Place* (Norman: University of Oklahoma Press, 1976). Sonnichsen's delightful essay, "From Savage to Saint: A New Image for Geronimo" (*Journal of Arizona History* 27 [1986]: 5–34) dissects the changing ways in which non-Apaches have perceived and appropriated the last great Chiricahua war leader. The entire issue of the journal, in fact, is devoted to Geronimo and his final surrender on September 4, 1886. It concludes with a useful bibliographic essay entitled "The End of the Apache Wars: The Basic Writings" (*Journal of Arizona History* 27 [1986]: 125–36).

To understand Geronimo, however, one needs to know something about *diyih* ('power'), which is a central concept in Apache religion. Most of the great Apache leaders, including Juh and Geronimo, had power of one kind or another. The best explanation of the importance of power in Apache culture is anthropologist Keith Basso's *The Cibecue Apache* (New York: Holt, Rinehart and Winston, 1970).

For accounts of the diversion of the Gila River and its disastrous impact on the Gila Pimas, see Paul Ezell's "History of the Pima" (*Handbook of North American Indians*, vol. 10: *Southwest*, 149–60 [1983]), Henry Dobyns's "Who Killed the Gila?" (*Journal of Arizona History* 19 [1978]: 17–30), Gregory McNamee's *Gila: The Life and Death of an American River* (New York: Orion Books, 1994), Amadeo Rea's *Once a River: Bird Life and Habitat Changes Along the Middle Gila* (Tucson: University of Arizona Press, 1983), and George Webb's *A Pima Remembers* (Tucson: University of Arizona Press, 1959).

✳ ✳ ✳ **6. The Freighters and the Railroads**

The best source on freighting in early territorial Arizona is Darlis Miller's *Soldiers and Settlers: Military Supply in the Southwest, 1861–1885* (Albuquerque: University of New Mexico Press, 1989), which covers New Mexico and West Texas as well. A brief introduction to the subject is Henry Walker's "Wagon Freighting in Arizona," (*The Smoke Signal* [Tucson Corral of Westerners], no. 28 [1973]). Additional information on Arizona freighting can be found in Walker's *The Wagonmasters: High Plains Freighting from the Earliest Days of the Santa Fe Trail to 1880* (Norman: University of Oklahoma Press, 1966), Miller's "Civilians and Military Supply in the Southwest" (*Journal of Arizona History* 23 [1982]: 115–38), Bruce Hilpert's "Proper in any Parlor: Furnishing Styles in Frontier Tucson" (*Journal of Arizona History* 22 [1981]: 129–46), and James Sherman and Edward Ronstadt's "Wagon Making in Southern Arizona" (*The Smoke Signal* [Tucson Corral of Westerners] Spring 1975).

Information on territorial Arizona's Mexican entrepreneurs can be found in Sheridan's *Los Tucsonenses*. Dean Smith's *The Goldwaters of Arizona* (Flagstaff, Ariz.: Northland Press, 1986) and the late Floyd Fierman's two books *Guts and Ruts: The Jewish Pioneer on the Trail in the American Southwest* (New York: KTAV Publishing House, 1985) and *Roots and Boots: From Crypto-Jew in New Spain to Community Leader in the American Southwest* (Hoboken, N.J.: KTAV Publishing House, 1987) discuss early Jewish businessmen in Arizona and New Mexico. Gerald Stanley's "Merchandising in the Southwest: The Mark I. Jacobs Company of Tucson, 1867 to 1875" (*American Jewish Archives* 23 [1971]: 86–102) and Dawn Moore's "Pioneer Banking in Tucson: Lionel and Barron Jacobs and the Founding of the Pima County Bank" (*Arizona and the West* 24 [1982]: 305–18) analyze the Jacob family. Larry Schweikart's *A History of Banking in Arizona* (Tucson: University of Arizona Press, 1982) also contains considerable information on early Jewish merchants and bankers.

Accounts of women on the Arizona frontier are few and far between. Sandra

Myres's *Westering Women and the Frontier Experience, 1800–1915* (Albuquerque: University of New Mexico Press, 1982) provides a fine overview of women in the West, but she has little to say about Arizona itself. Smith's *View from Officers' Row* includes the perceptions of army wives as well as army officers. The most famous such account is Martha Summerhayes's *Vanished Arizona: Recollections of the Army Life of a New England Woman* (Tucson: Arizona Silhouettes, 1960). The experiences of Indian women themselves are recorded in H. Henrietta Stockel's *Women of the Apache Nation: Voices of Truth* (Reno and Las Vegas: University of Nevada Press, 1991).

Susan Johnson's "Sharing Bed and Board: Cohabitation and Cultural Differences in Central Arizona Mining Towns, 1863–1873," in *The Women's West,* edited by Susan Armitage and Elizabeth Jameson, 77–91 (Norman: University of Oklahoma Press, 1987) examines the presence and perceptions of Mexican and Anglo women during the early territorial period. Donna Guy's "The Economics of Widowhood in Arizona, 1880–1940," in *On Their Own: Widows and Widowhood in the American Southwest, 1848–1939,* edited by Arlene Scadron, 195–223 (Urbana: University of Illinois Press, 1988) focuses on the period when Arizona's frontier ended and its extractive society developed. Two collections of oral histories—Mary Logan Rothschild and Pamela Claire Hronek's *Doing What the Day Brought: An Oral History of Arizona Women* (Tucson: University of Arizona Press, 1992) and Patricia Preciado Martin's luminous *Songs My Mother Sang to Me: An Oral History of Mexican American Women* (Tucson: University of Arizona Press, 1992)—also concentrate on the twentieth century. Nonetheless, both convey what life in rural Arizona was like for women, and both contain bits and pieces of information about the lives of the mothers, grandmothers, and great-grandmothers of the women who did the talking.

William Goetzmann's *Exploration & Empire* puts the early railroad surveys in the context of U.S. exploration in general during the nineteenth century. Richard Cowdery's master's thesis—"The Planning of a Transcontinental Railroad Through Southern Arizona, 1832–1870" (University of Arizona, 1948)—documents early interest in the thirty-second-parallel route. Russell Wahmann's master's thesis—"The Historical Geography of the Santa Fe Railroad in Northern Arizona" (Northern Arizona University, 1971)—surveys the construction of the thirty-fifth-parallel line.

Concerning the Southern Pacific, two basic sources are Stuart Daggett's dry but devastating *Chapters on the History of the Southern Pacific* (New York: Ronald Press Company, 1922) and Neill Wilson and Frank Taylor's popularly written *Southern Pacific: The Roaring Story of a Fighting Railroad* (New York: McGraw-Hill, 1952). The best account of the Southern Pacific in Arizona is

David Myrick's lavishly illustrated *Railroads of Arizona*, vol. 1: *The Southern Roads* (Berkeley: Howell-North Books, 1975).

James Marshall's *Santa Fe: The Railroad That Built an Empire* (New York: Random House, 1945) and Keith Bryant's *History of the Atchison, Topeka and Santa Fe Railway* (New York: MacMillan Publishing Company, 1974) provide two highly readable general accounts of the Santa Fe. More detailed information on the construction of the Santa Fe in Arizona can be found in two master's theses—Herbert Wisbey's "A History of the Santa Fe Railroad in Arizona to 1917" (University of Arizona, 1946), and Wahmann's thesis, noted above.

✻ ✻ ✻ 7. Cattle

J. J. Wagoner's *History of the Cattle Industry in Southern Arizona, 1540–1940* (Tucson: University of Arizona Press, 1952) remains the most comprehensive history of cattle ranching in the state. As the title indicates, however, it covers neither northern Arizona nor the past fifty years of cattle ranching in southern Arizona. Bert Haskett's "Early History of the Cattle Industry in Arizona" (*Arizona Historical Review* 6 [1935]: 3–42) contains valuable information but is marred by speculation and factual errors, especially concerning Spanish and Mexican ranching. Richard Morrisey's "The Early Range Cattle Industry in Arizona" (*Agricultural History* 24 [1950]: 151–56) briefly discusses the development of ranching in the late nineteenth century, while Larry Christiansen's "The Extinction of Wild Cattle in Southern Arizona" (*Journal of Arizona History* 29 [1988]: 89–100) points out how quickly the herds abandoned on the Mexican land grants disappeared. Darlis Miller's *Soldiers and Settlers* discusses the impact of army contracts on Arizona ranching.

Two works that examine the ecological impact of ranching on Arizona's vegetation are James R. Hastings and Raymond M. Turner's *The Changing Mile: An Ecological Study of Vegetation Change with Time in the Lower Mile of an Arid and Semiarid Region* (Tucson: University of Arizona Press, 1965) and Conrad Bahre's *A Legacy of Change: Historic Human Impact on Vegetation of the Arizona Borderlands* (Tucson: University of Arizona Press, 1991). James Wilson's dissertation, "Cattle and Politics in Arizona, 1886–1941" (University of Arizona, 1967), traces the political and economic evolution of the livestock industry. Jane Wayland's master's thesis, "Experiment on the Santa Cruz: Colin Cameron's San Rafael Cattle Company, 1882–1893" (University of Arizona, 1964), serves as a case study of one successful cattleman during a period of rapid change. She condensed her thesis in an article entitled "The San Rafael Cattle Company: A

Pennsylvania Enterprise in Arizona" (*Arizona and the West* 8 [1966]: 133–56), published under the name Jane Wayland Brewster.

Brief accounts of the conflict between the Aztec Land and Cattle Company and its neighbors are found in Don Dedera's *A Little War of Our Own: The Pleasant Valley Feud Revisited* (Flagstaff, Ariz.: Northland Press, 1988), the best history of the Pleasant Valley War, and Charles Petersen's *Take Up Your Mission: Mormon Colonizing Along the Little Colorado River* (Tucson: University of Arizona Press, 1973), a superb analysis of Mormon colonization in northern Arizona during the late nineteenth century. Historian Richard Maxwell Brown relies heavily on Dedera in his "Western Violence: Structure, Values, Myth" (*Western Historical Quarterly* 24 [1993]: 5–20). Bert Haskett's "History of the Sheep Industry in Arizona" (*Arizona Historical Review* 7 [1936]: 3–49) is the only synthesis of sheepraising in the state. The best survey of the drought and depression years of the 1890s is Diana Hadley's unpublished "Cattle and Drought in Arizona Territory, 1885–1903," supplemented by Forrestine Cooper Hooker's novel *The Long Dim Trail* (New York: Doubleday and Company, 1932).

The longstanding debate over the causes of arroyo cutting in the Southwest has generated an enormous amount of literature. The best recent analysis is Ronald Cooke and Richard Reeves' *Arroyos and Environmental Change in the American South-West* (Oxford: Clarendon Press, 1976). Analyses of the influence of El Niño–Southern Oscillation conditions upon the Southwestern climate are found in Julio Betancourt's "El Niño/Southern Oscillation (ENSO) and Climate of the Southwestern U.S.," presented at the Paleoclimate Workshop, and Robert Webb and Julio Betancourt's *Climatic Variability and Flood Frequency of the Santa Cruz River, Pima County, Arizona* (United States Geological Survey Water-Supply Paper 2379; Washington, D.C.: United States Government Printing Office, 1992).

❋ ❋ **8. Silver and Gold**

James Officer surveys Spanish and Mexican mining in *Hispanic Arizona*. A monograph that should bury all the legends of lost Jesuit mines (but probably never will) is Charles Polzer's "Legends of Lost Missions and Mines" (*The Smoke Signal* [Tucson Corral of Westerners], no. 18 [1968]). Pamela Renner's "La Paz: Gateway to Territorial Arizona" (*Journal of Arizona History* 24 [1983]: 119–44) is a good account of an Arizona boomtown that developed into an important commercial center along the Colorado River. Duane Smith's "The Vulture Mine: Arizona's Golden Mirage" (*Arizona and the West* 14 [1972]: 231–52) discusses both the myth and the reality of one of Arizona's most famous gold mines. Daniel Ellis Conner provides a firsthand glimpse of central Arizona's gold placer boom in the early 1860s in his *Joseph Reddeford Walker and the Arizona Adventure* (Norman: University of Oklahoma Press, 1956). Eldred Wilson's *Gold Placers and Placering in Arizona* (Bulletin 168, Bureau of Geology and Mineral Technology; Tucson: University of Arizona, 1978) describes the geology, technology, and history of placer gold mining in Arizona.

The most complete description of silver mining in territorial central Arizona is Robert Spude's "A Land of Sunshine and Silver: Silver Mining in Central Arizona, 1871–1885" (*Journal of Arizona History* 16 [1975]: 29–76). Gregory Dowell's "The Total Wreck: Arizona's Forgotten 'Bonanza' Mine" (*Arizona and the West* 20 [1978]: 141–54) describes the silver mine that underwrote the Empire Ranch during the early 1880s. Dale Nations and Edmund Stump's *Geology of Arizona* (Dubuque: Kendall/Hunt Publishing Co., 1981) surveys Arizona's geological chronology of landforms for general readers. There are also chapters on economic geology and environmental geology.

More ink has been wasted on the shoot-out at the O.K. Corral than on any other subject in Arizona history. Our national fascination with Wyatt Earp, Doc Holliday, and the Clantons has little to do with their historical importance and everything to do with the mythology of the Wild West. For those interested in the topic, however, the most balanced and scholarly treatment is Paula Marks's *And Die in the West* (New York: William Morrow & Co., 1989), an exhaustive exploration of the shoot-out and the social milieu that allowed it to happen. Concerning Tombstone in general, perhaps the best introduction is Odie Faulk's *Tombstone: Myth and Reality* (New York: Oxford University Press, 1972). "The Tombstone Discovery: The Recollections of Ed Schieffelin and Richard Gird," edited by Lonnie Underhill (*Arizona and the West* 21 [1979]: 37–76), provides a thoroughly annotated version of the reminiscences of the two men who discovered Tombstone's first mines. The same issue of *Arizona and the West* also contains Henry Walker's "Arizona Land Fraud: Model 1880; The Tombstone Townsite Company," which explores the conflict over land in Tombstone itself. Richard Lingenfelter's *The Hardrock Miners* (Berkeley: University of California Press, 1974) discusses the Tombstone strike and its impact on wages in mining camps across the West.

* * *   9. Copper

There is no good general history of the copper industry in Arizona. Frank Tuck's pamphlet "History of Mining in Arizona" (Phoenix: State of Arizona, Department of Mineral Resources, 1963), provides a brief chronology. Robert G. Cleland's *A History of Phelps Dodge, 1834–1950* (New York: Alfred A. Knopf, 1952) is a sympathetic company history, while H. H. Langton's *James Douglas: A Memoir* (Toronto: University of Toronto Press, 1940) presents Douglas in the best possible light. The development of several of Arizona's most important copper colonies is traced in Annie Cox's "History of Bisbee, 1877 to 1937" (master's thesis, University of Arizona, 1938); Robert Jeffrey's "The History of Douglas, Arizona" (master's thesis, University of Arizona, 1951); John Brogdon's "The History of Jerome, Arizona (master's thesis, University of Arizona, 1952); Roberta Watt's "History of Morenci, Arizona" (master's thesis, University of Arizona, 1956); and James Patton's *History of Clifton* (Greenlee County Chamber of Commerce, 1977). Carlos Schwantes's *Bisbee: Urban Outpost on the Frontier* (Tucson: University of Arizona Press, 1992) is an edited volume with chapters on various aspects of life in Arizona's largest copper town. The writing is clear, and the book is graced with many extraordinary historical photographs printed on glossy, high-quality paper.

There is also no comprehensive history of the Arizona constitutional convention or the political milieu out of which it arose. Wagoner's *Arizona Territory* provides an outline and sketches many of the players. John Goff's *George W. P. Hunt and His Arizona* (Pasadena: Socio-Technical Publications, 1973) focuses on the president of the convention, but the convention is not Goff's principal concern. Tru McGinnis's "The Influence of Organized Labor on the Making of the Arizona Constitution" (master's thesis, University of Arizona, 1930) and Alan Johnson's "Governor G.W.P. Hunt and Organized Labor" (master's thesis, University of Arizona, 1964) explore the development of the labor movement in Arizona during the late nineteenth and early twentieth centuries, including efforts to unionize Arizona miners. Joseph Parks's "The History of Mexican Labor in Arizona During the Territorial Period" describes the often antagonistic relationship between Mexican workers and organized labor. James Kluger's *The Clifton-Morenci Strike: Labor Difficulty in Arizona, 1915–1916* (Tucson: University of Arizona Press, 1970) analyzes organized labor's one major "victory" following statehood.

The only work that attempts to weave the many different strands together is James Byrkit's provocative *Forging the Copper Collar: Arizona's Labor-Management War of 1901–1921* (Tucson: University of Arizona Press, 1982). Byrkit examines how the copper companies, led by Phelps Dodge, broke the power of labor in Arizona during World War I. Phil Mellinger's "'The Men Have Become Organizers': Labor Conflict and Unionization in the Mexican Mining Communities of Arizona, 1900–1915" (*Western Historical Quarterly* 23 [1993]: 323–47) challenges several of Byrkit's conclusions, arguing that the successful strikes of 1915, not the Bisbee deportation of 1917, were the most significant episodes of Arizona labor history during the early twentieth century.

* * * 10. Oases in the Desert

Standard works on Native American agriculture in Arizona are E. F. Castetter and W. H. Bell's *Pima and Papago Agriculture* (Albuquerque: University of New Mexico Press, 1942) and *Yuman Indian Agriculture* (Albuquerque: University of New Mexico Press, 1951). Gary Nabhan's *Gathering the Desert* (Tucson: University of Arizona Press, 1985) contains wonderful essays on important and neglected native foods such as tepary beans, amaranth greens, and Sonoran panicgrass. Nabhan also corrects the historical misuse of the Tohono O'odham term *'Ak-ciñ*, which is usually transcribed *ak-chin*, in a technical article entitled "*'Ak-ciñ* 'Arroyo Mouth' and the Environmental Setting of the Papago Indian Fields of the Sonoran Desert" (*Applied Geography* 6 [1986]: 61–75). The best discussion of the relationship between Yuman agriculture, sex roles, and warfare is Clifton Kroeber and Bernard Fontana's *Massacre on the Gila: An Account of the Last Major Battle Between American Indians, with Reflections on the Origin of War* (Tucson: University of Arizona Press, 1986). John Hack's classic *The Changing Physical Environment of the Hopi Indians of Arizona* (Papers of the Peabody Museum of American Archaeology and Ethnology 35, no. 1 [1942]) and Richard Bradfield's *The Changing Pattern of Hopi Agriculture* (Royal Anthropological Institute of Great Britain and Ireland, Occasional Paper 30 [1971]) are two basic sources on Hopi farming.

A general discussion of irrigation on the northern frontier of New Spain is Michael Meyer's *Water in the Hispanic Southwest: A Social and Legal History, 1550–1850* (Tucson: University of Arizona Press, 1984). Sheridan's *Los Tucsonenses* discusses agriculture and water control in Sonoran Tucson. Stanley Crawford's *Mayordomo: Chronicle of an Acequia in Northern New Mexico* (New York: Doubleday, 1988) is a beautifully written account of an acequia system in twentieth-century New Mexico.

An early history of the Mormons in Arizona is James McClintock's *Mormon Settlement in Arizona*, first published in 1921 and reprinted by the University of Arizona Press in 1985. Peterson's *Take Up Your Mission* analyzes the first mission colonies in northern Arizona. A more technical discussion of those colonies is William Abruzzi's "Ecology, Resource Redistribution, and Mormon Settlement in Northeastern Arizona" (*American Anthropologist* 91 [1989]: 642–55), which focuses on their demographic, economic, and ecological aspects. Edward Lyman's "Elimination of the Mormon Issue from Arizona Politics, 1889–1894" (*Arizona and the West* 24 [1982]: 205–28) explains how the potentially explosive fight between Mormons and the Republican Party was defused.

A detailed history of agriculture and water control in the Salt River Valley has yet to be written. Karen Smith's *The Magnificent Experiment: Building the Salt River Reclamation Project, 1890–1917* (Tucson: University of Arizona Press, 1986) discusses the legal and political aspects of the struggle but pays little attention to the human drama. Luckingham's *Phoenix* contains useful information, but the focus is on Phoenix, not the Salt River Valley itself. Some of the most vivid descriptions of Salt River floods and their impact on valley settlers are found in David Myrick's encyclopedic *Railroads of Arizona*, vol. 2 (San Diego: Howell-North Books, 1980), which covers railroads in the Salt River Valley. Articles that treat various parts of the story include Merwin Murphy's "W. J. Murphy and the Arizona Canal Company" (*Journal of Arizona History* 23 [1982]: 139–70), Jack August's "Carl Hayden: Born a Politician" (*Journal of Arizona History* 26 [1985]: 117–44), Peter Booth's "Plain Folk and Christian Virtue: The Dunkard Colony in Glendale" (*Journal of Arizona History* 31 [1990]: 43–60), Karen Smith's "The Campaign for Water in Central Arizona, 1890–1903" (*Arizona and the West* 23 [1981]: 127–48), and Goeffrey Mawn's "Promoters, Speculators, and the Selection of the Phoenix Townsite" (*Arizona and the West* 19 [1977]: 207–24).

❋ ❋ ❋ **I I. Water and Cotton**

There is no full-scale biography of Carl Hayden. The best sources on Hayden's early life are Jack August's "Carl Hayden: Born a Politician" (*Journal of Arizona History* 26 [1985]: 117–44) and "'A Sterling Young Democrat': Carl Hayden's Road to Congress, 1900–1912" (*Journal of Arizona History* 28 [1987]: 217–42).

Karen Smith's *The Magnificent Experiment* describes the beginnings of the Salt River Project and the building of Roosevelt Dam. Luckingham's *Phoenix* also discusses the early development of the project and its impact on Phoenix. Smith's "The Campaign for Water in Central Arizona" (*Arizona and the West* 23 [1981]: 127–48) focuses on the competition between Gila Valley and Salt River Valley interests in the struggle to win federal support for reclamation and water control in their watersheds. Other books on the subject include Earl Zarbin's *Roosevelt Dam: A History to 1911* (Phoenix: Salt River Project, 1984) and *Salt River Project: Four Steps Forward, 1902–1910* (Phoenix: Salt River Project, 1986). All of these sources view both the project and the dam in a positive light.

More critical surveys of federal reclamation and Western water development are Donald Worster's *Rivers of Empire: Water, Aridity, and the Growth of the*

American West (New York: Pantheon Books, 1985) and Marc Reisner's *Cadillac Desert: The American West and Its Disappearing Water* (New York: Penguin Books, 1986). Neither discusses the early years of the Salt River Project in much detail, but both explore the assumptions and consequences of the policies that shaped the project. Donald Pisani provides a thoughtful critique of both books in "The Irrigation District and the Federal Relationship" in *The Twentieth Century West: Historical Interpretations,* edited by Gerald Nash and Richard Etulain, 257–92 (Albuquerque: University of New Mexico Press, 1989).

Arizona's first cotton boom and bust, like so many other aspects of Arizona history, has never received the attention it deserves. There is no single comprehensive treatment of the subject, and most of the information is scattered in general treatments of migrant labor in the United States or buried in obscure technical reports. Joseph McGowan's *History of Extra-Long Staple Cottons* (El Paso: Hill Printing Company, 1961), published by the Arizona Cotton Growers Association, traces the development of the Arizona cotton industry from its experimental stage in the early 1900s until the 1950s. B. Brooks Taylor's "Cotton" in *Arizona: The Grand Canyon State,* vol. 1 (Westminster, Colo.: Western States Historical Publishers, 1975), briefly summarizes that development. J. H. Collins's *A Study of Marketing Conditions in the Salt River Valley, Arizona* (Agricultural Experiment Station Bulletin No. 58 [Tucson: University of Arizona, College of Agriculture, 1918]) provides a fascinating glimpse of Salt River Valley agriculture at the beginning of the cotton boom. Malcolm Brown and Orin Cassmore's *Migratory Cotton Pickers in Arizona* (Washington, D.C.: U.S. Government Printing Office, 1939), prepared for the Works Progress Administration, documents the abysmal living conditions in the cotton camps. See also Marsha L. Weisiger's "Mythic Fields of Plenty: The Plight of Depression-Era Migrants in Arizona" (*Journal of Arizona History* 32 [1991]: 241–66) and Melissa Keane's "Cotton and Figs: The Great Depression in the Casa Grande Valley" (*Journal of Arizona History* 32 [1991]: 267–90).

Other general surveys of migrant labor in the United States that discuss the Arizona cotton industry include Carey McWilliams's pioneering *Ill Fares the Land: Migrants and Migratory Labor in the United States* (Boston: Little, Brown and Co., 1944); Mark Reisler's *By the Sweat of Their Brow: Mexican Immigrant Labor in the United States, 1900–1940* (Westport, Conn.: Greenwood Press, 1976); and Otey Scruggs's *Braceros, "Wetbacks," and the Farm Labor Problem: Mexican Agricultural Labor in the United States, 1942–1954* (New York: Garland Publishing, 1988). Scruggs pays particular attention to the role of Mexican labor during World War I and the 1920s in "The First Mexican Farm Labor Program" (*Arizona and the West* 2 [1960]: 319–26).

The best account of the San Carlos Project and its impact on the Gila Pimas is Robert Hackenberg's unpublished "A Brief History of the Gila River Reservation" (University of Arizona, Department of Anthropology, Bureau of Ethnic Research, 1955; a copy is held by the Arizona State Museum). David H. DeJong's "'See the New Country': The Removal Controversy and Pima-Maricopa Water Rights, 1869–1879" (*Journal of Arizona History* 33 [1992]: 367–96) examines government efforts to solve the Gila Pimas' water problems by removing them to Indian Territory in Oklahoma. Jack L. August, Jr., describes Carl Hayden's role in the San Carlos Project in "Carl Hayden's 'Indian Card': Environmental Politics and the San Carlos Reclamation Project" (*Journal of Arizona History* 33 [1992]: 397–442). The ecological consequences of upstream diversion and the construction of Coolidge Dam are documented in Amadeo Rea's *Once a River: Bird Life and Habitat Changes on the Middle Gila* (Tucson: University of Arizona Press, 1983).

The literature on the struggle for the Colorado River is immense. The finest account of the early battles is Norris Hundley's *Water and the West: The Colorado River Compact and the Politics of Water in the American West* (Berkeley: University of California Press, 1975). Additional sources concerning Arizona's opposition to the Colorado River Compact are Malcolm Parsons's "The Colorado River in Arizona Politics" (master's thesis, University of Arizona, 1947); Walter Rusinek's "Against the Compact: The Critical Opposition of George W. P. Hunt" (*Journal of Arizona History* 25 [1984]: 155–70); Thomas Smith's "Lewis Douglas, Arizona Politics, and the Colorado River Controversy" (*Arizona and the West* 22 [1980]: 125–62); John Goff's *George W. P. Hunt and His Arizona* (Pasadena, Calif.: Socio-Technical Publications, 1973); and Philip Fradkin's *A River No More: The Colorado River and the West* (Tucson: University of Arizona Press, 1984). Joseph Stevens's *Hoover Dam: An American Adventure* (Norman: University of Oklahoma Press, 1988) explores all aspects of the construction of the dam from the technological challenges to the landscaping of Boulder City, where most of the workers lived. Rich Johnson's *The Central Arizona Project, 1918–1968* (Tucson: University of Arizona Press, 1977) focuses on the project after World War II.

✳ ✳ ✳ 12. Climate

The best study of John C. Van Dyke and his encounter with the Sonoran and Mojave deserts is Peter Wild's *John C. Van Dyke: The Desert* (Boise State University Western Writers Series, no. 82; Boise: Boise State University, 1988). In 1976 the Arizona Historical Society in Tucson reprinted Van Dyke's *The Desert: Further Studies in Natural Appearances,* with an informative introduction by Lawrence Clark Powell. Ironically, Wild and Neil Carmony have now presented intriguing evidence that Van Dyke may rarely have left his brother's ranch and that many of his desert sojourns were imaginary in "The Trip Not Taken: John C. Van Dyke, Heroic Doer or Armchair Seer?" (*Journal of Arizona History* 34 [1993]: 65–80). Wild calls *The Desert* a "beautiful fraud."

Billy Jones's *Health-Seekers in the Southwest, 1817–1900* (Norman: University of Oklahoma Press, 1967) provides a well-written account of lung patients in Arizona and the rest of the Southwest, discussing nineteenth-century concepts of disease and the devastating impact of tuberculosis in the United States during the Industrial Age. Both Bradford Luckingham and C. L. Sonnichsen describe conditions within the tent cities in their general histories of Phoenix and Tucson, respectively. Articles about the lungers include Dick Hall's "Ointment of Love: Oliver E. Comstock and Tucson's Tent City" (*Journal of Arizona History* 19 [1978]: 111–30) and Alex Kimmelman's "Pastime Park: Tucson's First Veterans' Hospital" (*Journal of Arizona History* 31 [1990]: 19–42).

The literature on the Grand Canyon is almost as immense as the canyon itself, and like the canyon, it is filled with controversy and mystery. One of the most important issues is the authenticity of John Wesley Powell's diary of his first plunge down the Colorado in 1869. Powell claimed that the narrative was a daily journal "kept on long and narrow strips of brown paper, which were gathered into little volumes that were bound in sole leather in camp as they were completed." Martin Anderson's "John Wesley Powell's *Exploration of the Colorado River*: Fact, Fiction, or Fantasy?" (*Journal of Arizona History* 24 [1983]: 363–80) argues that the diary was written five years after the expedition and included observations and events from the second trip as well as the first. Powell made no mention of the trouble he had had with his nine-man crew, five of whom deserted and three of whom died while hiking out of the canyon. Powell knew that mutiny did not impress congressional committees or garner generous appropriations. As Jack Sumner, a member of the 1869 expedition, muttered, "There's lots in that book besides the truth."

Powell's *Exploration of the Colorado River of the West and Its Tributaries* (Washington, D.C.: U.S. Government Printing Office, 1875) and Clarence Dutton's *Tertiary History of the Grand Cañon District* (Washington, D.C.: U.S. Government Printing Office, 1882) are perhaps the two most basic sources on the geology, ethnology, and natural history of the Grand Canyon. Goetzmann's *Exploration and Empire* includes a superb chapter entitled "John Wesley Powell: The Explorer as Reformer." Other recent accounts of the canyon's natural and human history include Robert Euler and Frank Tikalsky's *The Grand Canyon: In-*

timate Views (Tucson: University of Arizona Press, 1992), river runner Michael P. Ghiglieri's *Canyon* (Tucson: University of Arizona Press, 1992), Louise Teal's *Breaking into the Current: Boatwomen of the Grand Canyon* (Tucson: University of Arizona Press, 1994), and Steven Carothers and Bryan Brown's scholarly *The Colorado River Through Grand Canyon: Natural History and Human Change* (Tucson: University of Arizona Press, 1991).

The best analysis of the early development of the Grand Canyon is Douglas Strong's two-part article "Ralph H. Cameron and the Grand Canyon" *Arizona and the West* 20 [1978]: 41–64, 155–72). Other articles on the period include Gordon Chappell's "Railroad at the Rim: The Origin and Growth of Grand Canyon Village" (*Journal of Arizona History* 17 [1976]: 89–107); Michael Pace's "Emery Kolb and the Fred Harvey Company" (*Journal of Arizona History* 24 [1983]: 339–62); Al Richmond's "The Grand Canyon Railway: A History" (*Journal of Arizona History* 27 [1986]: 425–38); and Debra Sutphen's "'Too Hard A Nut to Crack'": Peter D. Berry and the Battle for Free Enterprise at the Grand Canyon, 1890–1914" (*Journal of Arizona History* 32 [1991]: 153–72).

Earl Pomeroy's *In Search of the Golden West* (New York: Alfred A. Knopf, 1957), treats the development of tourism in the West with wit, verve, and insight. John Jakle's *The Tourist: Travel in Twentieth-Century North America* (Lincoln: University of Nebraska Press, 1985) is more pedestrian, but both books place tourism in broad social and economic contexts. Virginia Scharff provides a feminist perspective on automobile tourism in *Taking the Wheel: Women and the Coming of the Motor Age* (New York: Free Press, 1991).

Articles about tourism in Arizona include Jerome Rodnitzky's "Recapturing the West: The Dude Ranch in American Life" (*Arizona and the West* 10 [1967]: 111–26); Blake Brophy's "Tucson's Arizona Inn: The Continuum of Style" (*Journal of Arizona History* 24 [1983]: 255–82); Alex Kimmelman's "Luring the Tourist to Tucson: Civic Promotion During the 1920s" (*Journal of Arizona History* 28 [1987]: 135–54); Gerald Thompson's "'Greetings from Arizona': Postcards of the Grand Canyon State" (*Journal of Arizona History* 30 [1989]: 279–302); Kel Fox's "Of Dudes and Cows: The Foxboro Story" (*Journal of Arizona History* 32 [1991]: 413–42); and J. F. Elliott, Peter Wild, and Bruce Dinges's "*Progressive Arizona*: The Life and Death of a Sunbelt Magazine" (*Journal of Arizona History* 33 [1992]: 269–94). Two books on the impact of the Fred Harvey Company are D. H. Thomas's *The Southwestern Indian Detours* (Phoenix: Hunter Publishing, 1978) and Lesley Poling-Kempes's *The Harvey Girls* (New York: Paragon House, 1991).

Two articles in volume 9 of the *Handbook of North American Indians* (Washington, D.C.: Smithsonian Institution, 1979)—Albert Schroeder's "History of

Archeological Research" and Keith Basso's "History of Ethnological Research"—provide brief overviews of anthropological inquiry in the Southwest. J. J. Brody's "Pueblo Fine Arts" in volume 9 and Ruth Roessel's "Navajo Arts and Crafts" in volume 10 of the *Handbook* examine the development of Southwestern Indian arts and crafts in cultural and historical context. The *Handbook* also contains a large bibliography of the most important works on Native Americans in the Southwest. An excellent account of early research in the region is Curtis Hinsley's *Savages and Scientists: The Smithsonian Institution and the Development of American Anthropology, 1846–1910* (Washington, D.C.: Smithsonian Institution Press, 1981). Anthropologist Nancy Parezo's "Cushing as Part of the Team: The Collecting Activities of the Smithsonian Institution" (*American Ethnologist* 12 [1985]: 763–74) examines Cushing's early experiences in Arizona and New Mexico, while her essay "A Multitude of Markets" (*Journal of the Southwest* 32 [1990]: 563–75) gives a balanced view of the commercialization of Indian arts and crafts. Finally, Parezo's edited volume, *Hidden Scholars: Women Anthropologists and the Native American Southwest* (Albuquerque: University of New Mexico Press, 1993), discusses the experiences of women anthropologists like Matilda Cox Stephenson, Ruth Benedict, and Gladys Reichard.

George Webb's *Tree Rings and Telescopes: The Scientific Career of A. E. Douglass* (Tucson: University of Arizona Press, 1983) chronicles the contributions of the founder of dendrochronology. The discovery of the charcoal sample that extended Douglass's tree-ring calendar into the past by nearly 600 years is best told by Emil Haury, one of the archaeologists who found it, in "HH 39: Recollections of a Dramatic Moment in Southwestern Archaeology," reprinted in *Emil W. Haury's Prehistory of the American Southwest*, edited by J. J. Reid and David Doyel. Janice Bowers's *A Sense of Place: The Life and Work of Forrest Shreve* (Tucson: University of Arizona Press, 1988) focuses on Shreve but discusses the Carnegie Institution's Desert Laboratory as well. William G. McGinnies's *Discovering the Desert: The Legacy of the Carnegie Desert Botanical Laboratory* (Tucson: University of Arizona Press, 1981) popularizes some of the discoveries that Shreve and other scientists at the Desert Laboratory made.

There is no overview of the development of Arizona's federal lands. Mary Ellen Lauver's master's thesis, "A History of the Use and Management of the Forested Lands of Arizona, 1862–1936" (University of Arizona, 1938), analyzes the early policies that created the national forests and the opposition they engendered among Arizona miners and stock raisers. Charles Ames focuses on the evolution of the Coronado National Forest in southern Arizona in "A History of the Forest Service" (*The Smoke Signal* [Tucson Corral of Westerners], no. 16 [1967]). A good ecological history of Arizona has yet to be written.

*　*　*　13. The Depression and the New Deal

   Donald Worster talks about Walter Packard, his critique of California agribusiness, and his championship of agricultural collectives in *Rivers of Empire*. Edward Banfield's *Government Project* (Glencoe, Ill.: Free Press, 1951) analyzes the Casa Grande Valley Farms cooperative and why it failed.

  The best single source on the impact of the New Deal in Arizona is Leonard Arrington's "Arizona in the Great Depression Years" (*AR: Arizona Review* 17 [1968]: 11–19), which briefly describes federal expenditures for programs like the ccc and the aaa. The Autumn 1991 issue of the *Journal of Arizona History* (vol. 32) is devoted to the Depression in Arizona. Weisiger's "Mythic Fields of Plenty" and King's "Cotton and Figs" focus on Arizona agriculture and the conditions of farm workers. Peter Booth's "Cactizonians: The Civilian Conservation Corps in Pima County, 1933–1942" describes the ccc in southern Arizona.

  Two books by California muckraker Carey McWilliams—*Factories in the Field: The Story of Migratory Farm Labor in California* (Boston: Little, Brown, 1939) and *Ill Fares the Land*—discuss Arizona agribusiness and its exploitation of migrant laborers. Malcolm Brown and Orin Cassmore's *Migratory Cotton Pickers in Arizona* (Washington, D.C.: U.S. Government Printing Office, 1939) is a detailed statistical study of those workers during the disastrous harvesting season of 1937–38. Other studies of labor, land tenure, and agriculture include Philip Olson's master's thesis, "Agricultural Laborers: A Study of a Minority Group in a Small Arizona Community" (University of Arizona, 1956), which analyzes the social position of migrants in Eloy, and Philip Greisinger and George Barr's "Agricultural Land Ownership and Operating Tenures in Casa Grande Valley" (University of Arizona College of Agriculture Bulletin 175 [1941]).

  Abraham Hoffman's *Unwanted Mexican Americans in the Great Depression* (Tucson: University of Arizona Press, 1974) documents the repatriation of Mexican workers during the 1930s. No thorough account exists of the struggle to organize Arizona labor during the 1930s, but Michael Wade's *The Bitter Issue: The Right to Work Law in Arizona* (Tucson: Arizona Historical Society, 1976) and D. H. Dinwoodie's "The Rise of the Mine-Mill Union in Southwestern Copper," in *American Labor in the Southwest: The First One Hundred Years*, edited by James Foster, 46–56 (Tucson: University of Arizona Press, 1982) provide glimpses of those battles. Mario García's *Mexican Americans: Leadership, Ideology, & Identity, 1930–1960* (New Haven: Yale University Press, 1989) contains a more extended analysis of Mexican labor and the iummsw in El Paso.

  William Rowley's *U.S. Forest Service Grazing and Rangelands: A History* (College Station: Texas A & M University Press, 1985) and Lauver's "A History of the Use and Management of the Forested Lands of Arizona, 1862–1936" examine the conflict over grazing in the national forests from the 1890s to the 1930s. Haskett's "History of the Sheep Industry in Arizona" (*Arizona Historical Review* 7 [1936]: 3–49) recounts the early attempts to remove livestock from Arizona forest reserves and the roles E. S. Gosney and Gifford Pinchot played in keeping them there. Wagoner discusses the impact of the Taylor Grazing Act in his *History of the Cattle Industry in Southern Arizona, 1540–1940*. Diana Hadley goes into more detail in her *Environmental Change in Aravaipa, 1870–1970: An Ethnoecological Survey* (Safford, Ariz.: U.S. Bureau of Land Management, 1991).

Luckingham's *Phoenix* and C. L. Sonnichsen's *Tucson* both contain chapters on the impact of the Depression and the New Deal on those cities. Although much of the book is a diatribe against the Roman Catholic Church, Emmett McLoughlin's *People's Padre* (Boston: Beacon Press, 1954) vividly describes conditions in the slums of South Phoenix. Sheridan's *Los Tucsonenses* analyzes the subordination of working-class Mexicans in Tucson and also discusses the *mutualista* movement and other manifestations of Mexican protest during the 1930s.

Rothschild and Hronek's *Doing What the Day Brought* presents the experiences of twenty-nine Arizona women, all of whom lived through the Depression. Donna J. Guy's "The Economics of Widowhood in Arizona, 1880–1940" statistically documents the occupational subordination of women in Arizona from the arrival of the railroad to World War II. Marguerite Noble's *Filaree* (Albuquerque: University of New Mexico Press, 1985) fleshes out those figures by tracing the course of one Arizona woman's life during the first half of the twentieth century. The finest novel ever written about Arizona, it also provides a starkly honest view of how the extractive economy affected working-class people in the state. It is the single best antidote to the romanticization of Arizona's past that is currently available. See D. G. Kehl's "The Southwest Viewed from the Inside Out: A Conversation with Marguerite Noble" (*Journal of the Southwest* 36 [1994]: 131–47).

❋ ❋ ❋ 14. World War II and the Postwar Boom

The best analyses of how World War II changed the social and economic landscape of the American West are by Gerald Nash: *The American West Transformed: The Impact of the Second World War* (Bloomington: Indiana University Press, 1985); "Planning for the Postwar City: The Urban West in World War II" (*Arizona and the West* 27 [1985]: 99–112); and *World War II and the West: Reshaping the Economy* (Lincoln: University of Nebraska Press, 1990) even though Nash pays little attention to Arizona. His *The American West in the Twentieth Century: A Short History of an Urban Oasis* (Englewood Cliffs, N.J.: Prentice-Hall, 1973) provides a succinct introduction to twentieth-century Western history.

Steve Bergsman's "Del Webb" (*Phoenix,* August 1991, pp. 81–89) offers an entertaining overview of Webb's life. The critical source for Phoenix and Tucson during the war and the postwar boom are Luckingham's *Phoenix* and Sonnichsen's *Tucson.* Michael Wade's *The Bitter Issue* describes the successful assault on organized labor outside the mining communities after World War II. The best account of the 1946 IUMMSW strike against Phelps Dodge in Clifton-Morenci is Hector Galan's "Los Mineros," a television production for the American Experience series of the Public Broadcasting System.

Bob Cunningham's "The Box That Broke the Barrier: The Swamp Cooler Comes to Southern Arizona" (*Journal of Arizona History* 26 [1985]: 145–62) and Bert Fireman's "Urbanization and Home Comfort" (*Project Progress I: Progress and History in Arizona,* directed by William R. Noyes; Tucson: University of Arizona, 1973--74) discuss the impact of air-conditioning on Arizona's urban growth. Michael Konig's "Phoenix in the 1950s: Urban Growth in the 'Sunbelt' " (*Arizona and the West* 24 [1982]: 19–38) offers a short yet wide-ranging overview of the most explosive decade of growth in that city's history. Emmett McLoughlin's *People's Padre* (Boston: Beacon Press, 1954) and Mary Melcher's "Blacks and Whites Together: Interracial Leadership in the Phoenix Civil Rights Movement" (*Journal of Arizona History* 32 [1991]: 195–216) discuss the conditions of African Americans in Phoenix and their struggle for civil rights during the postwar period.

There is no comprehensive published history of Mexicans in Arizona after World War II. James Officer's dissertation, "Sodalities and Systemic Linkages," his *Arizona's Hispanic Perspective* (38th Arizona Town Hall; Phoenix: Arizona Town Hall, 1981), Raymond Flores's *The Socio-Economic Status Trends of the Mexican People Residing in Arizona* (1951; reprint, San Francisco: R and E Research Associates, 1973), and John Crow's *Mexican Americans in Contemporary Arizona: A Social and Demographic View* (San Francisco: R and E Research Associates, 1975) are the best places to start, but much more research needs to be done. Mario García's *Mexican Americans* and Juan García's *Operation Wetback: The Mass Deportation of Mexican Undocumented Workers in 1954* (Westport, Conn.: Greenwood Press, 1980) place the experiences of Arizona's Mexican population in national perspective.

The oral histories of Arizona women in Rothschild and Hronek's *Doing What the Day Brought* reflect the changes in sex roles brought about by World War II.

Karen Anderson's *Wartime Women: Sex Roles, Family Relations, and the Status of Women During World War II* (Westport, Conn.: Greenwood Press, 1981) analyzes those changes on a national level but also dissects the postwar retrenchment that occurred after the men came back from the war. Her "Western Women: The Twentieth-Century Experience" in *The Twentieth-Century West*, edited by Gerald Nash and Richard Etulain, 99–122 (Albuquerque: University of New Mexico Press, 1989) discusses the major trends, and major gaps, in the study of women in the American West.

*   *   *   **15. The Other Arizona**

The most readable introduction to the Native Americans of Arizona is Stephen Trimble's *The People: Indians of the American Southwest* (Santa Fe: School of American Research Press, 1993), which emphasizes the words of the Native Americans themselves. It is also graced by Trimble's black-and-white and color photographs. Thomas Weaver's edited volume *Indians of Arizona: A Contemporary Perspective* (Tucson: University of Arizona Press, 1974), which includes several chapters by Bernard Fontana, provides a basic introduction to the legal, economic, political, and social problems of modern Indians, but it is twenty years old and does not delve into the histories of individual tribes. Volumes 9 and 10 of the *Handbook of North American Indians* (Washington: Smithsonian Institution, 1979, 1983) contain at least one chapter on each tribe and numerous chapters on the Hopis, Navajos, and Pimas and Tohono O'odham (formerly called Papago). Edward Spicer's *Cycles of Conquest: The Impact of Spain, Mexico, and the United States on the Indians of the Southwest, 1533–1960* (Tucson: University of Arizona Press, 1962) remains the finest analysis of culture change and resistance among Southwestern Native Americans even though it was published more than three decades ago. Robert Trennert's *The Phoenix Indian School: Forced Assimilation in Arizona, 1891–1935* (Norman: University of Oklahoma Press, 1988) provides a critical but balanced history of that institution and its impact on Indian children, while *Born a Chief: The Nineteenth Century Hopi Boyhood of Edmund Nequatewa, As Told to Alfred F. Whiting*, edited by P. David Seaman (Tucson: University of Arizona Press, 1993) relates Nequatewa's escape from the school and return to the Hopi mesas. Kenneth Philp's *John Collier's Crusade for Indian Reform, 1920–1954* (Tucson: University of Arizona Press, 1977) examines Collier's ambivalent legacy in a sympathetic yet objective fashion.

The best source on Carlos Montezuma is Peter Iverson's biography, *Carlos Montezuma and the Changing World of American Indians* (Albuquerque: University of New Mexico Press, 1982). Iverson's *The Navajo Nation* (Albuquerque: University of New Mexico Press, 1981) discusses stock reduction and its aftermath, especially the growth of tribal government from the 1940s through the second administration of Peter MacDonald in the late 1970s. Other accounts of the Navajo during the twentieth century include Garrick Bailey and Roberta Glenn Bailey's *A History of the Navajo Years* (Santa Fe: School of American Research Press, 1986); Donald Parman's *The Navajos and the New Deal* (New Haven: Yale University Press, 1976); and Richard White's *The Roots of Dependency: Subsistence, Environment, and Social Change Among the Choctaws, Pawnees, and Navajos* (Lincoln: University of Nebraska Press, 1983). The data on Navajo versus Anglo mortality from alcohol-related causes comes from Stephen Kunitz and Jerrold Levy's *Careers of Navajo Drinkers: A 25-Year Study of Three Populations* (New Haven: Yale University Press, in press).

A number of works concentrate on the Forest Service and its inconsistent attempts to regulate grazing in national forests. The most comprehensive is Rowley's *U.S. Forest Service Grazing and Rangelands: A History* (College Station: Texas A & M University Press, 1985). Forest historian Michael Frome also includes chapters on grazing in his *Whose Woods These Are: The Story of the National Forests* (Garden City, N.Y.: Doubleday, 1962) and *The Forest Service* (Boulder, Colo.: Westview Press, 1984), as does Glen Robinson in *The Forest Service* (Baltimore: Johns Hopkins University Press, 1975). None of these sources focuses exclusively on Arizona, but most draw examples from the state.

The most comprehensive introduction to logging in Arizona is Robert Matheny's unpublished dissertation, "The History of Lumbering in Arizona Before World War II" (University of Arizona, 1975), which contains considerable information on Ayers and the Riordan brothers. See also Ellen Lauver's "A History of the Use and Management of the Forested Lands of Arizona, 1862–1936" (University of Arizona, 1938). The references on the Forest Service noted above all contain chapters on logging as well. A particularly critical study of modern timber cutting is Jack Shepherd's *The Forest Killers: The Destruction of the American Wilderness* (New York: Weybright and Talley, 1975). Unfortunately, it does not pay much attention to Arizona. The best overview of the modern Arizona lumber industry is a series of articles Ray Ring wrote for the *Arizona Daily Star* in 1984. The articles appeared in the February 5–12 issues of the newspaper and were reprinted as a supplement entitled "Taming the Forests." James McNary's *This Is My Life* (Albuquerque: University of New Mexico Press, 1956) contains many anecdotes about the development of Southwest Forestries from the author's decidedly favorable point of view.

Statistics on Arizona's population, economy, land tenure, and other topics can be found in three fundamental sources: *Arizona Statistical Abstract: A 1979 Data Handbook,* edited by Nat de Gennaro (Flagstaff: Northland Press, 1979), *The Arizona Atlas,* by Melvin Hecht and Richard Reeves (Tucson: University of Arizona, Office of Arid Lands Studies, 1981), and *Historical Atlas of Arizona,* by Henry Walker and Don Bufkin (Norman: University of Oklahoma Press, 1979). Ira Murphy's unpublished "Brief History of Payson, Arizona" provides a delightful historical sketch of Payson. It can be found in the main libraries of Arizona State University and the University of Arizona.

❋ ❋ ❋ 16. From the Southwest to the Sunbelt

Peter Wiley and Robert Gottlieb provide a short but pointed introduction to the manners and morals of modern Phoenix in their *Empires in the Sun: The Rise of the New American West* (New York: G. P. Putnam's Sons, 1982). Their portrait is considerably more critical than Luckingham's *Phoenix.* The circus of Arizona politics during the 1980s and early 1990s is described in Ronald J. Watkins's *High Crimes and Misdemeanors: The Term and Trials of Former Governor Evan Mecham* (New York: William Morrow and Co., 1990), which maintains a generally respectful attitude toward Arizona legislators, and Joseph Stedino's *What's In It For Me? How an Ex-Wiseguy Exposed the Greed, Jealousy, and Lust That Drive Arizona Politics* (New York: HarperCollins, 1992), which revels in their backstabbing and greed. Michael Lacey's "AzScam's Real Target: Union Leader Pat Cantelme; How the Cops Tried to Entrap an Innocent Man" (*New Times* 24 [Dec. 30, 1992–Jan. 5, 1993]: 3–10) argues that the powers behind AzScam—Phoenix police chief Ruben Ortega and Maricopa County attorney Richard Romley—pressured Stedino to go after firefighters' union leader Pat Cantelme.

Larry Schweikart's *A History of Banking in Arizona* (Tucson: University of Arizona Press, 1982) is a straightforward institutional account of Arizona banking in the days before deregulation. It has little to say about the savings and loan industry. Pam Hait's *The Arizona Bank: Arizona's Story* (Phoenix: Arizona Bank, 1987) is a well-written official history of one bank, focusing on the individuals like Rawhide Jimmy Douglas, Frank Brophy, and Lloyd Bimson who ran the institution from the early 1900s to the 1960s. Michael Binstein and Charles Bowden's *Trust Me: Charles Keating and the Great American Bank Robbery* (New York: Random House, 1993) dissects the world of Charles Keating with vivid but precise incisions. An ethnography of American business in the 1980s, it is structured around the portait of an obsessed and driven man who never seemed to be the sum of his parts.

Information about the collapse of Arizona thrifts comes from the following newspaper articles: Alan Thurber's "Banking Industry in Arizona Suffered Worst Year in 1989" (*Arizona Republic,* Dec. 24, 1989); the Associated Press's "U.S. Sues Western Savings for $1 billion" (*Arizona Daily Star,* June 15, 1992); Walt Nett's "Federal Suit Sifts Western Savings' Ruins" (*Arizona Daily Star,* June 21, 1992); Marian Frank's "Driggses Face Just Punishment in RTC Lawsuit" (*Phoenix Gazette,* June 21, 1992); and Walt Nett's "Failed S & L Executives Call RTC Suit 'Thin Soup' " (*Arizona Daily Star,* Oct. 11, 1992).

Information about Arizona's economy during the 1960s, 1970s, and 1980s is contained in *Arizona's Economy: Yesterday, Today and Tomorrow* (29th Arizona Town Hall, Research Report Prepared by Arizona State University; Phoenix: Arizona Academy, 1976); *Arizona's Changing Economy* (49th Arizona Town Hall, Research Report Prepared by Northern Arizona University; Phoenix: Arizona Academy, 1986); *The Many Faces of Economic Development in Arizona* (57th Arizona Town Hall, Background Report Prepared by the University of Arizona; Phoenix: Arizona Town Hall, 1990); "Special Report Star 200: The Major Employers of Southern Arizona" (*Arizona Daily Star,* March 29, 1992); and Richard Ducote's "Copper's Value to State Put at $6.56 Billion" (*Arizona Daily Star,* April 26–May 2, 1993). *Holding the Line: Women in the Great Arizona Mine Strike of 1983* (Ithaca, N.Y.: ILR Press, 1989) is Barbara Kingsolver's eloquent account of the strike against Phelps Dodge in Ajo and Clifton-Morenci.

The IRE's Arizona Project was published between mid-March and early April 1977 in a number of newspapers, including the *Arizona Daily Star,* which contributed two reporters to the team. Some of the articles were edited and cut by the *Star.* The *Arizona Republic,* on the other hand, refused to print the series at all even though Don Bolles worked for the paper. In a front-page statement, the paper claimed that it had not been "able to obtain sufficient documentation and proof to justify publication." None of the thirty-six reporters who participated in the project wrote a book except Michael Wendland of the *Detroit News.* Wendland's *The Arizona Project: How a Team of Investigative Reporters Got Revenge on Deadline* (Kansas City: Sheed Andrews and McMeel, Inc., 1977) borders on the novelistic. Like Stedino's book, it is a good read but contains many unsubtantiated statements and allegations. "The Arizona Report—Plus Five" (University of Arizona, Department of Journalism, 1982) is the edited transcript of a retrospective symposium five years after the series appeared.

Despite the IRE, however, there has never been a conclusive investigation of Don Bolles's murder. A decade after his death, the *Republic* published "The Long Goodbye: 10 Years Have Passed and Don Bolles' Murder Still Haunts the Valley" (June 1, 1986). Written by Charles Kelly and John Winters, the only *Republic* reporter to join the IRE team, the lengthy article summarizes the developments in the case to date and evaluates the different theories about who ordered Bolles's assassination and why they did. Both the *Scottsdale Progress* and the *New Times* challenged the dominant interpretation that Kemper Marley set the murder in motion as an act of "rangeland justice" in retaliation for Bolles's articles against him. After the *New Times* published its special report entitled "The Don Bolles Murder: Arizona's Shame" (June 1986), the *Progress* accused the *New Times* of plagiarism, distributing a statement to the Phoenix metropolitan media that said, "You take our work and use it without credit and imply that you did the extensive research that we spent eight years developing."

James Clarke's *Last Rampage: The Escape of Gary Tison* (Boston: Houghton Mifflin Company, 1988) is a fascinating account of Tison's brutal world, a world where land fraud and prison corruption are refracted through the personality of a domineering killer who grew up in the migrant camps of California and central Arizona. Jane Hill offers an amusing and acerbic sociolinguistic analysis of how Anglos in the Southwest use Spanish as an expression of dominance and contempt in "Hasta La Vista, Baby: Anglo Spanish in the American Southwest" (*Critique of Anthropology* 13 [1993]: 145–76).

The most detailed account of the struggle for the Central Arizona Project is Rich Johnson's *The Central Arizona Project, 1918–1968.* Johnson was the executive director of the Central Arizona Project Association, so his narrative is straightforward but favorably inclined toward the CAP. Norris Hundley's *Water and the West* also contains a chapter on *Arizona v. California.* More critical analyses can be found in Richard L. Berkman and W. Kip Viscusi's *Damming the West: Ralph Nader's Study Group Report on the Bureau of Reclamation* (New York: Grossman Publishers, 1973); Frank Welsh's *How to Create a Water Crisis* (Boulder, Colo.: Johnson Books, 1985), which also includes several chapters on the battle over Orme Dam; Philip Fradkin's *A River No More: The Colorado River and the West* (Tucson: University of Arizona Press, 1984), and Marc Reisner's *Cadillac Desert: The American West and Its Disappearing Water* (New York: Penguin Books, 1986).

Additional information on the CAP came from the following newspaper articles by Enric Volante: "Long-Planned CAP Water Finally Welcomed to Tucson" (*Arizona Daily Star,* Oct. 5, 1991); "CAP Costs Likely to Balloon, UA Report Says" (*Arizona Daily Star,* Dec. 1, 1992); and "Ex-UA Professor Predicted CAP Crisis in 1967" (*Arizona Daily Star,* Dec. 2, 1992). A useful potpourri of articles on Arizona water issues is *Arizona Waterline,* edited by Athia L. Hardt (Phoenix: Salt River Project, 1989). Dean Mann's *The Politics of Water in Arizona* (Tucson: University of Arizona Press, 1963) remains remarkably insightful three decades after it was published, while Helen Ingram's "Politics of Water Allocation," in *Value and Choices in the Development of the Colorado River Basin,* edited by Dean Peterson and A. Berry, 61–75 Crawford (Tucson: University of Arizona Press, 1978) extends the analysis one decade further.

As with all water issues in the West, the literature on Indian water rights is voluminous. Some key sources on those rights in Arizona are F. Lee Brown and Helen Ingram's *Water and Poverty in the Southwest* (Tucson: University of Arizona Press, 1987), which contains five chapters on the Tohono O'odham; Thomas R. McGuire's "Getting to Yes in the New West," in *State and Reservation: New Perspectives on Federal Indian Policy,* edited by George Pierre Castile and Robert L. Bee, 224–46 (Tucson: University of Arizona Press, 1992); and McGuire's incisive "Indian Water Rights Settlements: A Case Study in the Rhetoric of Implementation" (*American Indian Culture and Research Journal* 15 [1991]: 139–69) and *Indian Water in the New West,* edited by Thomas R. McGuire, William B. Lord, and Mary G. Wallace (Tucson: University of Arizona Press, 1993). The quote about Danny Lopez is taken from Bernard L. Fontana's *Of Earth and Little Rain: The Papago Indians* (Flagstaff, Ariz.: Northland Press, 1981; reprint, Tucson: University of Arizona Press, 1989).

✳ ✳ 17. The Political Ecology of a Desert State

See the citations to works by Worster, Reisner, and Pisani in the section on Chapter 11, above. Discussions of the controversy surrounding the Groundwater Management Act can be found in *Arizona Waterline,* edited by Athia Hardt (Phoenix: Salt River Project, 1989), and "The New Liquidity," by Clint Williams (*Arizona Trend* 4 [Jan. 1990]: 28–35). Charles Bowden's *Killing the Hidden Waters* (Austin: University of Texas Press, 1977) remains the best exploration of the philosophical and social costs of groundwater pumping in the Southwest and the mentality it reflects.

Index

Mormons in, 190, 196; tourism in, 240, 241; water control in, 201–3, 206–7, 208–12, 340, 343

Salt River Valley Canal, 199

Salt River Valley Water Users Association, 209, 211–12, 217, 223, 290, 359

Samaniego, Dolores Aguirre, 109

Samaniego, Mariano, 106, 109

Sam Hughes ditch, 350

San Agustín de Tucson. *See* Tucson

San Bernardino Ranch, 48, 49, 128

San Carlos, 208

San Carlos Apaches, 84, 85

San Carlos Creek, 85

San Carlos Lake, 218

San Carlos Project, 218, 347

San Carlos Reservation, 78, 84, 85, 87, 92, 130, 210, 246, 293; Chiricahua and, 90–91, 94

San Francisco, 33, 104, 114–15, 121

San Francisco Mountain Forest Reserve, 249, 259

San Francisco Peak, 82

San Francisco River, 43, 163, 172

San Ignacio de la Canoa grant, 48, 128, 129

San Ignacio del Babocómari grant, 128

San José de Sonoita grant, 48, 128

San Juan de las Boquillas y Nogales grant, 48, 128

San Pedro River, 16, 31, 43, 61, 196, 343; cattle on, 129, 140; military on, 79–80; O'odham on, 29–30, 38; Spanish on, 27, 35; stamp mills on, 153, 155–56

San Pedro Valley, 38, 48, 128, 145, 190

San Rafael Cattle Company, 49, 125

San Rafael de la Zanja grant, 48, 49, 125, 126, 128

San Rafael del Valle grant, 48, 128

San Rafael Valley, 48, 49, 127

San Simon Cattle Company, 132

San Simon Creek, 132, 141

San Simon Valley, 142–43

Santa Anna, Antonio López de, 56

Santa Catalina Mountains, 234, 248

Santa Cruz, Atanacia, 109

Santa Cruz, Petra, 109

Santa Cruz River, 30, 37, 38, 39, 48

Santa Cruz Valley, 14, 47, 53, 55, 213, 219; Hispanics in, 31–33; land grants in, 48, 128; livestock in, 127–28; water rights in, 350–51

Santa Fe Compact. *See* Colorado River Compact

Santa Fe, Prescott and Phoenix Railway, 166

Santa Fe Railroad. *See* Atchison, Topeka & Santa Fe Railroad

Santa Fe Trail, 42, 46, 106, 163

Santa María, 30

Santa Rita, 65

Santa Rita del Cobre, 45

Santa Rita Mountains, 106, 147

Santee, Ross: *Arizona: A State Guide,* 255

San Xavier del Bac, 31, 38, 47, 52; Apaches and, 54–55, 80; livestock and, 127, 129; water rights and, 351–52

San Xavier Reservation, 293, 350

San Ysidro Ranch, 130

Sasabe, 106

Sauer, Carl, 27

Savings and loan industry, ix; deregulation of, 318, 330–33

SAWRSA, 351–52

Sawyer, Mary, 152

Scalp hunters, 55, 62

Schieffelin, Albert, 146, 153

Schieffelin, Edward, 145–46, 152, 153

Schofield, John, 108

Schools: boarding, 290, 292–93; discrimination in, 264, 283, 285

Schultz, Bill, 322

Schuyler, Walter, 83

Scientists, 245–48

Scott, Tom, 115, 116